A WINTER
OF
DISCONTENT

A WINTER OF DISCONTENT

The Nuclear Freeze and American Politics

DAVID S. MEYER

PRAEGER

New York
Westport, Connecticut
London

Library of Congress Cataloging-in-Publication Data

Meyer, David S.
   A winter of discontent : the nuclear freeze and American politics / David S.
Meyer.
      p.   cm.
   Includes bibliographical references.
   ISBN 0-275-93305-9 (alk. paper). — ISBN 0-275-93306-7 (pbk. : alk. paper)
   1. Antinuclear movement—United States. 2. United States—
Military policy.   I. Title.
JX1974.7.M46   1990
327.1'74'0973—dc20   89-26588

Library of Congress Catalog Card Number: 89-26588

ISBN: 0-275-93305-9
       0-275-93306-7 (pb)

First published in 1990

Praeger Publishers, One Madison Avenue, New York, NY 10010
An imprint of Greenwood Publishing Group, Inc.

Printed in the United States of America

The paper used in this book complies with the
Permanent Paper Standard issued by the National
Information Standards Organization (Z39.48-1984).

10 9 8 7 6 5 4 3 2 1

Dedicated to the memories of my grandmothers,

Zeena Broder

and

Sylvia Harris

CONTENTS

FIGURES

ACKNOWLEDGMENTS

Many people helped with this book by generously granting time, information, insight, and encouragement. I want to acknowledge a debt of gratitude, recognizing I cannot hope to repay it.

Neta Crawford, Andy Markovits, Laura Reed, Mark Silverstein, and Howard Zinn read drafts of the book and made helpful suggestions. Will Hathaway collected piles of data on media coverage of the disarmament movement. Ted Dzielak of the National Lawyer's Guild, Anne Simon of the Center for Constitutional Rights, and Howard Zinn provided me with court papers and analyses of numerous cases, only a portion of which are discussed here. Pam Solo at the Institute for Peace and International Security discussed her research on the nuclear freeze movement with me and allowed me free access to her extensive files and to transcripts of interviews she conducted for her own work. Deb Mapes helped me find my way through the files.

During the book's long gestation period, I taught at Tufts University, the Harvard Extension School, Merrimack College, Northeastern University, and Boston University. I am grateful to many colleagues and students at these places whose energy and enthusiasm for work of this kind provided both encouragement and a constant challenge. As the book developed, Jeff Berry, Steve Carpenter, Maurice Coutts, Susan Eckstein, Lynn Eden, Richard Eichenberg, William Gamson, Joshua Goldstein, Margot Kempers, Karen Kispert, Thomas Linde, Sue Marsh, Katherine Magraw, Tony Messina, Steven Miller, Kent Portney, George Ross, Christine Rossell, Seth Shulman, Ralf Starkloff, and Ellen Sturgis all offered ideas, information, and reassurance at critical times.

I also worked at the Institute for Defense and Disarmament Studies during part of that time. Randy Forsberg helped me think through many of the ideas developed here and provided an environment in which relevant issues could be researched and discussed. Alan Bloomgarden, Phil Braudaway-Bauman, Carl Conetta, Matthew Goodman, Chalmers Hardenbergh, Laurie Ibarguen, Rob Leavitt, John Murphy, Bob Snope, Tom Stefanick, Peter Steven, Nancy Lee Wood, and Bart Wright helped with information and encouragement.

I also was fortunate to work with many thoughtful and committed people in Somerville Action for Nuclear Disarmament, the New England Campaign to Stop the Euromissiles, and Peace and Justice Summer. During the summer of 1982 I visited a number of peace movement organizations in Western Europe and was inspired and aided by numerous discussions with activists. Through all of this, I had the opportunity to discuss and argue protest movement strategies on both theoretical and practical levels. (I have since come to realize that I was generally wrong.) Peter Bohm, Dale Bryan, Neta Crawford, John Maher, Paula Schnitzer, Andie Stephens, Jean Stead, Helmut Sverre, and Carol Troyer-Shank were particularly helpful in this regard.

Margaret Coutts provided me with an unending stream of encouragement and support. Through what sometimes seemed like endless rough patches, she helped me maintain both a commitment to the work and an element of sanity in the rest of my life.

INTRODUCTION

In a televised October 1980 debate President Jimmy Carter charged that opponent Ronald Reagan had not devoted sufficient attention or seriousness to the problem of nuclear proliferation or the threat of nuclear war. Citing his daughter Amy, Carter claimed nuclear war was the central issue of the campaign. Reagan rebuffed Carter with a certainty most Americans apparently found reassuring, for they resoundingly rejected Carter at the polls less than two weeks later.

Less than two years after, on June 12, 1982, 1 million people marched in New York City to protest the Reagan administration's nuclear weapons policies. In the largest such demonstration in U.S. history, the protestors called for a bilateral freeze on the testing, production, and deployment of nuclear weapons and for a redirection of military spending to fund human needs. Since then national polls have consistently shown 70 percent to 80 percent popular support for those demands. Something happened. More quickly than even the most optimistic activists thought possible, large numbers of Americans became convinced that there was something wrong with current U.S. defense policy, that there was a more desirable alternative, and, perhaps most important, that they could do something about it.

Emerging seemingly out of nowhere, the nuclear freeze movement burst upon the political scene shortly after Ronald Reagan was first elected president. As with any social movement, activists espousing a wide range of goals engaged in an even greater variety of activities, in attempts to influence government policy. In relatively short order, organizations and individuals grouped under the banner of the freeze claimed numerous victories through Congressional resolutions, public opinion polls, and voter referenda. Despite the proliferation of antinuclear activity during the first Reagan term, the movement faded from the public eye with equally surprising alacrity. President Reagan won reelection in 1984 in a landslide despite widespread public opposition to his administration's nuclear security policies.

I began work on this book with three goals. First, I wanted to tell the story of the nuclear freeze and chronicle its meteoric life. Protest movements test both the stability of political institutions and the extent of democracy within a state. The development of dissent informs not only about the dissenters but also about the system with which they quarrel. Access to the arenas of decision making for all groups is critical to establish and maintain political legitimacy in a democracy.[1] The development of volatile and often extra-institutional protest indicates that citizens see a problem not only with a particular policy but also with the policy-making process.[2] The freeze movement challenged both the content of U.S. national security policy and the policy-making process. This book seeks to explore and explain that challenge, how it developed, and the way political institutions responded.

Second, by analyzing the freeze I mean to contribute to developing a theoretical framework for understanding other protest movements in the United States, their origins, development, and their potential political influence. Movements represent a peculiar mix of both institutional and extra-institutional political activity. As Charles Tilly writes:

> The social movement consists of a series of challenges to established authorities, especially national authorities, in the name of an unrepresented constituency. Its concrete actions combine various elements of the newer repertoire: public meetings, demonstrations, marches, strikes, and so on, combined with an attempt by leaders to link the actions organizationally and symbolically, as well as to bargain with established authorities on behalf of their claimed constituency. Although it does not have the official standing of an electoral campaign or a petition drive, the deliberately organized social movement occupies a recognized place in our contemporary array of means for acting collectively.[3]

This book explores the inventory of strategies from which the nuclear freeze movement drew and the ways in which a broad range of activities were linked. It also examines the political organization of the movement, the battles between various leaders to speak for it and its concerns, and the ways participating groups organized, mobilized, and operated within the constraints of U.S. politics. These constraints, the political dilemmas the movement confronted, and the choices it made are not peculiar to the freeze, but rather are endemic to movements in the United States.

Finally, I want to integrate analysis of peace movements into an understanding of the policy context in which they emerge. Through the nuclear freeze of the large numbers of Americans explicitly challenged long-standing and basic assumptions at the foundation of U.S. security policy. Protest movements and public opinion may play a role in determining the content of this crucial area in U.S. policy. The Harvard Nuclear Study Group suggests:

> American public opinion influences policy. How the individual votes, what policies elected officials believe the public supports, and the vigor of such demands, all can influence decisions in Washington ... the recent vacillation of American policy toward nuclear weapons has reflected the inconsistent messages politicians have received from the public on these issues.[4]

Simply, protest movements may matter. They can encourage political leaders to pursue dangerous and destabilizing policies, or they can aid in the development of arms control and disarmament initiatives and negotiated agreements that enhance both national and global security. This book and works like it should aid in assessing whether movements, and citizen activism generally, can help push governments toward safer, more secure, and more humane policies.

In Chapter 1, searching for a framework to use in understanding the freeze, I review other writing on social movements. I contend that although the choices activists make influence their prospects for success, the political system and public policy set a context that constrains these choices. Even though small groups have worked to organize opposition to the arms race generally and to U.S. strategic policy in particular, only sporadically have their efforts successfully reached the political mainstream. Visible changes in policy, political rhetoric, and the policy-making process can create a political space for movements. Within that window of opportunity, movements can mobilize dissent, make political gains, and alter the structure of opportunity for subsequent challenges.

Chapters 2, 3, and 4 explore the changes in political context that created an opportunity for a dissident movement explicitly concerned with nuclear weaponry and policy. The freeze emerged amid an ostensibly popular conservative revival. Ronald Reagan, who promised a more aggressive foreign policy and military posture, was elected president in 1980 by an overwhelming majority of voters. Despite rhetoric to the contrary, however, virtually all of his administration's policies that activists found provocative had their origins in previous administrations. Although marginally more bellicose, the differences were those of degree, not of kind. At the same time, the Reagan era ushered in an entirely new order of military spending, which was subjected to an unusual degree of scrutiny and criticism because of the recession of 1982. Further, by denigrating the arms control process and speaking carelessly, although often candidly, about nuclear strategy, administration officials undermined public support for their policies and for their stewardship of the U.S. arsenal. This political mismanagement of national security policy, both domestically and within the Atlantic alliance, in conjunction with real policy changes, afforded peace activists an unusual opportunity to mobilize opposition to both the Reagan program and to the assumptions at the core of U.S. national security policy.

Changes in policy, rhetoric, and economics can be manifest or managed in a wide variety of ways and may provoke a broad range of responses. Crucial to explaining and understanding a movement's development is the role played by mediating figures in shaping political opinions, legitimating dissent, and directing protest. Chapters 5, 6, and 7 examine the role of the media and of social, economic, and political elites in fostering and defining the expression of popular opposition to U.S. nuclear weapons policy during the first Reagan term. Mass opinion on nuclear issues has been remarkably consistent and contradictory over the past three decades. When dissident policy makers, excluded from access to government, brought their concerns to the general public, they nourished and exploited one facet of mass opinion. Their defections from support of the president's policies brought the movement support, media attention, and an influx of resources; they also shaped the movement's concerns, ultimately setting the boundaries of critical discourse. Mass media were also critical in defining the movement; after initially ignoring antinuclear activism, media overcovered the movement, magnifying its strength while minimizing and trivializing its criticisms of U.S. policy.

Social and political breakdowns, policy changes, and a schism in elite consensus all contribute to creating an opportunity for protest mobilization, but they do not create it. Within the context of a given historical opportunity, activists create movements by mobilizing and organizing protest, framing demands, and confronting mainstream politics. The freeze movement did not arise in a vacuum, nor was it simply a product of spontaneous eruptions of dissent. Rather, the freeze grew out of purposive efforts by individuals and organizations. The movement was deeply rooted in previous protest movements and the organizations they left behind. Chapter 8 reviews the history of peace and nuclear disarmament movements in the United States, examining the diverse resources, organizations, and networks available to the nuclear freeze. Chapters 9 and 10 analyze how the nuclear freeze proposal served as a vehicle to unite a broad and diverse coalition, allowing the movement to grow very quickly. Against this backdrop of unity, dramatic instances of civil disobedience and direct action, discussed in Chapter 11, served as exclamation points for the growing movement.

Chapters 12, 13, and 14 examine the interaction of the nuclear freeze movement with mainstream U.S. politics, analyzing the influence political opponents and supporters had in framing presentation of the nuclear freeze campaign and proposal, and the responses of U.S. politics and policy. National politicians were forced to respond to the freeze and did so in two basic ways. Some attacked the movement and the freeze proposal, accusing partisans of being naive or Communist inspired. Others supported some aspect of the large and diverse movement, perhaps only the activists' "genuine concern," anticipating a share of support or influence in return. These twin responses provoked internal conflict for the freeze coalition. Partly to answer or preempt conservative critics, groups with more modest goals distanced themselves politically and organizationally from those with broader concerns. At the same time, groups working for the freeze as part of a larger agenda, wary of cooptation, sought to push other issues, contending that the freeze was not enough.

The nuclear freeze came to obscure the activities of the groups that gave rise to it. The national campaign defined itself and its goals more narrowly, until winning passage of a Congressional freeze resolution overwhelmed all other goals. Divorced from its roots, the freeze was domesticated by mainstream politicians whose analysis of the arms race and arms control bore little relation to that of the freeze initiators. Legislators were comfortable voting for both a freeze resolution and the MX missile, for example, just as voters were comfortable supporting the freeze and Ronald Reagan. "Freeze" came to mean little more than support for some sort of arms control and a generalized opposition to nuclear war. Even politicians who could not support this diluted version had little difficulty dealing with it; they could oppose the freeze while articulating support for its new narrower goals. Indeed, in justifying his Strategic Defense Initiative, Ronald Reagan appropriated the language of the freeze. By proclaiming his new-found concern about the existence of nuclear weapons and the immorality of nuclear war, Reagan prevented the 1984 election from turning into a referendum on the nuclear freeze. He was aided in this regard by the timid campaign of Democrat Walter Mondale, whose support for the freeze was accompanied by endorsement of numerous contradictory policies. Taken from its political context, the freeze proposal and the movement lost political significance.

Chapter 15 presents an epilogue for the freeze, examining why a movement that had appeared so strong seemed to disappear so rapidly. While the freeze vanished from political discourse, the groups supporting it continued their own activities. Absent a unifying face, however, their efforts amounted to less than the sum of their parts. The fragmentation of the nuclear freeze coalition allowed its participating groups to be marginalized, depoliticized, or coopted. Many organizations survived at the expense of the movement that gave life to them.

Chapter 16 uses the freeze as a vehicle for understanding the ways in which U.S. politics engender and then absorb dissident movements. Although the freeze movement appeared unusual and dramatic at its height, it was not unique. Rather, it followed a trajectory of mobilization and institutionalization emblematic of protest in the Untied States. Although the freeze did not achieve its articulated goal of ending the arms race, it radically altered political discourse on nuclear weaponry and aided in restoring an arms control regime. The legacy of the movement — in the form of new discourse, a rejuvenated arms control process, the institutionalization of antinuclear concerns in research and education programs, and strengthened or new organizations — alters the political opportunities for subsequent antinuclear challenges.

NOTES

1. Seymour Martin Lipset, *Political Man,* Garden City, NY: Anchor, 1963, p. 65.

2. Theodore J. Lowi, *The Politics of Disorder,* New York: Basic, 1971, pp. ix–xi.

3. Charles Tilly, "Speaking Your Mind without Elections, Surveys, or Social Movements," *Public Opinion Quarterly,* Winter 1983, p. 466.

4. The Harvard Nuclear Study Group, *Living with Nuclear Weapons,* New York: Bantam, 1983, p. 10, and pp. 200–2 on public opinion.

ACRONYMS AND ABBREVIATIONS

ACA	Arms Control Association
ACDA	Arms Control and Disarmament Agency
ABM	Antiballistic Missile
AFSC	American Friends Service Committee
ALCM	Air Launched Cruise Missile
ATB	Advanced Technology Bomber
BUF	Black United Front
CALC	Clergy and Laity Concerned
CDI	Center for Defense Information
CLW	Council for a Livable World
CND	Campaign for Nuclear Disarmament
CNFMP	Coalition for a New Foreign and Military Policy
CoPD	Committee on the Present Danger
DOD	Department of Defense
END	European Nuclear Disarmament
ESR	Educators for Social Responsibility
FAS	Federation of American Scientists
FOE	Friends of the Earth
FOR	Fellowship of Reconciliation
ICBM	Intercontinental Ballistic Missile
IDDS	Institute for Defense and Disarmament Studies
INF	Intermediate Nuclear Forces
IPPNW	International Physicians for the Prevention of Nuclear War
IPIS	Institute for Peace and International Security
IPS	Institute for Policy Studies
LANAC	Lawyers Alliance for Nuclear Arms Control
LTB	Limited Test Ban
MAD	Mutually Assured Destruction

MfS	Mobilization for Survival
MIRV	Multiple Independently Targetable Reentry Vehicles
NATO	North Atlantic Treaty Organization
NCC	National Council of Churches
NWFC	Nuclear Weapons Freeze Clearinghouse
PSR	Physicians for Social Responsibility
SALT	Strategic Arms Limitation Talks
SANE	Committee for a Sane Nuclear Policy
SIPRI	Stockholm International Peace Research Institute
START	Strategic Arms Reduction Talks
TWPPC	Third World and Progressive Peoples Coalition
TNF	Theater Nuclear Forces
UCS	Union of Concerned Scientists
USCANW	United States Committee against Nuclear War
USPC	United States Peace Council
WAND	Women's Action for Nuclear Disarmament
WCC	World Council of Churches
WILPF	Women's International League for Peace and Freedom
WPA	Women's Pentagon Action
WPC	World Peace Council
WRL	War Resister's League

A WINTER
OF
DISCONTENT

NUCLEAR WEAPONS PROTEST AND SOCIAL MOVEMENTS

Since the dawn of the nuclear age, groups of Americans have consistently opposed the development of nuclear weaponry generally and U.S. national security policy in particular. Only sporadically, however, has that opposition reached beyond a few pacifist groups into the political mainstream. Indeed, the intensity and focus of even pacifist groups has waxed and waned in concert with the activity of more moderate organizations.[1] Periods of volatile dissident mobilization have alternated with times of relative quiescence, reflecting both the changing political climate and the tactical choices activists made. This chapter sets a theoretical context for understanding social movements in order to set a framework for analyzing the most recent period of antinuclear activism, the nuclear freeze movement.

SOCIAL MOVEMENTS

Social movements represent an unusual and invariably transient form of political participation that occurs when the state-sanctioned processes of popular participation cannot manage legitimate political conflict. Spilling over the boundaries of conventional politics and social life, movements bring new issues into the political system through a broad repertoire of activity.[2] As a result they also present a number of definitional problems.[3] Without dwelling on these issues, it is important to distinguish social movements from other political phenomena. To that end, I suggest six criteria that describe and define movements:

1. A social movement necessarily includes both political and personal transformation. These two aspects of conversion must be linked because a movement attempts to

change both state policy and the way participants live their lives.[4]

2. A social movement will use means additional to those offered and accepted by mainstream society to pursue its goals. Although various organizations within a movement may choose to participate in electoral competition, for example, a social movement will include nonconventional political behavior — demonstrations or civil disobedience, for example — as well.

3. A social movement must be in a dynamic state of interaction with the political mainstream. A movement not located toward the edge of legitimacy, demanding to effect structural political change, reaches an effective accommodation with society at large. It may still pursue certain reforms, but it can no longer be considered a movement. One that ceases to draw support, membership, or rhetoric from the mainstream ceases to be dynamic or moving.[5]

4. Social movements end when they are institutionalized, that is, when they have found a means of accommodation with established political institutions and society. There are two types of institutionalization. A movement or group is marginalized when forced so far to the edges of legitimacy that it no longer has any serious interaction with mainstream politics. It is then easily repressed or ignored. An organization is coopted when it limits its goals to those that can be achieved without threatening in any way the political structures of the state.[6] Cooptation does not necessarily mean that an organization, now functioning as an interest group, ceases to win meaningful political and social reforms. Indeed, it may be more effective at doing so. It will, however, abandon efforts or chances to change the structure of power and the process of decision making. Either process marks the end of a social movement. A successful movement will generally be split and undergo both processes throughout its life and, most certainly, in its demise. The end of the U.S. civil rights movement, for example, was marked by both the institutionalization and legitimation of the Southern Christian Leadership Conference and the effective disappearance of the Student Nonviolent Coordinating Committee.[7]

5. A movement may contain one or more social movement organizations, but it also includes activity generated outside them. Much movement activity is often unorganized or based in nascent, rather than established, groups.

Unorganized ghetto riots in the early 1960s, for example, proved to be a resource for organized civil rights groups. The degree to which an organization can credibly claim to speak for the unorganized is directly related to its prospects for success.[8]

6. The reality of a social movement includes specific policy demands made upon the state, but it is not limited to those claims. A social movement's program includes an often unspoken, yet shared culture and lifestyle. For example, Frank Parkin found that members of the British Campaign for Nuclear Disarmament (CND) generally shared both political and personal values not explicitly stated nor directly addressed in CND's literature or activity.[9]

Distinguishing social movements from other kinds of political phenomena is only the first step in developing a theory for understanding movements, their development, and their possible place in the policy-making process. Perhaps the most controversial and difficult aspect of analysis is identifying the factors that cause or allow social movements to emerge.

THE ORIGINS OF PROTEST MOVEMENTS: SOCIETAL BREAKDOWN

The wide range of writing on social movements generally splits on the issue of whether activists or states create dissident movements. As the Tillys point out, analysts tend to emphasize either a breakdown in the social or political institutions of a state or the solidarity or purposive organizing efforts of dissident political groups.[10] Within each general perspective, there is also a wide variety of perspectives and conflicts.

Breakdown theories are united in their assumption of the state's capacity to integrate or repress the potential for dissident mobilization. The first major wave of writing in this tradition came in an attempt to explain the emergence of fascist movements before World War II. "Mass society" theorists, including William Kornhauser, Hannah Arendt, and Eric Hoffer, argued that social movements were the product of a kind of collective anomie.[11] When a polity is unable to integrate some portion of its populace into intermediating institutions, linking the individual with the state, alienated individuals engage in unusual behavior, including suicide, crime, riots, and protest movements. Movements, according to this view, are essentially an irrational and undirected response to a failure of the state to deal with new problems or constituents.

The stresses creating social disequilibrium may include social, economic, or industrial modernization or stagnation or the rising expectations of personal advancement or progress the polity is unable to meet. The disjuncture between expectations and reality creates alienation, increased demands upon government, less respect for governmental authority, and dissident social mobilization. The stated goals of a movement or the grievances it purports to address are less important than the failure of the state to provide intermediary associations or integrating and stabilizing institutions. Dissident mobilization is seen as a product of aggregate psychological responses to unusual social circumstances.[12]

Marxist variants of breakdown theories are similarly state-fixated, with one important distinction. Rather than emphasizing the state's capacity to integrate and institutionalize new constituents or concerns, Marxist analysts emphasize the capacity of the state to repress dissent. Theda Skocpol, in a comparative study of revolutions, argues that while grievances based on class conflict may be inevitable and constant, only a state crisis creates the potential for revolution. She contends that these crises are generated exogenously, generally through foreign wars. By diverting the attention of those wielding state power and weakening the capacity of the state to repress dissent, foreign crises create the opportunity for inherent class conflict to express itself in revolutionary movements.[13]

Piven and Cloward use a similar approach to analyze protest movements of the poor in the United States. Noting that inequality is constant but movements are sporadic, they argue that movements emerge only when "large-scale changes undermine political stability."[14] Economic or geographic dislocation of a class, massive economic depression, and electoral instability may create the exceptional circumstances in which "the lower classes [are] afforded the socially determined opportunity to press for their own class interests."[15] Crises allow protest to emerge by weakening the authority of political institutions and disrupting the usual political process, thus allowing individuals to recognize their potential for political action. Crises also make elites and policy makers more sensitive, and possibly more responsive, to political disruption.[16]

Breakdown theorists, despite the numerous theoretical differences among them, share a focus on the state and large-scale social and economic dislocations as the causes of protest movements. Although the crises that create opportunity for social mobilization may be viewed as dangerous or fortuitous, in either case the responsibility for dissent lies with the state. State-centered theories can present the emergence and development of a movement as the product of historical inevitability, discounting the importance of choices made by movement activists, their interests and activities, and even politics. Despite the best efforts of analysts to formalize and quantify analysis of the conditions that create movements, the existence of political opportunity is ultimately signified by the presence of a movement, a tautology that calls into question the utility of a breakdown approach.

As example, an analyst of the peace movement writes, "A major stimulus of nuclear pacifism was undoubtedly *the need for a protest movement*. In the late 1970s, politically conscious individuals and organizations were in need of a cause. The end of the movement against the war in Vietnam had cut loose millions of such persons and scores of organizations. . . . The nuclear weapons state was the logical new target for this free-floating dissatisfaction."[17] Movements, from this perspective, appear and disappear with the tautologically determined need for them. Objects of protest are seen as virtually interchangeable and irrelevant.

Clearly this approach is problematic. On a theoretical level, political issues, tactics, strategies of mobilization, and the role of organization receive little analysis. Further, many of the basic tenets of breakdown approaches have not withstood empirical examination. Studies of movements and activists have shown, for example, that participants in protest movements are more, rather than less, likely to be psychologically stable, rational, and purposeful in their activity.[18] They are also more likely to belong to so-called intermediary organizations than nonparticipants.[19] Politically, breakdown approaches trivialize public policy and give would-be activists little help in understanding the possibilities and strategies for social change. Absent extraordinary circumstances, any options beyond conventional institutionalized politics or waiting are not clear. During times of upheaval, breakdown approaches emphasize the limits, rather than the possibilities, of creating change.[20]

THE ORIGINS OF PROTEST MOVEMENTS: SOLIDARITY

In contrast, solidarity or resource mobilization theories emphasize the process, rather than the context, of social mobilization. Protest is seen as a rational and purposive political tactic designed to win tangible political benefits. Movements arise not as a result of societal breakdown but through the directed efforts of activists and organizations to mobilize and apply their resources, including supporters, money, law, legitimacy, and communications networks, to their political purposes.[21] Protest is attractive as a political strategy to those who are unlikely to win through more conventional political strategies, either because of systematic exclusion from the political arena or a paucity of resources necessary for ongoing conventional participation.[22]

In certain respects, the solidarity theorists turn the analysis of breakdown approaches upside down. Breakdown theorists see extra-institutional protest resulting from a failure of the state; solidarity theorists emphasize the success of activists and organizations. Breakdown theorists see social networks and local organizations as integrating mechanisms that prevent anomie or alienation and the emergence of dissident movements; solidarity theorists view indigenous organizations as the foundation for the social integration and solidarity necessary to initiate, coordinate, and support dissident mobilization. As Aldon Morris argues in his study of the civil rights movement, "Mass protest is a product of the organizing efforts of activists functioning through a well-developed indigenous base."[23]

As described by Morris, a protest movement's emergence reflects the successful application of group resources toward the achievement of policy gains. Protest is politics by other means, a political tactic that enables the disadvantaged or excluded to win access or influence within political institutions. McAdam notes that resource mobilization theorists view the political arena as a slanted battleground monopolized by a relatively small number of interests. These interests dominate by virtue of their control of important political resources, particularly money, institutional position, and legitimacy. Groups use dissident extra-institutional mobilization as a tactical response to their exclusion from more conventional, institutional, and efficacious forms of political participation.[24]

Although critical of the pluralist view of the political arena in the United States, the resource mobilization perspective is compatible with pluralist analysis. Robert Dahl, in his classic study *Who Governs,* acknowledges the unequal dispersal of political resources but postulates the possibility of a sort of asymmetrical equivalence. "Individuals best off in their access to one kind of resource are often badly off with respect to many other resources," he writes. He contends that no group is without some politically significant resources that can be brought to bear on the policy-making process.[25]

The critical questions for a resource mobilization theorist, as for any political group as Dahl notes, involve how a group can maximize its influence by strategic management of its resources. To the extent that groups of the poor or otherwise disadvantaged lack status, money, access to policy makers, and other resources critical to success within political institutions, they must take advantage of the resources they do have, specifically, numbers of supporters, intensity of commitment, indigenous organization, and, perhaps most significantly, the capacity to disrupt the usual practice of politics.

For understandable reasons, this perspective is common among political activists. In contrast to the bleak prospect presented by breakdown theories, activists and organizations are responsible for creating their own opportunities.[26] The role of organizers is critical, as are the tactical choices they make. Issues of interest and the degree of opposition will change over time, but the strategic calculations of organizers, their choices of tactics, and their effectiveness in implementing them will determine success.

Clearly, however, the possibilities for change from below are limited by more than the imagination and abilities of organizers. Indeed, within the resource mobilization paradigm, many analysts stress the role of elite allies in supporting and responding to dissent. Support of elite actors, those with more resources or located closer to actual political power, is critical to a movement's success.[27] Indigenous resources are often only sufficient to leverage elite support, which leads to the application of greater resources to the political arena.[28] Lipsky contends, for example, that successful protest is contingent upon the activation of third parties or "reference publics."[29]

Of course, the responsiveness of elite and institutionalized actors to the demands and activities of protest movements is not constant. It is contingent upon the broader political climate, generally beyond the influence of indigenous organizations and activists. Although resource mobilization theorists acknowledge this, little within the approach contributes to understanding how the political context influences the mobilization and potential success of protest movements. Evans and Boyte, who emphasize the role of indigenous organizations, recognize the importance of political context, concluding that "under certain circumstances, communal associations become free spaces, breeding ground for democratic change."[30] Their analysis, however, does little to suggest what those circumstances might be, and how they could be recognized, created, or exploited.

Although useful in analyzing the relative efficacy of certain strategies and tactics within a period of mobilization, solidarity theories can ignore the important influences that state policies and responses can have on social movement strategy, tactics, and potential mobilization. As example, Paul Boyer notes that the decline of antinuclear protest in the 1960s was at least partly a response to a perceived decline in the threat of nuclear war, as well as the widespread feeling of urgency among activists to shift their primary efforts from the horrors of a war that might be to the horrors of the war in progress in Vietnam. Activists had not changed the tone of their fundraising appeals or scheduled their rallies in dimly lit neighborhoods; historical circumstances had changed.[31]

A comprehensive approach to the study of protest movements must include analysis at the levels suggested by both solidarity and breakdown theories. Particularly, it is important to understand the ways in which the "political opportunity structure"[32] shapes the options available to dissidents and the ways in which protest movements can alter the subsequent structure of opportunities.[33] Well-done historical analysis does this as a matter of course. E. P.

Thompson's *The Making of the English Working Class* and Lawrence Goodwyn's *Democratic Promise: The Populist Moment in America* analyze the range of choices available to dissident activists, the responses of the state and rival groups, and the restructuring of opportunities following a movement's institutionalization or demise. Although historical or journalistic analysis, when well executed, describes the interaction of political opportunity and political activism, integrating the levels of analysis is a difficult theoretical problem. The remainder of this chapter is an attempt to build a theoretical base for this study.

POLITICAL SPACE: THE OPPORTUNITY FOR MOBILIZATION

Movements appear when there are substantive issues and/or substantial constituencies not adequately integrated into the polity by existing linkage mechanisms. This offers an opportunity for a social movement, much as the particular coincidence of the orbits of the earth and the moon present the opportunity for a space shot. Movements, however, are the product of more than opportunity; they represent the efforts of groups and individuals not only to take advantage of opportunity but also to alter the subsequent opportunity structure. For, unlike the moon launch analogy, movements can change the distance between their concerns and government policy creating enhanced or denigrated opportunities for mobilization in the future.

Movements require a political space in which to mobilize activity, a breakdown in usual political process. Political space refers to the opportunities for legitimate mobilization within a society not monopolized by established linkage mechanisms. Legitimacy here applies only to those areas or constituencies a substantial portion of the populace believes merit state attention.[34] Mobilization means inducing people to undertake activity that is for them unusual, with a political intent. It also means applying resources, including media and finances, to pursuing a political goal.[35] Linkage mechanisms are the institutions, groups, and processes that connect people to the state.

A breakdown in the functioning of the state or society increases the political space available for dissident social movements. It does not, however, create these movements, nor does it ensure their success. It is nothing more than a window of opportunity. A movement's success in mobilizing or achieving policy goals is a function of how well it and its competitors — established parties and interest groups — respond to that limited opportunity and the extent to which they fill or expand the available political space.[36]

While the emergence of dissident social movements is a sure indicator of growing political space, the concept is not a simple tautology. It should be possible to observe opportunities, cracks in the veneer of society, before the emergence of a social movement or the restructuring of governmental institutions. Such cracks or opportunities are often underscored by the mass media or by the public and widespread defection of elites from support of government policy.[37] These signs enable us to assess both potential location and size of a nascent social movement and to evaluate how it might mobilize and direct its political impact.

The character of political space available for dissident movements is closely related to the nature of the ruling regime and the structure of its political institutions. Peter Eisinger, in a study of urban protest in the United States, noted that the character, intensity, duration, and frequency of protests were all related to the degree of access to local governmental institutions. Interestingly, protest occurred most frequently in cities with what he described as a mix of open and closed institutions.[38] The Tillys apply these findings to the analysis of national politics and note that although repression (and complete exclusion from the political process) can prevent the emergence of protest movements, extremely open systems can also preempt the development of extra-institutional protest by coopting nascent movements. They write, "highly tolerant regimes also diminish the effectiveness of those collective actions which have considerable probability of violence. They do this by multiplying the available paths to any particular objective, thus making the violence-strewn path less attractive."[39] Protest movements, then, are most likely and most effective in moderately tolerant states.

"Toleration," Charles Tilly writes, "is the space between repression and facilitation."[40] In liberal democratic states the boundaries of tolerance are generally fairly broad. This means that dissident movements may emerge using a very wide variety of tactics but that high cost and high risk strategies, such as violence, will be hard to sustain, simply because of the abundance of alternatives. Governments may play an active role in shaping the pattern of dissent, encouraging those activities least likely to be disruptive — and possibly least likely effective.[41] McAdam notes, for example, that President John F. Kennedy supported and encouraged the civil rights movement's focus on voter registration and voter education to funnel movement activity into less disruptive channels.[42]

The available avenues for political participation and influence shape emerging political space and the subsequent structure of dissent. The U.S. system of government, Lowi writes, "is almost perfectly designed to maintain an existing sate of affairs — any existing state of affairs."[43] The structure of U.S. political institutions, as explained and extolled by Madison in Federalist No. 10, serves not only to tolerate but also to embrace and institutionalize conflict. Once institutionalized, groups develop a stronger interest in maintaining the system of government and their place in it than in pursuing the issues and interests that led to their emergence.[44] Lowi argues that once movements enter the political system and become established organizations, they become obstacles to change: "Movements can succeed or fail; they can disappear and affect nothing thereafter, or they can persist, effect a change, and then defend the system and the changes they helped to effect. . . . The good democrat should try to foster new groups and distrust old groups."[45]

In the United States, mainstream political institutions are relatively quick to absorb, at least symbolically, the concerns and constituents of protest movements. Perhaps the best example of this is the two-party system. In a single member district system such as that of the United States or Great Britain, party rhetoric and politics generally veer to the increasingly nebulous center of the political spectrum; this is where elections are won.[46] Parties, with little purpose beyond forming parliamentary majorities and dispensing the patronage necessary to maintain their continued support, value electoral victories above all else. Under normal circumstances there is strikingly little difference between their rhetoric. Each takes for granted the voters on its extreme wing and seeks to steal support in the political center. Mainstream politicians are understandably reluctant to abandon the center and the appearance of moderation and potentially broad support that goes with it. Parties will only take the immoderate step of significantly differing from their competition when they believe they have something to lose by not doing so.

This loss may be votes, financial donations, or activist support. In any case, the shift from the center is brought about by a fear that activists on the margin of the party constituency will leave the fold if the party does otherwise. Party extremism, which opens legitimate political space in the center, is, however, a lagging indicator of political opportunity for social movements. The movement from the center is not as significant for movements as an opening at either extreme. The center is simply not the most conducive area for unconventional political mobilization. Politically significant space on the margins of U.S. politics can be opened in several different ways, each reflecting a failure of established mechanisms to integrate new issues or new constituencies into the political system. This failure can occur because established linkage mechanisms, such as parties and interest groups, are unable to meet the demands of new constituents or to address new issues successfully or because the established political organizations are unable to continue meeting the agreements of the old political consensus.

New issues can be carried by new constituencies, or they can be thrown into the public arena by foreign policy or technological crises.

The accident at the Three Mile Island nuclear power plant, for example, made nuclear power a mainstream political issue, hastening the demise of the movement against nuclear power, which had grown with the technology. The accident forced established political elites to address safety concerns that had previously been the rhetorical property of the antinuclear movement. The coincidence of the falling price of oil further undermined nuclear power development. A dissident movement was no longer needed to raise these issues. Significantly, although the threat of a nuclear accident did not increase after the accident, it became far more visible to mainstream politics.

Political space exists not only in the geography of political institutions but also in people's minds. The breakdown in legitimacy of the government, a particular industry, or the political process in general contributes to an environment in which people are more likely to participate in movement activity.[47] Movements rely on a breakdown in the hegemony of the dominant ideology and culture. This disruption creates the opportunity for individuals to acknowledge their own political concerns as distinct from those articulated by their government and to see themselves as members of a political and economic group with common interests and potential influence.

MOBILIZATION: THE MEANS OF PROTEST PRODUCTION

Opportunity, however, is not sufficient to make a movement. Political activists must mobilize resources to fill political space in order to generate meaningful protest. In this context, mobilization means applying resources, including people, finances, and publicity, to a political goal.[48] It includes a broad variety of activities, including attending meetings, writing letters, and throwing firebombs. Political space creates an opportunity for movements, but it does not mobilize resources; activists create movements by the political application of their assets.

Jo Freeman suggests that a social movement needs four essential conditions to emerge; (1) a preexisting communications network that is (2) cooptable to the ideas and purposes of the incipient movement; (3) a series of crises that motivates action people who are already involved in a network; and/or (4) subsequent efforts to organize spontaneous groups of people into a network. Freeman argues that organization and communication are not simply by-products of a social movement; they are the resources necessary to mobilize and leverage other resources.[49]

Successful movements build on the networks left by previous movements, those provided by groups well established within society and/or those located on the margins of mainstream politics. Despite frequent appearances to the contrary, movements do not spontaneously erupt. Rather, mobilization is contingent on the availability of people to mobilization and on the incipient movement's cooptation of the resources and networks of established organizations to its new purposes.[50] Such organizations provide new movements with a wealth of resources ranging from the most mundane such as office space, telephone lines, and mimeograph machines, to the more dramatic, including adherents and experienced organizers. They also serve to provide new movements with a carry-over of legitimacy.

The organizer's task is to induce others to contribute their efforts and resources to the movement's purposes. The obstacles to this kind of mobilization are numerous and exceptionally difficult to overcome. Not the least of these is the widespread apathy and nonparticipation characteristic of contemporary U.S. politics.[51] Organizers overcome these obstacles by producing inducements for activism. The first inducements for action to examine are a movement's explicit goals. Individuals will participate and take risks in order to increase the likelihood of achieving common political goals. This, however, may not be enough. In his theoretical exploration of voluntary action, Mancur Olson postulates that human beings act with an economic rationality and, therefore, participate in groups because of some potential benefit. Political gains by a group may be concentrated and accrue only to the members of a particular group, or they may represent public goods, accruing to all citizens.[52] In either case, the critical problem is the group of people who stand to benefit from the group's success, regardless of their contribution. The "free rider" recognizes that the marginal impact of his or her participation is unlikely to influence the prospects for political success, although such participation may be personally costly. Purposive or political goals, when viewed from a perspective of economic rationality, are therefore insufficient to mobilize participation.

Smaller groups, or those with smaller beneficiary constituencies, in which the efforts of a single member are more apparent and more likely significant, can overcome the free rider problem by stressing the costs of not winning or by using some means of social coercion. The free rider problem is far more difficult, however, for larger groups seeking public goods, such as a clean environment, automobile safety standards, or more complete labeling of packaged foods. The focus on collective benefits, characteristic of what Parkin terms "middle-class radicalism," provides the least stable base for sustained mobilization and the weakest prospects for success.[53]

Organizations can provide incentives to overcome the free rider problem. Material incentives, concrete benefits provided only to organization members, are most effective in this regard. Such things as journal subscriptions, insurance discounts, entertainment, job training, or free towing are far more likely to inspire and maintain individual participation than the pursuit of broader political goals. Groups engaged in extra-institutional mobilization, representing excluded policy alternatives or disadvantaged constituencies, are least likely to have sufficient wealth to offer much to would-be participants, especially given the greater extent of participation they require. Instead, insurgent groups depend upon solidarity (feelings of affiliation and social connection) and purposive incentives (prospects of progress toward achieving political goals) to inspire participa-tion.[54] As a result, dissident movements are by nature amateurish, dependent upon volunteers, purposive incentives, and symbolic benefits. As the costs of participation outweigh narrowly defined benefits, volunteers regularly "burn out" and leave active participation in the movement. (For the women's liberation movement in the early 1970s, Freeman claims, the average time of service was about two years.) As a result, there is a continuing need for fresh recruits, not only to invigorate, but simply to people, a movement.[55]

The problem of incentives and mobilization is particularly acute for a movement like the nuclear freeze, where the prospects for immediate success are very weak, links of direct relevance to most people's lives are difficult to make, the benefits are collective, and the capacity to generate material incentives is circumscribed. Although avoiding nuclear war is clearly a benefit to the entire human race, the marginal impact of an individual's participation is unlikely to influence the movement's prospect for success in any significant way. For this reason, the primary mobilizer for peace movements has historically been fear.[56] This, too, is exceptionally difficult to sustain.

ARENAS OF PARTICIPATION

The first obstacle for a movement is inducing people to participate, but mobilization refers to a wide variety of activity, with differing costs to the participants and potential influence on the political system. Attending a political meeting, for example, is one kind of mobilization. Even though this may be an unusual activity for an individual, it is unlikely to be visible, much less significant, to national policymakers. It requires little more than a slight curiosity and a minimal amount of spare time to attend a meeting or a demonstration. The costs are low, and the rewards, social activity, and solidarity reinforcement are immediate. Blowing up an office building, in contrast, requires a great deal more commitment, as the activist must devote large amounts of time and take very high risks. Although it is clearly easier to induce people to undertake low-intensity, low-risk activity, such activity is least likely to affect policy or subsequent mobilization. Groups that use higher-risk strategies of political participation, specifically the use of constraints or coercion against the state — or suffering such constraints from the state — are more likely to achieve favorable political results.[57] Such activities are understandably the most difficult to generate.

This represents one of many calculations activists must make in planning protest activity. Is it worthwhile to engage larger numbers of people in less-intense, less-threatening activity, or is it preferable to concentrate efforts on fewer people and more-intense activities? Living and growing movements include activities across a broad spectrum of cost and risk. This presents the state with a wide variety of action to counter; it also provides activists with a personal escalation ladder to correspond with their own changing commitments. As a movement's appeal fades, activity may be confined to a small and often marginalized group of people, or it may be restricted to conventional lower-risk activities. This escalates the movement's demise. A movement engaged exclusively in political violence or other intense activity from the committed few is unlikely to mobilize from the political mainstream and will likely face continually declining resources while provoking repression. A movement confined to low-intensity participation is not likely to threaten the state and its usual political processs in any way, and it will no longer be a movement.

In addition to the intensity level of activity, activists plan the arena in which they will confront the state and its policies. Here again, there are multiple options with multiple complications. Certain arenas — for example, electoral politics — require large-scale mobilization of very low-level activity and are likely to yield extremely limited benefits. The possible routes to influence, however, of less conventional political activity, such as civil disobedience, are far less clear, although clearly critical to developing and evaluating political strategies. Arenas are where movements meet the state. In the United States, available arenas include:

Elections. Movements can endorse candidates, mobilize voters, and contribute money to federal, state, or local political campaigns. Referenda can also be used in less conventional ways, such as creating "nuclear-free zones."

Lobbies. Movements can engage in conventional lobbying activities in attempts to influence policy makers.[58]

Streets. Movements may attempt to generate support by visibly presenting their grievances in highly public venues, demanding state response. Disruption of routine patterns of politics and life is the primary weapon in this context.[59] As street activity escalates in intensity, it is also likely to enter the legal system.

Sites. Movements seeking to promote justice can direct their activity directly at perceived injustice. Civil rights activists seeking to end segregation in the United States actively desegregated lunch counters, city buses, libraries, and many other public places. Opponents of nuclear power have physically attacked nuclear power stations. These activities are often less visible than assembling in front of the Lincoln Memorial or New York City's Central Park. Their directness does, however, have its own appeal and advantages. These efforts also often end in the legal system.

Markets. Movements often include activity explicitly directed against the economic functioning of the state or private corporations by staging economic boycotts.[60] This may prove to be the most effective way to change the conduct of a company marketing harmful products in the Third World or busting unions in the United States. When directed against the state, it may manifest as tax resistance and reach the legal system.

Legal System. Movements may actively challenge state policy in the courts or may end up in the courts after challenging policy elsewhere.[61]

Each of these arenas requires different resources for entrance and offers a limited number of responses. The choice of arena and activity structures a movement's development and limits the extent of potential gains. Accessibility, or the appearance of accessibility, directly affects the way fledgling movements define themselves and the way politics works in the United States.

THE ORGANIZATION OF PROTEST

The role of organizations in protest movements is both critical and extremely problematic. Movement organizations have been construed as both the source of dissident mobilization and the immediate obstacle to effective action.[62] A social movement is not limited to the efforts of established organizations; however, much of movement activity is coordinated by such groups.[63] The goals and organizational styles of a movement's component organizations have a large effect on the content, style, and eventual impact of a dissident movement.

The quintessential study of political organization, Robert Michels' *Political Parties,*[64] advanced the iron law of oligarchy. Michels concluded that power in organizations, regardless of how democratic their goals or ideology, inevitably concentrates in the hands of a few people. The leadership develops substantially different interests from rank and file members. The task of organizational maintenance substantially overshadows all other political goals, and although organizations tend to survive, survival is generally at the expense of the movements that create them. The inherent tendency toward conservatism of organizations has become a truism among analysts of organizations and movements.[65] Analytic approaches to oligarchic and bureaucratic processes often reflect political views of the larger society.

Wilson, for example, sees bureaucratization as a necessary stage in political development, arguing that moderation of rank and file demands is essential for organizational survival. He contends that the failure to develop centralized leadership within an organization inevitably leads to debilitating conflict, which prevents it from setting coherent, negotiable, and achievable goals.[66] Such organizations are unable to ensure their own survival, much less change government policy. He notes that organizations with multiple centers of power and rich diversity in membership are more likely to develop a large number of proposals for changing society, but they are far less likely to have any of those proposals accepted by the government. As example, he contrasts the National Association for the Advancement of Colored People (NAACP) with the Student Nonviolent Coordinating Committee (SNCC), pointing out that the latter, decentralized and democratically governed, was unable to adapt to a changing political climate for civil rights issues. SNCC disintegrated after a series of well-publicized internal conflicts. In contrast the NAACP has throughout its long history been able to adapt to changes in political climate and state policy and continually carve out a place for itself, the mark of success for Wilson. He writers, "In the long run . . . all organizations seek some form of accommodation with their environment, because the costs of sustaining indefinitely a combat-oriented organization are generally too high to be borne by the members."[57]

Piven and Cloward accept most of Wilson's analysis, but they derive entirely different prescriptions from it.[68] While they do not challenge Wilson's assertions regarding organizational survival, they question whether this is the sole criterion for success. SNCC's lifespan was limited, they acknowledge, but it surely helped to create a climate of national concern that enabled more moderate organizations to win policy concessions.[69] Organizations that survive, they argue, are those that so moderate their goals and tactics that they are no longer a threat to state policy. Organizational main-tenance and political mobilization are, if not antithetical, certainly separate. Elites, concerned with ensuring the survival of their organization, deemphasize and inhibit mobilization. At very best, they waste time and resources on activities that do not aid in mobilization. At worst, they moderate the demands and disruption of their claimed constituency, serving to minimize potential gains.

Movements, Piven and Cloward contend, should do what they do best: mobilize protest.

These drastically different views of organization both accept Michels' iron law as inevitable. This acceptance offers activists the choice of accepting more moderate approaches and goals or of ignoring the process of organization building and supporting unorganized activity or nascent political groups rather than established organizations.[70] Alternatively, they may challenge oligarchical tendencies directly by taking prophylactic measures, either explicitly rejecting all attempts at institutionalization or building in controls, such as rotation of leadership and professional positions or consensus rules, which keep decision-making power at the grassroots.

Gerlach and Hine contend that protest movements of the past two decades have adopted new organizational styles that run counter to more traditional bureaucratic models. New movements, they contend, reflect networks rather than organizations, and are "decentralized, segmented, and reticulate."[71] They frequently include several competing organizations and comprise a wide variety of political activities. Some of these component organizations are national and large, while others are locally based. In a living movement, organizations are constantly changing, reforming, and disintegrating. There are multiple leaders, none of whom has an exclusive claim to speak for the movement. The groups and leaders are linked through a network of concern, often cooperating in the service of shared political goals.

This style of organization offers several clear advantages over more conventional models and suggests the possibility of avoiding the worst consequences of Michels' iron law. Multiple activities in the service of a shared goal are likely to produce a synergistic effect, increasing the impact of the movement as a whole. A variety of tactical approaches and organizations increases the likelihood of discovering effective strategies and also the potential ways to appeal to new activists. The NAACP, SNCC, the Southern Christian Leadership Conference (SCLC), and the Congress of Racial Equality (CORE), for example, all appealed to different segments of society concerned with civil rights. The diverse efforts of all these groups made the civil rights movement more effective. The presence of more radical and threatening organizations and individuals made more moderate figures, like Martin Luther King, more attractive to mainstream society. Further, a movement with a number of leaders competing for support is less susceptible to cooptation than a conventional political organization. Finally, decentralized organizations may provide recruits with a sense of organizational efficacy, which may substitute for clear victories in the larger political arena and sustain activity.[72]

This decentralized structure, Gerlach and Hine contend, may simply occur de facto in contemporary movements, as happened in the civil rights and environmental movements. It may also be intentionally built into organizational structures, as in the movement against nuclear power. Opponents of nuclear power made a virtue of decentralization and participatory democracy, organizing protest through semiautonomous groups of 10–25 activists each. These affinity groups were tight units run by consensus. Strategy decisions about a particular activity were made by a consensus among representatives (spokes) from participating affinity groups. A group's consensus decision could theoretically be represented by any member of that group, and spokes were rotated frequently, generally from meeting to meeting, in order to develop a movement of leaders and to ensure informed and active participation.[73]

The decline of the movement, at least partly the result of its amorphous organization, reflects the problems with this organizational style. The loose structure of small groups was generally unable to respond to changes in the political environment, and there was no established group principally concerned with organizational survival. The rule of consensus ensured that anyone with concerns about the possibility, efficacy, or morality of a particular aspect of an action would be able to voice them. As a result, meetings were often exceedingly long and exceptionally tedious. This served to inhibit broadly coordinated creative responses to unexpected situations. In spite of the creativity displayed by individual affinity groups, the movement's actions veered toward an increasing sameness, a familiar style around which consensus could be built. Contingents intending to escalate the intensity of antinuclear activity to violence against property eventually succeeded in eliminating the strict rule of consensus, but at the cost of fragmenting the movement. Other groups negotiated with authorities on behalf of the movement to ensure nonviolence, minimize arrests, or gain maximum publicity and support. Each contingent organized successful events, but the movement as a whole lost cohesion and its capacity to mobilize.

Other movements' experiences with this decentralized model reflect the potential dangers. McAdam notes that the decentralization of control that characterized the civil rights movement during the late 1960s inhibited the development of a coordinated, powerful, and disruptive campaign at the national level. Activists increasingly picked local targets, ones unable to initiate broad policy reforms or grant meaningful concessions.[74] Frederick Miller's account of the demise of the Students for a Democratic Society demonstrates how a group that fails to formalize its organizational structure can be taken over by a small but determined and disciplined minority.[75] Jane Mansbridge notes that the decentralized structure of the campaign for the Equal Rights Amendment (ERA), while seen as an ideological virtue, created strategic and tactical problems that undermined the movement. The hierarchical structure of ERA opponents, she contends, was more effective at responding to new circumstances, training activists, dealing with the media, and providing continuity of leadership than the pro-ERA forces.[76] Further, the movement forfeited the capacity to define its own goals and image strategically. The responsibility for defining the movement and its goals devolved to the most activist and radical groups who advanced a vision that could not win the support needed for a constitutional amendment.[77] Finally, Gamson found that more hierarchically and bureaucratically structured groups are better suited to mobilize intense activity and to win real gains.[78]

The problems of both traditional and alternative organizational models offer no clear answers for activists and ensure an ongoing debate about efficacy and democracy within new movements. Continuous experimentation with new organizational models reflects a movement's struggle to maximize its mobilization and impact while still seeking organizational survival.

INSTITUTIONALIZATION: THE END OF MOVEMENT

As with the origins of social movements, their ends can best be understood by combining aspects of solidarity and breakdown theories. Social movements end when they lose their hold on a space at the edge of mainstream politics. They are no longer movements when they stop mobilizing, cease nonconventional activity, and fail to command attention from the mainstream. Although movements are transient, they do not vanish suddenly and without a trace; they leave extensive artifacts, often in the form of functioning political organizations, as well as the political acceptance of some of their concerns. Movements may end because activists and organizations make strategic and tactical choices that inhibit their ability to mobilize or command outside support. Movement ends may also be brought about by state response, including repression, cooptation, or acquiescence.[79] For contemporary movements like the nuclear freeze, decline is generally caused by some combination of all these things.

Protest movements are subjected to unusually strong external and internal pressures toward dissolution. States and intermediary institutions, particularly political parties, seek to regain the resources and legitimacy commanded by a movement by accommodating them, marginalizing them, or redefining their concerns and preempting them. When a movement's issues become less salient, each organization within a movement coalition, in order to maintain its own survival, is subjected to increasingly powerful pressures to specialize, distinguishing and distancing itself from the coalition in the process.[80]

All movement organizations share the common problem of ensuring the flow of resources in order to survive and to continue activity. There are a variety of resources and sources of support, however, so that groups can choose from a range of strategies to maintain some form of support. Activism from the grassroots is best sustained by a politics of polemic, in which enemies are vilified, demands escalated, the differences between movement goals and state policy magnified, and the efforts of competing organizations discredited. Such strategies may maintain the support of committed members, whose activity constitutes the leading edge of a social movement, but they are also likely to prevent the growth of support among larger numbers of weaker and more moderate supporters or to win recognition or support from the state or political elites. They are also more likely to invite repression. Groups choosing this approach, if they do survive, are effectively marginalized. They are no longer able to reach into the political mainstream for support or to influence mainstream political discourse. Alternatively, an organization may seek to cultivate the endorsement of weak supporters and elite allies. This entails following a more traditional model of political organization, abandoning comprehensive or radical demands, and emphasizing conventional forms of political participation. Although this course enhances the group's likelihood of survival and the chances of winning recognition and modest gains, they come at the expense of the broader vision that initially spawned the group; political goals ultimately atrophy in favor of organizational maintenance. These groups stop challenging conventional politics and are effectively coopted. Both marginalization and cooptation mean that a movement no longer poses an effective challenge to routine politics. Instead, it reaches an accommodation of sorts and is effectively institutionalized.[81]

These strategic decisions are not made in a political vacuum. The political opportunity structure for a movement organization is dynamic, influenced by the actions of other groups and the government. Governmental repression, by raising the costs of participation, can make political mobilization more difficult.[82] By adopting movement rhetoric, granting recognition and legitimacy to certain movement factions, reforming policy, and offering symbolic concessions, governments may also reduce the perceived need for a protest movement.[83] Mainstream organizations and political parties are often able to steal a movement's legitimacy and political space by incorporating only a small part of its concerns and promising better prospects for making some gains.[84]

Government responses are integrally related to the institutionalization of social movements. Since movements generally include multiple organizations and perspectives on politics, they will most commonly be institutionalized by both cooptation and marginalization. The narrow rim of legitimacy at the edge of U.S. politics cuts through the heart of movement consensus, incorporating some movement concerns, while allowing more volatile aspects to fall harmlessly off the edges of the mainstream. As a result, the movement coalition fragments, with the potential efficacy of each wing suffering.

The way in which marginalization and cooptation are mutually complementary is an essential feature of movements in the United States. In the struggle to gain and maintain widespread acceptance and support, social movement organizations will, in order to appear less threatening, become less threatening. Seeking to enhance their chances of survival, organizations coopt themselves, moderating their demands and tactics while disavowing other factions of the movement pursuing what were formerly shared goals. Criticism from mainstream counterparts, ostensibly working for the same goals, cuts into the legitimacy of more radical social groups and helps marginalize them.

The history of protest movements in the United States suggests that despite activists' best efforts, this process is inevitable. The nature of the political arena, which allows limited access to selected dissidents and provides opportunity for partial reforms, contributes heavily toward this tendency. Simply, the temptations of organizational security, widespread acceptance, mainstream legitimacy, access to political institutions, and real, though limited gains, are difficult to resist. Insurgent groups are thus incorporated into the structures that prevent substantive change. Participation in a protest movement involves the continuous calculation of what can be won at any given time. Maximum political efficacy means continuously fighting institutionalization at the possible cost of organizational destruction. It means sensing in some way when the opportunity for mobilization is ending and extracting the greatest possible concessions from the state in exchange for ending what is already ending. Neither dissident activists nor their opponents can make these judgments with certainty or precision. Rather, the process of institutionalization invariably includes continual testing and experimentation by movement leaders, opponents, and representatives of the state.

NOTES

1. Lawrence Wittner, *Rebels against War: The American Peace Movement, 1933–1983*, Philadelphia: Temple University Press, 1984, pp. 152, 246–47.
2. Theodore J. Lowi, *The Politics of Disorder*, New York: Basic, 1971, p. 54.

3. Roberta Ash Garner, *Social Movements in America,* Chicago: Markham, 1972; Charles Tilly, *From Mobilization to Revolution,* Reading, MA: Addison-Wesley, 1978; Paul Wilkenson, *Social Movement,* New York: Praeger, 1971.

4. This term is from Rudolf Bahro, *Socialism and Survival,* London: Heretic Books, 1982. See also Jo Freeman, *The Politics of Women's Liberation: A Case Study of an Emerging Social Movement and Its Relation to the Policy Process,* New York: David McKay, 1975, p. 3; Doug McAdam, "The Biographical Consequences of Activism," *American Sociological Review,* 54 (October 1989): 745–46.

5. Michael Lipsky, *Protest in City Politics: Rent Strikes, Housing, and the Power of the Poor,* Chicago: Rand McNally, 1970, p. 1.

6. Frederick Miller, "The End of SDS and the Emergence of Weathermen: Demise through Success," in Jo Freeman, ed., *Social Movements of the Sixties and Seventies,* New York: Longman, 1983, p. 283.

7. Doug McAdam, *Political Process and the Development of Black Insurgency,* Chicago: University of Chicago Press, 1982.

8. John D. McCarthy and Mayer N. Zald, "Resource Mobilization and Social Movements: A Partial Theory," *American Journal of Sociology* 82 (1977): 1212–41; Frances Fox Piven and Richard A. Cloward, *Poor People's Movements: Why They Succeed, How They Fail,* New York: Vintage, 1979.

9. See Frank Parkin, *Middle Class Radicalism,* New York and London: Praeger, 1968, p. 3.

10. Charles Tilly, Louise Tilly, and Richard Tilly, *The Rebellious Century: 1830–1930,* Cambridge, MA: Harvard University Press, 1975, pp. 4–6.

11. Hannah Arendt, *The Origins of Totalitarianism,* New York: Harcourt, Brace, 1951; Eric Hoffer, *The True Believer: Thoughts on the Nature of Mass Movements,* New York: New American Library, 1951; William Kornhauser, *The Politics of Mass Society,* Glencoe, IL: The Free Press, 1959. Charles Tilly contends that these analyses follow a Durkheimian tradition in *From Mobilization to Revolution,* pp. 18–21.

12. Several variants of this approach include Murray Edelman, *Politics as Symbolic Action: Mass Arousal and Quiescence,* Chicago: Markham, 1971; Ted Robert Gurr, *Why Men Rebel,* Princeton, NJ: Princeton University Press, 1970; Samuel Huntington, *Political Order in Changing Societies,* New Haven: Yale University Press, 1968; Neil Smelser, *Theory of Collective Behavior,* New York: Free Press, 1963. New social movement theory is based on the premise that the unusual circumstances, which create movements, have been institutionalized in "post-industrial society." These movements represent a force to create new social relations in a distorted society. See Alain Touraine, *The Voice and the Eye,* New York: Cambridge University Press, 1981.

13. Theda Skocpol, *States and Social Revolutions,* Cambridge: Cambridge University Press, 1979.

14. Piven and Cloward, *Poor People's Movements,* p. 28.

15. Ibid., p. 7.

16. Also see John Gaventa, *Power and Powerlessness: Quiescence and Rebellion in an Appalachian Valley,* Urbana, IL: University of Illinois Press, 1980; McAdam, *Political Process,* p. 48; J. Craig Jenkins and Charles Y. Perrow, "Insurgency of the Powerless: Farm Worker Movements (1946–1972)," *American Sociological Review,* April 1977, pp.57–85.

17. Paul Wehr, "Nuclear Pacifism as Collective Action," *Journal of Peace Research* 23 (June 1986): 104.

18. Kenneth Kenniston, *Young Radicals,* New York: Harcourt, Brace, and World, 1968.

19. Parkin, *Middle-Class Radicalism,* pp. 16–20.

20. Piven and Cloward, *Poor People's Movements,* p. 36.

21. McCarthy and Zald, "Resource Mobilization and Social Movements"; Anthony Oberschall, *Social Conflicts and Social Movements,* Englewood Cliffs, NJ: Prentice Hall, 1973.

22. William A. Gamson, *The Strategy of Social Protest,* Homewood, IL: Dorsey Press, pp. 141–43; Lipsky, *Protest in City Politics,* p. 1.

23. Aldon Morris, *The Origins of the Civil Rights Movement: Black Communities Organizing for Change,* New York: Free Press, 1984, p. xii; also see Sara M. Evans and Harry C. Boyte, *Free Spaces: The Sources of Democratic Change in America,* New York: Harper & Row, 1986; Pam Solo, *From Protest to Policy: Beyond the Freeze to Common Security,* Cambridge, MA: Ballinger, 1988, p. 180.

24. McAdam, *Political Process,* p. 20.

25. Robert A. Dahl, *Who Governs: Democracy and Power in an American City,* New Haven: Yale University Press, 1961, p. 228.

26. See Saul Alinsky, *Rules for Radicals: A Practical Primer for Realistic Radicals,* New York: Vintage, 1971.

27. McAdam, *Political Process,* p. 25.

28. Jenkins and Perrow, "Insurgency of the Powerless."

29. Lipsky, *Protest in City Politics,* p. 2.

30. Evans and Boyte, *Free Spaces,* p. 187.

31. Paul Boyer, "From Activism to Apathy: The American People and Nuclear Weapons, 1963–1980," *The Journal of American History,* March 1984, p. 821.

32. Peter K. Eisinger, "The Conditions of Protest Behavior in American Cities," *American Political Science Review* 67 (1973): 11–28.

33. C. Tilly et al. term such an approach "political process." *Rebellious Century,* p. 252; see also McAdam, *Political Process,* who attempts to refine an integrative theory.

34. Robert A. Dahl, *A Preface to Democratic Theory,* Chicago: University of Chicago Press, 1956, p. 138.

35. Tilly, *From Mobilization to Revolution,* pp. 7, 69.

36. Freeman, *Politics of Women's Liberation,* p. 44; McAdam, *Political Process,* p. 52.

37. Crane Brinton, *The Anatomy of Revolution,* New York: Vintage Books, 1965.

38. Eisinger, "Conditions of Protest Behavior," p. 23.

39. C. Tilly et al., *Rebellious Century,* p. 286. On opportunity structures and national politics, see also Herbert G. Kitschelt, "Political Opportunity Structures and Political Protest: Anti-Nuclear Movements in Four Democracies," *British Journal of Political Science,* January 1986, pp. 57-85; Sidney Tarrow, *Struggle, Politics, and Reform: Collective Action, Social Movements, and Cycles of Protest,* Ithaca, NY: Cornell University Center for International Studies, 1989, pp. 34–36.

40. Tilly, *From Mobilization to Revolution,* p. 107.

41. Gamson, *Strategy of Social Protest,* pp. 72–88; Tilly, *From Mobilization to Revolution,* pp. 114, 167.

42. McAdam, *Political Process,* p. 170.

43. Lowi, *Politics of Disorder,* p. 53.

44. Freeman, *Politics of Women's Liberation*, p. 5; McAdam, *Political Process*, p. 38; Tilly, *From Mobilization to Revolution*, p. 135.

45. Lowi, *Politics of Disorder*, p. 54.

46. Anthony Downs, *An Economic Theory of Democracy*, New York: Harper & Row, 1957.

47. Gaventa, *Power and Powerlessness*; Piven and Cloward, *Poor People's Movements*, pp. 2–3; McAdam, *Political Process*, p. 48.

48. Tilly, *From Mobilization to Revolution*, p. 69.

49. Freeman, *Politics of Women's Liberation*, pp. 48–49.

50. Morris, *Origins of the Civil Rights Movement*, pp. 282–85.

51. Dahl, *Who Governs*, pp. 198, 264, 276–301; Sidney Verba and Norman H. Nie, *Participation in America: Political Democracy and Social Equality*, New York: Harper & Row, 1987.

52. Mancur Olson, *The Logic of Collective Action*, Cambridge, MA: Harvard University Press, 1965, p. 14.

53. Parkin, *Middle-Class Radicalism*, p. 2; Gamson, *Strategy of Social Protest*, pp. 55–71.

54. James Q. Wilson, *Political Organizations*, New York: Basic Books, 1973, Chapter 3.

55. Freeman, *Politics of Women's Liberation*, pp. 96–101, 143–44; Lipsky, *Protest in City Politics*, p. 164.

56. Wittner, *Rebels against War*, pp. 167–69.

57. Gamson, *Strategy of Social Protest*, pp. 72–88. For a theoretical examination of the trade-offs involving participants' tactics and numbers, see James De Nardo, *Power in Numbers: The Political Strategy of Protest and Rebellion*, Princeton, NJ: Princeton University Press, 1985.

58. Kay Lehman Schlozman and John T. Tierney, *Organized Interests and American Democracy*, New York: Harper & Row, 1986, pp. 261–301.

59. Lipsky, *Protest in City Politics*, p. 187.

60. Gamson, *Strategy of Social Protest*, pp. 43–44, 82–86.

61. Joel F. Handler, *Social Movements and the Legal System: A Theory of Law Reform and Social Change*, Orlando, FL: Academic Press, 1978.

62. Compare Morris, *Origins of the Civil Rights Movement*; Piven and Cloward, *Poor People's Movements*, Chapter 4.

63. McCarthy and Zald, "Resource Mobilization and Social Movements."

64. Robert Michels, *Political Parties*, New York: Collier Books, 1962.

65. Freeman describes the "Weber-Michels" model in *Politics of Women's Liberation*, p. 100. See also McAdam, *Political Process*, p. 38; Tilly, *From Mobilization to Revolution*, p. 151.

66. See also Lipsky, *Protest in City Politics*, p. 11; Jane Mansbridge, *Why We Lost the ERA*, Chicago: University of Chicago Press, 1986, pp. 118–48.

67. Wilson, *Political Organizations*, p. 31. For his interpretation of SNCC's demise, see pp. 180–82.

68. Piven and Cloward, *Poor People's Movements*, p. 33.

69. See also Freeman, *Politics of Women's Liberation*, pp. 234–37.

70. Lowi, *Politics of Disorder*, p. 54; Piven and Cloward, *Poor People's Movements*, pp. xxi–xxiii, and passim.

71. Luther P. Gerlach and Virginia H. Hine, *People, Power, Change: Movements of Social Transformation*, Indianapolis, IN: Bobbs-Merrill, 1970, p. 33.

72. Parkin, *Middle-Class Radicalism*, pp. 20, 37–38.

73. See Lynn Dwyer, "Structure and Strategy in the Antinuclear Movement" in Freeman, ed., *Social Movements of the Sixties and Seventies,* pp. 148–61.

74. McAdam, *Political Process,* p. 16. Also see Lipsky, *Protest in City Politics,* p. 176.

75. Miller, "The End of SDS."

76. Mansbridge, *Why We Lost the ERA,* pp. 133–35.

77. Ibid., pp. 67–89, 268. Mansbridge calls this "decision by accretion."

78. Gamson, *The Strategy of Social Protest,* pp. 89–109.

79. Miller, "The End of SDS."

80. McCarthy and Zald, "Resource Mobilization and Social Movement," p. 1234.

81. Freeman, *Politics of Women's Liberation,* p. 154; Gamson, *The Strategy of Social Protest,* pp. 38–54; Lipsky, *Protest in City Politics,* p. 11; McAdam, *Political Process,* pp. 57–58; Emily Stoper, "The Student Non-Violent Coordinating Committee: Rise and Fall of a Redemptive Organization," in Freeman, ed., *Social Movements,* pp. 320–34; Tilly, *From Mobilization to Revolution,* p. 151.

82. Tilly, *From Mobilization to Revolution,* p. 100–1.

83. Freeman, *Politics of Women's Liberation,* Chapter 6; Lipsky, *Protest in City Politics,* p. 176; Mansbridge, *Why We Lost the ERA,* pp. 188–91.

84. See Goodwyn's discussion of the "shadow movement" following populism in *The Populist Moment,* pp. 215–30; see also Anthony M. Messina, "Postwar Protest Movements in Britain: A Challenge to Parties," *The Review of Politics,* Summer 1987, pp. 410–28.

2

NUCLEAR WEAPONS AND NATIONAL SECURITY POLICY: CONTINUITY AND CONFLICT

Despite conflict among policy makers about the political utility of nuclear weapons, U.S. national security policy, and the role of nuclear weapons within it, has been remarkably consistent. It has also been generally isolated from wider domestic political debate. Since Harry Truman ordered the *Little Boy* detonated over Hiroshima, nuclear weapons have consistently been used primarily not to protect the territorial security of the United States but to support conventional forces and foreign policy goals. Increasingly diverse and multifaceted nuclear capabilities have been the ultimate guarantor of U.S. military superiority in pursuit of a wide range of political and military goals. Given these broad objectives, Pentagon planners and elected officials involved in making policy have necessarily conceived the use of nuclear weapons considerably more flexibly and broadly than has the general public.[1]

This role of providing practically infinite threat escalation and military insurance means that nuclear weapons do not have to be detonated in order to be used.[2] The threat of nuclear strike, both explicit through deployment and implicit through possession, is but the most visible use of U.S. nuclear forces. In their study of the employment of U.S. military forces, Blechmann and Kaplan documented 19 distinct incidents in which nuclear weapons were "used" to support military and political objectives between 1946 and 1973.[3] The locales circle the globe, including South America (Uruguay), Central America (Cuba, Guatemala), Eastern and Western Europe (Yugoslavia, Turkey, Berlin), the Far East (North Korea, Taiwan, China), and the Middle East (Suez, Jordan). President Eisenhower believed that the skillful use of nuclear threats aided progress in negotiations to end the Korean War, and the Kennedy administration saw the resolution of the Cuban missile crisis as a textbook example of the political utility of nuclear threats used in the context of "flexible response."[4]

This approach to nuclear weapons did not change after 1973. Richard Nixon threatened North Vietnam with "measures of the greatest consequence" shortly after assuming the presidency,[5] and President Ford threatened the use of nuclear weapons in defense of South Korea. Both Presidents Carter and Reagan also acknowledged that they would use nuclear weapons to protect U.S. interests and political objectives in the Persian Gulf.[6] The explicit threat to employ nuclear weapons in a particular instance, however, represents only a portion of their utility. "Like Army ground troops deployed overseas," Blechmann and Kaplan note, "strategic nuclear forces serve vital political objectives on a continuing basis, perhaps obviating the need for discrete and explicit utilization."[7]

Nuclear weapons, then, are and have been used to deter far more than nuclear war. The U.S. nuclear arsenal is designed for "extended deterrence" of a broad spectrum of political and military actions including, but not limited to, Soviet conventional aggression in Europe and the Third World, and aggression of Third World nations against countries or business interests perceived to be "vital" to U.S. security interests.[8] Despite conflict among policy makers, U.S. foreign and military policy has long been predicated on the capacity and willingness to use nuclear weapons first[9] in pursuit of various political objectives, although the vast majority (81 percent by one estimate) of Americans remain unaware of this central principle.[10] Recognition of this central tenet is, however, crucial to a clear understanding of U.S. nuclear and military policy.[11]

Since nuclear weapons are intended for political and military use, that is, deterrence of conduct short of nuclear war, their efficacy is contingent upon an opponent's belief that the United States would indeed employ them in the service of a particular goal. If any military use of nuclear weapons inevitably leads to global destruction, then the number of political objectives justifying their employment would be clearly proscribed, and a list of such goals would be very short. Potential enemies recognizing this would not be readily deterred. If, on the other hand, nuclear weapons could theoretically be employed in a limited manner in pursuit of political ends without bringing about an apocalypse, their efficacy in deterring unwanted foreign initiatives would be greatly increased. If other nations believe that the United States would use nuclear weapons, they will refrain from behavior that might provoke a nuclear response. Only if they believe the United States lacks either the military hardware or political will to escalate to nuclear options will they risk goading the United States into using them. Paradoxically, the more conceivable use of nuclear weapons is, following this line of reasoning, the less likely it is that they will be used.[12] Consequently, according to the dominant consensus among policy makers, modernization and diversification of the U.S. nuclear arsenal are essential to prevent nuclear war.

Following this theory the United States has spent hundreds of billions of dollars to deploy nuclear weapons on an increasing variety of platforms, ranging from submarine launched ballistic missiles to nuclear land and sea mines, from intercontinental ballistic missiles to nuclear tipped torpedoes and air-to-air missiles. Each successive generation of weapons is designed to be more usable and, therefore, more credible than the preceding one. The destructive yield of these weapons has also been diversified, ranging from nine megatons (more than 60 times the yield of the Hiroshima bomb) to fractions of a kiloton.[13] The arsenal grew and grows out of a deliberate policy to provide numerous potential steps in a well-defined ladder of escalation, allowing for a graduated response to any imaginable contingency.[14]

CONFLICTS WITHIN THE CONSENSUS

This general goal and the pursuit of escalating nuclear capabilities have remained unchanged since the Eisenhower administration. There have, however, been differing emphases between, and indeed within, administrations as to the vigor with which strategic modernization and nuclear diversification have been pursued.[15] Conflicts about strategy have generally focused on two distinct but related issues: the political utility of nuclear weapons and the degree to which nuclear weapons should be integrated with conventional forces. The debates have consistently raged between those who advocated treating nuclear weapons as any other military hardware and those who saw their utility as heavily circumscribed. There has been no resolution.

Approaches to nuclear strategy are arrayed across a broad continuum, reflecting differing views of the utility of nuclear weapons, but for heuristic purposes we can identify three distinct approaches to nuclear deterrence.[16] The *minimum deterrence* view is based on the premise that nuclear weapons are fundamentally different from any other kind of weaponry and that their development has essentially made war unthinkable. Deployment of nuclear weapons is, however, the only effective way to deter another power from using nuclear weapons. According to this view, the United States must maintain a survivable "second strike" capacity, that is, the capability to absorb a nuclear "first strike" and then inflict "unacceptable" damage upon the aggressor. While there may be conflict about what level of damage an adversary would risk or about the best way to ensure the survival of a second strike force, this approach sets clear limits on the useful number of nuclear weapons.

Nuclear stability and national security can be achieved relatively cheaply and easily, with a minimum of highly destructive and invulnerable nuclear missiles, regardless of an adversary's capabilities.[17]

War fighters contend that the minimum deterrence position is inherently untenable. An opponent who has endured a U.S. nuclear attack may still maintain the capacity to attack the United States again. Thus a U.S. president is effectively held hostage to his own willingness to risk an all-out nuclear war by attacking civilian targets of even the most heinous enemy. By raising the stakes for employing U.S. nuclear weapons, their use becomes less credible. A president could be faced with the choice of acceding to enemy aggression or effectively inviting nuclear attack upon the United States. It is more effective, war fighters argue, and more ethical to maintain the capacity to engage in constrained nuclear exchanges and limited wars. A diversified and flexible nuclear arsenal must be developed in order to deny an enemy any kind of victory. In order to prevent nuclear war the United States must be prepared to fight such a war. A strategic balance or rough parity is necessary to ensure credible deterrence.[18]

A third group believes that capacity and willingness to engage in many levels of nuclear engagement is itself an insufficiently credible deterrent unless the United States has the capacity to escalate the conflict to a level at which it can prevail. This escalation dominance or *war winning* view essentially denies that nuclear weapons are unique or that nuclear war is unthinkable. The United States, advocates of this view hold, must develop tactics and strategies for nuclear weapons similar to those used for conventional weapons. A nuclear war can be "won" by inflicting "unacceptable" damage upon an enemy while limiting damage to the United States to an "acceptable" level. Nuclear weapons must be seen as another element in the U.S. arsenal and fully integrated with other military forces. The capacity to deny an enemy victory, seen as sufficient by war fighters, is essentially reactive and ignores broader U.S. interests. A war winning capability is necessary to ensure national security and the preservation of a wide range of foreign policy goals. War winners hold that this capability is achievable only through concentrated military research and development and, even more important, political will. In order to deter the Soviet Union or any other opponent, the United States must ensure not only the destruction but also paradoxically more important, the unambiguous defeat of an aggressor.[19]

Although each perspective carries with it clear implications regarding modernization, procurement, military spending, and arms control, the results of the conflict between them have been played out in a relatively consistent, although somewhat tempered, program of modernization within the boundaries of a war fighting paradigm. Debates between advocates of these three perspectives have continued unabated since the Eisenhower administration. As Lawrence Freedman notes, there has been no learning or evolution in nuclear strategy; the same issues continually recycle, no coherent strategy has been developed. The absence of an accepted strategic view of the utility of nuclear weapons has led to a persistent tendency to increase options available to policy makers by developing a wide variety of nuclear capabilities. As a result, technological innovation, rather than strategy, often seems to drive the U.S. national security posture.[20]

The Pentagon and private military contractors have provided a motor for this trend, seeking expanded forces and increasingly sophisticated weaponry with enhanced war fighting capabilities. Congress, for a variety of reasons including lack of understanding, domestic political considerations, and pork barrel politics, has rarely done more than "rubber-stamp Pentagon requests."[21] The executive branch of government has been primarily responsible for constraining the military buildup and expenditure countenanced by the Pentagon and defense industries.[22] Particularly, although not exclusively, within the war winning view, there is the potential for an unlimited military buildup in the ostensible pursuit of deterrence. Declaratory policy must then be read not only in light of addressing the Soviet Union and U.S. allies but also as part of the political struggle between the executive and the military services.

POLITICS AND NUCLEAR WEAPONS POLICY

The development of U.S. nuclear posture has reflected factors other than a consensus on strategy. To understand those factors, and to understand the extent to which President Reagan departed from the policies of his predecessors, it is useful to review briefly the approaches of postwar U.S. presidents to nuclear weapons.

Although Harry Truman is the only president to have employed nuclear weapons against an enemy, the Truman administration was initially unwilling to make the bomb the centerpiece of national security strategy or even to integrate nuclear weapons fully into the emerging strategy of containment. It is doubtful that U.S. possession of the bomb aided in postwar negotiations with the Soviet Union because an attack against the Soviet Union on the heels of World War II was seen as neither credible nor likely effective. By 1948, however, the developing Cold War and the Berlin Crisis pushed nuclear weapons to the fore. The Joint Chiefs of Staff developed the first targeting plan for nuclear attack on Soviet urban and industrial concentrations, and the adoption of NSC-30 was designed to make it clear to the Soviet Union that the United States would use the bomb.[23]

Under President Eisenhower and Secretary of State John Foster Dulles, U.S. nuclear superiority became the cornerstone of national security policy. Dulles' doctrine of massive retaliation called for nuclear weapons to substitute for conventional forces in deterring a broad range of aggressive behaviors. By the end of 1953, the chair of the Joint Chiefs of Staff could proudly announce, "atomic weapons have virtually achieved a conventional status within our armed forces."[24] Massive retaliation was predicated upon the ability of the United States to respond instantly and decisively against any enemy aggression, placing a heavy political burden on U.S. nuclear forces. Grouping together U.S. responses to a wide variety of enemies and threats under this doctrine, however, also limited the rationale for large standing conventional forces and allowed Eisenhower to make major cuts in Truman's proposed defense budgets without retreating from the doctrine of containment.[25]

Eisenhower's policies provoked a number of critics who noted that massive retaliation was not a credible threat against most kinds of aggression. Perhaps the most influential was Henry Kissinger, who argued that Eisenhower's "New Look" relied too much on nuclear weapons, which could not substitute for conventional forces in most situations. He also charged that massive retaliation did not deter revolutions in the Third World and neglected opportunities for arms control negotiations. Finally, in light of the Soviet Union's expected emergence as a nuclear power, Kissinger and others argued that massive retaliation would become even less tenable as a "missile gap" between Soviet and U.S. nuclear forces developed. The critics called for a new commitment to counter Soviet forces and for the development of more tactical options; a posture of "graduated deterrence" and a capacity to engage in limited wars would enhance the credibility and, thus, the efficacy of U.S. forces.[26]

The presidential campaign of 1960 saw both John Kennedy and Richard Nixon promising more active and aggressive foreign and military policies. Kennedy charged the Eisenhower administration with allowing a missile gap to develop, and he pledged to close it. Although Kennedy's Secretary of Defense Robert McNamara was apparently surprised to discover that the missile gap was illusory, he committed the United States to building a large force of intercontinental ballistic missiles (ICBMs) anyway, at least partly for what he acknowledged as domestic political reasons.[27] He also sought to expand tactical options by increasing the number, variety, and capabilities of tactical nuclear weapons and conventional forces and by integrating the two. This was aided by the willingness of Presidents Kennedy and Johnson to spend significantly more on defense than Eisenhower had.[28]

The strategic options available were also increased by a number of technological advances in missile guidance and fueling systems.

More accurate and reliable missiles allowed more flexible targeting of nuclear weapons with smaller yields, which would therefore be more "usable." McNamara introduced a "counterforce" policy, targeting Soviet weapons systems and command and control centers rather than cities (known as "countervalue" targets). In essence, this was an attempt to make nuclear weapons more like conventional forces. Nuclear war then, like conventional war, could theoretically be controlled within broad limits, isolated from population centers, and become more plausible. The initial rationale for counterforce targeting was "damage limitation." That is, by destroying Soviet nuclear forces, the United States could limit the amount of damage it would suffer from a Soviet attack, thus weakening the Soviet deterrent. Counterforce targeting also led, however, to the theoretical possibility of a "first strike" attack, leaving the victim without the will or capacity to do anything but accede to an aggressor's terms.[29]

Pursuing a fuller integration of nuclear weapons within the military arsenal and the multiplication of counterforce capabilities, McNamara presided over the development of the first detailed plans for an extended nuclear war. Adopted in July of 1962, SIOP-63 explicitly calls for the elimination of cities and population centers as potential targets.[30] Nuclear war was increasingly viewed less as an apocalyptic earth-ending phenomenon and more as war and politics by other means as McNamara developed a doctrine of "flexible response." This meant that the United States would pursue the capability to respond to any act of aggression with a combination of military and political measures in a graduated way, controlling the pace of escalation.[31] After years of effectively organizing the development and procurement of U.S. forces, it was officially adopted as NATO policy in 1967.[32] According to a distinguished group of veteran strategists, flexible response "permeates all aspects of American defense policy. . . . [and] relies heavily on the threat of first use despite the conspicuous lack of a plausible set of circumstances in which nuclear exchanges would not gravely risk catastrophic damage to the United States and its allies."[33]

While the Pentagon developed the arsenal to support flexible response and counterforce doctrines, McNamara himself came to doubt the utility of this posture, particularly as a means to organize defense planning. In order to make sense, counterforce required qualitative and quantitative superiority in weaponry.[34] In the face of the Soviet Union's developing nuclear arsenal, the costs of maintaining superiority grew untenable and the possibility of meaningful superiority became increasingly dubious. Further, given the levels of superpower armaments, superiority no longer clearly conferred any meaningful military or political benefits. Although technological innovation continued and counterforce options remained in Pentagon plans, McNamara began to see the attainment of a survivable second strike capacity, or a minimum deterrence posture, as a more desirable and viable alternative. He articulated this posture as Mutually Assured Destruction, whose telling acronym MAD has come to symbolize the nuclear dilemma for a wide variety of its critics.[35]

MAD also offered certain bureaucratic advantages. Flexible response offered little guidance in choosing among competing weapons systems because the multiplication of options was inherently desirable. In contrast, MAD could set clear limits on the necessary number and capabilities of the nuclear arsenal. McNamara used MAD to cap the growth in U.S. strategic forces and the military budget. It was specifically and successfully targeted at particularly expensive and, to the secretary's mind, useless projects in development at the Pentagon, most clearly, the B-70 strategic bomber. It is doubtful that MAD was ever really an operating strategic doctrine so much as a means to cap the appetite of Pentagon planners.[36] Along with a new posture of fixed structures for conventional forces, MAD was an attempt to limit weapons procurement and military spending without changing either foreign policy goals or basic military missions.[37] Counterforce weapons and plans have remained in the U.S. arsenal. MAD's effect on military spending, however, generated a certain amount of long-standing opposition, which later crystallized in support of the Reagan initiatives. Senator Jake Garn (R-UT), for example, criticized the former defense secretary because "McNamara did not start a single new strategic system during his seven years as defense secretary. More importantly, he formulated the theory of Mutually Assured Destruction which has had such a negative impact on defense spending."[38] Note that Garn does not suggest McNamara's policies harmed U.S. interests or security.

McNamara's approaches to nuclear weapons, as expressed by both MAD and flexible response, dominated U.S. policy even after he left office, schizophrenically coexisting within official U.S. national security policy for the better part of two decades. While the latter encouraged the development of a broad spectrum of nuclear options and war fighting plans, the former periodically provided a ready cap and criticism for plans or weapons systems judged excessively expensive or provocative. Although fundamentally in contradiction, one or the other was cited in support and/or criticism of virtually every nuclear project of the 1960s and 1970s. Antiballistic missiles were bad, for example, because they threatened MAD; battlefield nuclear weapons were desirable at the same time because they provided gradual and incremental intermediate steps in the escalation ladder.

Although nuclear superiority disappeared as a policy goal during McNamara's tenure, his successors all defined necessary nuclear capabilities as significantly more than minimum deterrence. As stated by Melvin Laird, who served under President Nixon, national security required strategic forces capable of "1) assured destruction and 2) flexible options; forces that are 3) equal to that of the Soviet Union and 4) perceived as equal; and forces that 5) contribute to crisis stability."[39] Without resolving deep conflicts about nuclear weapons, the articulation of strategic requirements variously described as "rough parity," "equivalence," or "sufficiency" allowed the United States to avoid making the cuts mandated by a true minimum deterrence posture without committing to the unrestrained buildup necessary to sustain even the fiction of a war winning strategy.[40]

The primary danger from the Soviet Union, planners now held, was not a nuclear first strike but restricted attacks. Deterrence thus required a limited war capability. Flexible response was restated as a war fighting doctrine designed to deny the Soviet Union any kind of military victory. In January 1974, Secretary of Defense James Schlesinger announced a Nuclear Weapons Employment Policy that repudiated MAD and called for the development of broader nuclear options. Signed by Nixon as National Security Decision Memo 242, it sets out limited targeting options for a prolonged limited nuclear war in Europe. Overshadowed at the time by the numerous problems plaguing the last years of the Nixon presidency, NSDM 242 did not draw a great deal of public attention at the time. Planning for limited wars has remained within the purview of U.S. nuclear strategy, although within the context of a war fighting, rather than war winning, paradigm, with credible deterrence as the primary goal.[41]

Under Presidents Nixon and Ford military spending decreased slightly, partly as a result of detente (a political means of pursuing containment), partly a result of their seeking nuclear "sufficiency" rather than superiority, and partly because of the activism of the post-Watergate post-Vietnam Congress.[42] The strategic buildup initiated under McNamara also slowed as the strategic nuclear triad was completed. During the 1970s the Soviet Union sought strategic parity by building up its own nuclear forces. In contrast to the United States, the Soviets concentrated their strategic forces primarily on land, which allowed them to build greater numbers and larger missiles more cheaply, albeit with greater vulnerability. Also unlike the United States, the Soviets did not replace outmoded weapons with more modern ones; they simply augmented their forces. As a result, the Soviets gained a numerical advantage in strategic nuclear launchers and the megatonnage of warheads they could carry. The United States meanwhile, by virtue of multiple independently targeted reentry vehicles (MIRVs), maintained an advantage in the number of nuclear warheads. Neither hardware advantage clearly translated into enhanced ability to prevail in a nuclear war or influenced the capacity of either superpower to pursue its political goals. It did, however, allow the perception of Soviet superiority, which translated into domestic political problems in the United States.[43] Ronald Reagan used the specter of nuclear inferiority and opposition to detente to challenge President Ford for the Republican presidential nomination in 1976.[44] Ford won the nomination, but he narrowly lost the final election to Jimmy Carter.

Upon entering office Jimmy Carter promised to give greater attention to international human rights, to reorganize U.S. military forces, and to move beyond the Republican efforts at arms control toward disarmament talks with the Soviet Union, pledging immediate efforts toward "the elimination of all nuclear weapons from this earth."[45] His Secretary of Defense, Harold Brown, however, was firmly grounded in the traditions of his predecessors. He continued most of the programs his predecessors had initiated while Carter finished negotiating the SALT II treaty that Nixon and Ford had pursued. Although there were slight differences in approach, the Carter policies, especially by the end of his term, were well within the war fighting paradigm. Carter presided over a substantial military buildup and reaffirmed a commitment to flexible response.[46]

This was demonstrated most clearly by Presidential Directive 59, which Carter signed on July 25, 1980.[47] PD 59 was essentially a restatement and refinement of the war fighting doctrine developed over the previous 20 years, which included contingencies for "securing" the Persian Gulf and acknowledged the potential use of strategic nuclear weapons against battlefield targets. Even with these two refinements, PD 59 did not represent a shift in strategic doctrine so much as a politically motivated restatement. As Brown stressed in a speech to the Naval War College, "Let me emphasize that PD 59 is not a new strategic doctrine."[48] Still, coming from the Carter administration as prospects of SALT II ratification were rapidly fading and as the Persian Gulf seemed quite likely capable of generating a nuclear contingency, PD 59's release tapped the first wave of massive discontent that would later crystallize in the nuclear freeze movement.

Given the potential political difficulties associated with the public announcement of PD 59, it is reasonable to question why Carter chose to float it in 1979 and then sign it amid much public debate in 1980, especially as it represented no significant changes in U.S. policy. Conceivably PD 59 was some sort of message to the Soviet Union regarding its conduct in Afghanistan or to the Iranian leadership about the U.S. hostages held in Teheran, but this is not likely. Any U.S. president has resources to send such messages more clearly and directly without risking the attention of the electorate. It seems far more likely that Carter chose this avenue for his message hoping for political benefits domestically. As Congressman Ronald Dellums writes:

Politicians from both major political parties have sustained and advanced themselves in office by following Senator Arthur H. Vandenberg's advice to . . . "scare the hell out of the country" when it comes to any public discussion of dealing with threats, real or imagined, to the "American way of life" at home and U.S. multinational interests abroad.[49]

Debates about national security can produce substantial electoral results, as John Kennedy demonstrated in 1960 when he made political capital of an illusory missile gap. Carter had already failed to gain Senate ratification of SALT II,[50] to free hostages from Iran, and even to reorganize military forces in the way he wanted.[51] On the eve of his reelection campaign, he faced serious challenges both from within his own party and from the Republicans; the economy was weak and his political popularity was low. PD 59 was most likely an attempt to wave the flag and assert his own toughness for political gains. By reemphasizing the harder line aspects of his foreign policy, he may have hoped to preempt, or at least mitigate, Republican criticism of his weakness. Possibly he intended to force an opponent, who was trying to gain support from those on his right, to stake out a foreign policy position beyond the pale of mainstream politics. (If this were the case, Carter succeeded.)

PD 59 was only one part of Jimmy Carter's domestic strategic policy. He also pushed for the development and deployment of Trident II D-5 and MX missiles (extremely accurate new multiple warhead counterforce strategic weapons),[52] orchestrated a plan to deploy intermediate-range nuclear weapons in Western Europe, coordinated a growth in NATO capabilities and Alliance spending, declared the Carter Doctrine, which defined the Persian Gulf as a vital interest, created a "Rapid Deployment Force" for protecting such interests, ordered a boycott of the Moscow Olympics in 1980 to protest the Soviet invasion of Afghanistan, provided for the development of cruise missiles, and increased real military spending by 5 percent above inflation in each of his last two years in office, budgeting the same increase for subsequent fiscal years.[53]

There was then a preliminary shift in emphasis in U.S. strategic policy before the emergence of the freeze movement. That shift, however, was incremental and effected during the Carter administration. This new strategic policy emphasis gave impetus and urgency to political activists, kindling the sparks that eventually coalesced into the nuclear freeze movement and related efforts, and created the opportunity for them to mobilize opposition. As Currie Burris, staff of Clergy and Laity Concerned (CALC) and one of the early freeze organizers, put it, "It just became a different climate for nuclear weapons work than ever before."[54] This change in climate caused activists to reevaluate their strategies.

Although Carter's new approach aided the development of a political movement, surely an unintended consequence, it did not bring him any clear political benefits. The more bellicose posture did not bring about any foreign policy triumphs, such as the release of hostages held in Iran, the withdrawal of Soviet troops from Afghanistan, or the ratification of SALT II, and it certainly did not help him at the polls. The new toughness did, however, succeed in aiding the erosion of his base of support within the Democratic Party, exploited by Senator Edward Kennedy who challenged Carter for the presidential nomination. At the same time, the more hawkish posture did not preempt candidate Reagan's criticism of Carter's foreign policy failures. Instead the Carter strategy robbed voters of any clear choice regarding foreign policy, as the incumbent chose to appear as a pale carbon of his challenger. The president was unable to compete with Ronald Reagan among voters who wanted a harder-line foreign policy and was increasingly unable to inspire support among those who did not. This the case, his election eve plea for concern about nuclear proliferation was doomed to fail.[55] Those already holding such concerns did not see the incumbent as an alternative worth much political effort. As *The Nation,* a voice in the latter group, laments in its postelection post-mortem:

> Although there was little to choose from between the two major parties on the war-peace issue, his [Reagan's] record, his pronouncements, his program, his advisers and his instincts make *nuclear war marginally more likely than it would have been under Jimmy Carter* (emphasis added).[56]

THE REAGAN DIFFERENCE

In fact, the increase of bellicose rhetoric and aggressive military posture under the new Reagan administration often appeared more than marginal. All aspects of the Reagan program had, however, begun under previous administrations. Reagan simply accentuated Carter's shift in emphasis. He increased the already increased military budgets and repudiated the SALT II treaty already withdrawn from Senate consideration. He supported every weapons program in development or procurement with vigor, revived a few that Carter had tried to cancel, although initially he added few of his own. Most significantly, the posture and policy of his administration developed without the moderating influence of any minimum deterrence advocates or arms control enthusiasts. There was no George Ball or Cyrus Vance within the Reagan camp. Candidate Reagan had run on a platform calling for the United States "to achieve overall military and technological superiority over the Soviet Union . . . to prevail in the event deterrence fails." President Reagan diligently set about trying to turn this campaign rhetoric into strategic reality.[57] For the first time, the war winners clearly dominated the strategic planning of an administration.

This was most clearly demonstrated by the presence of 51 members of the extremely hawkish Committee on the Present Danger (CoPD) in high level positions within the Reagan administration, with several others appointed to special advisory positions or bipartisan commissions.[58] CoPD had been formed in 1976 to oppose SALT II in particular and detente generally. As written in the group's founding document, "Our country is in a period of danger, and the danger is increasing . . . the principal threat to our nation, to world peace, and to the cause of human freedom is the Soviet drive for dominance based upon an unparalleled military build-up."[59] For CoPD, the buildup orchestrated in the last years of the Carter administration was far from sufficient as a response to this threat; rather, according to Eugene Rostow, CoPD cofounder and Reagan's first director of the Arms Control and Disarmament Agency, the 1970s represented a period of "unilateral disarmament," whose deleterious effects could only be overcome by a concerted and prolonged rearmament.[60]

The central tenets of CoPD faith include the belief that war with the Soviet Union is not only thinkable, but likely, and that military superiority is the only effective way to deal with the Soviets.[61] It is difficult to overestimate the impact CoPD had on Reagan administration policy; clearly it was quite substantial. Said Charles Tyroler II, CoPD director, "The leaders of the government . . . when they give a speech, in general terms, it sounds a lot like what we said in 1976. . . . And why wouldn't that be? They use the same stuff — and they were all members back then."[62]

CoPD members, however, had not lived in the political wilderness before the Reagan presidency. Rather, they had functioned in previous administrations, within the military and national security bureaucracy, and had cut their political teeth fighting policy battles with minimum deterrence advocates and war fighters. Neither the ideas nor their presentation was unprecedented. What was new was the degree of influence they had on policy. Never before had such ideas gone unchallenged within an administration. Herbert York described the phenomenon this way:

> What's going on right now is that the crazier analysts have risen to higher positions than is normally the case. They are able to carry their ideas further and higher because the people at the top are simply less well-informed than is normally the case . . . so when the ideologues come in with their fancy strategies and with their selected intelligence data, the

President and the Secretary of Defense believe the last glib
person who talked to them.[63]

The Reagan administration's exile of institutionalized opposition
fed the development of extra-institutional opposition. Increasingly
narrow access to policy-making levels within the executive branch
left a substantial wing of would-be policy makers with the need to
cultivate support outside government. Influence was not lost; the
minimum deterrence advocates had enjoyed little or no influence on
policy. They had won few victories in any previous administration.
Previously, however, their positions were always represented. It was
the new lack of access, rather than long-standing lack of efficacy,
that aided the movement's development. The freezing out of the
minimum deterrence school also had an impact on policy and the
way it was presented.

Unqualified acceptance of a nuclear war winning strategy
virtually necessitates an unconstrained military buildup. If the
United States must be prepared to prevail in any conceivable conflict,
from conventional skirmishes in the Third World to a full-scale
nuclear war, then a rationale or need can be found for any weapons
system, and no number is ever really sufficient. The two nuclear
powered aircraft carriers Carter had attempted to cut from the
budget, along with an additional one, were restored. Land based
intermediate-range missiles Carter had pledged to deploy in Europe
unless an arms control agreement could be reached were no longer
negotiable. The modernization program already proceeding under
Carter was accelerated for each leg of the strategic nuclear triad. In
the air, while Carter had called for the development of a new
advanced technology bomber and the retrofitting of existing B-52s
with long-range nuclear cruise missiles, Reagan endorsed 100 B-1
bombers in addition. At sea, development and acquisition of Trident
C-4 and D-5 missiles, the latter with counterforce accuracy,
proceeded apace. And on the land, the MX intercontinental ballistic
missile (ICBM), which was to be mobile in order to assure
survivability in the event of a Soviet attack, was redefined. Reagan
proposed alternative basing modes that, although cheaper and faster,
were highly vulnerable, thus undercutting the initial rationale for
the weapon.[64]

The MX, strongly supported by both Carter and Reagan against
widespread popular opposition, is perhaps the best illustration of the
different approaches taken by the two administrations. Since the
initial development of U.S. ICBMs, strategic planners have discussed
the development of a mobile missile that would be less vulnerable to a
theoretical Soviet first strike.[65] In the early 1970s this cause was
revived as some planners argued that ongoing improvements in the
accuracy of high yield Soviet "heavy" ICBMs directly threatened the

U.S. Minuteman force. Theoretically a preemptive Soviet first strike could "knock out" most of these most accurate U.S. strategic weapons, leaving a U.S. president with only less accurate submarine and air-based forces aimed at "soft" countervalue (cities, industrial sites, other population centers) targets remaining for retaliation. Understandably unwilling to take this option, which would invite similar re-retaliation, he would be forced to accede to whatever the Soviets demanded. This scenario posited a theoretical "window of vulnerability," which a mobile U.S. ICBM would close. (The CoPD coined this phrase, and Ronald Reagan used it in his 1980 campaign.) The Carter administration proposed several mobile basing options, including a rail-based "race track" as well as basing the missiles on flatbed trucks cruising the highways in the western United States. These proposals all met considerable opposition from virtually all quarters, partly because of the amount of land and money each required. Even Spencer Kimball, leader of the normally conservative Mormon church, forcefully and effectively opposed MX deployment in Utah.[66]

MX development was stalled before Reagan's election. The new president proposed a novel basing strategy, *Closely Spaced Basing,* nicknamed, *Dense Pack.* Under this plan, MX missiles would be clustered closely in a missile field under the rather questionable premise of fratricide, that is, Soviet missiles aimed at the field would destroy each other rather than most of the MX missiles. Nicknamed "Dunce Pack" by critics, this strategy was also abandoned. Reagan then appointed a commission headed by former (and future) National Security Advisor Brent Scowcroft.[67] The commission declared the window of vulnerability a myth, yet called for MX deployment anyway. Reagan chose to deploy the weapon in existing Minuteman silos, those same silos that both he and Carter had derided as vulnerable. Without in any way reducing the threat of a Soviet first strike, the Reagan administration committed to improving substantially U.S. counterforce capabilities based in fixed silos. Minuteman missiles, each equipped with three warheads, would be replaced by MX missiles each carrying 10 more accurate warheads. Although this deployment did not increase the survivability of the U.S. nuclear deterrent, it does increase Soviet vulnerability to some extent. The same weapon that Carter justified as a hedge against a Soviet first strike was used by Reagan to increase the credibility and threat of a U.S. first strike.

As the result of a combination of technological advances and political ideology, the Reagan administration advanced a set of policies that significantly increased the credibility of a U.S. first strike threat to wipe out Soviet nuclear forces.[68] This is, of course, a highly provocative strategy, predicated as it is on certain untestable assumptions not only about weaponry but also about the leaderships of the Soviet Union and the United States. Further, the Soviets faced with what they judge to be an impending U.S. first strike may think themselves compelled to attack first or risk losing their capability to do so.[69]

Such a posture can only be justified if one also believes that nuclear war is either inevitable or, at least, that the threat is sufficiently credible to have political utility. Both beliefs had wide adherence within the highest levels of the Reagan administration. The CoPD position had been that the threat of nuclear war could be used to "rollback" communism, even within the Soviet Union.[70] Reagan administration officials were not shy, at least initially, about spelling this out. In testimony before the Senate, national security aide Richard Pipes had cooly estimated a 40 percent chance of nuclear war with the Soviets, contingent entirely upon Soviet behavior. To avoid war, the Soviets could abandon communism and change their system of government.[71] Pipes' views were common in the Reagan administration. Caspar Weinberger sold the Reagan administration strategy and budget to Congress by emphasizing the urgency of the threat of an imminent war with the Soviet Union for which the United States was not adequately prepared. "I only hope we have enough time," he repeatedly declaimed.[72]

Isolated aggressive policy and budget initiatives become more understandable when seen in the context of this larger world view. Stepped up programs of aggression in Central America, Afghanistan, and Angola make more sense if one believes a great war is inevitable, as does a laissez-faire attitude toward nuclear proliferation,[73] even if that means allowing the sale of fissile materials to South Africa.[74] The same is true of a similar marketplace attitude to the sales of arms.[75] It is also true of a massive increase in civil defense and nuclear crisis relocation preparations, which makes sense only if one believes it is possible to save "80 percent of the American population in an all-out nuclear war."[76]

It must again be emphasized that each of the Reagan programs had theoretical and bureaucratic roots in the policies of previous administrations, and that the shift to a more hawkish foreign policy posture was begun in the last years of the Carter administration. The combination of each of these incrementally more aggressive steps in virtually every aspect of U.S. foreign and military policy, however, abetted by technological advances in weaponry and unrestrained by criticism or serious scrutiny within the Reagan administration, created a fundamentally different public posture. An escalating series of incremental changes produced a change in kind, the explicit adoption of a war winning approach. Politically, this allowed debates about nuclear weapons and nuclear strategy to expand beyond the circles of experts and policy makers and become public political issues. Not only was the posture problematic, the growth of military spending to support a war winning posture, in the context of domestic budget cuts, further politicized nuclear issues.

NOTES

1. See, for example, Peter Pringle and William Arkin, *SIOP: The Secret U.S. Plans for Nuclear War,* New York: Norton, 1983; Scott D. Sagan, "SIOP-62: The Nuclear War Plan Briefing to President Kennedy," *International Security,* Summer 1987, pp. 22–51.

2. Herman Kahn provides the most explicit description in *On Escalation: Metaphors and Scenarios,* New York: Praeger, 1965.

3. Barry M. Blechmann and Stephen Kaplan, *Force without War: The Political Use of U.S. Military Forces,* Washington, D.C.: The Brookings Institution, 1978, pp. 47–48.

4. Lawrence Freedman, *The Evolution of Nuclear Strategy,* New York: St. Martin's, 1983, pp. 84–85; John Lewis Gaddis, *Strategies of Containment: A Critical Appraisal of Postwar American National Security Policy,* Oxford University Press, 1982, pp. 231–32.

5. Richard Nixon, *RN: The Memoirs of Richard Nixon,* New York: Grosset and Dunlap, 1978, pp. 396–404.

6. McGeorge Bundy et al., "Back from the Brink," *The Atlantic Monthly,* August 1986; Gaddis, *Containment,* p. 345; Robert Komer, "What 'Decade of Neglect'?" *International Security,* Fall 1985, p. 73.

7. Blechmann and Kaplan, *Force without War,* p. 49.

8. On extended deterrence and U.S. policy goals, see Randall Forsberg, "The Freeze and Beyond: Confining the Military to Defense as a Route to Disarmament," *World Policy Journal,* Winter 1984, pp. 285–318. Freedman, *Evolution of Nuclear Strategy,* pp. 73, 82–84; Gaddis, *Containment,* pp. 148–52; The Harvard Nuclear Study Group, *Living with Nuclear Weapons,* New York: Bantam Books, 1983, pp. 135–42; Henry A. Kissinger, *Nuclear Weapons and Foreign Policy,* New York: Harper and Brothers, 1957; Warner Schilling, "U.S. Strategic Nuclear Concepts in the 1970s: The Search for Sufficiently Equivalent Countervailing Parity," *International Security,* Fall 1981, p. 58.

9. Frank Blackaby, Jozef Goldblat, and Sverre Lodgaard, eds., *No First Use,* London: Taylor and Francis, 1984; McGeorge Bundy, George Kennan, Robert McNamara, and Gerard Smith, "Nuclear Weapons and the Atlantic Alliance," *Foreign Affairs,* Spring 1982, pp. 753–68; Freedman, *Evolution of Nuclear Strategy,* p. 238; Gaddis, *Containment,* p. 102.

10. Bundy, "Back from the Brink," pp. 35–41. The figure cited is from a Yankelovich poll, May 1984, asking whether respondents thought it was U.S. policy to use nuclear weapons first. Details of the poll are in *Voter Options on Nuclear Arms Policy,* published by The Public Agenda Foundation, in collaboration with the Center for Foreign Policy Development at Brown University, May 1984.

11. Graham T. Allison, Albert Carnesdale, and Joseph S. Nye, Jr., eds., *Hawks, Doves, and Owls: An Agenda for Avoiding Nuclear War,* New York: Norton, 1985, p. 230.

12. Freedman, *Evolution of Nuclear Strategy,* pp. 373–74; Gaddis, *Containment,* pp. 203, 219–20.

13. For information on the U.S. nuclear arsenal, see William M. Arkin, Thomas R. Cochran, and Milton Hoenig, *Nuclear Weapons Databook, Vol. 1: U.S. Forces and Capabilities,* Cambridge, MA: Ballinger, 1983.

14. Gaddis, *Containment,* p. 101; Kahn, in *On Escalation,* for example, postulates a 44-rung escalation ladder, with nuclear weapons first employed at rung 15.

15. See Jeffrey D. Porro, "The Policy Wars: Brodie vs. Kahn," *Bulletin of the Atomic Scientists,* June/July, 1982, p. 16.

16. I am grateful to Randall Forsberg for suggesting these analytic categories. Also see Freedman, *Evolution of Nuclear Strategy,* p. 396. Charles L. Glaser advances a similar typology and provides more extensive treatment of the positions and their implications in "Why Do Strategists Disagree about the Requirements of Strategic Nuclear Deterrence?" in Lynn Eden and Steven E. Miller, eds., *Nuclear Arguments: Understanding the Strategic Nuclear Arms and Arms Control Debates,* Ithaca: Cornell University Press, 1989, p. 114.

17. Freedman, *Evolution of Nuclear Strategy,* p. 135; Gaddis, *Containment,* p. 80; Schilling, "U.S. Strategic Nuclear Concepts," p. 59; Jeremy Stone suggests it would take only about 4 percent of current U.S. strategic forces to fulfill this role in Ronald V. Dellums et al., eds., *Defense Sense: The Search for a Rational Military Policy,* Cambridge, MA: Ballinger, 1983, p. 135.

18. Freedman, *Evolution of Nuclear Strategy,* pp. 68, 232; Gaddis, *Containment,* p. 203; Schilling, "U.S. Strategic Nuclear Concepts," p. 56.

19. Freedman, *Evolution of Nuclear Strategy,* pp. 134-37; Colin S. Gray, "National Style in Strategy," *International Security,* Fall 1981, pp. 21-47.

20. Freedman, *Evolution of Nuclear Strategy,* pp. xv, 233; Gaddis, *Containment,* pp. 354-55.

21. The phrase in this context is from Robert C. Aldridge, "America's Strategic Arsenal," in Dellums, *Defense Sense,* p. 15. See Arnold Kanter, *Defense Politics: A Budgetary Perspective,* Chicago: University of Chicago Press, 1979, pp. 39-44, on Congressional response to presidential budgets. See Douglas C. Waller, "The Impact of the Nuclear Freeze Movement on Congress," in Steven E. Miller, ed., *The Nuclear Weapons Freeze and Arms Control,* Cambridge, MA: Ballinger, 1984, on the institutional biases of Congress on nuclear weapons issues. On pork barrel politics, see Gordon Adams, *The Iron Triangle: The Politics of Defense Contracting,* New York: Council on Economic Priorities, 1981; Kenneth A. Bertsch and Linda S. Shaw, *The Nuclear Weapons Industry,* Washington, D.C.: Investor Responsibility Research Center, 1984.

22. This responsibility and power of the president is a central theme of Alain Enthoven and K. Wayne Smith, *How Much Is Enough? Shaping the Defense Program, 1961-1969,* New York: Harper & Row, 1971. The authors, Pentagon efficiency experts during the Kennedy and Johnson administrations, discuss Secretary of Defense McNamara's strategies for overcoming institutional opposition from the services and Congress to "rationalize" defense forces.

23. Freedman, *Evolution of Nuclear Strategy,* pp. 48-55.

24. Ibid., p. 77.

25. Ibid., pp. 76-90; Gaddis, *Containment,* pp. 128, 147-52, 171.

26. Freedman, *Evolution of Nuclear Strategy,* pp. 97-103; Gaddis, *Containment,* p. 165; Kissinger, *Nuclear Weapons.*

27. David Halbertstam, *The Best and the Brightest,* Greenwich, CT: Fawcett Crest, 1972, pp. 28-29, 91, 296-300.

28. Freedman, *Evolution of Nuclear Strategy*, pp. 227–41; Gaddis, *Containment*, pp. 175, 202–5, 215.

29. Freedman, *Evolution of Nuclear Strategy*, pp. 123–27, 237; Robert C. Aldridge, *The Counterforce Syndrome: A Guide to U.S. Nuclear Weapons and Strategic Doctrine*, Washington, D.C.: Institute for Policy Studies, 1978.

30. Gray, "National Style," p. 39; Pringle and Arkin, *SIOP*; Sagan, "SIOP-62."

31. Freedman, *Evolution of Nuclear Strategy*, pp. 228–38; Gaddis, *Containment*, pp. 100, 231–32.

32. "The Nuclear Freeze Proposal: Pro and Con," *Congressional Digest*, No. 8–9 (1982), p. 199; Harvard Nuclear Study Group, *Living with Nuclear Weapons*, pp. 85–92.

33. Bundy et al., "Back from the Brink," p. 36.

34. Freedman, *Evolution of Nuclear Strategy*, p. 241.

35. Freedman, *Evolution of Nuclear Strategy*, pp. 241–48; Gaddis, *Containment*, pp. 219–20; Gray, "National Style," pp. 37–42; Schilling, "U.S. Strategic Nuclear Concepts," p. 59.

36. Adam Garfinkle, *The Politics of the Nuclear Freeze*, Philadelphia, PA: Foreign Policy Research Institute, 1984, p. 127; Fred Kaplan, "Going Native without a Field Map," *Columbia Journalism Review*, January/February 1981. On the B-70, see Enthoven and Smith, *How Much Is Enough?* pp. 243–51; Nick Kotz, *Wild Blue Yonder: Money, Politics and the B-1 Bomber*, New York: Pantheon, 1988, pp. 48–68.

37. James Fallows, *National Defense*, New York: Random House, 1981, p. 24.

38. Ibid., p. 162.

39. Schilling, "U.S. Strategic Concepts," p. 59.

40. Ibid., p. 78; Freedman, *Evolution of Nuclear Strategy*, pp. 341–43; Gray, "National Style," p. 42.

41. Fallows, *National Defense*, p. 143; Freedman, *Evolution of Nuclear Strategy*, pp. 374–78; Colin S. Gray and Jeffrey G. Barlow, "Inexcusable Restraint; The Decline of American Military Power in the 1970s," *International Security*, Fall 1985, pp. 41–42.

42. Gaddis, *Containment*, pp. 321–23.

43. Freedman, *Evolution of Nuclear Strategy*, pp. 344–46; Schilling, "U.S. Strategic Concepts," pp. 64–68.

44. Lloyd N. Cutler and Roger C. Molander, "Is There Life after Death for SALT?" *International Security*, Fall 1981, p. 6.

45. *Public Papers of the Presidents of the United States, Jimmy Carter, 1981, Volume 1*, Washington, D.C.: U.S. Government Printing Office, p. 3.

46. Gaddis, *Containment*, p. 345; Robert Komer, "What 'Decade of Neglect'?" pp. 73–74; Schilling, "U.S. Strategic Concepts," p. 59.

47. On PD 59, see Harold Brown, *Department of Defense Annual Report, Fiscal Year 1982*, pp. 38–45; Freedman, *Evolution of Nuclear Strategy*, p. 393; Gray and Barlow, "Inexcusable Restraint," pp. 41–42; Kaplan, "Going Native," p. 24; Komer, "What 'Decade of Neglect'?"; Schilling, "U.S. Strategic Concepts," pp. 72–73. For analysis of the political and military context surrounding PD 59, see Richard Falk, "Lifting the Curse of Bipartisanship," *World Policy Journal*, Fall 1983, p. 139.

48. Speech, August 20, 1980, Office of the Assistant Secretary of Defense (Public Affairs), News Release No. 344-80.

49. Dellums, *Defense Sense*, pp. xxi–xxii.

50. Carter suggests that his all-out effort to win ratification of the Panama Canal treaties ultimately cost him support for SALT II in the Senate; he had depleted his stock of bargaining chips with Congress. See *Keeping Faith: Memoirs of a President,* New York: Bantam, 1982, p. 224. Interestingly, Carter does not mention PD 59 in his memoirs.

51. Carter was unable, for example, to prevent Congress from reinstating funding for two $3.6 billion aircraft carriers he had previously cut; see David S. Meyer, "Aircraft Carriers: $3 Billion Flagpoles," *Defense and Disarmament News,* April/May 1985. Further, opposition from European allies forced him to suspend neutron bomb production, also seen as a sign of weakness in his resolve. Carter, *Keeping Faith,* pp. 225–29.

52. Gordon Adams and David Gold, "Derail the MX," *The Nation,* November 10, 1979, p. 461; Carter, *Keeping Faith,* p. 224.

53. On Carter's domestic strategic policy, see Bundy et al., "Back from the Brink," p. 41; George Kistiakowsky, "The Good and the Bad of Nuclear Arms Control Negotiations," *Bulletin of the Atomic Scientists,* May 1979, p. 10; Michael T. Klare, "The Brown Doctrine: Have RDF, Will Travel," *The Nation,* March 8, 1980; Klare, "Potomac War Fever: Letter from Washington," *The Nation,* February 10, 1979, p. 107; Robert Scheer, *With Enough Shovels: Reagan, Bush, and Nuclear War,* New York: Random House, 1982, pp. 69–70.

54. Quoted in Robert Leavitt, "Freezing the Arms Race: The Genesis of a Mass Movement," Kennedy School of Government Case Study, Harvard University, 1983, p. 8.

55. Carter discusses his decision to cite his daughter's concerns during the presidential debate in *Keeping Faith,* pp. 564–65.

56. "Protest and Survive," *The Nation,* January 24, 1981, p. 67. See also the magazine's near endorsement of Carter, which was both late and lukewarm, "The Reagan Danger," November 1, 1980, p. 425.

57. Scheer, *With Enough Shovels,* p. 127; Leavitt, "Freezing the Arms Race," p. 8; "Nuclear Politics," *The Nation,* August 30, 1979, p. 169. On these goals see Desmond Ball, "Can Nuclear War Be Controlled?" *Adelphi Papers,* London: International Institute for Strategic Studies, Fall 1981.

58. Scheer, *With Enough Shovels,* pp. 144–46, contains a list of these appointments.

59. Max M. Kampelman, ed., *Alerting America: The Papers of the Committee on the Present Danger,* Washington, D.C.: Pergamon-Brassey, 1984, introduction.

60. Scheer, *With Enough Shovels,* p. 212. See also Lawrence J. Korb and Linda P. Brady, "Rearming America: The Reagan Administration Defense Program," *International Security,* Winter 1984/85, pp. 3–18; Gray and Barlow, "Inexcusable Restraint"; Elmo R. Zumwalt, Jr., "Heritage of Weakness: An Assessment of the 1970s," in W. Scott Thompson, ed., *National Security in the 1980s: From Weakness to Strength,* San Francisco: Institute for Contemporary Studies, 1980, pp. 17–51. This collection also includes pieces by several Reagan appointees, including Kenneth Adelman, Richard Burt, Fred Ikle, and Paul Nitze.

61. Scheer, *With Enough Shovels,* p. 5; see also Robert Sherrill, "Gene Rostow's Propaganda Club," *The Nation,* August 11–18, 1979.

62. Scheer, *With Enough Shovels,* pp. 36–37.

63. Ibid., p. 13, quotation from April 1982 interview.

64. For a variety of perspectives on this strategic modernization and its relation to strategy, see Hans Bethe, "Meaningless Superiority," *Bulletin of the*

Atomic Scientists, October 1981, p. 1; Michael T. Klare, ed., "The New Arms Technology," Special Issue, *The Nation,* April 9, 1983; Korb and Brady, "Rearming America"; Christopher E. Paine, "Arms Buildup," *Bulletin of the Atomic Scientists,* October 1982, p. 5; Barry Posen and Stephen Van Evera, "Defense Policy and the Reagan Administration: Departure from Containment," *International Security,* Summer 1983, pp. 3–45; Schilling, "U.S. Strategic Concepts," pp. 72–78.

65. On the military rationale and political history of the MX, see Carter, *Keeping Faith,* p. 241; Garfinkle, *Politics of the Nuclear Freeze,* pp. 184–92; David Gold, Gail Shields, and Christopher Paine, *Misguided Missile: An Analysis of the Proposed MX Missile System,* New York: Council on Economic Priorities, 1981; Gary Hart, *A New Democracy,* New York: Quill, 1983, pp. 164–66; William Kincaide, "Another Summer of the MX," *Bulletin of the Atomic Scientists,* August/September 1981, p. 50; Herbert Scoville, *MX: Prescription for Disaster,* Cambridge, MA: MIT Press, 1981.

66. William Appleman Williams, "Regional Resistance: Backyard Autonomy," *The Nation,* September 5, 1981, p. 162.

67. Scowcroft Commission, "Report of the President's Commission on Strategic Forces," Washington, D.C.: Office of the Secretary of Defense, 1983.

68. The introduction of extremely accurate MX, Pershing II, Trident II, and cruise missiles, especially in conjunction with increased antiballistic missile and antisatellite capabilities can be seen as part and parcel of a first strike strategy; Scheer, *With Enough Shovels,* p. 32, quotes Undersecretary of Defense for Research and Engineering Richard DeLauer in October 1981 as saying that Trident II may provide the United States with a usable first strike capability. Also see Robert C. Aldridge, *First Strike: The Pentagon's Strategy for Nuclear War,* Boston: South End Press, 1983; Edward J. Anderson, "First Strike: Myth or Reality," *Bulletin of the Atomic Scientists,* November 1981, p. 6.

69. Freedman, *Evolution of Nuclear Strategy,* pp. 134–39.

70. Posen and Van Evera, "Defense Policy."

71. Scheer, *With Enough Shovels,* p. 13.

72. Nicholas Lemann, "The Peacetime War: Caspar Weinberger in the Pentagon," *The Atlantic Monthly,* October 1984, pp. 71–94.

73. Ronald Reagan really did say, "I just don't think it's any of our business." New York *Times,* February 1, 1980, quoted in Mark Green and Gail MacColl, *There He Goes Again: Ronald Reagan's Reign of Error,* New York: Pantheon Books, 1983, p. 44.

74. New York *Times,* May 19, 1982, p. 7.

75. Michael T. Klare, "Opening the Floodgates: 'Arms Diplomacy' of the Reagan Administration," in Dellums, *Defense Sense,* p. 89. See also Klare's *The American Arms Supermarket,* Austin: University of Texas Press, 1985.

76. Scheer, *With Enough Shovels,* pp. 107–9. In the spring of 1982 Reagan presented a $4.3 billion ["1982 dollars"] seven-year program for civil defense that represented the first major spending increase for these programs in 20 years. These programs are described and criticized by Jennifer Leaning, Matthew Leighton, John Carpenter, and Herbert L. Abrahms, "Programs Surviving a Nuclear War: A Critique," *Bulletin of the Atomic Scientists,* July 1983.

3

MILITARY SPENDING: HOW MUCH IS TOO MUCH?

> Some day there is going to be a man sitting in my chair who has not been raised in the military services and who will have little understanding of where slashes in their [the military's] estimates can be made with little or no damage. If that should happen while we still have the state of tension that now exists in the world, I shudder to think what could happen in this country.
> — Dwight D. Eisenhower[1]

> Defense is not a budget item. You spend what you need.
> — Ronald Reagan[2]

> The worst thing that could happen is for the nation to go on a defense spending binge that will create economic havoc at home and confusion abroad and that cannot be wisely dealt with by the Pentagon.
> — Melvin Laird[3]

While the strategic doctrines employed by the Reagan administration were rooted in those of previous administrations, the same is not true of its budgets. The Reagan budgets initiated and sustained a level of military spending unprecedented in modern U.S. history. The high costs of preparing to prevail at every level of nuclear conflict while maintaining the capacity to fight limited wars engendered and enlivened Reagan's political opposition.[4] The widespread perception that military spending was out of control called into question other aspects of the Reagan military program. Perhaps most significantly, although strategic doctrine and military policy remain esoteric even to policy makers, dollars are immediately intelligible and become especially important during a recession. Within the context of the 1982 recession, conflicts about the level and goals of military spending opened numerous rifts in the support for the administration's policies. The military budget served as a lightning rod for criticism of Reagan's military and domestic priorities.

MILITARY BUDGETS

Between the end of World War II and the beginning of the Reagan presidency, peacetime military spending remained generally consistent.[5] From fiscal years 1954–1980, peacetime military budget authority ranged from \$189–\$220 billion annually.[6] Wartime budgets were higher, reaching a peak of \$325 billion in 1952 at the height of involvement in the Korean War and a lower but more sustained level of about \$250–\$260 billion in the late 1960s, at the height of U.S. involvement in Vietnam. As U.S. involvement in these wars waned, military budgets declined more sharply, returning to their normal peacetime level. The level of spending varied relatively little under different administrations; indeed, Republican Presidents Eisenhower and Nixon presided over somewhat lower peacetime military budgets than did Democrats Kennedy, Johnson, and Carter.[7]

Contrary to popular rhetoric, U.S. military expenditures historically have not directly robbed government spending in other areas such as social welfare. Rather than making the choice between guns and butter, the United States has generally increased or decreased military budgets in concert with spending on social welfare programs. Bruce Russett notes that between 1941 and 1979, increased military spending has been accompanied by increased federal

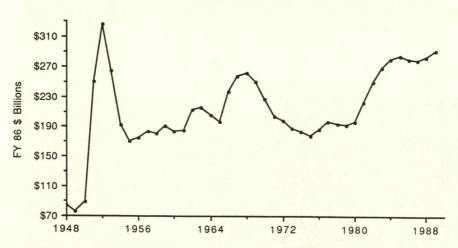

FIGURE 1 — U.S. Military Budget Authority, 1948–1989 (Constant Dollars)
(*Source*: Department of Defense, TOA by Program, FY 1986 and 1989.)

spending on social programs. There have been brief periods in which military expenditures and social welfare spending have been inversely related under Republican administrations; Presidents Eisenhower, Nixon, and Ford presided over real cuts in military spending while social welfare spending remained relatively constant.[8]

Perhaps even more than with domestic programs, politicians have frequently pointed to the "top line" or military budget totals as an indication of their commitment to security. The enormity of even the normal level of military spending, the length of time it takes to buy major weapons systems, and the technological and bureaucratic complexity of U.S. military programs all contribute to keeping political debate at a very general level. Beneath the top line, however, the broad global objectives of postwar foreign policy have encouraged the Pentagon to develop an unending stream of weapons systems and programs for responding to any number of contingencies. The justification of "national security," rarely defined in detail, has placed enormous pressure on elected officials to acquiesce to Pentagon proposals. Congress as an institution has historically been unable or unwilling to refuse the military, and the vast majority of budget and program cuts have been effected by the chief executive.[9] Every modern administration has developed its own way of doing this.

President Eisenhower used the doctrine of massive retaliation to lower the costs of implementing a policy of containment. Smaller numbers of nuclear weapons substituted for relatively more expensive and extensive conventional forces, as nuclear weapons produced "more bang for the buck." Eisenhower possessed both the will and the political credibility to preside over deep cuts in Truman's proposed budgets, imposing a strict ceiling on total military expenditures. Although strongly committed to keeping the top line below these ceilings, the former general exercised little control or influence over how the money was allocated among the services or which programs were prioritized. Instead, he allowed the services wide discretion over allocations, feeding interservice rivalry.[10]

In contrast, John Kennedy entered office committed to a more aggressive foreign policy supported by higher levels of spending. The first Kennedy budgets showed substantial increases as Secretary of Defense Robert McNamara presided over the establishment of the strategic nuclear triad, consisting of weapons based on long-range bombers, submarines, and intercontinental ballistic missiles. McNamara contended that the defense budget could be properly determined only by clearly establishing U.S. security needs, finding the best systems to meet those needs, and funding them rather than by imposing a politically determined top line and allowing the services to squabble for shares of it. To do this, he established a policy of civilian review and a *Planning Programming-Budgeting System* (PPBS) to produce objective analysis of defense requirements and the most efficient means of meeting them. As two of his aides explain, "The fundamental idea behind PPBS was decision making based on explicit criteria of the national interest in defense programs, as opposed to decision making by compromise among various institutions, parochial, or other vested interests in the Defense Department."[11]

These claims were met by skepticism from the military. Said one Air Force officer, "McNamara always insisted that there was no budget ceiling, but regularly made all kinds of cuts to get under it."[12]

McNamara also tried to restrain military growth by imposing fixed structures on the services, limiting the number of divisions, ships, fighter and bomber wings, and bases. By capping the numerical growth of the armed forces, McNamara tried to restrain budget growth, although extra funds could be allocated for unforeseen contingencies, including the war in Vietnam. This strategy backfired, however, as Pentagon planners designed increasingly sophisticated and expensive weapons systems. If there were to be only a limited number of fighter planes, for example, the Air Force and the Navy wanted exceptional performance characteristics that would theoretically allow them to be more versatile. As a result, each individual weapon became more expensive. The leaders of the armed forces also sought to upgrade and replace old equipment more frequently. This increased the amount of money spent annually on developing and buying new weapons without increasing the size of U.S. forces or even their actual performance in combat.[13] Indeed, the more complex weapons broke more frequently, used more fuel, were more difficult to operate, and required more frequent maintenance and more skilled operators. All of this further increased the military budget. In effect, fixed structures brought about an infinitely escalating technology-driven buildup, limited only by the imagination of weapons designers and force planners.

Under President Nixon, Defense Secretary Laird proposed that instead of fixed structures, the president set a top line for the military budget, which would then be allocated in relatively consistent shares to the services. This allowed each service far more discretion regarding budget management, opting for some combination of numbers and performance characteristics. Under this system, additional money spent on the war in Vietnam would be compensated by cuts in strategic weaponry or forces in Europe. Laird's intent was to soften the Pentagon's commitment to the war in Southeast Asia by making the services sacrifice other programs in order to conduct it. By allowing the services greater discretion about spending priorities, Laird managed to reduce defense budgets while still maintaining a good working relationship with the Pentagon.[14] The decreasing U.S. military involvement in Vietnam and the climate of detente, aided by a volatile post-Watergate Congress, brought about the modern low in military spending in 1975.

Although they emphasized different programs, both Presidents Ford and Carter set out to effect significant budget increases from that low point. Ford followed Nixon's style, leaving the planning to the Pentagon, but Carter worked at restructuring Pentagon demands. In general, he advocated greater spending for operations and maintenance, training, personnel, and the development of smaller, less complex systems. His budgets provided for real spending increases; the money was directed toward the maintenance and actual readiness of fighting forces, rather than toward less immediately usable strategic weapons or research and development. This changed slightly in the last year of his administration, when responding to both the Soviet invasion of Afghanistan and the Republican assault on his presidency, Carter called for even larger increases in spending for operations and maintenance, as well as for the development of several strategic systems, including the MX and the Trident C-4 and D-5 missiles.[15] The top line, while still within the peacetime norm, began to increase rapidly.[16]

THE REAGAN BUDGETS

Candidate Reagan had called for a real increase (after inflation) in military spending of about 7 percent annually over the already increased Carter budgets. Matters were complicated because Carter, in the last days of his administration, proposed larger increases in military spending. The Reagan administration, however, did not acknowledge it at the time.[17] The Reagan administration set about keeping the candidate's campaign promise regardless. Reagan's transition team proposed a special "get well" package for the military to begin even before the new president took office. There was no question within the administration about the direction of spending, but there was considerable conflict about the base line to which increases would be added. According to then budget director David Stockman, there was a consensus on a 7 percent real increase in spending when he and Defense Secretary Weinberger met late one evening in January 1981 to finalize the details. Stockman claims that because of fatigue and a calculator error, he mistakenly agreed to use the recently inflated Carter budgets plus the Reagan "get well" package as a base line upon which subsequent increases would be added. The actual increases were fully twice what Reagan had promised during the campaign.[18] These increases in military spending were in the context of real cuts elsewhere in the federal budget, particularly social welfare programs. This was the first time since 1941 that military spending had increased at the direct expense of social welfare programs.[19]

Once proposed, however, Weinberger refused to concede even the smallest portion of the increases, which amounted to a full 50 percent increase in budget authority between 1980 and 1985. Even after Stockman pointed out his mathematical errors to the president, Reagan consistently supported Weinberger's budget requests. By 1982 the budget had passed the peacetime norm; in 1983 budget authority reached the level achieved during the Vietnam War. For fiscal 1986, Reagan called for budget authority to surpass the previous spending peak of the Korean War (1952). Each year the Reagan administration called for further increases, arguing that the magnitude of the Soviet threat demanded extraordinary responses. To a remarkable degree, in his first term Reagan was successful in getting what he wanted for the Pentagon even though since World War II the military budget had never previously increased in more than three successive years.[20]

Caspar Weinberger's role in this was critical and surprising in light of his experience in the Nixon administration. As budget director, Weinberger had developed a reputation as a sharp fiscal manager and fierce budget cutter, earning the nickname "Cap the Knife," opposing wasteful spending in the Pentagon as well as elsewhere, including the B-1 bomber he would come to resurrect. Indeed, although his government experience was extensive, beyond his own brief naval service he had no experience or expertise in military matters. It is likely that this, as well as his tight-fisted reputation, made him a more attractive candidate for the Defense job. He was not widely seen as steeped in the ways of the Pentagon, and his credentials for fiscal stinginess were impressive. He would likely be a particularly effective spokesman for increased military spending; after all, a budget cutter like Weinberger would not ask for funding his department did not need. This image was extremely short-lived, however, and soon "Cap the Knife" became known as "The Shovel" within the Reagan administration.[21]

While Weinberger was not familiar with the details of the military budget or the workings of the Pentagon, he was willing to depend upon others who were, particularly Texas Senator John Tower. When the Republican Party gained control of the Senate in 1980, Tower became chair of the Armed Services Committee. The hawkish senator taught an eager Weinberger about Defense; Tower also arranged briefings for him by William Van Cleave (the only official witness to testify against SALT I) and other members of "Team B," a group of Committee on the Present Danger members who had been responsible for revising upward CIA projections of Soviet strength during the 1970s.[22] Weinberger became a true believer virtually immediately, and with the zeal of the newly converted, began to proselytize while demanding more money for the military. Several weeks into the job, Weinberger began telling friends that he was shocked the Soviet Union was so far ahead of the United States and that he only hoped the United States had enough time to catch up.[23]

Given this apocalyptic premise, it is not surprising that Weinberger defined his position as more political than administrative. He was far more concerned with getting the funds he believed necessary to the Department of Defense than overseeing the details of expenditure; he left that to the Pentagon. Generating high spending itself was his part in the battle to counter the Soviet threat, to demonstrate U.S. resolve, and perhaps to bankrupt the opponent who might try to keep up.[24] This entailed so much money that days before Reagan entered office, the services were asked to design more programs to absorb the windfall. Alone among Cabinet secretaries, Weinberger refused to develop a "cut list" of unnecessary or redundant projects. According to Stockman, defense "requirements" were developed to consume the hyper-inflated budget's top line.[25]

The secretary's dealings with the Congress and the public were not much different. Weinberger warned about the Soviet threat. His reports to Congress emphasized superpower global competition more vehemently and exclusively than did those of any of his predecessors. While short on detail, they were overflowing with zeal and enthusiasm about "restoring" U.S. military power after a period of alleged "neglect."[26] One tool in this campaign was *Soviet Military Power,* a new DOD publication. With slick pages and numerous photographs, *Soviet Military Power* described and evaluated Soviet weapons systems and policies in far greater detail than the secretary's report to Congress provided on U.S. weapons and policies.[27] Soviet weapons, actions, intentions, and even the existence of the Soviet Union were shown as justification for any and every U.S. military initiative.

While Weinberger stonewalled Stockman and the Congress, he was an extremely effective salesman to the president. Weinberger's tenure working for Governor Reagan in California taught him the most effective ways to influence his boss. The secretary's briefings to Reagan were light on detail and heavy on imagery. Stockman describes a typical Weinberger presentation including a series of flip-chart graphics showing a Soviet tank factory superim-posed on a map of Washington. Different budget proposals were also compared in dramatic fashion. Weinberger's charts represented the Carter defense program with an unarmed pygmy. Stockman's OMB proposals were represented by a Woody Allen caricature carrying a small gun. Only with the Pentagon's proposals, the charts showed, could the United States achieve GI Joe stature.[28]

Even the armed forces were surprised at the new secretary's effectiveness at bringing in more money than even they could imagine spending. As one former Pentagon officer described it, "Suddenly money was available. There are cheaper designs that could have been looked at, but they just dusted off the old plans. Under Carter's zero-base budgeting, they had priority bands — band one, band two, band three. There was a lot of crap from band five and six that got funded."[29]

Money was thrown at the Department of Defense faster than the Pentagon could spend it. Pentagon planners, perhaps sensing that the political honeymoon producing these windfalls would one day end, front-loaded their budgets, emphasizing research and development and the procurement of new weapons. These investment accounts, those devoted to construction and future forces, spend out at a slower pace than money allocated to current forces (personnel, operations and maintenance, supplies, and training). Procurement of new weapons led the way, comprising fully one-third of the fiscal 1986 budget authority. By the end of the first Reagan term, there was a backlog of more than $200 billion appropriated that had not yet been spent, more than $50 billion not obligated to specific contracts or weapons systems. Overall investment accounts reached 50 percent of the total military budget in fiscal 1986 for the first time since the Korean War, an emphasis William Kaufmann described as "truly remarkable and very likely unfeasible."[30]

In this way, the military received much higher budgets, yet a significant portion was not immediately spent. Meanwhile, large sums were committed to starting the production and procurement of new systems, that portion of the budget most susceptible to cost overruns and most difficult to control. Beginning construction of a battleship, for example, consumes only a small part of the ship's total cost. Once begun, however, sunken costs, institutional inertia, and Congressional pork barrel politics make cutting the system almost impossible. The Reagan budgets were committed not only to growth but also to unprecedented sustained growth, even if at the expense of combat readiness.[31]

Spending on controversial, expensive strategic nuclear programs, including the MX and the Trident, increased dramatically. Although this increase generated a great deal of publicity,[32] such programs still consumed a relatively small share of the budget.[33] These items were also slow in coming into line, so that the actual military implications of increased spending were not immediately visible. It is not clear that the inflated Reagan budgets bought many more or even better weapons, much less the ever-elusive national security. James Fallows notes that the Reagan budgets produced no appreciable change in U.S. military posture or capabilities. Forces were not significantly expanded, and combat readiness probably declined. He suggests that "military buildup" is a misnomer and that the policies are better described as a "spend-up," with much more money chasing only slightly more military hardware. The Navy under Reagan, he notes, bought 23 percent more ships than under Carter but spent 48 percent more for them; the Army bought 40 percent more helicopters, costing 150 percent more; the Air Force bought 12 percent fewer planes, spending 75 percent more.[34] Driving up the cost of the individual weapons was a tendency to "gold plate" or incorporate expensive and possibly unnecessary features.[35]

The process of spending more for less was particularly visible and controversial in spare parts and common household items. Mini-scandals broke when it was revealed that the Pentagon had paid $600 for a toilet seat, $400 for a hammer, and $7,000 for a coffee pot designed to continue operating even if the plane that carried it was destroyed.[36] These excesses, while constituting a small portion of the Reagan budgets, naturally drew political fire, as they were more immediately intelligible to the general public and to Congress than the appropriate cost of a fighter plane or ballistic missile. Congressional candidates enjoyed grandstanding with these boondoggles, as they afforded the opportunity to criticize Reagan's military spending without addressing the potentially controversial foreign policy goals it served. Across the country newspaper photographs showed U.S. senators peeking out through overpriced toilet seats. Although everyone knows that $600 was too much for a toilet seat, approximating the cost and means of ensuring national security is a more difficult subject to broach in a campaign for elected office.

These Reagan budgets and concomitant waste were shocking to most Americans. Even while in office, Stockman noted that there was "a swamp of $10 to $20 to $30 billion worth of waste" in the military budget.[37] Reformers of all political persuasions have made proposals for sifting through that swamp and developing a "leaner, meaner military budget" without the waste.[38] The more pertinent question, however, is whether, given U.S. military goals, such excess and waste are inevitable. This is the argument of Earl C. Ravenal, who opposes high military spending, global military objectives, and extended deterrence.[39] Ravenal argues that the scope of U.S. objectives makes the potential military budget limitless and that a certain level of waste is inevitable in any budget of this size. Edward Luttwak, who strongly supported the Reagan administration foreign policy objectives and spending, agrees:

> We must reject the suspect prescriptions of James Fallows and his ilk [military reformers], who would launch us on a quest for cheap solutions to problems that have none, and for many things to cut from the budget. . . . If the price of a wise strategy, of better operational methods, and of more ingenious tactics is indeed the neglect of micro-management, then so be it. We

would then have good reason to welcome a little more "waste, fraud, and mismanagement" in the Pentagon.[40]

Luttwak's approach, political rhetoric to the contrary, was shared by the dominant forces within the Reagan administration. Defense of the free world, in their view, does not come cheaply.[41] The cost of the Reagan program brought the broad strategic objectives and the means used to achieve them into question for many Americans, especially as budgets for many other popular programs were slashed. This new public scrutiny, bringing military spending to the attention of much larger numbers of people, was an opportunity for an emerging dissident movement.

THE RECESSION OF 1982

The much-vaunted economic recovery at the center of the Reagan program was quite long in coming. By almost any measure, the economy got worse during the early years of Reagan's presidency. Unemployment increased from an average less than 7 percent under Carter to 10.7 percent early in 1982, and it was substantially worse for women and minorities. While inflation was substantially cut, ultimately reaching negative numbers in early 1983, interest rates skyrocketed, dramatically increasing the real cost of credit to more than 14 percent in early 1982. As a result, housing starts declined as the economy stagnated. Simply, the triumph over inflation was no real victory for people who borrowed money. These statistics reflect a recession that reached its nadir in 1982. In addition to objective declines, public opinion surveys show that large numbers of people lost confidence in the ability of the Reagan administration to improve their economic prospects. After a brief period of optimism following Reagan's election, confidence in the economy waned, bottoming out at the end of 1982.[42]

The relationship between military spending and the economic recession is by no means as clear as critics suggested. Indeed, Caspar Weinberger has suggested that military spending can serve as a sort of Keynesian stimulation for the economy as a whole, leading to increased employment and economic growth. As the recession deepened early in Reagan's first term, Weinberger and other administration officials were virtually forced to reiterate this dubious proposition to increasingly less credulous audiences.[43]

Political activists have often pointed to high military spending as a means of mobilizing opposition to the arms race. An excellent example of this is the work of Jobs with Peace, a group that argues military spending robs the economy and that limiting defense expenditures and redirecting government spending can lead to economic growth and reduce unemployment.[44] Others concerned with particular economic issues have attempted to link their causes with that of disarmament activists. William Winpisinger, president of the International Association of Machinists and Aerospace Workers, signed on the nuclear freeze effort early, arguing that the union's cause was intimately connected with that of the peace movement.[45] The Reagan recession offered ample opportunity for these linkages. Several analysts have argued that the recession aided the nuclear freeze movement's early growth.[46] This potential link, between the recession and a protest movement not explicitly addressing economic issues, merits examination.

Clearly the greatest amount of movement activity, at least as measured through media coverage of the movement, took place during the worst part of the recession.[47] It is probably a mistake to treat this relationship as causal, implying that the economic recession generated discontent that at this time manifested in an antinuclear movement. At the same time, there probably is some sort of relationship. There are several possible explanations. Possibly it is all a coincidence, akin to occasional proliferations of sunspots; however, the sharp decline in reported activity as the economic recovery swung into play calls this interpretation into question. A conspiracy theorist might see extensive coverage of the nuclear freeze movement as means for diverting public attention from pressing economic issues, but this connection also does not seem credible. The relationship is probably somewhat more complex.

It is important to recall that candidate Reagan's primary appeal was on economic issues; even before he took office, large sectors of the public were wary about his ability to manage international affairs and the arms race. A poll taken October 20, 1980 (before the candidates' televised debate) showed that fully 43 percent of the population believed that Reagan was more likely than Carter to lead the country into war.[48] The administration's failure to make quick progress on improving the economy probably increased public distrust of its ability to manage other problems. Perhaps the recession effectively invalidated a tacit agreement made between Reagan and much of the public, that voters would ignore their foreign policy concerns if the president could improve their economic prospects. His failure to do so thereby unleashed a large number of long-standing, but previously unvoiced, concerns.

There is also the issue of budget transfers. President Reagan slowed the growth of overall federal spending in an attempt to finance his military budget increases and a large tax cut. Federal spending on social welfare, human services, employment training, school lunches, and numerous other projects was cut. No previous administration had so clearly increased military spending at the expense of social welfare programs.[49] This naturally created political opposition that, for many of the reasons listed above, was targeted at military policy and nuclear weapons. Advocates of all the programs shortchanged on the Reagan domestic agenda had common interest in opposing increased military spending. As one critic observed, the "antinuclear movement has become a magnet attracting a great variety of local coalitions . . . that now begin to see the relationship of the local agenda to the national agenda."[50] Ronald Reagan was like an economics teacher for the movement, said Randy Kehler, national coordinator of the nuclear freeze campaign. "The disarmament movement has been trying for years to make these connections, but he made them much better than we ever could."[51]

Those disaffected by Reagan's economic policies were not only human services advocates but also a large segment of the business community, troubled by the costs of the Reagan military program and especially the mounting federal deficit. Democratic political activist Harold Willens founded Business Executives for Nuclear Arms Control (BENAC), arguing that the arms race hurts the economy and is not conducive to doing business.[52] Along this line, the recession marked the beginning of the disintegration of Reagan's virtual monopoly of support among the business community, especially in those parts of the United States most adversely affected by the new restructuring of the nation's economy. Ferguson and Rogers note that Democratic business elites looked upon this as a political opportunity. Rather than forwarding a yet undeveloped economic plan, long-time business Democrats like Averell Harriman and Thomas J. Watson, Jr., began criticizing Reagan where he was most vulnerable, on the issue of arms control.[53]

This led to a rapid expansion of the movement beyond the traditional peace constituency, infusing a flow of new constituencies including high-status establishment figures. In addition to the new legitimacy, this development also brought in a flow of money, an obvious asset for the movement. The recession provoked the mobilization of several groups not previously interested in military issues or in working together, and these new alliances increased the visibility, volatility, and overall potential of the antinuclear movement.

There is also one other possibility, that the recession called into question the immediate future for many people. Perhaps desperation that one could not get a good job (or any job), afford a home, or live better than one's parents served as a stimulus for mobilization to preserve any kind of a future. Desperation about economic well-being may well have translated into desperation about being at all. The Reagan administration initially was particularly inept at assuaging such fears.

NOTES

1. Quoted in Jonathan Alter and Phil Keisling, "35 Ways to Cut the Defense Budget," *The Washington Monthly,* April 1982, p. 12.

2. Quoted in David Stockman, *The Triumph of Politics: Why the Reagan Revolution Failed,* New York: Harper & Row, 1986, pp. 290–91.

3. Quoted in Washington *Post,* November 19, 1980, p. A17.

4. President Nixon's diplomatic opening to China allowed the United States to reduce its military requirements from the ability to fight 2 1/2 wars to 1 1/2 wars, mandating preparations for war with the Soviet Union and an unspecified less powerful enemy. The 2 1/2-war capability was resurrected by Secretary of Defense Caspar Weinberger in justifying the early Reagan administration budgets. See Jimmy Carter, *Keeping Faith: Memoirs of a President,* New York: Bantam, 1982, pp. 192–93; James Fallows, *National Defense,* New York: Random House, 1981, p. xv; Richard A. Stubbing, with Richard A. Mendel, *The Defense Game,* New York: Harper & Row, 1986, pp. 58–60.

5. On U.S. military spending, see Congressional Budget Office, *An Analysis of the President's Budgetary Proposals,* Washington, D.C.: Congress of the United States, annual since 1977; William W. Kaufmannn, *The 1985 Defense Budget,* Washington, D.C.: The Brookings Institution, 1984 (also editions for 1984 and 1986); Stubbing, *Defense Game,* pp. 29–51.

6. These figures are derived from Department of Defense, *Total Obligational Authority (TOA) by Program, 1945–86,* published in 1985, and the updated 1989 edition, published in 1988. Unless otherwise noted, all figures cited here represent constant (adjusted for inflation) FY 1986 dollars.

7. John Lewis Gaddis, *Strategies of Containment: A Critical Appraisal of Postwar American National Security Policy,* Oxford University Press, 1982, pp. 204–5, suggests that Democratic presidents practicing Keynesianism more generally have felt less fiscally constrained than Republicans have.

8. Bruce Russett, "Defense Expenditures and National Well-Being," *American Political Science Review,* December 1982, pp. 767–77. For a cross-national analysis of the relationship, or nonrelationship, of defense and social welfare expenditures, see William K. Domke, Richard C. Eichenberg, and Catherine M. Kelleher, "The Illusion of Choice: Defense and Welfare in Advanced Industrial Democracies, 1948–1978," *American Political Science Review,* 77, no. 1, pp. 19–35.

9. This is a central theme of Alain C. Enthoven and Wayne K. Smith, *How Much Is Enough?: Shaping the Defense Program, 1961–1969,* New York: Harper & Row, 1971. For analysis of Congressional responses to presidential budget requests, see Arnold Kanter, *Defense Politics: A Budgetary Perspective,* Chicago: University of Chicago Press, 1979; Stubbing, *Defense Game,* pp. 90–98.

10. Lawrence Freedman, *The Evolution of Nuclear Strategy,* New York: St. Martin's, 1983, p. 78; Gaddis, *Containment,* pp. 152, 171; Kanter, *Defense Politics,* pp. 68–70.

11. Enthoven and Smith, *How Much Is Enough?,* p. 33.

12. Kanter, *Defense Politics,* pp. 74–75.

13. Fallows, *National Defense,* p. 24; Nicholas Lemann, "The Peacetime War: Caspar Weinberger in Reagan's Pentagon," *The Atlantic Monthly,* October 1984, p. 86; Stubbing, *Defense Game,* pp. 263–87.

14. Freedman, *Evolution of Nuclear Strategy*, pp. 341–43; Melvin R. Laird, "A Strong Start in a Difficult Decade: Defense Policy in the Nixon-Ford Years," *International Security*, Fall 1985, pp. 5–26; Stubbing, *Defense Game*, pp. 304–6.

15. Robert Komer, "What 'Decade of Neglect'?" *International Security*, Fall 1985, p. 74.

16. William Kaufmannn, who supported increased defense spending, criticized the magnitude of the Carter buildup, writing, "The amounts involved, even without further increases, are huge by any standard." See *Defense in the 1980s*, Washington, D.C.: The Brookings Institution, 1981, pp. 3–4.

17. Lemann, "Peacetime War," p. 71; Kaufmann, *Defense in the 1980s*, pp. 4–6; Stockman, *Triumph of Politics*, pp. 107–9. Stockman described this as an "up yours" gesture to the incoming president.

18. Stockman, *Triumph of Politics*, pp. 131–32. Stubbing notes that the institutional conflict between the budget director and the Secretary of Defense is often resolved by the strength of their respective relationships with the president, *Defense Game*, pp. 83, 368–98. While Stockman barely knew Reagan before his appointment, Weinberger had been Governor Reagan's budget director in California, and their personal and professional relationship spanned 20 years.

19. Russett, "Defense Expenditures," p. 771.

20. Fallows, *National Defense*, p. 11; Lawrence J. Korb and Linda P. Brady, "Rearming America: The Reagan Administration Defense Program," *International Security*, Summer 1987, p. 5.

21. Lemann, "Peacetime War," p. 75; Stockman, *Triumph of Politics*, pp. 277–78; Stubbing, *Defense Game*, p. 84.

22. Lemann, "Peacetime War," pp. 71, 74; On Team B, also see Robert Scheer, *With Enough Shovels to Go Around: Reagan, Bush, and Nuclear War*, New York: Random House, 1982. Scheer devotes a chapter to the CIA reestimates. Also, see Stubbing, *Defense Game*, pp. 12–13.

23. Lemann, "Peacetime War," p. 76.

24. Ibid.; Stubbing, *Defense Game*, pp. 368–98.

25. Stockman, *Triumph of Politics*, pp. 277–78.

26. Although accepted as gospel by Reagan administration officials, the "decade of neglect" remains controversial; see Komer, "What 'Decade of Neglect'?"; Warner Schilling, "U.S. Strategic Nuclear Concepts in the 1970s: The Search for Sufficiently Equivalent Countervailing Parity," *International Security*, Fall 1981; Stubbing, *Defense Game*, p. xiii.

27. The accuracy of this detail is extremely controversial; see Tom Gervasi, *Soviet Military Power: The Pentagon's Propaganda Document, Annotated and Corrected*, New York: Vintage, 1987; Kaufmann, *1985 Defense Budget*, p. 45.

28. Stockman, *Triumph of Politics*, pp. 290–91.

29. Quoted in Lemann, "Peacetime War," p. 72.

30. Kaufmannn, *1985 Defense Budget*, p. 3. Also see James Fallows, "The Spend-Up," *The Atlantic Monthly*, July 1986, p. 27; Randall Forsberg and David S. Meyer, "Defense Spending: Can We Budge It?" *Defense and Disarmament News*, June/July 1984; Christopher E. Paine and Gordon Adams, "The R&D Slushfund," *The Nation*, January 26, 1980, p. 72; Stubbing, *Defense Game*, pp. 43–44.

31. Gordon Adams and the Defense Budget Project, *The FY 1985 Defense Budget: The Buildup Continues*, Washington, D.C.: Center for Budget and Policy Priorities, 1984.

32. See, for example, Gordon Adams and David A. Gold, "$50 Billion That Can Go: How to Cut the Defense Budget — Now," *The Nation,* December 11, 1982, p. 609; Alter and Keisling, "35 Ways to Cut"; David Gold, Christopher Paine, and Gail Shields, *Misguided Missile: An Analysis of the Proposed MX Missile System,* New York: Council on Economic Priorities, 1981; John David Isaacs, "Reagan's Defense Budget," *Bulletin of the Atomic Scientists,* May 1981; Christopher E. Paine, "Arms Buildup," *Bulletin of the Atomic Scientists,* October 1982, p. 5.

33. Admiral Eugene LaRoque notes that more than 70 percent of the military budget is used in preparation for foreign wars and that "actual defense of the United States costs about 10 percent of the military budget and is the least expensive function performed by the Pentagon," in Ronald V. Dellums et al., eds., *Defense Sense: The Search for a Rational Military Policy,* Cambridge, MA: Ballinger, 1983, pp. 113, 109–24, and passim. Also see Forsberg and Meyer, "Military Spending."

34. Fallows, "The Spend-Up," pp. 27–28. Also see Congressional Budget Office, *Defense Spending: What Has Been Accomplished,* Washington, D.C.: U.S. Congress, April 1985.

35. This is a central theme of Fallows's *National Defense.* Also see Alter and Keisling, "35 Ways to Cut"; and, for example, Gregg Easterbrook, "Why DIVAD Wouldn't Die," *The Washington Monthly,* November 1984; Dina Rasor, ed., *More Bucks, Less Bang: How the Pentagon Buys Ineffective Weapons,* Washington, D.C.: Fund For Constitutional Government, 1983; Scott Shuyer, "The Navy's Plane Stupidity," *The Washington Monthly,* October 1985.

36. See Lori Comeau, *Nuts and Bolts at the Pentagon: A Spare Parts Catalogue,* Washington, D.C.: Defense Budget Project, 1984, for a surprisingly exhaustive list of similar expenditures.

37. Quoted in Gordon Adams, "What Do Weapons Secure," *Bulletin of the Atomic Scientists,* April 1982, p. 8.

38. For two divergent and thoughtful attempts to develop this kind of military, see Fallows, *National Defense*; Kaufmann, *The 1985 Military Budget,* p. 46. Kaufmannn proposes savings of $174 billion over five years.

39. Earl C. Ravenal, *Defining Defense: The 1985 Military Budget,* Washington, D.C.: The Cato Institute, 1984.

40. Edward Luttwak, "Why We Need More 'Waste, Fraud, and Mismanagement' in the Pentagon," *Commentary,* February 1982.

41. Korb and Brady, "Rearming America."

42. "Opinion Roundup," *Public Opinion,* August/September, 1985, pp. 21–24.

43. Others have suggested that high military spending is the necessary cost of maintaining an empire and compliant allies in the Third World ready to provide open markets and cheap labor and raw materials. See Paul Baran and Paul Sweezy, *Monopoly Capital,* New York and London: Monthly Review Press, 1966, Chapter 7. Also see these alternative perspectives: Gordon Adams, *The Iron Triangle: The Politics of Defense Contracting,* New York: Council on Economic Priorities, 1981; Robert DeGrasse, *Military Expansion, Economic Decline,* New York: Council on Economic Priorities, 1983; Seymour Melman, *The Permanent War Economy,* New York: Simon and Schuster, 1974; Hugh G. Mosley, *The Arms Race: Economic and Social Consequences,* Lexington, MA: Lexington Books, 1985.

44. See, for example, Jobs with Peace, *Towards a Boston Peace Budget,* Boston, 1982.

45. Dellums et al., *Defense Sense,* pp. 197–204.

46. Thomas Ferguson and Joel Rogers, "Big Business Backs the Freeze," *The Nation,* July 19/26, 1986, pp. 43–47; Adam Garfinkle, *The Politics of the Nuclear Freeze,* Philadelphia: Foreign Policy Research Institute, 1984, pp. 106–10; Frank Riessmann, "The Antinuclear Movements: Why Now?" *Social Policy* 13 (Summer 1982): 2; Paul Walker, "Teach-Ins on American Campuses," *Bulletin of the Atomic Scientists,* February 1982, p. 10.

47. See Chapter 7 for a more detailed discussion.

48. *Public Opinion,* December/January 1981, p. 24. On the eve of the election, November 1, this percentage declined to a still very substantial 35 percent, remarkable in light of Reagan's victory margin. A Washington *Post*/ABC poll reported that 45 percent of those surveyed said they believed that the risk of war would increase under Reagan's presidency, Boston *Globe,* May 24, 1982.

49. Russett, "Defense Expenditures."

50. Riessmann, "The Antinuclear Movement," p. 2.

51. Mary Kaldor, Randy Kehler, Mient Jan-Faber, "Learning from Each Other," *END Bulletin* , February/March 1983, p. 22.

52. Garfinkle, *The Politics of the Nuclear Freeze,* pp. 106–10. See also Harold Willens, *The TrimTab Factor: How Business Executives Can Help Solve the Nuclear Weapons Crisis,* New York: William Morrow, 1984. Such arguments have previously buttressed business support for peace movements. See C. Roland Marchand, *The American Peace Movement and Social Reform, 1898–1918,* Princeton, NJ: Princeton University Press, 1972, p. 98, for a discussion of business support for the peace movement before World War I.

53. Ferguson and Rogers, "Big Business Backs the Freeze."

4

THE ARMS RACE AND DOMESTIC POLITICAL MISMANAGEMENT

Nuclear weapons policy is generally not the subject of broad public debate. Previous administrations have worked hard to keep this so, assuaging or exploiting nuclear fears by a careful combination of arms control negotiations, tempered political rhetoric, and careful maintenance of alliance support. An administration's strategically expressed sincere concerns about the costs and dangers of the arms race and nuclear weapons can go a long way toward preempting the development of dissent. In contrast, the Reagan administration's political style provoked opposition. The administration's explicit denigration of the arms control process and frequent cavalier statements about the feasibility of nuclear war from top administration officials drew additional scrutiny to Reagan's nuclear weapons policies. Opposition movements first emerged strongly in Western Europe and soon spread to the United States. The Reagan admin-istration's failure to use established processes for managing the politics of the arms race brought about domestic political fallout.

POLITICAL BENEFITS OF ARMS CONTROL

Arms control has historically been used to temper the costs and the hostility of military competition between the superpowers. This ongoing process of communication, negotiation, and the search for common objectives between the superpowers also mitigated and moderated public concern about the arms race during the 1960s and 1970s. The Reagan administration's visible disdain for the entire process enhanced the development of political space for opposition. The political costs of the administration's approach to arms control become clear in light of its contrast with the previously bipartisan practice of arms control.

First, it is essential to understand the goals of arms control in the modern era. Despite widespread perceptions to the contrary, they do not include nuclear disarmament or world peace. Rather, arms control is a means for managing the international competition by reducing the likelihood of war, the costs of preparing for war, and the damage caused in the event of war.[1] Arms control agreements between the Soviet Union and the United States, in order to gain the assent of both superpowers, must be limited to a small number of common objectives, comprising those listed above and limiting the spread of nuclear weapons technology to other nations. These common interests also include facilitating the maintenance and modernization of each superpower's strategic and tactical nuclear forces. Arms control is not a means for pursuing nuclear disarmament but an alternative to it, another means for implementing U.S. foreign policy programs, including containment.[2] Christopher Paine writes that given these objectives, the term "arms control" is a misnomer, noting "The National Center for Disease Control in Atlanta . . . does not interpret its mission as mandating the introduction and controlled spread of new forms of disease."[3]

The conduct of arms control has also served to preempt or coopt opposition to the arms race, playing on the notion that pursuit of broad and comprehensive goals may preclude "pragmatic" and desirable arms control.[4] Many apparently agree with the Harvard Nuclear Study Group that nuclear disarmament, although an attractive notion, is not a realistic or achievable goal and that "the danger of focusing on utopian objectives is they can take attention away from practical and positive steps that can be taken now. Such actions may only produce incremental steps toward the goal of national security. But incremental steps matter."[5]

Pursuit of incremental steps has slowed the momentum for broader, perhaps utopian goals. The call for the international control of nuclear weapons in the immediate postwar period, led by a number of scientists involved in developing the bomb, was derisively labeled as naive and subsequently quashed.[6] Later, President Eisenhower appointed Harold Stassen as a special advisor on nuclear disarmament, ostensibly embracing the concerns that spurred the scientists' movement. In 1955, however, Stassen announced that nuclear disarmament was unattainable and that the best security program would focus on strengthening deterrence and guarding against surprise attack.[7]

This kind of government approach to arms control and disarmament has led disarmament advocates such as Alva Myrdal to wish for a boycott of the term "arms control." "It is nothing but a euphemism," she writes, "serving regrettably to lead thinking and action towards the acceptance as 'arms control measures' of compromise with scant or nil disarmament effect."[8] Government pursuit of arms control, when successfully conducted, has preempted the development of stronger calls for disarmament.[9]

In the atmosphere of increased public concern and activism against nuclear weapons testing, President Kennedy founded the Arms Control and Disarmament Agency (ACDA) in 1961 to coordinate pursuit of measures more modest than a nuclear test ban. In doing so, he effectively tied one wing of the peace movement to the left of the Democratic Party and his administration and provided an institutional venue for antinuclear activism.[10] Since the creation of ACDA, a number of agreements have been concluded, placing numerical limits on superpower nuclear forces and limiting some of the most dangerous and disruptive by-products of the arms race, most notably, atmospheric testing. Arms control efforts, however, are equally notable for what they have not addressed: the ongoing nuclear competition, technological advances in arms technology, and the drive by both superpowers to deploy nuclear weapons in an increasing variety of roles. Every arms control achievement is distinguished by a corresponding development in the arms race left untouched.

The Limited Test Ban Treaty (LTB), signed by Kennedy in 1963, ended above-ground testing and thereby reduced the radioactive and political fallout of nuclear testing. Importantly, the number of nuclear tests increased after the treaty's ratification; testing moved underwater and underground. The level of public concern and activism, however, declined precipitously. Myrdal writes, "The public was too easily satisfied with the ostrich-like solution of driving the tests underground — which had no effect on the major objective, to hamper and curtail nuclear-weapons development."[11] The Strategic Arms Limitations Talks (SALT) I and II agreements negotiated by Presidents Nixon, Ford, and Carter set numerical constraints on strategic weapons while explicitly ignoring the most destabilizing technological advances, including MIRVs (multiple independently targeted reentry vehicles), cruise missiles, and other counterforce weapons such as the MX and Trident missiles. In 1972, President Nixon signed the Antiballistic Missile (ABM) Treaty, which limited then-undeveloped systems and technologies, setting a numerical ceiling on these weapons higher than either superpower has yet approached.[12]

Even these rather modest achievements did not come easily. Success within the arms control process requires not only agreement between the superpowers but, at least in the United States, the alignment of a constellation of domestic support among the military, Congress, and the public.[13] This must be orchestrated and utilized by a chief executive both committed to and competent in the process of arms control. No arms control agreement has ever been approved without exceptionally strong and determined leadership from the

Oval Office.[14] Not only must the president negotiate an acceptable agreement with the Soviet Union; he must also be able to counter or preempt domestic opposition, demonstrating clearly that he is not capitulating U.S. military preparedness to the perceived red menace. Given the political environment surrounding foreign policy issues in U.S. politics, this can be exceptionally difficult.[15] Most significant in this regard is winning the support of the military. Historically, this has entailed providing a "sweetener" for the Joint Chiefs of Staff and the Pentagon along with any arms control agreement.[16] Increased nuclear testing bought the LTB support in 1963; support for the B-1 bomber and accelerated development of Trident I was traded for SALT I. President Carter made deals with the Senate in which he granted support for the MX, Trident II, and cruise missiles, increased spending on civil defense, and the neutron bomb in an ultimately futile attempt to win support for SALT II.[17] The cost of these domestic bargaining chips is substantial. One analyst confessed, "I'm terrified of SALT III, because it could bankrupt us."[18]

The desire for arms control bargaining chips, for use in dealing with both the military and the Soviet Union, has actually fed the momentum of the arms race. Seeking to bargain from a position of strength, arms controllers may support the development of numerous weapons otherwise judged redundant or destabilizing, promising or planning to trade them later. In practice, however, negotiations generally legitimate rather than limit existing weapons or those already in development. Once in the development stage, new weapons develop not only strategic rationales but also bureaucratic constituencies and institutional support, making trading or cancelling them virtually impossible. In effect, the arms control process is used to justify increasing spending and the development of new weapons. According to George Rathjens, "If you're an advocate of a weapons program and you're in trouble getting it through you try the arms control justification."[19]

These factors have led disarmament proponents to question the utility of the arms control process as it has operated. As Jane Sharp writes, "Arms control diplomacy . . . encourages the acquisition of new systems to increase bargaining strength or negotiations in specific force categories." Numerical limits, she adds, drive the technological arms race by encouraging each side to increase its strategic capabilities while staying under a numerical ceiling.[20] The arms control process is based on a supposition of perpetual superpower nuclear competition, which can be managed but not halted.

Arms control itself will not end nor even significantly restrain the nuclear arms race. It may, however, inhibit the development of opposition movements, whose partisans may have unrealistically high expectations of potential gains that can be made through the arms control process.[21] These factors, along with the large military buildup that President Carter presented with SALT II, led many liberals to give only lukewarm support to the treaty. Marcus Raskin, for example, suggested that SALT II was worth ratifying but not worth the cost of the buildup that would come with it.[22] Jerome Grossman, president of the Council for a Livable World, an organization that normally provides strong support for arms control efforts, chose not to push for SALT II ratification, encouraging activists to follow his lead. He feared the identification of the disarmament lobby with Carter's military buildup and a very limited treaty, which would probably not be ratified in any case.[23]

The lack of strong usport from such quarters was probably one of many factors contributing to the difficulties SALT II faced in the Senate. Carter's strong personal commitment to the treaty and identification with it aided in undermining support for ratification as the president's base of support eroded. The taking of hostages in Iran contributed to the rise of hawkish anti-arms control sentiments. When the Soviet Union invaded Afghanistan in January 1980, Carter formally withdrew the already doomed treaty from Senate consideration.[24]

THE REAGAN APPROACH TO ARMS CONTROL

The prospects for arms control preceding the 1980 election appeared dismal; the election of Ronald Reagan made things worse and appear much worse. Candidate Reagan had castigated Carter's weakness in standing up to the Soviet Union, likening arms control to appeasement. Although Carter's campaign rhetoric grew increasingly hawkish, it could not match the polemic thrust provided by the Reagan team. Reagan interpreted his landslide victory as a broad mandate of support for his foreign and domestic policies, among them opposition to arms control. Indeed, he had ample electoral evidence to use. In addition to his landslide in both the popular and electoral college vote, the Republicans also won control of the Senate. Ousted from the Senate were several notable arms control advocates, including Democrats Birch Bayh (Indiana), Frank Church (Idaho), John Culver (Iowa), Warren Magnuson (Washington), George McGovern (South Dakota) and Gaylord Nelson (Wisconsin), and Republican Jacob Javitts (New York). In all cases they were replaced by Republicans either indifferent or hostile to the arms control process.

Upon inauguration, President Reagan implemented the arms control policy he had promised. His appointments to key arms control positions, and the steady stream of rhetoric criticizing both the Soviet Union and the arms control process generally, made any prospect of agreements or even serious negotiations appear doubtful. Reagan cleared moderates and liberals out of ACDA, replacing them with Committee on the Present Danger (CoPD) veterans who frequently had little background and no interest in arms control.[25] Initially these officials were candid about their contempt for the process. Eugene Rostow, ACDA director and cofounder of CoPD, testified in his confirmation hearings that the last successful arms control agreement had been signed by the United States and Canada in 1817.[26] Finding nothing positive about arms control in this century, Rostow asserted that useful negotiations with the Soviet Union could proceed only after they have been "contained," as the Truman Doctrine demanded. This might mean a limited nuclear war with "only 10–100 million casualties," he estimated, acknowledging that prospects for arms control were not very good.[27] Rostow and others from CoPD believed that a strong and unabated U.S. military buildup could force the Soviet Union to liberalize or at least bankrupt itself. Arms control undermined these objectives and was therefore dangerous and undesirable. Indeed, Rostow saw his ACDA appointment as an opportunity to proselytize against arms control.

When the freeze movement began to gain momentum, Rostow directed his efforts to countering its impact on domestic politics. Reporter Robert Scheer uncovered a Rostow memo to that effect, which he published in the Washington *Post*. The memo outlined a possible administration effort to answer and overwhelm the nonpartisan Ground Zero week by a series of speeches and television appearances by administration officials and ostensibly unattached conservatives, including George Will. Rostow thought that a widespread educational campaign on nuclear issues like the one Ground Zero promised was a threat, which "would produce an eruption of the issue of nuclear war . . . [and a movement] which includes such perennial elements as the old-line pacifists, the environmentalists, the disaffected left, and various communist elements."[28]

Rostow's perspective on arms control and arms control advocates was hardly unique among top level Reagan administration officials. Another CoPD member, Paul Nitze, was appointed to head Theater Nuclear Forces (TNF) negotiations. At his confirmation hearings Nitze testified that serious arms control could only take place after a prolonged U.S. buildup, which he estimated could take ten years.[29] Serving in President Truman's administration, Nitze had predicted a Soviet first strike by 1954. At that time, he suggested in a memo to the president that the United States engage in arms control negotiations but avoid agreements. He proposed that the United States make proposals that sound reasonable but which were unlikely to be accepted by the Soviet Union. "Of course, should the Russians show unexpected flexibility," he reasoned, "we would have to consider very seriously whether we should accept such agreements."[30] (Rostow and Nitze were later replaced, at least partly for showing some support for a tentative agreement on intermediate-range missiles.)[31]

Reagan's chief strategic negotiator was Edward Rowny, who had been the representative of the Joint Chiefs of Staff to the SALT negotiations from 1973 until June 30, 1979, when he resigned to oppose the Joint Chiefs and the SALT II treaty. Said Rowny, "I have had little to say about arms control. I have done this because my 6 1/2 years with SALT have led me to the conclusion that we have put too much emphasis on the *control* or arms and too little on the *provision* of arms."[32]

Upon taking office, Reagan immediately took SALT II "off the shelf" where Carter had left it, and abandoned the agreement.[33] He did not present his own START (Strategic Arms Reduction Talks) proposals until a speech at his alma mater, Eureka College, on May 9, 1982. This mild attempt at maintaining the appearance of interest in arms control occurred only after the freeze movement was well underway. It seems that someone in the Reagan administration had read Nitze's ancient memo and decided there was political advantage in at least presenting a facade of arms control efforts. Almost as if to demonstrate that these extremely unbalanced proposals would not lead to some sort of agreement,[34] the administration simultaneously unveiled (later disproven) allegations of Soviet treaty violations and chemical warfare in the form of "Yellow Rain."[35] The START proposals were probably designed to be rejected, in an attempt to place the public relations onus of concessions on the Soviet Union. Clearly START was directed more at the U.S. public than at the Soviet Union. In summary, from the outset the Reagan administration did virtually everything it could to prove that it had no intention of reaching any kind of arms control agreement with the Soviet Union, perhaps far too explicitly to be politically wise.

SYMBOLIC POLITICS: MISMANAGED POLEMICS

It was not actual policies that undermined Reagan's support among the general public so much as the administration's presentation of those policies. The provocative nature of the administration's military and arms control policies was emphasized by the administration's rhetoric and style. Extreme anti-Soviet barbs were accompanied by an apparently cavalier attitude toward the dangers of nuclear war and nuclear weapons. Indeed, the Reagan administration's departure from previous U.S. strategic policy was not nearly as striking as its new and distinctive rhetoric. The president and many of his appointees demonstrated neither concern or competence in their confirmation hearings and subsequent speeches. They gave most Americans every reason to believe that the

Reagan administration was not capable of managing this most crucial set of issues.[36]

Reagan's own misstatements were only the most visible from an administration prone to overstatement and polemics. Reagan termed the Soviet Union an "evil empire" and the Soviets "godless monsters," proudly proclaiming that "we have a different regard for life than those monsters do," paradoxically attempting to justify a more hostile, militaristic, and threatening U.S. posture.[37] A candidate for office might derive domestic political benefits from this tone, but it was more problematic from a sitting president. It was not simply the unabashed hostility of his tone, however, but also factual errors that grated. Reagan falsely asserted, for example, that the United States had unilaterally disarmed in the 1970s and that submarine-launched ballistic missiles are recallable. He admitted that it was several years before anyone in his administration realized that most Soviet strategic nuclear forces were based on land, by way of explaining the administration's slow start in the arms control process. His grasp of the growing dissident movement in the United States was no more astute. Reagan claimed that Leonid Brezhnev first proposed a nuclear freeze, that those Americans who supported it were being "duped" by Soviet agents,[38] and that the Catholic bishops' pastoral letter criticizing his policies was actually supportive.[39] He joked about nuclear war, while providing for the sale of fissile materials to South Africa.[40] Oddly, his advisors were no better, and often they were worse.

Defense Secretary Caspar Weinberger announced the production of the controversial neutron bomb on the anniversary of the bombing of Hiroshima. Arms negotiator Edward Rowny suggested that arms control was possible only after a prolonged period of unilateral Soviet disarmament, while Eugene Rostow, Richard Pipes (a member of the National Security Council), and others suggested that the Soviet Union would have to transform its political nature before any agreements would be possible. Pipes claimed that this was a reasonable expectation, estimating the chance of nuclear war at about 40 percent. Meanwhile Secretary of State Alexander Haig pointed out that current U.S. plans included the possibility of firing a "nuclear warning shot" somewhere in Europe.[41]

Others suggested that a limited nuclear war was not only possible but likely. During Rostow's confirmation hearings, Senator Claiborne Pell (D–RI) asked ACDA's new director whether either country might survive a nuclear war. Rostow's reply focused on the resilience of the human race, noting that "ten million casualties on one side and one hundred million on the other . . . is not the whole of the population."[42] Louis Giuffrida, director of the Federal Emergency Management Agency, explained that although "nuke war" would be messy, it was not necessarily "unmanageable."[43] FEMA, allocated an unprecedented $4.2 billion to provide for civil defense and crisis relocation in the event of a nuclear war, engaged in such ill-fated public education efforts as producing a film to "paint a rosier picture of nuclear war."[44] Casualties could be limited to a mere 10 million, according to T. K. Jones, a Defense undersecretary. All that was needed was "enough shovels to go around" so that people could improvise fallout shelters. Jones asserted that the United States could recover from such a war in two to four years.[45]

While there was certainly the problem of defending and implementing controversial policies, there was an even larger public relations problem. Like a number of officials in previous administrations, Reagan's appointees believed that the United States must be prepared to fight and win different kinds of nuclear wars. Unlike their predecessors, however, they were not reluctant to say so. Reagan himself was explicit on this matter, stating at an October 1981 press conference that the exchange of tactical nuclear weapons on the battlefield need not bring one of the superpowers to "push the button."[46]

These beliefs and this rhetoric had been developed and honed by CoPD during years of political opposition to arms control and detente under Presidents Ford and Carter. The tone may have made for effective campaign rhetoric, sharply schematizing the political landscape and impressing potential supporters of the need to sign on, but it was far less effective as the language of governance. Administration officials' polemics drew attention to extremely difficult and controversial problems they were now responsible for managing. The administration's embrace of political confrontation aided opponents outside government. As an example, upon hearing that four former high-level strategic policy makers were about to publish an article calling for the United States to declare it would not use nuclear weapons first,[47] Secretary of State Alexander Haig called a press conference to announce in no uncertain terms that the United States would surely not do so.[48] Haig effectively promoted the article, bringing it readers and media attention it might otherwise have had difficulty attracting. This is just one of many examples of high-level Reagan officials virtually seeking confrontation not only with peace movement advocates but also with advocates of previously mainstream strategic positions.

The Reagan administration's approach seemed to trivialize widespread, long-standing, and legitimate fears of nuclear holocaust. In even the most diplomatic and sympathetic of the administration's early comments, high-level officials met these concerns with extremely faint cautions and disclaimers. Top Reagan advisor Ed Meese acknowledged that nuclear war "*may* not be desirable."[49] Charles Kupperman, executive director of an ACDA advisory committee and a CoPD veteran described nuclear war as essentially "a physics problem," which the United States could resolve and win. It is, he explained, the difference between 20 million and 150 million casualties.[50]

It should not be surprising that talk like this, probably even more than the administration's policies, terrified large numbers of people into concern and political mobilization. The policies after all represented nothing totally new and were not widely understood. The biggest difference was one of style and rhetoric. While government officials formerly spoke of "options," the Reagan appointees were much more graphic and forthright in discussing nuclear warning shots or acceptable casualties numbered in the tens of millions. Questions about the administration's capacity to manage the arms race and relations with the Soviet Union were underscored by the administration's failure in domestic diplomacy. Basically the administration was unable to sell the general public the basic premise that its policies were only marginally different from those of its predecessors — even though this was generally the case. Partly this was because the administrators were unwilling to yield what they considered to be the moral and political high ground. They were also unable or unwilling to sugarcoat or soften their rhetoric and management style. This unwillingness to compromise, if only through the time-worn pacifiers of conducting arms control negotiations and occasional conciliatory rhetoric, had a political price: the mobilization of a hostile mass movement. Freeze activist John Isaacs suggested that the movement would never have materialized if Reagan had simply "kept his mouth shut for the first six months in office."[51] Reagan administration rhetoric became the most powerful recruiting device for the nuclear freeze.

RIFTS WITHIN THE ALLIANCE: PEACE MOVEMENTS IN WESTERN EUROPE

The political fallout from the Reagan policies and politics was first visible in the form of emerging peace and antinuclear movements in many Western European countries. They were provoked by a number of U.S. policies and rhetoric as well as issues specific to each country. There was, however, one common catalyst: President Carter's December 1979 announcement of a "dual track" decision to deploy intermediate-range nuclear missiles in five European countries. This decision, to begin preparations for deploying Pershing II and ground-launched cruise missiles while negotiating with the Soviets to limit this class of weaponry, immediately generated widespread opposition. No doubt this was exacerbated by the subsequent announcement of PD 59 and discussion of limited nuclear wars.

The decision and the way it was made, appearing to have been dictated by the United States to quiescent but unenthusiastic allies, were controversial. The lack of visible consultation among the allies generated nearly as much antipathy as the missiles themselves.[52] The Reagan administration's approach only made things worse. Alexander Haig's speculations on a nuclear warning shot disturbed many Americans, but their concerns were mild compared to those who lived in the potential theater for such a demonstration. Many Europeans were understandably uncomfortable with loose talk about limited nuclear wars while preparing to host the weapons that would fight them. Meanwhile the prospects for an arms control agreement that might forestall deployment, perhaps slight under Carter, became unimaginable under President Reagan. This gave a new impetus to the developing European peace movements.[53]

The tactics and political style of the European movements varied from country to country and organization to organization. In the Netherlands opposition was coordinated by the Dutch Interchurch Peace Council (IKV), with strong support across the political spectrum. In Italy, much of the opposition was organized by the Communist Party; antinuclear sentiment aided in the formation of a new political party in West Germany, the Greens. The movement in Great Britain was funneled primarily through old organizations, especially the Campaign for Nuclear Disarmament (CND), but new organizations and approaches were also created, including the peace camp movement and an umbrella organization intended to unify the European movements, European Nuclear Disarmament (END). Across the continent, there was a proliferation of antinuclear activity. Very large demonstrations were staged in many European capitals in late 1981 and early 1982, drawing 300,000 people in Bonn, 250,000 in London, 250,000 in Paris, 200,000 in Rome, and more than 400,000 in Amsterdam.[54]

Antinuclear organizations in the United States seized upon the news from Europe even as the European movements began, attempting to draw attention to the issue. The *Bulletin of the Atomic Scientists,* for example, published a special European Nuclear Disarmament issue in December 1980. Peace groups in the United States tried to use the European activism as a means for igniting protest in the United States. "This movement has created hope," one activist wrote, "and therein lies the hope for us all. They send us a challenge: Why do you not scream, America?"[55]

While most of the protest of the European movements was directed at the European governments preparing to accept the new missiles (Belgium, Great Britain, Italy, the Netherlands, and West Germany), European activists also tried to influence public opinion in the United States. European disarmament activists thought this might help change the conduct of the U.S. government, which they saw as the moving force behind the dual track decision. Leaders of European governments and movements, including long-time disarmament advocates like Swedish Prime Minister Olof Palme and British historian E. P. Thompson, published articulate appeals calling for action in the United States.[56] Thompson seemed to be everywhere, publishing prolifically and visiting the United States for several speaking tours. Most visible was the collection of essays he edited with Dan Smith, *Protest and Survive*, which achieved mass circulation quickly and went through several paperback editions.[57] Nuclear disarmament, Thompson argued, was necessary to break the hegemony of *both* superpowers on Europe and their own citizenries and was inextricably linked with the struggle for human rights.[58]

Thompson was not alone; many Western European activists trooped through the United States and the media spreading different iterations of antinuclear concern. Petra Kelly, a spokesperson for the antinuclear West German Green Party, became a media darling, as much because of her father (a retired U.S. Army officer) and excellent English as her powerful speaking style and political positions.[59] Scores of less famous Western European activists, including clergy and several former NATO generals, visited the United States to publicize their cause and ask for help in ending the arms race, and more immediately, in stopping the deployment of Pershing II and cruise missiles.[60] These visits were usually coordinated by U.S. movement organizations, eager to promote the development of a movement on home soil. The American Friends Services Committee (AFSC) and Clergy and Laity Concerned (CALC) for example, sponsored a 52-city tour for ten European activists between March 21 and April 3, 1982.[61]

The European movements presented the first wave of concern about nuclear weaponry that sensitized the general public and the press about the concerns soon to be represented by the nuclear freeze movement. They not only suggested the possibility of a U.S. movement but also prepared the potential audience for activist efforts already underway.

NOTES

1. Thomas C. Schelling and Morton H. Halperin, *Strategy and Arms Control*, New York: Twentieth Century Fund, 1961.

2. John Lewis Gaddis, *Strategies of Containment: A Critical Appraisal of Postwar American National Security Policy*, New York: Oxford University Press, 1982, p. 324.

3. Christopher E. Paine, "Conceptual Foundations of a Comprehensive Nuclear Freeze," in Steven E. Miller, ed., *The Nuclear Weapons Freeze and Arms Control*, Cambridge, MA: Ballinger, 1984.

4. See, for example, Christopher M. Lehman, "Arms Control vs. the Freeze," in Miller, ed., *Nuclear Weapons Freeze*, pp. 65–71. Lehman was Reagan's director of the Office of Strategic Nuclear Planning.

5. Harvard Nuclear Study Group, *Living with Nuclear Weapons,* New York: Bantam, 1983, pp. 18–19. This theme is the central concern of Graham T. Allison et al., eds., *Hawks, Doves, and Owls: An Agenda for Avoiding Nuclear War,* New York: Norton, 1985.

6. Lawrence Wittner, *Rebels against War: The American Peace Movement, 1933–1983,* Philadelphia: Temple University Press, 1984, pp. 144–50.

7. Lawrence Freedman, *The Evolution of Nuclear Strategy,* New York: St. Martin's, 1983, pp. 198–99.

8. Alva Myrdal, *The Game of Disarmament: How the United States and Russia Run the Arms Game,* New York: Pantheon, 1982, p. xxxiv.

9. See, for example, Jane M. O. Sharp's analysis of the political context surrounding conventional arms control negotiations in Europe, "Security Through Detente and Arms Control," in David Holloway and Sharp, eds., *The Warsaw Pact: Alliance in Transition?* Ithaca: Cornell University Press, p. 173.

10. Wittner, *Rebels against War,* p. 277.

11. Myrdal, *Game of Disarmament,* p. 95. See also Paul Boyer, "From Activism to Apathy: The American People and Nuclear Weapons," *The Journal of American History* 70 (March 1984): 821; Robert A. Divine, *Blowing on the Wind: The Nuclear Test Ban Debate, 1954–1960,* New York: Oxford University Press, 1978; George Kistiakowsky, "The Good and the Bad of Arms Control Negotiations," *Bulletin of the Atomic Scientists,* May 1979; Glen T. Seaborg, *Kennedy, Khrushchev, and the Test Ban,* Berkeley, CA: University of California Press, 1981; Wittner, *Rebels against War,* pp. 277–78.

12. On the negotiations and implications of the ABM and SALT I treaties, see John Newhouse, *Cold Dawn: The Story of SALT,* New York: Holt, Rinehart and Winston, 1973; Gerard Smith, *Doubletalk: The Story of SALT I,* New York: Doubleday, 1980. On SALT II see Strobe Talbott, *Endgame: The Inside Story of SALT II,* New York: The Free Press, 1979; Cyrus Vance, *Hard Choices: Critical Years in America's Foreign Policy,* New York: Simon and Schuster, 1981, pp. 99–119, 349–67.

13. Steven E. Miller, "The Viability of Nuclear Arms Control: U.S. Domestic and Bilateral Factors," *Bulletin of Peace Proposals* 16 (1985).

14. McGeorge Bundy, "Nuclear Arms Control: Nothing until Everything?" in Miller, ed., *Nuclear Weapons Freeze.*

15. As example, President Ford chose not to finish negotiations with the Soviet Union on SALT II because he feared the strength of Ronald Reagan's conservative challenge for the Republican presidential nomination, Harvard Nuclear Weapons Study Group, *Living with Nuclear Weapons,* p. 10; Miller, "Viability of Nuclear Arms Control," p. 268; Strobe Talbott, *Deadly Gambits: The Reagan Administration and the Stalemate in Arms Control,* New York: Alfred A. Knopf, 1984, p. 218.

16. The Joint Chiefs, by withholding support for broader measures, can also limit the scope of arms control agreements. Lack of military support stopped Kennedy from pursing a comprehensive test ban and Nixon from seeking a ban on MIRVs; see Steven E. Miller, "Politics over Promise: Domestic Impediments to Arms Control," *International Security,* Spring 1984, p. 69.

17. Jimmy Carter, *Keeping Faith: Memoirs of a President,* New York: Bantam, 1982, p. 239; Vance, *Hard Choices,* p. 68.

18. Quoted in James Fallows, *National Defense,* New York: Random House, 1981, pp. 169–70.

19.　Quoted in Robert Leavitt, "Freezing the Nuclear Arms Race: The Genesis of a Mass Movement," unpublished Kennedy School of Government Case Study, Harvard University, 1983, Section II, p. 21. The accuracy of Rathjens's comments is disturbingly demonstrated by Representative Les Aspin's trade of support for the MX missile in exchange for promises of arms control. See Aspin, "The MX Bargain," *Bulletin of the Atomic Scientists,* November 1983, p. 52. Also see Kosta Tsipis's rejoinder, "Not Such a Bargain After All," in the same issue, p. 54; and Elizabeth Drew, "A Political Journal," *The New Yorker,* June 20, 1983.

20.　Jane M. O. Sharp, "Arms Control Priorities," *Bulletin of the Atomic Scientists,* August/September 1981, p. 26. Also see Sharp, "Bargaining Chips: Dumb or Devious?" *Foreign Service Journal,* March 1984; Gaddis, *Containment,* p. 324; Myrdal, *Game of Disarmament,* p. xxvi.

21.　Miller, "Viability of Nuclear Arms Control," p. 270.

22.　Marcus Raskin, "Countering Counterforce, SALT II: A Call to Disarm," *The Nation,* July 28/August 4, 1979, p. 72. Also see Richard Falk, "Surviving SALT II," *The Nation,* October 27, 1979, p. 391.

23.　Leavitt, "Freezing the Arms Race," p. 10.

24.　Carter, *Keeping Faith,* p. 224; Talbott, *Deadly Gambits,* pp. 219–22.

25.　Adam M. Garfinkle, *The Politics of the Nuclear Freeze,* Philadelphia: Foreign Policy Research Institute, 1984, p. 92.

26.　Duncan Clarke, "Arms Control and Foreign Policy under Reagan," *Bulletin of Atomic Scientists,* November 1981, p. 12.

27.　John David Isaacs, "Three Rs of Arms Control: Reagan, Rostow, and Rowny," *Bulletin of the Atomic Scientists,* August/September 1981, p. 5.

28.　Washington *Post,* May 9, 1982.

29.　Robert Scheer, *With Enough Shovels: Reagan, Bush, and Nuclear War,* New York: Random House, 1982, pp. 90–93.

30.　Ibid. Soviet General Secretary Gorbachev's acceptance of Reagan's "zero option" in the Intermediate Nuclear Forces negotiations created this kind of dilemma for the United States.

31.　Rostow was replaced by the far less experienced Kenneth Adelman, who was less sympathetic to arms control. Adelman barely won confirmation from a Republican-dominated Senate; the vote in committee for confirmation was an unusually close 9–8. Garfinkle, *Politics of the Nuclear Freeze,* pp. 187–89. For an overview of the TNF negotiations and the Reagan administration's approach to arms control, see Talbott, *Deadly Gambits.*

32.　Isaacs, "Three Rs of Arms Control," p. 5. Also see Clarke, "Arms Control and Foreign Policy," p. 12.

33.　The Reagan administration explicitly recognized no responsibility to abide by the limits of the unratified SALT II agreement. Despite a concerted buildup, however, the United States did not exceed the treaty's numeric ceilings until 1986.

34.　On the proposals and the negotiations, see Christopher E. Paine, "A False START," *Bulletin of the Atomic Scientists,* August/September 1982, p. 11; I. F. Stone, "Behind the Reagan START," *The Nation,* May 22, 1982, p. 602; Talbott, *Deadly Gambits,* pp. 263–76. Also see Philip Braudaway-Bauman, Randall Forsberg, and John Murphy, "Strategic Forces of the United States and Soviet Union: Projections through 1985," Institute for Defense and Disarmament Studies Occasional Paper No. 4, 1985.

35.　Garfinkle, *Politics of the Nuclear Freeze,* p. 158. On yellow rain see Lawrence Eagelburger's testimony before a House subcommittee on arms control,

"Yellow Rain: The Arms Control Implications," *Department of State Bulletin,* April 1983; Peter Pringle, "Political Science: How the Rush to Scientific Judgment on Yellow Rain Embarrassed both U.S. Science and the U.S. Government," *The Atlantic Monthly,* October 1985.

36. See James Clotfelter, "Disarmament Movement in the United States," *Journal of Peace Research* 23 (June 1986): 97–101; Lt. Col. Thomas P. Elliot et al., "What Are the Implications for U.S. Defense Policy of Growing Nuclear Dissent in the United States?" The Naval War College National Defense University Strategic Study, April 1983. Also see Gerard Smith's evaluation of Reagan rhetoric in Scheer, *With Enough Shovels,* p. 158.

37. Scheer, *With Enough Shovels,* p. 31.

38. Garfinkle, *Politics of the Nuclear Freeze,* p. 158. For "evidence" see John Barron, "The KGB's Magical War for Peace," *Reader's Digest,* October 1982, pp. 206–59.

39. National Conference of Catholic Bishops, *The Challenge of Peace: God's Promise and Our Response,* Washington, D.C.: U.S. Catholic Conference, 1983.

40. Mark Green and Gail MacColl, *There He Goes Again: Ronald Reagan's Reign of Error,* New York: Pantheon, 1983, pp. 42–48.

41. Alexander Cockburn and James Ridgeway, "The Freeze Movement Versus Ronald Reagan," *The New Left Review* 137 (January/February 1983): 8–10. Isaacs, "Three Rs of Arms Control"; Scheer, *With Enough Shovels,* pp. 65, 210.

42. Scheer, *With Enough Shovels,* pp. 87–88.

43. Ibid., p. 5.

44. Quoted in Ronald V. Dellums et al., eds., *Defense Sense: The Search for a Rational Military Policy,* Cambridge, MA: Ballinger, 1983, p. 20.

45. Jones is quoted in Dellums et al., *Defense Sense,* p. 30; Fallows, *National Defense,* p. 160; Scheer, *With Enough Shovels,* p. 18.

46. Leavitt, "Freezing the Arms Race," p. 32.

47. See McGeorge Bundy, George Kennan, Robert McNamara, and Gerard Smith, "Nuclear Weapons and the Atlantic Alliance," *Foreign Affairs* 60 (1982): 753–68.

48. Scheer, *With Enough Shovels,* p. 98.

49. Francis C. Brown III, "Media Coverage of the American Nuclear Freeze and Antinuclear Movements," unpublished thesis, Woodrow Wilson School of Public and International Affairs, Princeton University, 1985, p. 26.

50. Dellums et al., *Defense Sense,* p. 132; Scheer, *With Enough Shovels,* pp. 130-31.

51. Leavitt, "Freezing the Arms Race," p. 28.

52. For a sampling of diverse perspectives on the military and political implications of the dual track decision, see Paul Buteaux, *Strategy, Doctrine, and the Politics of Alliance: Theater Nuclear Force Modernization in NATO,* Boulder, CO: Westview Press, 1982; Diana Johnstone, *The Politics of the Euromissiles,* New York: Schocken Books, 1984; Olive M. McGraw and Jeffrey D. Porro, eds., *Nuclear Weapons in Europe: Modernization and Limitation,* Lexington, MA: Lexington Press, 1982; Andrew J. Pierre, ed. *Nuclear Weapons in Europe,* New York: Council on Foreign Relations, 1984; Jeffrey Record, *NATO's Theater Nuclear Force Modernization Program: The Real Issues,* Cambridge, MA: Institute for Foreign Policy Analysis, 1981; Alan Wolfe, "European Rearmament: No GLICIMS for NATO," *The Nation,* November 25, 1979, p. 513.

53. Some supporters of the dual track decision had second thoughts when Reagan entered office. See, for example, Helmut Schmidt, "Saving the Western World," *The New York Review of Books,* May 31, 1984, p. 25.

54. Michael Clarke and Marjorie Mowlam, eds., *Debate on Disarmament,* Boston: Routledge & Kegan Paul, 1982; Mary Kaldor and Dan Smith, eds., *Disarming Europe,* London: Merlin Press, 1982; Sverre Lodgaard and Marek Thee, eds., *Nuclear Disengagement in Europe,* Philadelphia: Taylor and Francis, 1983; Alva Myrdal et al., *The Dynamics of European Nuclear Disarmament,* Chester Springs, PA: Dufour Editions, 1982; Dorothy Nelkin and Michael Pollock, "The Atom Besieged: Antinuclear Movements in France and Germany," *Bulletin of the Atomic Scientists,* August/September 1983. Also see *Disarmament Campaigns,* an IKV-supported monthly magazine covering disarmament organizations worldwide.

55. Marta Daniels, "Disarmament: A View from Europe," *Peacework,* December 1981.

56. Olof Palme, "The Slick Slide into Armageddon," *The Nation,* January 3–10, 1981, p. 7. E. P. Thompson, "The END of the Line," *Bulletin of Atomic Scientists,* January 1981, p. 9; Thompson, "A Letter to America," *The Nation,* January 24, 1981, p.65.

57. E. P. Thompson and Dan Smith, eds. *Protest and Survive,* New York: Monthly Review Press, 1981. The title was a satirical twist on a British civil defense pamphlet, "Protect and Survive."

58. E. P. Thompson, *Beyond the Cold War: A New Approach to the Arms Race and Nuclear Annihilation,* New York: Pantheon, 1982.

59. Petra Kelly's politics and style can best be gleaned from her book, *Fighting for Hope,* Boston: South End Press, 1984. Kelly's celebrity earned a profile in *People,* November 22, 1982, p. 136.

60. Gert Bastian, Nino Pasti, et al., *Generals for Peace,* New York: Universe Books, 1984.

61. Howard Smith, "Disarming Europeans," *The Village Voice,* April 27, 1982.

5

PUBLIC OPINION: VOLATILITY AND CONSISTENCY

I'd like to believe that people in the long run are going to do more to promote peace than our governments. Indeed, I think that people want peace so much that one of these days governments had better get out of their way and let them have it.
— Dwight D. Eisenhower[1]

It is initially surprising to see how frequently disarmament advocates quote the former president and Commander of Allied Forces in Europe. Eisenhower spent almost all his adult life in the military. As president he presided over the chilliest period of the Cold War, set in motion development of U.S. strategic nuclear forces, and introduced Richard Nixon and John Foster Dulles to the executive branch of government. Posthumously, however, he has been resurrected as an advocate for disarmament, democracy, and social welfare. Eisenhower articulated an extremely appealing notion — that the government of the United States, indeed the governments of the world, will ultimately respond to the wishes of the general public.

By predicting government responsiveness "one of these days," however, Eisenhower acknowledged that the U.S. government frequently does not respond to the wishes of the American people and that public opinion may not always translate into public policy. Mass opinion and policy may diverge in many areas, but this divergence is particularly visible in the areas of security policy and nuclear weapons. Just as the development of U.S. nuclear weapons policy has proceeded relatively consistently amid conflict and debate, so have the basic assumptions and values of public opinion remained constant underneath apparent shifts in preference about particular policies. There has been remarkably little connection between public opinion, often based on misinformation and misconception, and the conduct of policy. No opinion shift on nuclear issues took place either before or during the nuclear freeze movement, so we must look elsewhere to explain the movement's rise and development.

PUBLIC OPINION AND GOVERNANCE

Leadership in a democracy is inherently problematic. It is not clear whether elected officials have an obligation to accede to public preferences, to act on behalf of their view of public interest regardless of popular opinion, or to educate the public to support the official view. It also is not clear which of these approaches best describes the actual relationship of public opinion to policy in the United States. Before examining the shape of public opinion on nuclear weapons policy, it is useful to review basic theories of the relationship between opinion and policy.

The textbook notion of democracy is that government policy is the product of a political process in which citizens have a variety of resources for attempting to influence its development and content. Political participation serves as an input to governmental institutions, which then translate popular demands into policy. The most commonly used and visible means of participation is voting. By choosing officials who represent their views, the theory goes, citizens influence the shape of politics and policy. Candidates for office will support policies they deem acceptable to a winning coalition of voters. Those who do not will lose their seats to others more attuned to the voting public. Since public opinion ranges across a broad political spectrum, office seekers will attempt to position themselves toward the middle of this spectrum and attempt to draw from a wider base of support than do their opponents. Policy then will follow a moderate course, pushed incrementally by changes in the electorate and public opinion. This theory, most clearly articulated by Anthony Downs, is based upon certain assumptions that are problematic, particularly in the area of national security issues.[2] Among the questionable assumptions are that voters rationally choose among candidates based upon issue preferences, that office seekers are candid about their positions, and that voters are informed about candidate positions and policy issues.

Benjamin Page and Robert Shapiro present a slightly less formalistic view of this process.[3] They argue that, after a fashion, there is a congruence between public opinion and public policy, with policy generally lagging behind shifts in public opinion. This roughly coincides with the Downsian view, but Page and Shapiro do not cite the source of all change at the ballot box. They claim that often regardless of campaign promises, once elected policy makers respond to shifts in public opinion, bringing their attention to issues raised by public concern, and generally responding to policy problems in ways most of the public finds acceptable.

This is "an eighteenth-century" view of public opinion, according to C. Wright Mills, who is far more cynical about democratic processes. "Decisions," he argues, "are made by those in authority," who then use the apparatus of the state to implement those decisions and the mass media to legitimate them. Elections, ostensibly the contest between competing ideas, are rituals of participation that have little effect on the actual content of policy. Policy reflects elite consensus and elite interests, whether implemented by the elite themselves or by quiescent managers. Public opinion is shaped to support these policies and meaningful access for "the people" to answer back is systematically unavailable.[4]

Policy and public opinion congruence, critics argue, may not indicate a causal relationship compatible with classical democratic theory. V. O. Key and others have argued that the reverse is the case. Policy makers influence popular beliefs and the resulting government is one "not *by* public opinion, but *of* public opinion."[5] By virtue of their access to media, information, and a limited wellspring of political legitimacy, elected officials can influence the development of public opinion, shaping the development of political concerns and the definitions of the possible.

This relationship is especially true when the electorate is not particularly informed or interested in most policy questions, and many may not even have opinions on many issues. In foreign policy matters, where the issues may "get too complicated, remote, or vague," most Americans are often willing to give the government a broad grant of trust.[6] Even when public opinion is strong and the issues clearer, elected officials, particularly presidents, have significant power to shape public opinion or exploit contradictions within it. The historical record shows that presidents have been willing and able to present information, or even conceal, distort, or invent information, in such a way to draw support for their programs. Certainly this was the case in candidate John Kennedy's use of the illusory missile gap, President Johnson's Gulf of Tonkin Resolution, and President Nixon's secret bombing of Cambodia.

Despite their differences, the theories outlined above all share a common assumption: that there must be some relationship between public opinion and policy. For Downs, policy is driven by public opinion as government responds to the wishes of the people. For Mills and Key, government shapes the will of the people to fashion sufficient support and legitimacy for the policies favored by elected officials. Page and Shapiro are somewhere in between, suggesting mutual influence between government and public opinion. An additional possibility to be considered, however, is that in the case of national security and nuclear issues, there is no necessary relationship between popular sentiment and policy. In this view, government serves as a steward for the people, pursuing policies it judges to be in their best interest, neither shaping nor responding to popular will.[7] James Madison expresses this possibility as a goal in Federalist Paper No. 10. Madison explains that the goals of the Constitution include protection of the public interest against factions including both minorities and majorities. Although popular participation and democracy can minimize the undue influence of minorities, majorities present a greater danger. He writes:

> When a majority is included in a faction, the form of popular government . . . enables it to sacrifice to its ruling passion or interest, both the public good and the rights of other citizens. To secure the public good, and private rights, against the danger of such a faction, and at the same time to preserve the *spirit* and the *form* of popular government, is then the great object to which our inquiries are directed.

In other words, government must be protected from the influence of the people, even as it needs to appear that it is not. Although Madison certainly did not have nuclear policy in mind, his analysis is helpful in understanding the ways in which the government he crafted responds (or does not respond) to issues he could not imagine. Essentially, Madison and the other framers were interested in creating some degree of popular participation in governance while ensuring that the public interest as they saw it was protected from majority tyranny. Among the devices Madison developed to check majority will are the system of representation, the separation of powers, and the inclusion of a large enough number of disparate interests such that "make it less probable that a majority of the whole will have a common motive to invade the rights of other citizens; or if such a common motive exists, it will be more difficult for all who feel it to discover their own strength, and to act in unison with each other."[8] While Madison's primary concern was property rights, latter-day Madisonians make the same arguments about nuclear policy; essentially, majorities are not equipped to make decisions in the public interest.[9] If Madison's system works as intended, policy making may sometimes be effectively insulated from popular influence.

In explaining the relationship between public opinion and nuclear policy, advocates of each basic approach can find evidence to support their views. Candidates for office do tell the voting public what they believe it wants to hear, even if this sometimes means appearing to adopt new stances. Elected officials attempt to respond in some way to new directions in public opinion, although such responses need not include changing policy. Elected officials also try to shape public opinion to support particular policies, with varying degrees of success. Overall, however, Madison's explanation of a schism between policy and public opinion is very powerful. Since its inception U.S. nuclear policy has been remarkably consistent regarding goals and means of achieving them. Despite periodic surface shifts in preferences on particular issues, underlying public opinion regarding nuclear weapons has been equally consistent although generally opposed to, and ill-informed of, government policy.

SHIFTS IN POPULAR SENTIMENT

Before Ronald Reagan's first election, there was an apparent shift in public opinion on defense and foreign policy issues. Some aspects of this shift boded well for Reagan's approach to the upcoming campaign. First, support for ratification of SALT II decreased dramatically. From 75 percent popular approval in December 1978, support for the treaty eroded to 43 percent in September 1980.[10] This drop in support can be attributed to world events, Carter's wounded presidency, and a concerted public relations attempt by treaty opponents led by the Committee on the Present Danger. Along with opposition to SALT II came increased support for higher military spending, peaking with popular approval of 60 percent.[11] There was also increased interest in foreign affairs. A January 1980 CBS/New York *Times* poll reported that fully 42 percent of the population said foreign policy was the most important problem facing the nation.[12] President Carter responded to events and these opinion shifts, increasing military spending, taking a tougher rhetorical stance against the Soviet Union, and shelving SALT II.

As one portion of the public was apparently becoming disenchanted with the arms control process and the position of the United States in the world, others were responding to the turn of world events and the Carter administration's new hawkish bent in a different way. One activist wrote, "Fear of war, like a low-grade fever has spread across the country since last December. . . . The message is that the issue of war versus peace is now so urgent that all our other national problems must be put on the back burner."[13]

This was not simply activist polemic or wishful thinking. Public support for a more hawkish posture was accompanied by greater fears of war and stronger opposition to military solutions for foreign policy problems. Even as polls showed support for higher military spending, they also showed at least equally strong antipathy toward use of U.S. weapons or troops abroad. From a series of questions about the contingencies short of attack on the United States in which the public would approve the use of U.S. combat forces, only one possibility drew more than 40 percent support. According to *Public*

Opinion, 54 percent of the population favored the use of force if the Soviet Union were to invade Western Europe.[14] This scant majority is an astonishingly small margin of support for a policy that has been a cornerstone of security policy since World War II. As for using U.S. forces to defend vital interests declared by U.S. presidents in the Persian Gulf or South Pacific, there is nothing even approaching a substantial element of support. By the end of 1981, before the nuclear freeze even appeared on national opinion questionnaires, 76 percent of those polled favored the "Kennan plan," an immediate 50 percent bilateral cut in the nuclear arsenals of both superpowers.[15] Support was even higher (82 percent) among college-educated respondents.

Opinion analysts could easily find contradictory tendencies within U.S. public opinion. Certainly the Reagan election did not resolve any trends clearly. Before the Reagan/Carter debate in October 1980, 43 percent of those polled acknowledged a fear that as president Ronald Reagan would lead the United States into war. Reagan's appearance on television was apparently only moderately comforting, as this figure declined to a still very substantial 35 percent on the eve of the election.[16] This widespread fear of Reagan, even in light of his impending electoral landslide, hardly lends credence to the notion that his victory at the polls was a mandate for his national security policy.

The rise of strong antiwar, pro-military, and anti-interventionist sentiment nationally may be interpreted as a reaction to the confusing events of the late 1970s. Perhaps opinion became increasingly polarized with the turbulence of the times, as both so-called hawks and doves became increasingly dissatisfied with the results of U.S. foreign and military policy. This view, although understandable, is probably mistaken. There is indeed a great deal of volatility regarding attitudes toward particular events, potential enemies, support for a given weapons system, or even whether military spending should be increased or decreased. Public preferences can also be mobilized by movements or elected officials, but beneath all of this there is an underlying stability.

U.S. public opinion on national security issues since the advent of the nuclear age has been relatively consistent and deeply ambivalent.[17] "American opinion on nuclear weapons and war," writes Everett Carll Ladd, "has changed scarcely at all over nearly four decades."[18] He notes that there has always been a widespread uneasiness about nuclear weapons. In 1950 most Americans favored efforts to reach "an agreement with Russia before we try to make a hydrogen bomb." Similarly, most endorsed a Comprehensive Test Ban in 1958, fully five years before President Kennedy negotiated the Limited Test Ban treaty. At the same time, Ladd found an equally long history of distrust of the Soviet Union, technical means of treaty verification, and legalistic solutions to national security problems.[19]

Elsewhere he argues that this stability holds true for virtually all political issues, remarking, "how little the nation's attitudes and values have shifted in the face of the kaleidoscopic changes in the political setting."[20]

Other opinion analysts have found both the same consistency and ambivalence in U.S. public opinion. Daniel Yankelovich and John Doble, for example, argue that most Americans are torn between a fear of nuclear war and a distrust of the Soviet Union, both so deep that they can do nothing to ameliorate one without exacerbating the other. Ultimately this is paralyzing.[21] Yankelovich found that most Americans supported unilateral initiatives to end the arms race, 43 percent (and 55 percent of those 18–30) agreeing even to the proposition that "the United States should lead the world out of the nuclear arms race by unilaterally reducing our stockpile of nuclear weapons." Nonetheless, he argues, distrust of the Soviet Union is great enough to threaten support for arms control.[22]

Misinformation and mistrust are not limited to public perceptions of the Soviet Union. Louis Harris describes the ambivalence in terms of two consistent and strongly held opinions, that the Soviet Union is hostile and cannot be trusted (85 percent) and that weapons are dangerous. He reports that 81 percent want the superpowers to agree to stop making nuclear weapons while 82 percent oppose the United States disarming unilaterally. Harris claims that peace movement initiatives must be couched in language respecting this ambivalence toward arms control and nuclear weapons.[23] Regardless of how careful the language, however, popular sentiment on specific policies is extremely volatile.

Just as support for SALT II disappeared suddenly, a strong consensus for higher military spending, for example, evaporated almost as soon as Ronald Reagan started submitting budgets to Congress. By 1982, 38 percent of the U.S. population did not trust President Reagan to make the right decisions regarding nuclear policy; another 32 percent believed that Reagan favored the nuclear freeze — even as the president was clear in stating that he did not.[24] Widespread concern about nuclear weapons, exceptionally strong during the early 1980s, evaporated during Reagan's second term, with most people believing that both superpowers were reducing their nuclear arsenals, although this was not the case. On nuclear issues, ambivalence and distrust are often accompanied by misinformation, as "volatile opinion is often murky opinion."[25]

BROAD AND SHALLOW FREEZE SUPPORT

Misinformation, in conjunction with strong opinions about war, weapons, and the Soviet Union, helps explain why the nuclear freeze so quickly achieved massive popular support, at least as measured in polls. In May 1982 an AP/NBC poll showed 83 percent supported the nuclear freeze proposal.[26] The Washington *Post* found 79 percent support for the freeze, while CBS/New York *Times* found 77 percent support.[27] Gallup polls showed 60 percent support even among such traditionally conservative groups as self-identified evangelical Christians.[28] In the population at large, Gallup found 71 percent support for the nuclear freeze, with marginally higher support (75 percent) in the East and Midwest, among college-educated respondents, and those between 18–29. Among professionals, Gallup found 78 percent support for the nuclear freeze, and among trade union members, 74 percent support. In all cases, support was even higher when a provision about assured verification was added and somewhat lower when the question was cast in terms of "freezing Soviet advantages."[29]

The level of consistent strength in all the polls is staggering. In 1982 *The Gallup Report* reported that 45 percent favored a unilateral nuclear freeze, regardless of whether the Soviet Union agreed to reciprocate (supported by 61 percent of white females).[30] At the same time, Harris found that 56 percent of voters would make the nuclear freeze a litmus test issue in the upcoming Congressional election, refusing to vote for candidates who did not support it.[31] The poll numbers seemed to get stronger and stronger, regardless of what any political opponents did. In June 1984, at the outset of President Reagan's successful reelection campaign, Peter Hart found that 80 percent of Illinois residents supported the nuclear freeze proposal and that 61 percent supported a one-year unilateral U.S. freeze.[32] This compares quite favorably with popular support for other social movements. In 1971, for example, at the height of the antiwar movement, 41 percent of the population supported withdrawal of U.S. troops from Vietnam within one year.[33]

The stability of antinuclear sentiment in U.S. public opinion supports the theory that mass opinion on these issues has little if any influence on policy. Seeing these attitudes in conjunction with equally widespread public apathy toward foreign affairs and outright hostility toward the Soviet Union help explain why this is the case. Fear of nuclear armaments and distrust of foreign governments, even among a substantial majority of Americans, does not necessarily translate into support for proposals for disarmament or arms control, nor for politicians who advocate this approach. These attitudes are apparently as likely to translate into support for candidates who promise "peace through strength."[34] In policy preferences and elections, images of character, political style, and rhetoric dominate. When issues arise at all in political campaigns, those more visibly immediate to daily life, such as housing or jobs, draw the most attention.

When an aspect of military policy or a particular arms control proposal comes to the forefront of popular political discourse, it is generally for a very limited time, before other concerns of U.S. political life push it back into the hands of policy makers and a small group of experts. Political leaders manage information to forge supportive political coalitions, and not only details but even the most basic assumptions of strategic nuclear policy are generally never communicated to the public at large. If fully 81 percent of the U.S. public is unaware of extended deterrence and the declared willingness of the United States to use nuclear weapons first, it is clear that the public is effectively denied meaningful discussion or even explanation of nuclear policy.[35]

This is true not only of the general public but also of most elected officials. Policy makers' debate about strategy is generally centered on extremely complicated questions of technique: do satellites provide sufficient verification for a treaty? will mobile single warhead missiles be more effective than stationary multiple warhead missiles? can submarine-launched missiles become sufficiently accurate to develop hard target capabilities? will building a weapons system bring jobs to my state? — to note but a few examples. Questions regarding the broad lines of policy effectively escape scrutiny while decisions often hinge on the most instrumental rationales.[36] Those relatively few members of the public or Congress able to maintain an interest must fight through such obstacles, the roadblocks of classified information, and most significantly, the unwillingness of political leaders even to discuss the broader goals of U.S. nuclear policy. Phrases like "national security" or "vital interests" are virtually guaranteed to end debate.

These factors effectively insulate the policy-making process from the potential impact of public opinion. Steven Miller explains,

> The great emphasis placed on public opinion reflects an exaggerated notion of its significance in the policy process. . . . U.S. policy makers can choose from among a wide range of confrontational or conciliatory policies with considerable prospect of adequate public support . . . critics of the direction of policy must do battle with the tradition that in matters of defense the President almost always gets what he wants.[37]

It is also often hard to discern what is actually happening in matters of international security policy. Much of what constitutes policy is substantially symbolic. Summits, cultural exchanges, and public posturing constitute the bulk of international relations visible to the public. Miller notes that this is particularly true of arms control. Although public sentiment may drive a government into arms control negotiations, he acknowledges, it can have little influence on what actually occurs in those negotiations. Failure to achieve agreement may be the result of unreasonable demands or lack of political will on one or both sides. Successful public relations efforts probably have more influence on public perceptions than on the content of negotiations. This can make arms control negotiations a powerful domestic political tool with potentially no international significance. Miller argues that this is the case with the Reagan administration, which seemed to begin arms control negotiations "at least in part to defuse the vigorous antinuclear movement that had arisen in 1980–1981."[38]

If the impact that public opinion has on nuclear weapons policy is, at most, unclear, its relationship to social mobilization is much the same. As opposition to the Vietnam War showed, majority public opinion support is not necessary to generate a volatile movement. By the same token, majority public support, at least as measured in opinion polls, does not necessarily generate a dissident movement. Since the freeze movement was neither preceded nor accompanied by any great shift in public attitudes, it should be clear that a movement can fade even without policy reforms, even as public support shown in polls remains constant. Social movements require not only some element of public opposition to a particular policy, but, more important, the spread of a belief that dissident mobilization may be legitimate, necessary, and at least potentially effective. As one analyst notes, the freeze did not grow out of a change in attitudes toward nuclear weapons, but was "a move from a feeling of powerlessness and consequent behavioral apathy to awareness, active concern, and involvement."[39] We must look beyond mass opinion to find the sources that generate and support this kind of movement.

NOTES

1. Quoted in Otto Klineberg, "Public Opinion and Nuclear War," *The American Psychologist* 39 (1984): 1247.

2. Anthony Downs, *An Economic Theory of Democracy*, New York: Harper & Row, 1957.

3. Benjamin I. Page and Robert Y. Shapiro, "Effects of Public Opinion on Policy," *The American Political Science Review*, March 1983.

4. C. Wright Mills, "Mass Media and Public Opinion," *Power, Politics, and People*, New York: Ballantine, 1963, pp. 580–82.

5. V. O. Key, Jr., "Public Opinion and the Decay of Democracy," in Edward C. Dreyer and Walter A. Rosenbaum, eds., *Political Opinion and Electoral Behavior*, Belmont, CA: Wadsworth, 1966, p. 417. Also see Murray Edelman, *Politics as Symbolic Action*, Chicago: Markham, 1971; John Gaventa, *Power and Powerlessness: Quiescence and Rebellion in an Appalachian Valley*, Urbana: University of Illinois Press, 1980; Benjamin Ginsberg, *The Captive Public: How Mass Opinion Promotes State Power*, New York: Basic, 1986.

6. John E. Mueller, *War, Presidents, and Public Opinion,* New York: John Wiley and Sons, 1973, p. 2.

7. For a theoretical exposition and criticism of this possibility, see Robert A. Dahl, *Controlling Nuclear Weapons: Democracy Versus Guardianship,* Syracuse, NY: Syracuse University Press, 1985.

8. Federalist Number 10.

9. See Graham T. Allison, Albert Carnesale, and Joseph S. Nye, Jr., eds., *Hawks, Doves, and Owls: An Agenda for Avoiding Nuclear War,* New York: Norton, 1985. The authors contend most people either expect more from nuclear weapons than they can safely provide (hawks) or believe that, given the dangers of nuclear war, it is best to eliminate nuclear weapons and abandon any political role they might serve (doves). Both popular factions, they argue, are naive, and policy should be made by those (owls) who recognize both the political necessity and practical limits of nuclear weaponry. For a thoughtful exploration of the conflict between democratic processes and expert decision making, see Dahl, *Controlling Nuclear Weapons.*

10. William Schanbra, "More Bucks for the Bang: New Public Attitudes toward Foreign Policy," *Public Opinion,* January/February 1979; *Public Opinion,* October/November 1979, p. 40. For a comprehensive historical overview of public opinion on nuclear issues, see Thomas W. Graham, *American Public Opinion on NATO, Extended Deterrence, and Use of Nuclear Weapons: Future Fission?* Cambridge, MA: Harvard University Center for Science and International Affairs, 1989.

11. *Public Opinion,* December/January 1980.

12. *Public Opinion,* February/March 1980.

13. Sandy Close, "Apocalypse Now: War and Peace and the Left," *The Nation,* March 29, 1980, p. 353.

14. *Public Opinion,* December/January 1980.

15. Gallup poll reported in Chicago *Sun Times,* December 13, 1981; Washington *Post,* December 22, 1981. George Kennan advances this plan in "A Modest Proposal," *The New York Review of Books,* July 16, 1981, p. 14. See also his *The Nuclear Delusion: Soviet American Relations in the Atomic Age,* New York: Pantheon, 1982.

16. *Public Opinion,* December/January 1981, p. 24.

17. Klineberg, "Public Opinion and Nuclear War," p. 1245.

18. Everett Carll Ladd, "The Freeze Framework," *Public Opinion,* August/September 1982, p. 26.

19. Ibid.

20. Everett Carll Ladd, "Public Opinion: Questions at the Quinquennial," *Public Opinion,* April/May 1983, p. 20.

21. Daniel Yankelovich and John Doble, "The Public Mood: Nuclear Weapons and the USSR," *Foreign Affairs* 63 (Fall 1984): 33–46.

22. The Public Agenda Foundation, *Voter Options on Nuclear Policy,* Providence, RI: Center for Foreign Policy Development, May 1984.

23. Louis Harris, "Public Opinion and the Freeze Movement," in Steven E. Miller, ed., *The Nuclear Weapons Freeze and Arms Control,* Cambridge, MA: Ballinger, 1984, pp. 39–41.

24. Royce Crocker, "Nuclear Disarmament, 1982: Public Opinion Issue," *Congressional Research Service Brief No.* IB82064, January–May 1982.

25. Daniel Yankelovich and Richard Smoke, "America's 'New Thinking'," *Foreign Affairs*, Fall 1988, p. 12.

26. Boston *Globe*, May 17, 1982.

27. *Public Opinion*, October/November 1982, p. 34, chronicles a number of relevant and interesting poll results.

28. Boston *Globe*, July 5, 1983.

29. *The Gallup Report*, No. 208, January 1983, pp. 10–11. Also see Robert Leavitt, "Freezing the Arms Race: The Genesis of a Mass Movement," unpublished Kennedy School of Government Case Study, Harvard University, 1983, Section B.

30. *The Gallup Report*, No. 206, November 1982, p. 8.

31. Quoted in Alexander Cockburn and James Ridgeway, "Redbaiting the Freeze," *The Village Voice*, August 10, 1982, p. 10.

32. Peter D. Hart Research Associates, June 1984.

33. *The Gallup Report*, No. 206, November 1982.

34. James Clotfelter, "Disarmament Movements in the United States," *Journal of Peace Research*, June 1986, p. 99.

35. Public Agenda Foundation, *Voter Options: Women's Action for Nuclear Disarmament, Turnabout: Emerging New Realism in the Nuclear Age*, Boston: WAND Education Fund, 1986, pp. 5, 15. WAND found that even in 1986, 75 percent of those surveyed mistakenly believed it was U.S. policy to use nuclear weapons only in response to the first use of nuclear weapons by another country.

36. Nick Kotz, *Wild Blue Yonder: Money, Politics, and the B-1 Bomber*, New York: Pantheon, 1988.

37. Steven E. Miller, "The Viability of Nuclear Arms Control: U.S. Domestic and Bilateral Factors, *The Bulletin of Peace Proposals* 16 (1985): 265.

38. Ibid., p. 267. Strobe Talbott shares this view, *Deadly Gambits: The Reagan Administration and the Stalemate in Arms Control*, New York: Alfred A. Knopf, 1984, pp. 173–79, 279.

39. Klineberg, "Public Opinion and Nuclear War," p. 1246.

6

THE DEFECTION
OF THE ELITE

If massive shifts in public opinion did not elicit the freeze movement, we must look beyond the general public to find the sources of support for dissident mobilization. Organization, political development, and even modernity, Michels and others have argued, have combined to place increasing concentrations of political and economic power in the hands of fewer and fewer individuals.[1] The political realignment inaugurated with the advent of the nuclear age and the bipolar international arrangement that grew out of World War II accelerated this consolidation and concentration of power. The dominance of an interventionist foreign policy and the increasing political influence of what Eisenhower termed the "military-industrial complex" also contributed to insulating foreign and military policy from democratic political influence.[2]

Although there is both an appearance and a limited reality of pluralism, decisions on crucial matters are effectively isolated from public input or politics as commonly construed. Even though many people hold positions ostensibly proximate to political and economic power, the broad outlines of U.S. military, political, and economic policy reflect both the politics and the interests of a very small group of people, which also holds by far the greatest concentration of wealth and power. What Mills called the "power elite" holds governing power above and beyond the conflicts that dominate everyday politics. By virtue of its controlling influence of government, business, and the media, this group can also maintain the appearance of pluralistic debate and the scope of emerging political demands. So great is their domination, argue elite theorists, that the power elite can normally effectively preempt, repress, or coopt dissident movements.

THE ROLE OF ELITES IN SOCIAL MOBILIZATION

This analysis may explain why protest movements do not occur, but it is less powerful in explaining why they sometimes do. In order for a successful movement to emerge, something must break elite unity and control over the state and society. Theda Skocpol contends that conflicts within the leadership or dominant classes of a regime create political and administrative crises that allow revolutions to take place. These crises, she argues, result from international challenges, which either preoccupy or divide the ruling classes, weakening the state's capacity to respond to internal dissent.[3]

Crane Brinton gives greater importance to ideas and intellectuals, defining "the transfer of allegiance of intellectuals" as the "most reliable symptom" of a society ripe for revolution.[4] Brinton's "intellectuals" are individuals with the resources to treat ideas in some serious fashion and were proximate, although not party, to political decision making. Before a revolution, he argues, a number of these individuals abandon the failing old regime and defect to insurgent movements. They bring with them, Brinton argues, ideas, political resources, and legitimacy.

Frances Fox Piven and Richard Cloward concur that upheaval and subsequent defection of elites create the opportunity for social movements and that elite support is critical to a movement's potential success. Rather than ideas, however, they emphasize the material bases of politics, arguing that the economic dislocation of elites during the Depression, for example, aided the mobilization of dissident movements by the poor in the 1930s.[5] Elite interests, however, constrain the potential gains movements can make. The only route to influence for movements of the disadvantaged or excluded is mobilizing elite support on their behalf.[6]

Identifying which elite are relevant to a movement's success is a difficult problem, made more difficult by the competing definitions of elite. Mills and Skocpol, for example, postulate a finite number of people relatively proximate to state power. In contrast, Piven and Cloward and Michael Lipsky define elite somewhat more broadly. Rather than seeking to identify an inner circle making or bene-fiting from the political order, they mark people with a dispropor-tionately large share of political resources, including status, money, and political access, who can aid or constrain a movement's development.

The more inclusive definition suggests a broader analysis of movements and their potential influence. It allows us, for example, to note that leaders of insurgent movements often share more in common with their opponents than with the participants in move-ments they lead. Dissident leaders generally come from privileged backgrounds, with a certain measure of economic affluence and social status. Kenneth Keniston, in his study of dissident youth during the 1960s, notes that movement leaders uniformly shared backgrounds of relative affluence, which "provided them not only with economic security, but with the preconditions for the independence they exhibit in later life: families generally free from acute anxiety over status, thoughtful and well-educated parents, schools and colleges that — whatever their limitations — exposed them to many of the riches of world tradition, and the extraordinary privilege of a lengthy adolescence and youth in which to grow, to become more complex, to arrive at a more separate selfhood."[7]

For Keniston elite status, privilege, and education provided individuals with the security and leisure useful to develop dissent. This includes not only knowledge of the way politics and society work but also the essential belief that one has the capacity to alter the status quo. This analysis is compatible with Ronald Inglehart's concept of "post-materialist" concerns. Inglehart argues individuals have a hierarchy of personal and political concerns. Primary concerns, naturally enough, include food, clothing, shelter, and security. It is only after these needs are satisfied that an individual can approach more abstract political issues, such as the content of defense policy or the structure of political institutions.[8] Insurgent leaders, then, would naturally come from a background that affords them the opportunity to develop these larger social concerns.

There is also a more cynical view, however, that dissident elites use movements to pursue personal political and economic goals. Brinton notes that revolutionary leaders come almost exclusively from exceptionally privileged backgrounds and that the social status provided by wealth, education, and even social graces, aids in their legitimacy and consequently in political mobilization. Their goals, however, may be narrower than those they articulate to win public support. As example, Brinton acknowledges that the leaders of the U.S. war for independence, almost without exception, benefited personally in terms of social, political, or economic advancement as a result of the revolution's success.[9] In essence, one group of elites used or generated a certain amount of social unrest as a route to economic advantage or political power.

Similarly, people in positions of privilege may use movements as a defense against threats to their positions, trying to protect their positions of power, or at worst, to make the most of a bad situation. James Fallows, for example, in discussing youth protest against the war in Vietnam, discounts post-materialist morality or separate selfhood as primary motivators; he argues privileged youth got involved in the antiwar movement in response to the widening scope of the draft. (Indeed, President Nixon acknowledged that by establishing an all-volunteer armed forces, he hoped to defuse the antiwar protests.)[10] They joined the resistance not because of moral concerns, Fallows contends, and not to gain new advantages but simply to maintain the status quo at a time when their positions were threatened.

The same may apply to those far more privileged. Elites generally have an obvious and strong interest in preserving social and political institutions and systemic stability. In times of political upheaval, elites primarily interested in stability may adopt a variety of strategies, including offering real or symbolic concessions, and "making efforts to channel the energies and angers of the protestors into more legitimate and less disruptive forms of political behavior . . . by coopting them."[11] This may appear as a defection, but it is, in fact, a limited alliance, which may undermine the legitimacy and breadth of the protestors' public support and simultaneously make repression of more extreme dissident groups possible.[12] A limited defection, then, may actually serve to enhance political stability and defuse a movement's more volatile aspects. An apparent transfer of allegiance or a defection may actually be something quite different.

It may be nothing more than a rear-guard action against a new ascendent group, designed not to empower new groups but to prevent the entrenchment of a new elite. In the case of the nuclear freeze, this seems to provide a powerful explanation. Many of the architects of U.S. defense policy for the 20 years before Reagan's presidency attacked the new administration's policies. This was at least partly a reaction to the presence of a new contingent, represented by the Committee on the Present Danger and its fellow travelers, in an unaccustomed position of power. The old guard, while ostensibly allied with those demanding radical changes in U.S. defense posture, was far more concerned with restoring previous foreign and military policies.

An element of elite support for a social movement can be a powerful resource, legitimating and inspiring further activism. For this reason, dissidents often seek elite support for their actions and goals, even to the extent of falsely claiming their allegiance.[13] More commonly, movement organizations may define themselves in ways they believe will be more attractive to elites, choosing less threatening goals and tactics. Organizations choose whether to attempt to influence, displace, or join the ruling political elite.[14] If a group takes the first strategy, attempting to win elite sympathy to influence policy, its chances for success are substantially increased. Elites often act as bargaining agents and intermediaries for movements, often winning palpable, although necessarily limited, reforms. Partly for this reason, groups that espouse more limited goals are more likely to survive and to succeed than groups with broader and more comprehensive goals.[15]

Although these realities seem to support the virtues of moderation for protest movements and vindicate a strategy of thinking small, the record is more ambiguous. William Gamson found that groups that use disruptive tactics, including initiating or suffering violence, were also more likely to achieve some measure of success.[16] These tactics, however, especially violence against persons and property, are those most likely to alienate potential allies among the elite.[17] For this reason organizations often resist such risky tactics or a broader definition of their goals. This is particularly true of professional organizers because of their interest in maintaining their organizations. As Piven and Cloward argue, "In the largest part organizers tended to work against disruption because, in their search for resources to maintain their organization, they were driven inexorably to elites, and to the tangible and symbolic supports that elites could provide."[18]

Negotiating an effective relationship with elite supporters is inherently problematic. Maintaining support often means eschewing the most disruptive (and often most effective) tactics. Paradoxically, institutional disruption is the most effective means of winning political concessions, but it is also the riskiest and is the strategy least likely to gain elite support. This situation presents dissident activists with a constant dilemma: should they limit their goals to seek elite support, abandoning more comprehensive goals and potentially effective tactics, or should they forego elite support and play the high stakes roulette of political disruption, the response to which cannot be accurately predicted, thereby risking organizational survival and the limited gains that might otherwise be won? This discussion and dilemma provides a backdrop for discussion of elite support for the nuclear freeze.

SCIENTISTS AND NUCLEAR EXPERTS

Antinuclear movements in the United States have always been spearheaded by an extremely visible contingent of one kind of elite or another. Scientists have been among the most active and credible spokespeople for these movements and have often played a critical role in focusing public attention on the dangerous capabilities of nuclear weapons. Albert Einstein, whose endorsement helped bring additional government support to develop nuclear weapons, was among the early vocal critics of U.S. nuclear policy. In 1954, along with Linus Pauling, Bertrand Russell, 50 Nobel laureates, and 9,000 other scientists, he signed a petition calling for an end to nuclear testing. Their opposition began to bring mass attention to the dangers of a possible nuclear war and of "peaceful" tests conducted by both superpowers. Their fame and their expertise brought attention and credibility to their dissent. By conveying information to nonexperts, dissident scientists opened the political debate. By the early 1960s, the scientists were joined in their opposition by several political figures, including Eleanor Roosevelt, Socialist Norman Thomas, Democrat Adlai Stevenson, and Republican Alf Landon, as well as a smattering of celebrities, including actor-singer Harry Belafonte.[19]

Scientists played a similar role in opposing the development of antiballistic missile systems in the late 1960s. They organized public meetings, gave expert opinion in television interviews, testified at Congressional hearings, and publicly questioned the assertions of the administration experts during the Johnson and Nixon presidencies. As in the campaign against testing, efforts often focused on translating the technical debates over ABM into more accessible and concrete images,[20] broadening the political debate to include the general public. Activism began with successful attempts to prevent ABM deployment in particular communities.[21]

In addition to visibility and credibility, scientists have also provided the antinuclear movement with organizations, most notably the Union of Concerned Scientists (UCS) and the Federation of Atomic Scientists (FAS), and information, often published in the very topical *Bulletin of the Atomic Scientists*. The strong role played by scientists in U.S. antinuclear movements can be explained in a variety of different ways. The status and legitimacy of scientists often afford their expressions of concern a broad hearing. Even more than other antinuclear activists, scientists are better educated and wealthier than most Americans, afforded more control of their work lives, and therefore more likely to have the resources necessary for participation in post-materialist political issues. Finally, scientists may be involved in disproportionate numbers because they can clearly understand the implications of nuclear war, or at least can generate concrete images of what a nuclear exchange would be like.[22]

Throughout the life of the freeze movement, nuclear scientists and strategic experts were extremely visible in attacking the Reagan administration's nuclear policies, if not always supporting the nuclear freeze proposal. Some had "defected" from dominant foreign policy consensus long before. They included Robert Aldridge, who had designed portions of the Polaris and Poseidon systems for Lockheed, and Daniel Ellsberg, who had dramatically made his break from the Rand Corporation, Henry Kissinger, and Richard Nixon with the release of the Pentagon papers. Other dissident scientists included former presidential science advisors George Kistiakowsky and Jerome Wiesner,[23] whose more moderate political views afforded them great credibility from mainstream press.

Early freeze supporters included Philip Morrison, George Rathjens, and Jeremy Stone; as the movement's momentum grew, increasing numbers of scientists signed on. In a reprisal of his role nearly 30 years earlier, two-time Nobel prize winner Linus Pauling joined 96 other Nobel laureates in calling for a nuclear freeze.[24] Among the notable scientists endorsing the freeze were Hans Bethe, Harrison Brown, Karl Menninger, George Wald, Bernard Feld (also editor of the *Bulletin of the Atomic Scientists*), Carl Sagan, and Jonas Salk.[25] These scientists were able to bring legitimacy and media attention to growing opposition to the administration's nuclear policies. In some cases they were also able to direct research projects to inform the debate. Most notable among these projects was work to examine the long-term effects of nuclear war on global climates, adding the element of "nuclear winter" to the political debate.[26]

In addition to using scientific expertise to direct public attention to relevant nuclear issues, scientists also used their professional status to organize educational efforts. UCS sponsored a Veterans' Day "Convocation on the Threat of Nuclear War," in November 1981. The Convocation, which involved teach-ins at 151 college campuses, was nonpartisan and intended as a set of educational events on a variety of nuclear issues. (UCS actually opposed the nuclear freeze as an arms control proposal.)[27] The Convocation was not a freeze event, but it aided the freeze movement by bringing attention to U.S. nuclear policy. Public discussion of the "increasing threat" of nuclear war clearly encouraged exactly the kind of citizen education and activity that would form the core of movement activity. Freeze activists used the UCS events, recognizing that broad and informed public discussion of these issues could only help their cause.

In April 1982 Roger Molander announced the formation of another educational organization, Ground Zero, and a similar and larger series of educational events. Ground Zero week involved informational programs in 30 cities, 30 college campuses, and more than 1,000 high schools and was widely seen as a nuclear freeze event. It was immediately followed by the publication of a Ground Zero reader, *Nuclear War: What's In It for You,* which went into its second printing after only two days. Molander's legitimacy and the newsworthiness of his group were the result of his service in the Arms Control and Disarmament Agency, the Pentagon, and on the National Security Council under Presidents Nixon, Ford, and Carter. Although he was clear about his opposition to the freeze proposal, his activities and those of his "nonpartisan, nonadvocacy" organization served to stimulate and reinforce the development of an oppositional movement because Molander and Ground Zero forcefully raised questions about Reagan administration policy.[28]

Molander was not alone among former security planners in raising questions about or even criticizing the administration's nuclear policies. Indeed, as Cockburn and Ridgeway commented, "it is remarkable how many out-of-power cold warriors have suddenly seen light on the road to Damascus."[29] Some signed on quickly to the freeze or even offered similarly comprehensive proposals. George

Kennan, the primary architect of President Truman's containment policy, proposed deep cuts of up to 50 percent in superpower strategic arsenals well before the freeze movement gained any widespread recognition.[30] Other early supporters included former U.S representative to the United Nations Averell Harriman, former state department officials George Ball and Warren Christopher, former Secretary of Defense Clark Clifford, and former arms control negotiators William Foster and Paul Warnke.[31]

Support for the freeze movement among former policy makers grew quickly after Senators Edward Kennedy and Mark Hatfield introduced the nuclear freeze resolution in the Senate and soon included ACDA veterans Herbert Scoville, Jr., Richard Barnet, Marcus Raskin, Paul Walker, and former CIA director (and founding member of the Committee on the Present Danger) William Colby. Hodding Carter, Townsend Hoopes, Henry Cabot Lodge, and former U.N. Ambassador Donald McHenry also endorsed the freeze resolution. Admiral Hyman Rickover, so-called "father of the nuclear navy," endorsed the freeze as he retired, adding bitter criticisms of Reagan's military policies and calling for the elimination of nuclear weapons altogether. Other retired or retiring military leaders who endorsed the freeze included Rear Admiral Gene R. Laroque, Rear Admiral Gene Carroll, Admiral Noel Gayler, and Major General William Fairbourn.[32]

It was not necessary to endorse the freeze, however, to undermine public support for the Reagan program and thus aid the freeze movement. McGeorge Bundy, National Security Advisor to Presidents Kennedy and Johnson, was among the many defense experts who became vocal critics of the administration's nuclear and strategic policies. Along with Kennan, former Defense Secretary Robert McNamara, and SALT I negotiator Gerard Smith, Bundy published a very visible article advocating the adoption of a nuclear "no first use" strategy.[33] The so-called "gang of four" did not endorse the freeze; indeed, in public appearances for years following, McNamara was thorough in presenting his opposition to the freeze proposal. Their criticisms of the president and U.S. strategic posture, however, effectively encouraged and legitimated other more comprehensive criticisms. This was also true of the parting shot at the Reagan administration's nuclear plans taken by the retiring chairman of the Joint Chiefs of Staff, General David C. Jones. He noted that "it would be throwing money in a 'bottomless pit' to try to prepare the United States for a long nuclear war with the Soviet Union."[34]

A broad spectrum of experts in nuclear strategy, foreign policy, and arms control joined in criticizing various aspects of the Reagan program. The cumulative effect of biting criticisms from a wide spectrum of both domestic and foreign experts encouraged an equally broad spectrum of nonexpert criticism. Dissent was further encouraged when Alva Myrdal, perhaps the most radical of the expert critics, was awarded the Nobel Peace Prize in 1982.[35] Essentially, it became quite reasonable to be concerned about, and critical of, the Reagan military program.

EXPANDING THE ELITE OPPOSITION

The circle of defecting elites can be drawn much wider to include elites other than scientists and strategic planners. The relevant defectors include advantaged groups and individuals who would normally have absolutely no role in, or even informed opinion about, military and strategic policy. These people normally support U.S. policy simply by ignoring it. The Reagan era and the freeze movement were characterized by the spread of antinuclear concerns far beyond the experts.

Expertise is not the only asset that draws public attention. For example, it is easy to see the political significance of both of President Reagan's daughters, neither known as a nuclear expert, publicly signing petitions to place the nuclear freeze referendum on the California ballot. This rather mild action brought publicity to the freeze movement, partly by exposing cracks in the political consensus where one would least expect them, within the Reagan family. One daughter, actress Patti Davis, regularly spoke at rallies in opposition to her father's nuclear policy and even arranged a notoriously unsuccessful audience with the president for antinuclear activist Helen Caldicott.[36]

Similarly, although somewhat less dramatically, Betty Bumpers, married to Senator Dale Bumpers (D-AK), founded an antinuclear group, Peace Links, with the wives of several other senators. Although most of the women were married to arms control supporters, their independent stance on security policy encouraged movement politics.[37] This is also true of Ariela Gross, who was among a group of outstanding high school students selected for special recognition as "presidential scholars." Gross used the opportunity to circulate a petition in support of the nuclear freeze among the other scholars.[38] Simply by having a public position on nuclear policy, certain individuals drew attention to the movement and its cause. This attention, of course, includes not only media coverage but may also bring about increased popular participation, financial donations, and even greater public discussion of the policies at issue.

Patti Davis was not the most famous actress or entertainer committed to the nuclear freeze. Paul Newman had been among the most visible participants at the Center for Defense Information's first nuclear war conference in 1979.[39] Television producer Norman Lear contributed and raised money for the nuclear freeze referendum campaign in California, and Ed Asner videotaped an encouraging message for petition parties. Martin Sheen produced *From in the King of Prussia,* a film dramatizing the trial of the Plowshares Eight in which he played the trial judge. Sally Fields, Celeste Holm, Tony Randall, Susan Sarandon, and Meryl Streep lent their efforts to the freeze movement, as did musicians Stevie Wonder, Yo-Yo Ma, Leonard Bernstein, Jackson Browne, Harry Belafonte, Joan Baez, and Pete Seeger.[40] By raising and donating money, appearing at demonstrations, publicly addressing nuclear issues, or even committing civil disobedience, these people were able to direct public attention, political resources, and popular legitimacy to the antinuclear movement. Just as actors and celebrities made personal appearances and sometimes chose roles to aid the movement and musicians played music at demonstrations, others also tried to make a connection between their work and nuclear issues.

Medical doctors were probably the most visible. In the late 1970s, Australian pediatrician Helen Caldicott revived the moribund Physicians for Social Responsibility (PSR) while working to publicize the dangers of nuclear radiation. Her early work focused primarily on radiation generated by nuclear power stations, but Caldicott consistently stressed a connection between nuclear power and nuclear weapons. As a result of her efforts, PSR took on a new life. Throughout the early 1980s physicians repeated Caldicott's basic message, that the effects of nuclear war would be beyond the capacity of any remaining hospitals and doctors to treat.[41] To complement their activities, Bernard Lown and Soviet cardiologist Vladimir Chazov cofounded International Physicians for the Prevention of Nuclear War (IPPNW) in 1980. The group followed Caldicott's strategy of stressing the unmanageable medical consequences of nuclear war but operated in an international context, holding conferences and meeting with groups of physicians from other nations, including those of the East bloc.[42] Well before the freeze movement emerged, PSR ran a full page advertisement in the New York *Times* calling for the United States and the Soviet Union to meet to discuss substantial reductions in their nuclear arsenals.[43] With the Council for a Livable World (CLW), PSR organized a national conference to discuss ways to end the arms race.[44]

Like physicians, prominent lawyers also used their professional expertise and status to question U.S. nuclear policy. At a convocation of lawyers and legal scholars assembled to discuss nuclear weaponry, keynote speaker Arthur Miller suggested that nuclear weapons were inherently unconstitutional, as their use would preclude Congress from exercising its constitutional responsibility to declare war.[45] Legal scholars examined what they considered to be relevant issues for the antinuclear movement. Richard Falk testified in civil disobedience cases, arguing that international law, particularly the Nuremberg Principles, might not only justify, but potentially require citizens to disobey the law to stop Trident missile deployment.[46] Scholars examined the legal issues inherent in tax resistance as a means of protesting the nuclear arms race and the "necessity" or "competing harms" defense in civil disobedience cases.[47]

Beyond scholarship, individual lawyers and nonprofit groups litigated on behalf of the antinuclear movement, challenging the government on relatively technical issues,[48] attacking core issues of government policy,[49] and defending civil disobedience. Former Attorney General Ramsey Clark represented the Plowshares Eight.[50] The National Lawyers Guild began publication of *Peace and Disarmament News,* a newsletter dedicated to reporting what lawyers could do to help the antinuclear movement or to affect U.S. policy. The Meiklejohn Civil Liberties Institute compiled a data bank of briefs and decisions from antinuclear cases, intended to aid sympathetic lawyers and scholars.

Alan Scherr, a Boston attorney, founded the Lawyers Alliance for Nuclear Arms Control (LANAC) in 1981. Modeled after PSR, it was explicitly intended to educate both lawyers and the general public about relevant legal issues and how the law might be used to challenge government policy and encourage arms control and nuclear disarmament.[51] At least one legal scholar, David Kennedy, publicly questioned the political utility of litigation and legal expertise altogether, arguing that the law was an extremely limited tool in changing policy and that no one could be convinced by anyone else's legal argument anyway. According to Kennedy "deference to the political structure is no more helpful than utopian speculation." Kennedy suggests that lawyers should acknowledge this, "take a walk on the wild side," and work as citizens against U.S. policy.[52]

The active and public defections within the legal and medical communities, while including a small percentage of practitioners in each field, were substantial enough to give impetus to the developing social movement. Partly this was because they encouraged people in other fields to follow suit. Teachers, for example, formed another profession-based group, Educators for Social Responsibility (ESR). Under its auspices, teachers assigned elementary school students to write letters to the president about nuclear policy. Others designed curricula for high school and college students dealing with nuclear strategy and weaponry, crisis relocation plans, political conflict, and "concepts of peace."[53] Terry Herndon, director of the National Education Association, worked to have nuclear issues curricula implemented in schools across the country.[54] ESR and concerned teachers, by raising questions about U.S. nuclear policy in the classroom, were pointing to cracks in the apparent consensus and legitimizing dissent.

Like physicians, lawyers, and teachers, many other concerned citizens formed groups, often organized according to vocation, ranging from high technology professionals to black veterans, from mental health workers to business executives, from civil rights activists to psychologists. The nuclear freeze movement was characterized and abetted by the publicized defection of larger numbers of these concerned individuals identifying not only their political opposition but also their professional opposition, using the skills, expertise, and status associated with their professional identities.[55]

THE FREEZE GETS RELIGION

Of the proliferation of vocation-based groups, none was more visible or more critical than associations of clerics. Many clergy, religious leaders, and church institutions began to question not only Reagan administration policy but also the very precepts upon which U.S. foreign policy is based. They often prescribed political action ranging from voting to civil disobedience. This prescription gave the antinuclear movement a large share of political and moral legitimacy and aided in gaining adherents and media attention. Although there is an antiwar and pacifist tradition within virtually all the major religions in the United States, this tradition rarely emerges in institutional conflict with national policy. Even the historic peace churches, including the Quakers, Mennonites, and Brethren, have reached an accommodation with the secular state, rendering quiescence in exchange for recognition and generally benign neglect. The cooperation that government demands has ranged from individual income taxes to tacit approval of government activities to the outright endorsement of controversial policies, the last demonstrated most clearly by Cardinal Spellman's blessing of B-52 bombers bound for Vietnam.

Throughout U.S. history small numbers of people of all faiths have challenged the government through public protest, civil disobedience, and tax resistance to live up to their religious ideals. These dissidents, however, have always been the minority, generally disinherited by the institutionalized churches of their own faiths. Martin Luther King's classic "Letter from Birmingham City Jail," for example, was written to explain his civil disobedience to angry and unsupportive church superiors. Interestingly, the civil rights and antiwar movements during the 1960s probably involved the greatest extent of institutional religious opposition to government policy in U.S. history. This was duplicated during the nuclear freeze movement, according to Baptist minister and U.S. Representative William Gray (D-PA).[56]

The participation of the churches was probably even greater during the nuclear freeze movement. Although members of the clergy had been involved in peace movements and social justice struggles, their numbers were always relatively small, and their places within church hierarchies generally either low or marginal. Organizations such as Clergy and Laity Concerned (CALC), the Southern Christian Leadership Conference (SCLC), Pax Christi, and the American Friends Services Committee (AFSC) were formed precisely because the mainstream organizations were reluctant to engage in social protest. This was not so for the freeze movement. All the activist groups were actively engaged in the movement, but religious participation was not limited to them. There was significant support and activity from the National Conference of Catholic Bishops, the National Council of Churches of Christ, United Presbyterians, the Episcopal House of Bishops, the United Methodist Council of Bishops, and the American Baptists. All endorsed the nuclear freeze resolution in one form or another in 1981, well before the peak of movement activity.[57]

The rash of endorsements and social activity erupting in 1981 was actually the product of work that had been going on since the end of the Vietnam War. Groups like Pax Christi and Sojourners, which had been active in the antiwar movement, shifted their efforts to nuclear issues in the 1970s. The Riverside Church, led by antiwar movement veteran William Sloane Coffin, also established a disarmament program at the same time. As their activities continued throughout the 1970s, their ideas percolated up through their church hierarchies, perhaps aided by the election of Jimmy Carter, a self-proclaimed reborn Christian who explicitly endorsed the idea that moral and religious concerns had a central place in politics. The arms race was unsurprisingly often targeted for opposition. As the Second Vatican Council announced in 1965, "men should be convinced that the arms race in which so many countries are engaged is not a safe way to preserve a steady peace. Far from being eliminated (through the arms race), the causes of war threaten to grow gradually stronger."[58]

The change was not in theory but in action. Suddenly, it seemed, religious leaders were trying to nudge U.S. policy in the direction of their gospel of peace. By 1979, even conservative evangelist and long-time cold warrior Billy Graham was talking about the evils of nuclear war and the need for detente and disarmament — on a crusade in the Soviet Union. Human survival is certainly the most basic value underlying most religions, and it was to this, rather than to analyzing the dynamics of nuclear strategy, that most active clerics turned their attention. As J. Brian Hehir, who drafted the Catholic bishops' pastoral on nuclear weapons, testified before Congress, "Protecting human dignity is a thoroughly Gospel task. It can't be done outside the political arena. That's why the church does it. It's not trying to impress people with being au courant."[59] This approach was demonstrated with increasing frequency not only in the United States but throughout the world; virtually every nation's nuclear disarmament movement during the 1970s and early 1980s contained a significant faction of previously mainstream clergy.[60]

The basic moral concern of acting for peace and to preserve life was far more readily understandable than the intricacies of deterrence theory, and easily far more appealing. Throughout the 1970s, increasing numbers of clergy made discussion of nuclear arms policy an important part of their moral and spiritual teachings. As the last hopes for SALT II ratification collapsed, the urgency and relative dissidence of these teachings naturally increased. The Reagan administration's failure to grant these concerns even rhetorical acknowledgment added impetus to growing numbers of increasingly critical religious leaders. Their self-defined moral concerns were politicized by the new administration's neglect and occasional criticism.

Religious faith also provides a more easily sustainable motivation for activism than do more instrumental or pragmatic incentives. Religiously motivated people were among the first to address passionately the dilemmas of the nuclear age partly because they were not necessarily searching for battles that could be easily won. Religious faith can make political activity personally rewarding, even when it does not seem to be immediately or even potentially efficacious. It can justify and even encourage actions against both the state and the odds, which gain meaning for activists in the context of religious commitment rather than realpolitik.[61] Clerical status also gives individuals a certain legitimacy to address moral issues, a legitimacy not generally accorded to other professions. The structure of clerical life may also provide activists greater freedom to structure their lives and priorities, often by renouncing certain secular pursuits, such as wealth, job security, and in the case of Roman Catholics, a traditional family.[62] This may afford the opportunity to act aggressively on behalf of their beliefs, taking large risks with small prospect of immediate return.

Since the 1960s Daniel and Philip Berrigan have placed direct action on behalf of their beliefs at the center of their lives. In September 1980, along with six others of the Plowshares Eight, the Berrigan brothers broke into a General Electric plant in King of Prussia, Pennsylvania.[63] By itself, this dramatic action was not a harbinger of an emerging movement. Indeed, the Berrigan brothers had committed such acts of civil disobedience fairly consistently since their protests against the Vietnam War in the 1960s. Their activities have consistently generated discussion among people sharing their political or theological sympathies, but only occasionally has it gone beyond this small group.[64]

The Plowshares' actions were not, however, isolated incidents of witness. They were accompanied by other strains of antinuclear activism, first from traditional pacifist groups. The AFSC virtually commissioned *The Call to Halt the Arms Race,* the first freeze document. During the summer of 1980, AFSC, CALC, and the pacifist Fellowship of Reconciliation (FOR) endorsed the freeze and committed to work for it. Shortly thereafter Harvard Divinity School Professor Harvey Cox presented the nuclear freeze to the World Council of Churches (WCC), and along with Pax Christi, Sojourners, and the Riverside Church, it chose to make the proposal a priority by May 1980.[65] To reach the political mainstream, however, the nuclear freeze movement had to move beyond these natural and historic allies.

Freeze activists from the outset worked to gain acceptance and aid for their cause in their own churches. Organizers brought the freeze to their local parishes, distributing the proposal and supporting literature, and working to get the churches to endorse the proposal at their annual conferences. By the end of 1981, the freeze proposal was endorsed by the United Presbyterian Church U.S.A., the Union of American Hebrew Congregations, the United Methodist Church, and the institutional establishments of the Lutheran, Unitarian Universalist, and Greek Orthodox churches. In addition to formal institutional endorsements, the freeze was buoyed by individual endorsements from mainstream religious leaders. Among those who spoke on its behalf were Bishop James Armstrong, president of the National Council of Churches; James Crumley, president of the Lutheran Church; Father Theodore Hesburgh, president of Notre Dame University; Archbishop Iakonos of the Greek Orthodox Diocese of North and South America; Eugene Picket, president of the Unitarian Universalist Association; and Rabbi Walter Wurtzberger, president of the Synagogue Council of America.[66]

At the parish level of each denomination there was equal, if not greater, commitment to the nuclear freeze and opposition to the Reagan nuclear agenda. More than half the Roman Catholic bishops personally endorsed the freeze by the middle of 1982; many called for unilateral initiatives to end the arms race or embraced more radical means of political action.[67] Archbishop John Quinn of San Francisco blasted "the obsessive drive for security through nuclear weaponry," calling upon the superpowers to renounce explicitly the use of nuclear weapons and contending that the arms race prevented social justice for the poor and disadvantaged.[68] Berrigan-style sentiments as well as direct action and support for direct action were emerging from surprisingly high places in church hierarchies.

In 1981 Archbishop Quinn encouraged Roman Catholics across the country to take political action, including civil disobedience, to stop the arms race.[69] When guards went on strike at the Pantex plant in Amarillo, Texas, where all U.S. nuclear warheads are made, they were supported by all 12 Roman Catholic bishops in Texas, who also criticized Pantex and its work. Amarillo Bishop Leroy Matthiesen urged the workers "involved in the production and stockpiling of nuclear bombs to consider what they are doing, to resign from such activities, and to seek employment in peaceful pursuits." He then set up a counseling center and a fund to help those so inspired to change jobs.[70] Archbishop Raymond Hunthausen of Seattle, Washington, calling the Trident submarines based in nearby Everett "the Auschwitz of the Puget Sound," announced a personal campaign of income tax resistance and urged others to join him. He began withholding half his federal income tax and sending it to the World Peace Tax Fund. He also supported local civil disobedience actions of the Puget Sound Peace Camp and the Ground Zero Campaign against the White Train. The leaders of the Lutheran, Methodist, and Presbyterian churches in Seattle publicly announced support for Hunthausen.[71]

Almost as if to show that Hunthausen and Matthiesen were not out of step with the church hierarchy, the National Conference of Catholic Bishops began work on a pastoral letter addressing nuclear issues at the end of 1981. The first draft, released in June 1982, questioned the morality of deterrence and endorsed an immediate freeze on superpower nuclear arsenals followed by deep cuts.[72] The Reagan administration attacked the document, but subsequent drafts were even tougher, calling for decisive and even unilateral actions to end the arms race. It is hard to estimate the potential effect of such pastoral letters on public opinion and policy, but it was at least significant enough to motivate President Reagan to claim it supported his policies. On May 4, 1983, shortly before the publication of the final draft, Reagan announced, "I have some information in advance about it which indicates that it really is a legitimate effort to do exactly what we're doing." Archbishop John R. Roach, president of the Council of Bishops, and Cardinal Joseph Bernardin, chair of the committee that wrote the pastoral, immediately called a press conference to announce that Reagan was misinformed and that the pastoral called for substantially different policies than those the president advocated.[73] Similar pastoral letters were issued by the Episcopal House of Bishops, the United Methodist Council of Bishops, and the National Council of Churches of Christ.

These efforts supported the development of the nuclear freeze movement. At minimum, the criticisms from religious leaders kept debate about nuclear issues in the news. Clerics taking a stand on U.S. nuclear policy was newsworthy in and of itself, and this drew media and public attention to the movement's concerns. For example, the Catholic bishops' pastoral letter alone generated 32 New York *Times* stories in the eight months before its publication in May 1983, nine of them on the front page.[74] Further, the character of clerical opposition to U.S. nuclear policy, generally grounded in spiritual language and virtually never touching the minutiae of nuclear weaponry or strategy, was accessible to the general public. It prevented the Reagan administration from claiming a moral high ground and encouraged many to develop their own opinions rather than ceding that authority to elected officials.

Churches and religious groups also offered organizational resources to the movement, including meeting sites, office equipment, and mailing lists. Clerical and lay organizers working for the nuclear freeze were sometimes partially supported by their churches. The parishes provided natural organizing units in congregations and regular means for reaching, educating, and mobilizing people through newsletters, services, and sermons. It is difficult to calculate the impact these things might have on public opinion and political action over an extended period of time. Even in a short time, however, the combination of organization and moral authority held by churches within certain areas could prove to be insurmountable. For example, when Spencer Kimball, leader of the normally very conservative Mormon church, devoted his efforts to preventing MX missile deployment in Utah, he mobilized popular opinion and political resources so forcefully that the Department of Defense quickly changed its plans.[75]

BUSINESS AND THE NUCLEAR FREEZE

Less visible than clerical support, but equally important to development of the nuclear freeze movement, was a schism among large segments of the corporate elite about nuclear issues. Big business, a major source of support for Reagan's presidential campaign, was far from monolithic in its support of his military and nuclear policies. Defectors within the business elite criticized the administration's military policies, founded and funded oppositional organizations, subsidized research projects, and supported candidates opposed to the Reagan military agenda. In addition to aiding the antinuclear movement, the Reagan administration was robbed of unanimous support from a sector where such support was expected.

The roots and significance of this defection are both broad and deep. Business leaders became increasingly politicized in the 1970s, exploiting the campaign reforms of 1974 to increase their political influence. Thomas Byrne Edsall argues the business community gradually gained an influence on U.S. politics and policy it had not enjoyed since before the New Deal. "The political stature of business rose steadily from the early 1970s . . ." he writes, "until, by the end of the decade, the business community achieved virtual dominance of the legislative process in Congress."[76] Reagan's 1980 landslide was one expression of this increased influence. Still, there were significant business interests hesitant to support the full extent of the Reagan revolution. Some were deterred by ideology, others by their need for trade with the Soviet Union and the Eastern bloc, others by their business interests' need for government investment, and still others were troubled simply by the sheer magnitude of the new federal deficit the military buildup fed. These concerns generated a schism within the corporate elite most visible on military and arms control issues.[77]

Democratic party leaders, recognizing that the active politicization of business hurt the party, were faced with a dilemma. They could either try to energize and activate their natural constituencies of working class and poor people and minorities or attempt to compete with the Republicans for support among the middle and upper-middle classes and business interests. While the first strategy was targeted at a larger group of potential supporters, those people were far less likely to vote, work in campaigns, or to contribute money to candidates than were those targeted by the second. After the Carter debacle in 1980 both business and labor leaders in the Democratic Party supported the election of Charles Manatt as the new party chair, whose explicit intention was to regain support from business and middle-class voters.[78]

New business interest in arms control and some restraint of military spending offered both the Democrats and the emerging freeze movement several resources. First, several business-funded foundations began supporting research and public education on arms control issues. In the early 1980s the Rockefeller Foundation instituted a major grant program for research on arms control issues, shortly followed by the Rockefeller Family Fund, the Ford Foundation, the Carnegie Endowment for International Peace, and the MacArthur Foundation. Business Democrats were well represented on the boards of trustees for each of these foundations and clearly influenced funding choices. Between 1982 and 1984 annual funding for research on international security and nuclear issues tripled, increasing from $16.5 million to $52 million. The Stern Fund, the CS Fund, and the Field Foundation provided the early bankroll for most of the emerging freeze organizations.[79] By funding established scholars at universities and mainstream think tanks and, on occasion, movement partisans, these foundations ensured not only that arms control would be on the political and academic agenda but also that it would be in the news.

The MacArthur Foundation's award of "genius" grants to Randall Forsberg and H. Brian Hehir (who had instigated the Catholic bishops' pastoral letter) gave the recipients not only the opportunity to pursue their work but also a broader public platform from which to articulate their views. Alan Kay, an electronics entrepreneur, provided the start-up funds and continuing support for Forsberg's Institute for Defense and Disarmament Studies (IDDS) in 1980 and 1981 and also provided the seed money for the Nuclear

Weapons Freeze Clearinghouse (NWFC).[80] Democratic business elites, such as Averell Harriman and Thomas J. Watson, Jr., began directing their criticisms of the Reagan administration to the areas of arms control and international relations. Jerome Wiesner, board member of the MacArthur Foundation and former Democratic presidential policy advisor, and Paul Walker, who worked in ACDA in the Carter administration, in conjunction with the Council for a Livable World set up PeacePac, which supported arms control supporters — usually Democrats — in Congressional races. They were shortly joined by a wide spectrum of supporters from corporate America.

The embrace of segments of the corporate elite was not an unambiguous blessing. Although it offered money, media attention, and some elements of mainstream legitimacy, this support came at a cost. The bulk of business support went to older, more established, and more conservative organizations within the larger antinuclear movement.[81] Although strengthening these organizations initially contributed to the health of the movement as a whole, it also meant that the more radical aspects of movement analysis and action were deemphasized, indeed, often preempted. The case of the California nuclear freeze referendum campaign is telling.

In early 1981 Jo and Nick Seidita of Los Angeles began a grassroots referendum campaign to support the nuclear freeze. They were joined in September by Harold Willens, a millionaire who had long been an arms control advocate within the Democratic Party establishment, as a fundraiser in both Carter campaigns and a delegate to the first United Nations Special Session on disarmament in 1978.[82] Willens' participation in the freeze campaign was welcomed as it meant an infusion of money, media attention, and mainstream legitimacy, but there was also a certain amount of trepidation within the campaign as Nick Seidita lost his seat on the new executive board of the campaign, replaced by better-known and more mainstream activists. Seidita, who remained active in the California freeze, said:

> Everybody bowed and scraped their foreheads on the floor when Harold Willens came into the campaign. He's name, and he's money and he's connections. . . . Now that's important. . . . But this campaign cannot succeed if it turns into a media debate between the haves and the have-nots. They'll beat our ass every time. . . . The beginning of this campaign was an authentic grassroots beginning. If it doesn't stay that way, it doesn't have a future.[83]

Willens did alter the grassroots style, however, and it is likely that these changes helped the campaign grow. He personally hired Bill

Zimmerman, a media consultant, and Craver, Matthews, Smith, and Company, a direct mail firm, to aid the referendum effort. He commissioned polls, sought endorsements, directed public relations, considered campaign strategies, and perhaps most important, raised a great deal of money. This led to a media campaign and a very rapid expansion of support; in less than three months the freeze gathered more than 500,000 signatures to put the issue on the ballot.

It was not only campaign style that received a makeover. Willens also successfully shaped the California freeze resolution in the image he thought most palatable to people like himself. He prevented the freeze from being linked to any other issues, defining it in as limited and moderate a way as possible. He urged other nuclear freeze campaigns to follow his example, writing in a letter to the *Bulletin of the Atomic Scientists* in May 1982, "All will depend on our campaign, and we must keep it as hard-nosed and free from peace rally rhetoric as possible." He compared the California resolution favorably to those on the ballot in Massachusetts and Connecticut for two basic reasons: the California question had a paragraph mandating adequate U.S. verification of the freeze and did not have a clause calling for the transfer of funds used in the arms race to civilian use. The economic transfer clause "would lose us at least 9.7 percent of the voters," he explained, so "we are limiting ourselves to a few key points and backing them with the most conservative authorities we can find."[84]

The nuclear freeze was in this way designed to be as inoffensive as possible to the largest number of people. Discussions of massive direct action campaigns or advocacy of unilateral initiatives were purged from the mainstream of the freeze, not only in California, but across the United States, as the Willens style came to dominate. Local activists found it difficult to refuse the generosity and energy of business sponsors, and the compromises needed to maintain their support seemed minor in light of the potential gains available with such an alliance. Indeed, freeze resolutions passed at almost every level of government in the United States with ease, doubtlessly aided by the Willens approach. The problem was that the moral and political clarity of the movement and the freeze idea itself were obscured. As Ferguson and Rogers contend, the freeze

> moved far from the intentions of its original champions. Few of the business groups and foundations that now helped push it along wanted to explore the relations between multinational business, the use of force in U.S. foreign policy and social class. Accordingly, the critical content of the early freeze proposals largely evaporated. Allying with the freeze became little more than a way of expressing disapproval of a military buildup of the scale Reagan projected.[85]

Politicians flocked to this approach; candidates and office holders from every level of government were quick to express their support for the nuclear freeze. Initially targeted at the left end of the Democratic spectrum, the freeze proposal now drew support from moderate Republicans and conservative Democrats. A freeze resolution was introduced into Congress in March of 1982, but its image was so tepid it was no longer clear what the proposal or the movement meant. It was variously coupled with a conventional arms buildup and the creation of a new single warhead ICBM. The nuclear freeze became an all-purpose political pablum, which did not clash with any other proposal or approach. Politicians found they could justify support for even the most heinous and wasteful military programs by also supporting a freeze.

Elite nuclear freeze support was a response to the perceived excesses of the Reagan administration. The freeze itself, which had been written as part of a comprehensive and detailed approach to nuclear disarmament, was coopted and became shorthand for opposition to some element of the Reagan program, essentially robbed of its political context. The alliance between freeze organizers and business executives and, subsequently, national politicians put the freeze on the front pages and the floor of Congress, but in a stripped-down version without the meaning the early supporters intended. It is doubtful that this bargain was a fair one; freeze advocates got only the most superficial support in exchange for surrendering their language and the heart of their campaigns.

NOTES

1. Classic texts on elite theory include Robert Michels, *Political Parties*, New York: Collier, 1962; C. Wright Mills, *The Power Elite*, New York: Oxford University Press, 1962; Gaetano Mosca, *The Ruling Class*, ed. A. Livingston, New York: McGraw-Hill, 1939; Vilfredo Pareto, *The Mind and Society: Treatise of General Sociology*, New York: Harcourt, Brace & World, 1935.

2. "Farewell Address, January 17, 1961," in *Public Papers of the Presidents of the United States: Dwight D. Eisenhower*, Washington, D.C.: U.S. Government Printing Office, 1961, pp. 1035–40.

3. Theda Skocpol, *States and Social Revolutions*, Cambridge: Cambridge University Press, 1979, p. 47.

4. Crane Brinton, *The Anatomy of a Revolution*, New York: Vintage, 1965, p. 251.

5. Frances Fox Piven and Richard A. Cloward, *Poor People's Movements: Why They Succeed, How They Fail*, New York: Vintage, 1979, p. 44.

6. Michael Lipsky, *Protest in City Politics: Rent Strikes, Housing, and the Power of the Poor*, Chicago: Rand-McNally, 1970, p. 172.

7. See Kenneth Keniston, *Young Radicals*, New York: Harcourt, Brace & World, 1968, p. 230.

8. Ronald Inglehart, *The Silent Revolution: Changing Values and Political Styles among Western Publics*, Princeton, NJ: Princeton University Press, 1977.

Also see Frank Parkin, *Middle-Class Radicalism: The Social Bases of the British Campaign for Nuclear Disarmament,* New York: Praeger, 1968.

9. Brinton, *Anatomy of a Revolution,* p. 102.

10. James Fallows, *National Defense,* New York: Random House, 1981, p. 136; Richard Nixon, *RN: The Memoirs of Richard Nixon,* New York: Grosset and Dunlap, 1978, p. 399.

11. Piven and Cloward, *Poor People's Movements,* p. 30.

12. Ibid., pp. 29–32. Also see Michels, *Political Parties,* pp. 172–73; Charles Tilly, *From Mobilization to Revolution,* Reading, MA: Addison-Wesley, 1978, p. 114.

13. Piven and Cloward, *Poor People's Movements,* p. 13. Also see Eric Hobsbawm and George Rude, *Captain Swing,* New York: Pantheon, 1968, p. 65.

14. Roberta Ash Garner, *Social Movements in America,* Chicago: Markham, 1972, p. 230.

15. William A. Gamson, *The Strategy of Social Protest,* Homewood, IL: The Dorsey Press, 1975, pp. 41–50.

16. Gamson, *Strategy of Social Protest,* pp. 72–88. See also David Garrow, *Protest at Selma,* New Haven: Yale University Press, 1978. Garrow argues that Martin Luther King intentionally sought out Bull Connor, Selma's Commissioner of Public Safety, as a political opponent. King believed that Connor was prone to violent overreaction and that this violence would draw attention and sympathy to the suffering and, consequently, the cause of civil rights activists.

17. Lipsky, *Protest in City Politics,* p. 171.

18. Piven and Cloward, *Poor People's Movements,* p. xxii.

19. Paul Boyer, "From Activism to Apathy: The American People and Nuclear Weapons, 1963–1980," *The Journal of American History,* March 1984, p. 821; Lawrence Wittner, *Rebels against War: The American Peace Movement, 1943–1983,* Philadelphia: Temple University Press, 1984,

20. Concrete imagery of nuclear realities has proven to be a strong motivation for activism. See Seymour Feshbach and Michael J. White, "Individual Differences in Attitudes towards Nuclear Arms Policies: Some Psychological and Social Policy Considerations," *Journal of Peace Research* 23 (June 1986): 129–39; Susan Fiske, Felicia Pratto, and Mark Pavelchak, "Citizens' Images of Nuclear War: Content and Consequences," *Journal of Social Issues* 39 (1983). To manage nuclear issues, politicians and nuclear experts use language that obscures nuclear realities. See Carol Cohn, "Sex and Death in the Rational World of Defense Intellectuals," *Signs,* Summer 1987, pp. 687–718; Glenn D. Hook, "Making Weapons Easier to Live With: The Political Role of Language in Nuclearization," *Bulletin of Peace Proposals* 16 (1985).

21. Joel Primack and Frank von Hippel, *Advice and Dissent: Scientists in the Political Arena,* New York: Basic, 1974, pp. 59–73, 178–95.

22. Feshbach and White, "Individual Differences," p. 130.

23. Jonathan D. Auerbach, "Nuclear Freeze at Crossroads," Boston Sunday *Globe,* June 22, 1986; Michael Kazin, "How the Freeze Campaign Was Born," *The Nation,* May 1, 1982, p. 523. A scientist can achieve maximum exposure with a defection only once in his or her career and may subsequently be excluded from access to classified information, policy makers, and political legitimacy; Primack and von Hippel, *Advice and Dissent,* p. 102.

24. New York *Times,* September 4, 1982, p. 3.

25. Adam Garfinkle, *The Politics of the Nuclear Freeze*, Philadelphia, PA: Foreign Policy Research Institute, 1984.

26. On nuclear winter, see Paul R. Ehrlich, Carl Sagan, Donald Kennedy, Walter R. Roberts, et al., *The Cold and the Dark: The World after Nuclear War*, New York: Norton, 1984; see also P. R. Ehrlich et al., "The Long-Term Biological Consequences of Nuclear War," *Science* 222 (1983): 1293–300; Jeannie Peterson, ed., *The Aftermath: The Human and Ecological Consequences of Nuclear War*, New York: Pergamon Press, 1983; Carl Sagan, "Nuclear War and Climatic Catastrophe," *Foreign Affairs*, Winter 1983/84, pp. 257–92.

27. See also the Federation of American Scientists, *Seeds of Promise: The First Real Hearings of the Nuclear Arms Freeze*, Andover, MA: Birch House, 1983; for the UCS position, see Daniel Ford, Henry Kendall, and Steven Nadis, *Beyond the Freeze*, Boston: Beacon Press, 1982.

28. Robert Leavitt, "Freezing the Arms Race: The Genesis of a Mass Movement," unpublished Kennedy School of Government Case Study, Harvard University, 1983, p. 28; Earl Molander, "Democracy in Military Policy . . . Leading the Leaders," in Ronald V. Dellums et al., eds., *Defense Sense: The Search for a Rational Military Policy*, Cambridge, MA: Ballinger, 1983, pp. 266–72; Roger Molander, *Nuclear War: What's in It for You*, New York: Pocket Books, 1982; Keith Payne and Colin Gray, eds., *The Nuclear Freeze Controversy*, New York: University Press of America, 1984, p. 79; Robert Scheer, *With Enough Shovels: Reagan, Bush, and Nuclear War*, New York: Random House, 1982, p. 11.

29. Alexander Cockburn and James Ridgeway, "The Freeze Movement Versus Ronald Reagan," *The New Left Review* 137 (January/February 1983): 9.

30. Kennan himself had much earlier "defected" from supporting the way in which the United States implemented containment. See George Kennan, "Foreign Policy and Christian Conscience," *The Atlantic Monthly*, May 1959, p. 45; also his "A Modest Proposal," *The New York Review of Books*, July 16, 1981, p. 14; Wittner, *Rebels against War*, pp. 254–55.

31. Auerbach, "Nuclear Freeze at Crossroads."

32. Cockburn and Ridgeway, "The Freeze Movement," p. 9; Dellums et al., *Defense Sense*, p. 122; Garfinkle, *Politics of the Nuclear Freeze*, p. 14; Kazin, "How the Freeze Campaign Was Born," p. 523; Otto Klineberg, "Public Opinion and Nuclear War," *The American Psychologist* 39 (1984): 1248. Also New York *Times*, January 29, 1981, p. 3; January 30, 1981, p. 8.

33. Bundy et al., "Nuclear Weapons and the Atlantic Alliance," *Foreign Affairs* 60 (1982): 753–68.

34. Washington *Post*, June 19, 1982.

35. Klineberg, "Public Opinion and Nuclear War," p. 1248.

36. Francis C. Brown III, "Media Coverage of the American Nuclear Freeze and Antinuclear Movement," unpublished thesis, Woodrow Wilson School of Public and International Affairs, Princeton University, 1985, p. 78; Kazin, "How the Freeze Campaign Was Born," p. 524; New York *Times*, June 9, 1981, Section 2, p. 4; June 16, 1981, Section 2, p. 19.

37. See Betty Bumpers, "For My Part, Peace Is the Ultimate Issue," *Glamour*, October 1982. Discussion of nuclear politics in generally apolitical magazines like *Glamour* demonstrates the movement's permeation into mainstream politics and culture.

38. See her description of events, Ariela Gross, "Freezing Reagan: Showdown at the White House" *The Nation*, August 6–13, 1983, p. 99.

39.   Gene LaRoque and Richard Barnet, "The First Nuclear War Conference," *Bulletin of the Atomic Scientists,* April 1979.

40.   Brown, "Media Coverage," p. 137; Garfinkle, *Politics of the Nuclear Freeze,* p. 92; Kazin, "How the Freeze Campaign Was Born," p. 523.

41.   Pam Solo, *From Protest to Policy: Beyond the Freeze to Common Security,* Cambridge, MA: Ballinger, 1988, p. 36. Helen Caldicott's books give a good flavor of the tone and content of her speeches; see *Missile Envy: The Arms Race and Nuclear War,* New York: William Morrow, 1984; *Nuclear Madness,* New York: Bantam, 1981. On the medical consequences of nuclear war, see H. Jack Geiger, "The Illusion of Survival," *Bulletin of the Atomic Scientists,* June/July 1981, p. 16; John Gofman, *Radiation and Human Health,* San Francisco: Sierra Club, 1981. (Both Geiger and Gofman were veterans of the movement against nuclear power.) Also see Ruth Adams and Susan Cullen, eds., *The Final Epidemic: Physicians and Scientists on the Medical Consequences of Nuclear War,* Chicago: Bulletin of the Atomic Scientists, 1981; Eric Chivian et al., *Last Aid: The Medical Dimensions of Nuclear War,* San Francisco: W. H. Freeman, 1982.

42.   IPPNW, *The Soviet Response to Medical Efforts for the Prevention of Nuclear War,* Boston: IPPNW, 1981. IPPNW was awarded the Nobel Peace Prize in 1985.

43.   New York *Times,* March 2, 1980, Section 4, p. 22.

44.   New York *Times,* September 27, 1980, p. 27.

45.   Arthur S. Miller, "The Constitutional Challenge of Nuclear Weapons," in "Nuclear Weapons and Constitutional Law: Symposium," *Nova Law Journal* 7 (Fall 1982): 1.

46.   Ted Dzielak and Lynn Greiner, "Moral Victory against Trident Terror," *National Lawyers Guild Notes,* November/December 1982, pp. 2–3. Also see *U.S. v. May, Federal 2nd* 622 (1980): 1000, rejecting Falk's arguments.

47.   Robert C. Aldridge and V. Stark, "Nuclear War, Citizen Intervention, and the Necessity Defense," *Santa Clara Law Review* 26 (Spring 1986): 299; Charles Di Salvo, "Saying 'No' to War in the Technological Age: Conscientious Objection and the World Peace Tax Fund Act," *De Paul Law Review* 31 (Spring 1982): 497. Michael L. Kessler, "Antinuclear Demonstrations and the Necessity Defense, *State v. Warshow,*" *Vermont Law Review* 5 (Spring 1980): 103.

48.   See, for example, "Weinberger v. Catholic Action of Hawaii," *US* 454 (1981): 139.

49.   See, for example, "Greenham Women against Cruise Missiles v. Ronald Reagan et al.," *Federal Supplement* 591 (1984): 1332.

50.   "Commonwealth of Pennsylvania v. Berrigan et al.," *Atlantic Reporter 2nd Series* 472 (1984): 1099.

51.   Alan B. Sherr, "Nuclear Arms Control and the Role of the Legal Community," in "Are Nuclear Weapons Legal under Existing Law?: Symposium" Special Issue, *Brooklyn Journal of International Law* 9 (Summer 1983): 209.

52.   David Kennedy, "A Critical Approach to the Nuclear Weapons Problem," *Brooklyn Journal of International Law* 9 (Summer 1983): 309.

53.   Also see Educators for Social Responsibility, *Perspectives: A Teaching Guide to Concepts of Peace,* Cambridge, MA: ESR, 1983; Barry H. Feriman, "Survival of the Species: A Classroom Project," *Bulletin of the Atomic Scientists,* November 1981, p. 20; Roberta Snow and Elizabeth Lewis, *Decision Making in a Nuclear Age,* Cambridge, MA: ESR, 1982; Daniel C. Thomas and Michael T. Klare, *Peace and World Order Studies: A Curriculum Guide,* Boulder, CO:

Westview, 1989; John Zola and Reny Sieck, *Teaching about Conflict, Nuclear War, and the Future,* Boulder, CO: Center for Teaching International Relations, 1984.

54. Albert Shanker, president of the American Federation of Teachers, opposed Herndon's effort, arguing that children were becoming unnecessarily frightened of nuclear war. See Garfinkle, *Politics of the Nuclear Freeze,* pp. 30–31.

55. Klineberg, "Public Opinion and Nuclear War." For a comprehensive listing of active groups, see IDDS, *Peace Resource Book,* Cambridge, MA: Ballinger, 1986.

56. Dellums et al., *Defense Sense,* p. 235.

57. Brown, "Media Coverage," pp. 31–32; Cockburn and Ridgeway, "The Freeze Movement," p. 17.

58. Quoted in Archbishop John R. Quinn, "The Cross of Iron," in Dellums et al., *Defense Sense,* p. 224.

59. Quoted in *Time,* "God and the Bomb: The Bishops Debate Nuclear Morality," November 1982, pp. 75–77.

60. Bernd W. Kubbig and Thomas Risse-Kappen, "Living Up to the Ethical Dilemmas of Nuclear Armament: The Churches as Pace-setters of Current Thinking on Peace and War," *Bulletin of Peace Proposals* 15 (1984): 65; Kjell Skjelsbaek, ed., "Ethical and Moral Issues of War and Peace: The Role of the Churches," Special Issue, *Bulletin of Peace Proposals* 15 (1984).

61. See Daniel Berrigan and Robert Coles, *The Geography of Faith,* Boston: Beacon Press, 1971, p. 90.

62. Ibid., pp. 42–45.

63. New York *Times,* September 10, 1980, p. 16.

64. For example, see William VanEtten Casey and Philip Nobile, eds., *The Berrigans,* New York: Avon, 1971.

65. Garfinkle, *Politics of the Nuclear Freeze,* pp. 22–23; Leavitt, "Freezing the Arms Race," pp. 17–19; Solo, *From Protest to Policy,* pp. 44–48.

66. Brown, "Media Coverage," p. 31; Garfinkle, *Politics of the Nuclear Freeze,* p. 91; Leavitt, "Freezing the Arms Race," p. 29.

67. Cockburn and Ridgeway, "The Freeze Movement," p. 18.

68. Dellums et al., *Defense Sense,* pp. 221–26; Kazin, "How the Freeze Campaign Was Born," p. 524.

69. New York *Times,* October 4, 1981, p. 41.

70. "Bishops at the End of the Line," *Sojourners,* February 1984, p. 21; Cockburn and Ridgeway, "The Freeze Movement," p. 17; Leavitt, "Freezing the Arms Race," p. 29; New York *Times,* September 29, 1981, Section 4, p. 2; February 14, 1982, p. 28.

71. *Sojourners,* February 1984; Wallace Turner, "Tax Refusal Completes Prelate's Moral Journey," New York *Times,* April 19, 1982, p. A19; New York *Times,* July 13, 1981, p. 8.

72. For differing interpretations of the politics surrounding the pastoral, see Richard B. Miller, "Catholic Bishops on War," *Bulletin of the Atomic Scientists,* May 1983, p. 9; Marcus Raskin, "The Church vs. the Bomb," *The Nation,* January 29, 1983; Peter Steinfels, "Pastoral Proceeding," *The New Republic,* May 30, 1983, pp. 15–17; *Time,* "God and the Bomb." The pastoral was ultimately published as *The Challenge of Peace: God's Promise and Our Response,* Washington, D.C.: U.S. Catholic Conference, 1983.

73. Cockburn and Ridgeway, "The Freeze Movement," p. 17; Mark Green and Gail MacColl, *There He Goes Again: Ronald Reagan's Reign of Error,* New York: Pantheon, 1983, p. 48.

74. Brown, "Media Coverage," p. 129.

75. See William Appleman Williams, "Regional Resistance: Backyard Autonomy," *The Nation,* September 5, 1981, p. 162.

76. Thomas Byrne Edsall, *The New Politics of Inequality,* New York: Norton, 1984, pp. 107–8, 109–40; also see Larry J. Sabato, *Pac Power,* New York: Norton, 1985, pp. 160–87; Michael Useem, *The Inner Circle: Large Corporations and the Rise of Business Activity in the U.S. and U.K.,* New York: Oxford University Press, 1984.

77. Frank Riessmann, "The Antinuclear Movement: Why Now?" *Social Policy* 13 (Summer 1982): 3.

78. Edsall, *New Politics of Inequality*; Thomas Ferguson and Joel Rogers, *Right Turn: The Decline of the Democrats and the Future of American Politics,* New York: Hill and Wang, 1986.

79. Cockburn and Ridgeway, "The Freeze Movement," p. 17; Thomas Ferguson and Joel Rogers, "Big Business Backs the Freeze," *The Nation,* June 19/26, 1986, pp. 43–47.

80. Fox Butterfield, "Anatomy of a Nuclear Protest," *New York Times Magazine,* July 11, 1982; Garfinkle, *Politics of the Nuclear Freeze,* p. 85; Solo, *From Protest to Policy,* p. xiii.

81. Ferguson and Rogers, "Big Business."

82. Cockburn and Ridgeway, "The Freeze Movement," p. 10; Kazin, "How the Freeze Campaign Was Born."

83. Garfinkle, *Politics of the Nuclear Freeze,* p. 86.

84. Harold Willens, "Letter," *Bulletin of the Atomic Scientists,* May 1982, p. 57.

85. Ferguson and Rogers, "Big Business," p. 46.

7

THE PUBLIC FACE OF
THE NUCLEAR FREEZE

In order to be effective or even simply to be sustained, protest must be projected to a broader audience. The mass media can magnify, minimize, or ignore dissident activity. Through coverage of political issues, the media can draw attention to or obscure particular areas, set the tone and intensity of political debate, and shape popular perceptions of the potential limits or necessity for change.[1] Protest movements need media attention, but that attention can undermine the achievement of their goals and even their definitions of those goals. For these reasons, the story of the nuclear freeze is told and shaped by its relationship with media.

MEDIA AND POLITICS

Mass media have enjoyed increasing influence on politics in the United States. As Americans grow increasingly isolated from each other, television and, to a lesser extent, newspaper have come to fill a gap in social life. While this applies to entertainment, spirituality, and sports, it is particularly true of politics. The decline in strength for political parties and membership organizations has left an opening in the U.S. political scene. Most people no longer learn about political issues primarily from other people, either opinion leaders or party functionaries. Instead individuals now have a direct source of information in television and print news.[2]

Mass media play a critical role in setting the political agenda for most Americans, that is, deciding which political issues are significant and merit attention. Television and print media have tremendous influence on what Americans think is important. In addition to influencing which issues receive attention and action, television news programs and newspapers frame the way those issues will be treated. By identifying political problems, presenting a relatively narrow inventory of legitimate solutions, and through their portrayal of certain proposals and political actors, the media have a clear impact on the shape of public opinion[3] and, consequently, on policy as well.

Given this critical role in politics, it is important to recognize possible biases of the media, particularly of television news, the primary source of political information for most Americans. Long ago Marshall McLuhan observed that the very nature of this medium mandated certain biases. Television, he argued, was ill suited for offering perspective or depth, and it was ahistorical. The size of the screen made detail or precision impossible, and the intense nature of the medium demanded short duration of particular stories or shots, as the viewer's attention span became progressively shorter. Most obviously, television was biased to favor hype.[4] Relatively recent technological innovations, including videocassette recorders, remote control devices, and satellite and cable television, all providing increased program alternatives, intensify these inherent biases. Television today is even less equipped or disposed to show depth or detail; it must be consistently more and more visually stimulating and sensational, its messages compressed into an even shorter period of time.[5]

Beyond the medium's stylistic biases, there is also the issue of potential political biases. To an even greater extent than newspapers, television news is predisposed to emphasize institutional views of news events, particularly those of the government. The president and members of Congress have inherent news legitimacy, in addition to easily accessible offices and dramatic backdrops. Politicians manage the news by providing dramatic information and events at times and in ways appealing to television producers. By acceding to the style and timing needs of the media, a clever politician can influence the substance and perspective of the news projected to his benefit.[6] In addition to an inherent bias in favor of both political institutions and hype in general, critics have suggested there is a conservative pro-business slant as well. Television stations are owned by large corporations and are themselves business ventures oriented to making profits. To a large extent, featuring dramatic and graphic perspectives that attract viewers serves this goal. Networks may also be interested in shaping the news in such a fashion that it supports a political climate favorable to their continued profitability; this includes preempting extensive coverage of threatening ideas in nonthreatening ways.[7]

The mass media in the United States simultaneously represent both a tremendous resource and a substantial obstacle to any protest movement. This is true regardless of the movement's concerns; it is especially so for a movement focused on international and military issues. Unlike housing or medical care, for example, few Americans have any direct experience with nuclear weaponry or "the Soviet threat," nor do many have the inclination or expertise to evaluate military strategy and hardware. As a result, the media play a role even larger than usual in evaluating dissent on military and foreign policy issues. The media offer the potential to make these generally distant and abstract issues immediate and concrete. Television particularly might conceivably help issues of nuclear strategy assume a political importance equal to perhaps taxes or housing. The print media can question administration statements on the military and arms control by presenting alternative viewpoints, which may gain comparable legitimacy. Further, media outlets can report movement activities and analyses in such a way that they become legitimated and encouraged.

Alternatively, the mass media may report administration policies with deference and movement activity with hostility. Worse still for activists, media may simply ignore extra-institutional activity and criticism altogether. This last strategy is most common, unless a movement grows so big that neglect becomes impossible. As Robert Spiegelman writes, "Until social movements actually do mobilize enormous crowds, nationwide mass media ignore them." Once forced into the media's public eye, there is a wide inventory of media strategies that effectively "depoliticize, defuse, and coopt" social movements.[8]

MEDIA COVERAGE AND THE NUCLEAR FREEZE

The Reagan administration's proposed military buildup received an unprecedented degree of media scrutiny when the president presented his first budget to Congress. This drew public and media attention to the magnitude of the buildup and, to a lesser extent, to the theories underpinning it. Public scrutiny invited critical attention, and the mass media were willing to present the criticisms of established military and political figures. Effectively, this suggested a direction for dissent. The first shot in the media coverage was a five-part CBS documentary on U.S. military policy, *The Defense of the United States*. Presented in June 1981, the feature was unusually thorough by television standards. The documentary described the potential impact of a 15-megaton nuclear warhead detonating on Omaha, Nebraska. The horrific consequences were described in graphic detail by long-time antinuclear activist Dr. Jack Geiger in a manner that would be replicated by PSR speakers across the country.

The documentary effectively put defense politics and military spending on the political agenda for many Americans. Unlike most public affairs programming, the series was produced and scheduled to draw as large an audience as possible. Hosted by CBS lead anchorman Dan Rather, it was run on five consecutive evenings during prime time viewing hours and had good production values. The series was also uncharacteristically critical. CBS examined many of the premises at the roots of the Reagan defense plan and found them dubious. This was a tremendous change from the coverage that had characterized Presidents Ford and Carter's efforts to increase military capabilities and budgets. The documentary openly questioned the Reagan buildup and the administration's loose rhetoric about limited and winnable nuclear wars.[9] Rather concluded the series with these comments: "The nation is about to commit itself to the biggest defense spending buildup in our history. . . . Yet, for a commitment of this magnitude, we have heard little debate about alternatives."

This sort of criticism from a television network was unprecedented. As Thomas Powers wrote, "CBS made two essentially political decisions before commencing *The Defense of the United States,* neither of them a big deal for a writer speaking to a small audience, but acts of independence for a broadcasting network. The first was to dwell on the consequences of nuclear war, the cost in human terms — not to touch on it in passing but to make it the point. . . . The second decision was to treat the Soviet Union as a great power like any other, not the source, but the other *half* of this great conflict."[10] The documentary and its unusual approach encouraged and legitimized what nuclear freeze activists had been trying to do for more than a year, and in five hours reached a substantially broader spectrum and greater number of people than the fledgling movement could have hoped to approach.

At that point antinuclear activism was still largely ignored by national media. Dramatic instances of antinuclear civil disobedience had periodically drawn some national coverage, especially when they prominently featured the arrest[11] of well-known figures such as author Grace Paley,[12] Daniel Ellsberg,[13] or the Berrigan brothers.[14] The stories, however, always lacked any hint of a political context. They were treated as the quirky pursuits of semicelebrities and rarely given prominent placement or in-depth treatment. Reports on the protests were never connected with even the most superficial discussion of the politics they were directed against; in the news, the actions were depoliticized.

By the end of Carter's presidency, freeze organizers had already begun grassroots campaigns and had successfully made use of local newspaper coverage. Conferences, educational events, petition campaigns, and symbolic demonstrations were all reported by local media outlets, and this fed the early growth of the movement. The decision to use local media was both ideological and pragmatic. Many activists argued that such a regional approach was inherently more democratic than appealing directly to national media outlets.[15]

Activists also recognized that opposition to U.S. military policy was paradoxically more attractive news to local outlets than to national media. Papers and reporters accustomed to dealing with such issues as school bonds and zoning laws were apparently grateful for the opportunity local activism provided to write about national issues. Freeze activists were cognizant of this and targeted their actions accordingly, even when it came to international tours. Activists made certain they expanded any itinerary beyond big cities so that it would include media markets in which their activities would be sure to qualify as news. An example of the success of this strategy, a two-week tour of European activists, sponsored by the AFSC and CALC, generated more than 1,000 press clippings, almost all of them in local papers.[16] Especially at the outset, organization and leadership were extremely decentralized, and this aided in gaining local coverage. Town newspapers could interview and write about the people who were making important decisions about movement activity.

MAKING THE NATIONAL NEWS

The downside of the emphasis on local organization and leadership was that it made getting national media attention more difficult. Absent easily identifiable leaders, established offices, and a consistent public relations effort, the national nature of antinuclear activity was easily ignored by mainstream media, which gave sporadic attention only to the most dramatic of local actions. The early days of the freeze movement were thus both unencouraged and unencumbered by national media attention. This allowed local

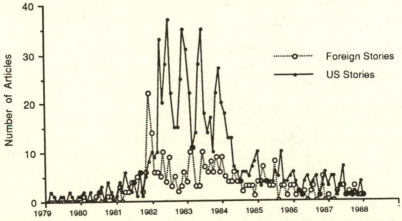

FIGURE 2 — Periodical Coverage of Nuclear Weapons Protest, 1979–1988 (*Source:* Reader's Guide to Periodical Literature.)

activists and a few national political figures to have the most influence in defining the movement and its goals. National media began to cover antinuclear sentiment and the freeze movement only when the issue was forced on the front pages by West European disarmament movements.

In November 1981 news of large demonstrations in many Western European capitals found its way to front pages in the United States, clearly preceding any media recognition of comparable activism at home. The European antinuclear movements demonstrated rifts in the mainstream consensus on nuclear issues, and this animated and energized the emerging U.S. movement.[17] The emergence of the European movement penetrated not only the conscience of the general public but also that of U.S. journalists. The European movements provoked journalists and the mass media to look for something comparable in the United States. The demonstrations also drew attention to nuclear issues and encouraged activists working in the United States.

The number of stories on the antinuclear movement can be found in the indexes of national media outlets, in this case, *The Reader's Guide to Periodical Literature,* New York *Times,* and *CBS News.*[18] This approach also provides a gauge for the degree to which the movement had entered the scope of mainstream politics and had thus won media attention. Before looking at general trends, it is interesting to note the differences between the three sources. *The Reader's Guide,* representing a large number of diverse publications, began coverage of the antinuclear movement earliest and showed the least dramatic peaks of the three. One peak is during the summer of 1982, when the movement's largest demonstration took place in New York City. The second smaller peak in magazine coverage occurs in November and December of the same year, when the freeze passed in several state and local referenda, followed by another surge in coverage in the spring of 1983, when the freeze was debated in Congress. The New York *Times* shows the same peaks, with a more dramatic increase in coverage for the June 12 demonstration, exaggerated by the number of local stories on the demonstration. Movement news, in this case, included stories detailing garbage clean-up and police coverage for the demonstration, for example, surely not critical to the movement's development. *CBS News* was last to cover the movement, and its index shows peaks similar to the other sources, although its most dramatic expansion of coverage reflects a television event, ABC's screening of the television movie *The Day After* in November 1983. Print media were apparently less interested in the program than a competing network.

From the data a picture of how the story percolated up to national attention emerges. From 1979 through most of 1980, there was a

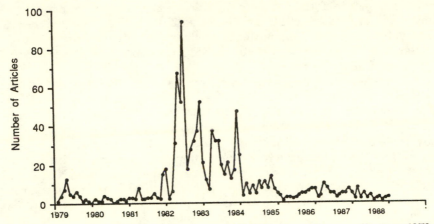

FIGURE 3 — New York *Times* Coverage of U.S. Nuclear Weapons Protest, 1979–1988 (*Source:* New York Times Index.)

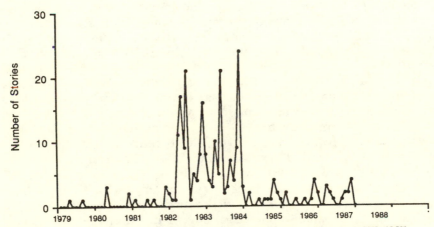

FIGURE 4 — *CBS News* Coverage of U.S. Nuclear Weapons Protest, 1979–1987 (*Source:* CBS News Index.)

consistent and rather small number of stories in magazines and newspapers indexed under "Antinuclear Movement." Closer inspection shows that the vast majority dealt with protests against nuclear power in the United States. In December of 1980 most of the stories so indexed deal with movements in other countries, generally Western Europe and Japan. This continued throughout 1981, as one-half to three-quarters of the magazine articles on the antinuclear movement deal with activities and protests in other countries.

National media found it astonishingly easy to ignore what was happening at home. As late as March 1982, when 300 activists met in Georgetown for the first national nuclear freeze campaign strategy conference, the growing nuclear freeze movement drew absolutely no attention from national media.

Coverage of antinuclear weapons protest really commenced in the fall of 1981 with reports on the Western European movements. The fall demonstrations were colorful and dramatic, as many demonstrators deliberately played to the media with outlandish costumes and signs and slogans in English. Foreign correspondents from the United States wrote about them, often comparing them to the 1960s antiwar demonstrations in the United States. In November 1981, the European antinuclear movement was the subject of a cover story in *Time* magazine; there was no mention of comparable activity in the United States.

The first event in the United States to receive much national media attention was the UCS Veteran's Day Convocation, also in November of 1981. In contrast to coverage of the European demonstrations, however, reports emphasized the moderate nature of the event; the New York *Times* explicitly contrasted the mood and rhetoric of the convocation events with the more confrontational style of 1960s-style protests, stressing the activists' attempts to reach "middle Americans."[19] The media highlighted the participation of stars of a sort: Carl Sagan, Jerry Brown, Gary Hart, and Paul Warnke. Unlike their presentation of events in Western Europe, national media portrayed antinuclear concerns in the United States as exceedingly wholesome, mainstream, and safe. There was no mention of the nuclear freeze or even much suggestion that the event, attended by an estimated 100,000 students, had anything to do with political opposition to the Reagan military program.

The traditional left press in the United States, consisting of left and liberal magazines with general circulation, such as *The Nation, The Progressive,* and *Mother Jones,* was not much quicker to catch the story. Even small-circulation movement publications, such as WRL's *WIN* or the New England AFSC's *Peacework* directed little attention to the freeze movement's early development; they focused instead on other issues, including opposition to nuclear power and the draft.[20] While civil disobedience actions and campaigns against particular weapons systems received broader coverage in these outlets than in the mainstream press, the freeze movement escaped attention at these early stages. It was not until March 1982, when New England town meetings began endorsing the freeze resolution, that either the left or the mainstream press was virtually forced to take notice of the movement. The *Times* then reported the opening of the Nuclear Weapons Freeze Clearinghouse in St. Louis, which had taken place two months earlier. It was May before *The*

Nation published any real treatment of the movement and September/October before *Mother Jones* devoted a special issue to the disarmament movement.

The town meeting endorsements, followed shortly by the introduction of the freeze resolution into Congress, allowed the freeze to break through national media's neglect. The number of magazine and newspaper articles increased dramatically, and national television news took notice for the first time. On its nightly news broadcast in March and April of 1982, CBS ran a total of 28 stories on antiweapons protest in the United States; it ran 17 stories in the previous 38 months. Magazines and newspapers increased their coverage of the movement and of the Reagan program correspondingly.[21] Mainstream media acknowledged that widespread dissatisfaction with the Reagan military program was percolating up through the political system.[22] Left media realized at the same time that the nuclear freeze movement was the most viable vehicle for this dissatisfaction, partly because mainstream media recognized it as such.

Throughout the spring and summer of 1982, media coverage of the freeze continued at a high level, as networks and newspapers competed for fresh perspectives and distinctive angles on this emerging story. The active participation of large segments of institutionalized religion helped a great deal. In addition to giving the movement a large share of legitimacy, it also gave the news stories an element of drama. Further, it gave the media an identifiable "beat" with which to identify the movement. The Catholic bishops' pastoral, for example, probably seemed far less important to national affairs editors and reporters than to those covering religion. The latter group was also more likely to give antinuclear clergy sympathetic treatment and to push managing editors for prominent placement of their stories. The pastoral drew 32 New York *Times* stories between October 1982 and May 1983 when it was released, nine of them on the front page, as well as 13 other stories about Catholics and the antinuclear movement.[23]

The level of coverage magnified the movement's strength. Christopher Paine, an early freeze activist with the Federation of American Scientists, described the media's new interest in the movement as an example of the "hula hoop syndrome," or a faddishness in media coverage. "The intense coverage we got in the period from February 1982 to April of 1983 was just way out of proportion to our actual strength at that time."[24] Molander and Ground Zero, for example, were featured prominently in early coverage, although Molander was not involved in the freeze and Ground Zero was a very small organization. The new and unexpected wave of attention given antinuclear sentiments and the freeze movement in 1982 was a mixed blessing for the movement. While it did make recruiting activists, gaining support from politicians, and fundraising easier, it also generated heightened expectations, expectations many activists believed were premature and beyond the movement's capacity to meet.

Randy Kehler, then national coordinator of the freeze, recognized this while it was happening and wondered if the movement was ready for the accelerating political demands of a political and media campaign at the national level. At the same time he realized that, aided by the media, events had begun to move beyond the control of the organizers. "I feel like I'm on a comet," he told reporters in March 1982, "but I don't know whether I'm leading it or on its tail."[25] National attention and the Congressional resolution came well before activists originally intended, but there was little the freeze leaders could do about either. Just as the campaign accelerated beyond their expectations and capabilities, so too did media image making. In 1982, the public image of the nuclear freeze was increasingly defined by national media rather than by those in the campaign. The activist initiators rode the coattails of media and political celebrities as well as they could.

IMAGES OF THE FREEZE

The media selected spokespeople who reinforced whatever image of the nuclear freeze they wished to project. The most frequently quoted were Senator Edward Kennedy and Representative Ed Markey, both Democrats from Massachusetts. They were relatively late arrivals to the nuclear freeze, however, and could be considered strong supporters only in a Congressional context. Outside Congress, Roger Molander of Ground Zero and Helen Caldicott were most frequently quoted.[26] *Time* magazine featured Molander and Caldicott prominently in its coverage of the freeze, terming them as the two who best typify the protestors' concerns and labeling Molander as "the single most visible (and thoughtful) leader in the nebulous movement" although Molander was candid about his opposition to the proposal.[27] *Newsweek* featured a roundtable discussion on the freeze proposal, featuring one supporter, Paul Warnke, and four opponents: Molander, Gary Hart, Richard Perle, and Edward Luttwak. Said Luttwak, "This colossally insane proposal . . . is the politics of unilateral surrender masquerading as responsible leadership."[28] Freeze supporters were given short shrift whenever the actual proposal, rather than the movement, was discussed.

Forsberg and Kehler were rarely quoted by television news or the press. Nor was the freeze proposal often described, much less explained or substantively evaluated. The first widely available discussion of what a freeze might actually entail did not appear until November 1982, when *Scientific American* published an analysis and explanation by Forsberg.[29] The drama of the movement, in contrast, received sensationalistic coverage for a time. Helen Caldicott was a freeze supporter and certainly among the most powerful speakers on its behalf, but her analysis and rhetoric were almost antipolitical. This, in addition to her charisma, was apparently attractive to the media. Of several dozen speakers at the June 12, 1982, rally in New York City, both CBS and the New York *Times* chose the same Caldicott quote to anchor their reports. "We're thinking of our babies. There are no Communist babies; there are no capitalist babies. A baby is a baby is a baby."[30] While this is undoubtedly true, it gave the viewer or reader little sense of the analysis of the freeze movement's goals or analysis. Similarly, *Newsweek*'s first story on the freeze led with the drama of a disabled Vietnam veteran collecting signatures for a freeze petition despite severe hip pain.[31]

Perhaps this should not be surprising as mass media are certainly more interested in, and adept at, covering events or personalities than issues of any kind. Movements must recognize this and adapt accordingly in order to get coverage, although they can be undone by the compromises made for mass attention. Activists may find themselves modifying their rhetoric or political tactics and depending on media-approved spokespeople far more than they would want. Over time, however, moderation and celebrities make the movement less newsworthy, as the media grow tired of familiar angles and approaches. Elite supporters may reward moderation and "responsibility," but media coverage prizes overstatement and confrontation. As movements try harder and harder to gain any media recognition, these efforts may undermine organizational maintenance and efficacy.[32] As Todd Gitlin points out in his analysis of media and the New Left, media have an insatiable appetite for escalation and new news. "Where a picket line might have been news in 1965, it took tear gas and bloodied heads to make headlines in 1968. If the last demonstration was counted at 100,000, the next would have to number 200,000; otherwise it would be downplayed or framed as a sign of the movement's waning."[33]

Gitlin's observations hold true for the freeze. Movement events received extensive coverage in 1982 and 1983, but they were rarely presented as part of a larger whole, much less in a political context that considered the relationship of antinuclear forces to U.S. politics and policy. Movement events were often determined by media interest rather than by concerns about building public support or advancing clear political analysis. Even a successful media event, then, may have little impact on the movement's long-range goals. For example, before the freeze became a media delight, activists began planning the movement's first national demonstration. The June 12, 1982, demonstration gained tremendous media attention, not only in New York, but nationally. The message emerging from it, however, although sent by some one million people, was far from clear. What was originally conceived as a building block in the campaign's development was portrayed as a show of strength and, subsequently, as the movement's zenith. Stories stressed that the freeze did not know what it would do next, even though the campaign was still in the early stages of a multi-year plan. The media's "unmodulated celebration of the rally's size and 'good behavior'," wrote one critic, "smothered and obliterated the urgency and terror that had brought so many together."[34] The substance of the speeches, and even the slogans, was rarely reported.

Almost as if to stress that the freeze was neither radical nor threatening, coverage in *The Times* and on CBS News stressed that most of the marchers were white and middle class and that all of them were peaceful and well-behaved. The movement was further divorced from its own self-definition by coverage portraying it not as a disarmament movement but as a campaign for the United States to return to previous arms control and security policies. As *The Times* editorialized before the demonstration, "The freeze movement members are not lobbying for a specific piece of legislation. They are people, ordinary citizens pressing for something much less intricate. They want to put nuclear restraint back on track, to give diplomacy and peace a chance."[35] Freeze activists were in fact increasingly focusing their efforts on passing a particular piece of legislation, and their goals were somewhat more ambitious. Contrasts with the demonstrations of the 1960s were also plentiful, as if to emphasize that the freeze would not cause the social discomfort of movements past. The nuclear freeze could then become as American as Mom and apple pie, and just as appealing — but not very threatening or even urgent.

The media anointed the nuclear freeze as a relatively wholesome fad that was hardly political. Bruce Morton, in his commentary on *CBS Nightly News* just before the June 12 demonstration, pronounced the movement a radical chic affair, counting off a facetious checklist. "Do famous people talk to famous talk show hosts about it?" he asked, while the screen showed that they did. "Do famous people sing for the movement? . . . Does the movement have rock stars? . . . And the toughest test of all, does it have Pete Seeger? There hasn't been a cause since the Great Depression that got anywhere without Pete Seeger."[36] The camera shifted to the folksinger as strains of banjo music played in the background, almost as if to say that the upcoming demonstration would be good wholesome fun.

Somewhat intimidated by the success of the June 12 demonstration, and by the intensity of political conflicts glossed over by both activists and the media, activists were reluctant to call for another national demonstration. Although activities proceeded apace both locally and in Washington, D.C., all that followed was far less dramatic than the New York demonstration. Media coverage leveled off and began to fade. Good wholesome fun soon becomes tedious to report, and the media focused on the especially dramatic or quirky aspects of antinuclear activity. Thus, the Berrigan brothers and their Plowshares action received publicity over a period of years as the trial and appeals wound through the legal system while the success of nuclear freeze resolutions nationally in November 1982 received only one story from the New York *Times* and CBS.[37] Such things as the development of peace studies curricula, the creation of oppositional think tanks and alternative military policy discussion groups, the growth of antinuclear and arms control PACs, or the efforts of freeze activists at political conventions were seen as even less newsworthy.

Editorial judgments are only sometimes aligned with the potential political impact of a story or even the number of people involved. There was always room for a headline like "Andre the Seal Swims for Peace." *The Times* devoted more extensive coverage to an antinuclear protestor's 39-day fast and the shadows painted on Wall Street to simulate the results of nuclear vaporization than to 25,000 people demonstrating in the streets of Chicago. This was even more true of television news, which looked for stories that would be visually dramatic, such as a man climbing 26 stories of a 45-story building to hang a nuclear freeze poster, or the arrest of a civil disobedient married to the Minneapolis chief of police. In almost all cases, the political dimensions of the story were subordinate to human interest or personality issues, such as the deteriorating health of the antinuclear faster, how one actually climbs a skyscraper, or who made the chief's dinner when his wife was in jail.

The focus on novelty and personality was demonstrated with haunting clarity when Norman Mayer, a man overwhelmed by his concern about nuclear war, parked a van he said was filled with explosives next to the Washington Monument. He wanted to hold the monument hostage in order to force a nationwide debate on nuclear weapons policy. After a few hours police killed Mayer when he tried to drive away in the empty van. His action, however, received national publicity for weeks following. The ensuing stories did not, as he presumably would have wished, deal with his concern but with his pathology.

Mayer's action aside, after national media first discovered the freeze, most news on antinuclear concerns or the antinuclear movement was focused on privileged groups or individuals far outside the movement's organizations or direct concerns. Jonathan Schell's ruminations on life in a nuclear world, originally published in *The New Yorker,* drew a great deal of attention when published in book form as *The Fate of the Earth.*[38] Despite Schell's call to "reinvent politics," however, there was little in the way of political analysis in his book. Similarly, an ABC produced drama dealing with the effects of a nuclear war on Lawrence, Kansas, generated tremendous attention in the media and among the general public. *The Day After,* aired November 20, 1983, drew an estimated audience of more than 100 million people, with 46 percent of all television households watching.[39] There was controversy surrounding the airing of the film, as some conservative forces argued that allowing the possibility of a nuclear attack on Lawrence distorted the fact that nuclear deterrence worked. They feared that a dramatization of the horrors of nuclear war would support the efforts of freeze advocates. In newspaper and television reports, those who supported airing the program were termed "pro-freeze," regardless of their attitudes toward arms control or the movement.[40] Mass media now defined the term "nuclear freeze" more vaguely; it came to mean simply concern about the dangers of nuclear war.

The movie itself lacked both a political context and dramatic intensity, no mean feat given the subject. Nonetheless, it is likely that depictions of people being vaporized grabbed the attention of many viewers. Immediately following the television movie, ABC ran a discussion program hosted by Ted Koppel, who welcomed the audience by telling them not to worry, Lawrence remained. The program featured a videotape of Secretary of State George Shultz explaining that the Reagan administration was continuing to work to avert nuclear war. His comments were followed by a panel discussion, featuring Henry Kissinger, Robert McNamara, Carl Sagan, and author Elie Wiesel.

The panel was notable in having no one representing the freeze proposal, then polling more than 75 percent popular support nationally. Although Sagan supported the freeze, Koppel as moderator confined the scientist's comments predominantly to the issue of nuclear winter. The panelists discussed the movie and nuclear issues as though there were not a mass movement underway. The nuclear freeze proposal was introduced by a question from the floor some 45 minutes into the program. In response, both McNamara and Kissinger explained why it was not a good idea. Antinuclear activists who complained to ABC were told that their humanitarian views were represented by Wiesel, who candidly admitted during the program that he knew little of the details or even broad outlines of nuclear strategy.

The Day After dramatically demonstrated what had happened to the freeze movement in mass media. Widespread concern about nuclear war and nuclear armaments were acknowledged as legitimate, appropriated by mainstream politics, as demonstrated by Shultz, Kissinger, and McNamara. Coverage of nuclear weapons and arms control issues increasingly focused on such official sources. The freeze proposal was not granted similar legitimacy. The media consulted "experts" not convinced by the freeze proposal, and this influenced editorial treatments of the freeze as an arms control proposal and of the movement. Extra-institutional protest, debilitating fear, or opposition beyond the boundaries of the two political parties was not necessary, nor even desirable, mainstream media implied; the government could protect national interests.

The discussion after *The Day After* was not anomalous. Indeed, it reflected an approach common within mainstream media. The number of stories about the antinuclear movement continued at a relatively high level, but increasingly they were dominated by mainstream political figures who had no interest in the nuclear freeze as originally defined. As left journals tried to move beyond the freeze in 1983 and 1984, linking concern about nuclear armaments to campaigns against war in Central America and the Middle East, mainstream media treated the freeze as a symbolic demonstration of nuclear fear unconnected with any other political issues, even those dealing with the specifics of nuclear armaments.[41]

The approach of the mass media, effectively to depoliticize the freeze proposal and thereby trivialize the then acceptable freeze movement, had the effect of exacerbating developing rifts within the movement. On one side, many of the organizations initially supporting the freeze attempted to move beyond the proposal and make use of the political support it had gained by linking it to other issues. The freeze organization had, however, effectively deserted them, choosing to make support for the freeze proposal a litmus test, unconnected with other political issues that might temper its strength. Meanwhile, the media had legitimated and appropriated the nuclear fear underlying much freeze support and had translated it into a humanitarian concern that had little to do with policy. This concern was expressed as so moderate and apolitical that it could continue to demonstrate very high levels of support in public opinion polls without having any effect on politics or policy.

NOTES

1. Michael Lipsky, *Protest in City Politics: Rent Strikes, Housing, and the Power of the Poor,* Chicago: Rand-McNally, 1970, pp. 169–72.

2. Thomas Byrne Edsall, *The New Politics of Inequality,* New York: Norton, 1984, pp. 34, 105–6.

3. Todd Gitlin, *The Whole World Is Watching: Mass Media in the Making and Unmaking of the New Left,* Berkeley: University of California Press, 1980, pp. 6–7; Shanto Iyengar, Mark D. Peters, and Donald Kinder, "Experimental Demonstrations of the 'Not-So-Minimal' Consequences of Television News Programs," *American Political Science Review,* December 1982, pp. 848–58; J. M. McCleod, L. B. Becker, and J. F. Byrne, "The Political Consequences of Agenda Setting," *Mass Communications Review,* Spring 1976, pp. 8–15; D. L. Shaw and M. E. McCombs, eds., *The Emergence of American Political Issues,* New York: West Publishing, 1977.

4. Marshall McLuhan, *Understanding Media,* New York: Signet, 1964, pp. 268–94.

5. Gitlin suggests that newspapers are not much better, *Whole World,* p. 301.

6. Harvey G. Zeidenstein, "New Media Perceptions of White House News Management," *Presidential Studies Quarterly,* Summer 1984.

7. Gitlin, *Whole World,* p. 10; Michael Parenti, *Inventing Reality,* New York: St. Martin's, 1986.

8. Robert Spiegleman, "Media Manipulation of the Movement," *Social Policy,* Summer 1982, p. 10. See also Jo Freeman, *The Politics of Women's Liberation: A Case Study of an Emerging Social Movement and Its Relation to the Policy Process,* New York: David McKay, 1975, pp. 111–14. Freeman contends that media coverage trivialized the women's liberation movement, ignoring substantive demands and focusing instead on "bra stories." Gitlin discusses the devices used by media to defuse movements, *Whole World,* pp. 27–28.

9. Alexander Cockburn and James Ridgeway, "The Freeze Movement versus Ronald Reagan," *The New Left Review* 137 (January/February 1983): 7; Thomas B. Elliot et al., "What Are the Implications for U.S. Defense Policy of Growing Nuclear Dissent in the United States?" The Naval War College National Defense University Strategic Study, April 1983; Francis C. Brown III, "Media Coverage of the American Nuclear Freeze and Antinuclear Movement," unpublished thesis, Woodrow Wilson School of Public and International Affairs, Princeton University, pp. 82–83.

10. Thomas Powers, "Sticking to the Grim Point," *The Nation,* July 25–August 1, 1981, p. 86.

11. "Arrests," Gitlin notes "allow non-celebrities to become newsmakers," *Whole World,* p. 42.

12. New York *Times,* February 2, 1979, p. 25, and subsequent stories on February 12, 13, and 22.

13. New York *Times,* April 30, 1979, Section 4, p. 8.

14. New York *Times,* September 10, 1980, p. 16.

15. Also see William Appleman Williams, "Letter," *The Nation,* February 14, 1981.

16. Howard Smith, "Disarming Europeans," *The Village Voice,* April 27, 1982.

17. Brown, "Media Coverage," p. 28; Ronald Dellums et al., eds., *Defense Sense: The Search for a Rational Military Policy,* Cambridge, MA: Ballinger, 1983, p. 270; Michael Kazin, "How the Freeze Campaign Was Born," *The Nation,* May 1, 1982, p. 523. Frank Riessman, "The Antinuclear Movement: Why Now?" *Social Policy,* Summer 1982, p. 3; William Sweet, "Europe's Peace Movement: Topic or Target," *Columbia Journalism Review,* September/October 1983, p. 46.

18. On methodological issues, see Jorg Becker, "Methodological Problems of Dealing with Disarmament in the Press," *Current Research on Peace and Violence* 6 (1983): 29–52; Gitlin, *Whole World,* pp. 293–305; Doug McAdam, *Political Process and the Development of Black Insurgency,* Chicago: University of Chicago Press, p. 267.

19. Brown, "Media Coverage," pp. 94–96.

20. *WIN* indexed only nine articles on nuclear weapons during 1981 — one critical of the freeze proposal in contrast with more than 37 articles in 1983 (indexes published December 15, 1981, and December 15, 1983).

21. The Boston *Globe,* for example, published a special magazine supplement dealing with both the antinuclear movement and the policies that appeared to have

inspired it, "War and Peace in the Nuclear Age," October 17, 1982.

22. Antinuclear issues even received increased attention in contemporary humor, as *The National Lampoon's* parody of *Newsweek* featured a cover story on the opposition of fashion models to U.S. nuclear policy, entitled "Nuclear Arms and Terrific Legs," Fall 1982.

23. Brown, "Media Coverage," p. 129.

24. Quoted in ibid., p. 106.

25. Judith Miller, "Effort to Freeze Nuclear Arsenals Spreads in U.S.," New York *Times,* March 15, 1982.

26. Brown, "Media Coverage," p. 74.

27. Quoted in Spiegleman, "Media Manipulation," p. 10.

28. *Newsweek,* "A Complex of Tricky Issues," April 26, 1982.

29. Randall Forsberg, "A Bilateral Nuclear Weapons Freeze," *Scientific American,* November 1982, p. 2.

30. Brown, "Media Coverage," p. 123.

31. *Newsweek,* "A Matter of Life and Death," April 26, 1982, pp. 20–26.

32. Lipsky, *Protest in City Politics,* p. 171.

33. Gitlin, *Whole World,* p. 182.

34. Spiegleman, "Media Manipulation," p. 10.

35. New York *Times,* "Ferocious Mr. Reagan and the Freeze," March 16, 1982.

36. *CBS Nightly News,* June 8, 1982.

37. Brown, "Media Coverage," p. 90.

38. Jonathan Schell, *The Fate of the Earth,* New York: Alfred A. Knopf, 1982.

39. In the spring of 1982 an episode of a television drama dealing with the potential for nuclear war in a fictional Middle-Eastern country drew comparable controversy although a much smaller audience. See Todd Gitlin, "The Screening of Lou Grant," *The Nation,* June 26, 1982, p. 775.

40. Brown, "Media Coverage," pp. 133–35.

41. A notable exception is *The National Catholic Reporter,* which continued to report extensively on the antinuclear movement in 1983 and 1984, consistently tying antinuclear concern to political action.

8

THE ROOTS OF A NUCLEAR DISARMAMENT MOVEMENT

The nuclear freeze movement was built on the political foundations of previous disarmament movements. Although small groups have been engaged in antinuclear activism consistently, their efforts have generally been marginalized. Twice previously in the postwar period, however, antinuclear activism emerged in large-scale protest movements. In both cases, new information or political mismanagement altered the political landscape on nuclear issues, and dissident organizations were successful in overcoming their internal problems to force partial redress of their grievances. New organizations were created that worked in concert with older established groups. Government responses, the Limited Test Ban (LTB) treaty of 1963 and the ABM and SALT treaties of 1972, while modest compared to movement demands, were sufficient to recapture domination of political space and defuse the antinuclear triggers. Also in both cases, the movements left behind a set of resources that would prove instrumental in the development of subsequent protest movements: a network of organizations, a core of experienced political activists, a communications network linking those organizations and individuals, and a history and inventory of mobilization strategies.[1]

Throughout the 1970s these organizations worked, often independently, to oppose various aspects of U.S. nuclear and military policy and to bring attention to a variety of other political issues. They remained separated, however, by differences on both goals and tactics; the potential peace movement coalition ranged from absolute pacifist organizations to others concerned with more efficient and cost effective means of organizing U.S. military posture. These groups roughly split into two factions, which generally had little contact with each other and no clear common goals. As a result, neither faction was able to present a cohesive political challenge to government policy. One broad faction, comprising pacifist and left groups offering a comprehensive critique of the basic tenets of U.S. military policy, was generally marginalized, receiving little attention or credence from governmental institutions, the media, or most people. Another set of organizations pursued more modest goals, seeking solutions to the dangers of the arms race through arms control and international law. Their proximate goals usually included support for a provision in a particular treaty or opposition to a specific weapons system. This "liberal internationalist" wing found a means of coexistence within the world of Washington lobbyists, establishing alliances, aiding candidates, and occasionally influencing the content of legislation.[2]

Although usually divided, together both wings of the peace movement represented an extensive network, which would support the nuclear freeze movement's rapid growth. United through common efforts, this network had the potential to produce a movement broader and more powerful than any previous effort. Given the diverse interests represented by the component groups, however, finding a common program to unify and mobilize these networks was extremely difficult. Activists made a number of attempts, including the campaign against the B-1 bomber, the formation of Mobilization for Survival, and the efforts against the Rocky Flats nuclear plant in Colorado. Each campaign had its own successes and limits, but all served to lay a groundwork of cooperation that made the freeze possible.

ANTINUCLEAR HISTORY: THE TEST BAN CAMPAIGN

The history of peace movements in the United States is older than the country itself and includes draft resistance from traditional peace churches, abolitionist movements, anticonscription riots during the Civil War, and socialist and union activity at the outset of the twentieth century.[3] Tactics included public education and moral suasion, sit-down strikes, tax resistance, and electoral activity. Two distinct strains unite this broad collection of political concern: deep cynicism about the state as an agent of policy, particularly concerning violence and war, and the imperative of individuals and communities to challenge the state's claim to define public morality.

The advent of the nuclear age drastically changed the context surrounding these movements, heightening both the scope and intensity of the threat of war and distancing individuals even further from the policy-making process. Peace movements, however, maintained essentially the same set of organizations and constituencies: middle-class sympathizers of the peace churches and the political left. Like other dissident groups, the early antinuclear movements had mostly volunteer leadership and always inadequate funding and staffing. For the most part they remained on the margins of U.S. politics, exercising little influence on either policy or mainstream political debate.[4] Although Hiroshima and Nagasaki had demonstrated the truly awesome potential of nuclear weapons, widespread public fear did not make antinuclear activism a high priority issue for most Americans. Politicians helped keep the public scared more of the Soviet Union and communism than of the nuclear menace. They were greatly aided in this effort by the Soviet Union. By stressing the potential benefits of the "peaceful atom," politicians in the 1950s were also able to legitimate expanded research and development of nuclear technologies.

Antinuclear sentiment developed into antinuclear movements only when a generalized fear of nuclear weaponry was provoked by more immediate manifestations of the arms race. In the 1950s and early 1960s, these were nuclear testing and civil defense planning. The civil defense shelter in the backyard, nuclear attack drills in public schools, and radioactive fallout from nuclear tests all served to give a generalized fear of nuclear war concrete targets. This expanded the potential constituency available for political mobilization and increased the likelihood and intensity of participation. By 1959, fully 77 percent of Americans favored a moratorium on nuclear testing.[5]

The Test Ban movement grew in the early 1960s, spurred by increased testing, technological advances in weaponry, and, perhaps most significantly, the political momentum given the arms race by the Kennedy administration. Fear of nuclear war and opposition to nuclear testing increased throughout the late 1950s and early 1960s and began seeping into popular culture, as demonstrated by the popularity of novels and movies dealing with the end of the world, including *Fail Safe, On the Beach,* and *Cat's Cradle.*[6] In the Test Ban campaign, as in subsequent antinuclear movements, political concern and fear was most prevalent among the well-educated middle classes and liberals generally.[7]

As concern about nuclear issues spread, an increasing number of organizations began organizing around these issues. Long-established peace groups, like the American Friends Services Committee (AFSC), the Fellowship for Reconciliation (FOR), the War Resister's League (WRL), and the Women's International League for Peace and Freedom (WILPF), had long included nuclear issues in their work. These groups called for unilateral disarmament and linked their antinuclear efforts to other foreign policy issues and questions of social justice.[8] In the 1950s McCarthyism effectively pushed such groups onto the political margins, and even after the worst of the red scare had passed, they were unable to reach deeply into the mainstream for support. Antinuclear concern was also represented by the Federation of American Scientists (FAS), which had been formed in 1946 by scientists involved in developing the first atomic bomb.[9] As fears of nuclear fallout increased, antinuclear concern soon grew beyond the boundaries of these groups, and new organizations grew up to articulate it.

The Committee for a Sane Nuclear Policy (SANE) was founded in 1957, in an attempt by Norman Cousins (editor of the *Saturday Evening Post*) and Clarence Pickett (AFSC) to broaden the base of the antinuclear movement. Instead of unilateral actions, SANE advocated a worldwide comprehensive Nuclear Test Ban. By the end of the decade, physicians who supported the Test Ban began publicizing the potential consequences of nuclear war through articles and speeches. They powerfully dramatized the deleterious effects of nuclear testing by demonstrating the presence of Strontium-90 in the baby teeth of children growing up near radioactive fallout. This group grew into Physicians for Social Responsibility (PSR) in 1960, and although small in number, it had a powerful impact on the Test Ban campaign. The following year physicist Leo Szilard started the Council for a Livable World (CLW), which also attempted to broaden the appeal of the movement. Women Strike for Peace was also founded at this time, and by organizing more than 100,000 women to demonstrate in 60 cities for the Test Ban, it escalated the tactics of the movement as a whole.[10]

This pattern of organizational and tactical proliferation, repeated in both the anti-ABM campaign of the late 1960s and the nuclear freeze movement, helped the Test Ban movement. Under the umbrella of a campaign to stop nuclear testing was a wide variety of activity, offering potential activists a broad array of choices for political participation. In addition to enhancing mobilization, this coalition approach also increased the movement's visibility, allowing it to penetrate into many different aspects of U.S. political culture. This style of organization was also a political necessity. The red scares of the 1950s had tainted a number of the older groups for many Americans. Established organizations are also bound to varying extents to a particular agenda and style of operation. They are frequently unable to shift tactics and emphases quickly enough to take advantage of new political opportunities. New groups, without political history and often with far more moderate goals and analyses, could develop new approaches and escape popular prejudices.

SANE, for example, "relied on its access to Washington power wielders and its ability to influence the educated middle class through the prestige of its sponsors."[11] This approach, dependent upon elite approval and support, made it extremely sensitive to charges of communist infiltration. In response to such allegations,

SANE purged itself of elements its leadership deemed undesirable. In McCarthyesque fashion Cousins asked staff members about previous allegiance to the Communist Party, firing those who gave the wrong answer or no answer at all. The purge split SANE, but in the short term mobilization increased. The national office of SANE, now apparently responsible and respectable, continued to mobilize elite support and maintained access to policy makers. Many SANE chapters, however, especially those on college campuses, were frustrated by this tactical and ideological timidity and broke with the national organization. Freed from the limits of the national office, grassroots activism increased and diversified.[12]

The Test Ban movement was defused and dissipated by a variety of factors. Chief among these was the LTB treaty, signed by President Kennedy, Soviet Premier Khrushchev, and British Prime Minister Macmillan on September 24, 1963. The antinuclear campaigns of the 1960s and their influence on both public opinion and political discourse had been instrumental in building support for the treaty and its ratification. Although a comprehensive test ban had been a "least common denominator" strategy to unite a diverse coalition, the LTB agreement fell substantially short of even these limited goals; the total number of tests conducted by both superpowers immediately increased. Nonetheless, by ending atmospheric testing, the LTB removed the most visible and unpopular aspect of U.S. nuclear policy. The end of atmospheric fallout significantly cut political fallout domestically as well.[13] The Cuban missile crisis, which shortly preceded progress in the test ban negotiations, also probably had a demobilizing effect. Perhaps Kennedy's forceful and confident public handling of the affair impressed the U.S. public with his ability to manage these critical issues effectively. Alternatively, perhaps the crisis increased popular distrust of the Soviet Union to the extent that more comprehensive bilateral treaties were no longer viable concerns for mass mobilization. Perhaps the close brush with nuclear war convinced many that nuclear policy was now effectively removed from the sphere of their influence, that the future was now truly out of their hands.

The groups that coordinated the Test Ban campaign now lost their capacity to mobilize people and public attention; they adapted to changed circumstances in different ways. PSR became moribund, its already small membership declined to less than 100 physicians. CLW and FAS established smaller but relatively stable presences in Washington as interest groups dedicated to lobbying Congress on arms control measures. Many of the other groups adapted their agendas to changing political circumstances by addressing new issues. The rising concern with civil rights and the war in Vietnam effectively limited the activist appeal of nuclear issues, as activists turned to more immediately urgent issues. Many of the campus-based SANE groups became the core of student activism in the Free Speech Movement and in what would eventually become the New Left.[14] The national office of SANE eventually took the word "nuclear" out of its name and focused its efforts on opposing U.S. participation in the Vietnam War. The traditional peace movement organizations also shifted their efforts to more pressing issues, responding not only to changing government policies but also to changes in the patterns of popular concern.[15] Essentially, these organizations derived their legitimacy and their support from effectively representing the concerns of their constituencies. As the political landscape changed, so did activist priorities, and organizations had to respond and adapt accordingly.

ANTINUCLEAR MOVEMENTS: ACCOMPLISHMENTS AND ARTIFACTS

The same pattern of mobilization was repeated during the campaign against antiballistic missile systems, which ran its course between 1969 and 1972. Unlike U.S. strategic missiles, which are located in sparsely populated areas in the western United States, ABM fields for population defense would necessarily be located near cities, precisely where they would be most likely to disrupt daily life and encounter opposition. Preparations to develop potential ABM sites near major cities, again making the nuclear threat more immediate and visible, spurred public concern about nuclear weapons generally and about ABM in particular.

SANE and Clergy and Laity Concerned (CALC), an organization developed in opposition to the Vietnam War, organized meetings against ABM development in 1969. FOR and AFSC also augmented their own antiwar work by organizing against the ABM. In contrast to the Test Ban campaign, much of the opposition to ABM development was locally based and oriented, directed to keeping ABM systems out of particular cities and towns. Citizens in Glenview, Illinois, for example, passed a resolution stating their opposition to ABM deployment literally in their own backyards.[16] Nuclear scientists were extremely visible in voicing concern about the technological feasibility, strategic desirability, and cost of the ABM. A new organization, the Union of Concerned Scientists (UCS), coordinated opposition to ABM development in the scientific community. UCS ran public education campaigns, making full use of the scientific expertise and credibility of its membership. It commissioned studies on the costs and strategic implications of ABM, lobbied legislators, and testified before Congress. The organization's work in educating the public and Congress was probably critical in securing ratification for the SALT I and ABM treaties.[17]

As with the LTB, the SALT I and ABM agreements served to defuse public opposition to U.S. nuclear policy, even though the treaties provided for significantly fewer limits than the anti-ABM movement had demanded. SALT I allowed MIRV development, establishing high numerical ceilings for strategic warheads; the ABM agreement allowed each side to defend one missile site and one population center with a total of 100 ABMs. Nonetheless, the president and the political establishment were able to reclaim dominance of political discourse through arms control efforts. By adopting some portion of movement demands, President Nixon was able to defuse antinuclear sentiment enough to limit the potential of dissident mobilization. Nixon also astutely moved potential ABM sites from suburban locales by redefining the goals of the program. Rather than population defense, the ABM would be called upon to defend U.S. ICBMs and would be based near far less visible strategic missile fields.[18]

Movement organizations survived the end of the movement, readjusting their political agendas and tactics to the modest changes in policy they had helped bring about. UCS shifted its concerns to nuclear power, pointing out safety problems in plant design and waste disposal. FOR, AFSC, CALC, SANE, and others redirected their full efforts to ending U.S. participation in the Vietnam War. The political shifts of the 1970s left what had been the disarmament and arms control movement once again split into two distinct camps. One, anchored by Washington-based lobbying groups and nuclear scientists, advocated arms control measures and was essentially reformist and moderate in tone and tactics. The other wing of the movement was anchored by religious activists and others descended from the New Left and antiwar movements of the 1960s. Suspicious of traditional arms control, these groups generally saw nuclear issues as intimately linked to other political problems. They distrusted Washington politics and often used more radical tactics to present their concerns.[19] For the most part, they had far less access to policy makers, media attention, mainstream legitimacy, and financial support than did the arms control lobby.

The end of the Vietnam War and draft registration caused many movement organizations to reevaluate their goals and redirect their efforts. In order to continue their work, political organizations had to redefine it. AFSC, CALC, the Coalition for a New Foreign and Military Policy (CNFMP), FOR, SANE, WILPF, and WRL turned their efforts to building local movements responsive to a wide range of political concerns. There were ideological underpinnings to these decisions, particularly issues of democracy that had been raised by the student movements of the 1960s, but this redirection was also good practical politics.[20] In the absence of an overriding national issue that could mobilize broad participation, organizations found it easiest to gain support by allowing local groups to respond to local issues. These local groups also had lower expenses, encountered less significant and powerful opposition, and could provide more direct benefits and political victories to participants. In addition to numerous new community organizations, the environmental and women's movements also benefited from the experiences, organizations, and activists who protested the Vietnam War. The campaigns against the B-1 bomber and nuclear power are most closely related organizationally, tactically, and ideologically to the nuclear freeze campaign that would follow them.

In 1972 AFSC initiated a campaign against development and procurement of the B-1 bomber. The B-1 was an extremely visible and politically vulnerable target. Intended to replace the B-52 force as the air-based leg of the strategic nuclear triad, the B-1 was virtually certain to be obsolete by the time it was deployed. It was exceptionally expensive by any standard and filled no strategic role that could not be accomplished more cheaply and effectively by other weapons. By 1976 the coalition against the B-1 comprised more than 40 national groups, including a pacifist core and feminist, environmental, labor, and religious constituencies in 160 communities across the nation. The effort was so strong and the claims of B-1 so weak that Congress delayed appropriations for the bomber program pending the results of the presidential election. President Carter canceled the B-1, but in conjunction he provided for retrofitting B-52 bombers with long-range nuclear-armed cruise missiles (ALCM) and for research and development of an advanced technology bomber, variously known as ATB, B-2, and Stealth. (Ronald Reagan later resurrected the B-1, while maintaining cruise missiles and research and development on the Stealth.)[21] Despite hedges Carter built into his decision to cancel the B-1, activists considered the campaign a major success. No previous movement had ever made such a clear impact on the fate of a weapons system in development. The B-1 campaign also established a political network that activists hoped would be useful for future campaigns.

The movement against nuclear power, using local and visible targets, also worked through a broad coalition of national and local groups, with significant decision-making power based in localities. The movement included many of the scientists who had been involved in stopping the ABM. Absent much political activity on nuclear weapons, the campaign against nuclear power gave them a means of educating the public on the dangers of radiation and nuclear waste. The antinuclear power movement also included many veterans of earlier social movements who "had been radicalized during the protest action of the 1960s," observes Dorothy Nelkin. "Nuclear power is a visible and accessible target through which they can express their desire for social change."[22] Just as nuclear power could be clearly linked to nuclear weapons politically, it also provided an opportunity to discuss environmental issues, the power of corporations, grassroots democracy, and U.S. political economy.

The movement against nuclear power was exceptionally decentralized. Most efforts were directed locally to stop the construction or operation of a particular power station. The site-based approach allowed the movement to criticize the dangers or inefficiencies of a specific plant while begging larger questions of the viability or desirability of nuclear power. Throughout the 1970s, local groups used these campaigns to forge broad coalitions, including environmentalists, labor activists, and community groups, coalitions that probably would not survive the strains of a national campaign. Decentralized organization also encouraged a diversity of tactics, which were responsive to the salient issues and available resources in each locality. Antinuclear activists sponsored referenda in nine states calling for such things as a ban on nuclear power within the state, imposing tight regulations on site approval, and prohibiting power companies from imposing a surcharge on their customers to cover the costs of "construction works in progress." Most were unsuccessful. In states without referenda provisions, antinuclear power activists lobbied to push their bills through state legislatures.[23]

Civil disobedience also became a keystone of many campaigns. It began one night in 1973 when Sam Lovejoy knocked down a weather tower near his home in Montague, Massachusetts. The tower had been placed to gather information for the planned construction of a nuclear power station on the Montague plain. Lovejoy turned himself in to the police that evening, and in his trial argued that it was not he but nuclear power that was in the wrong. The judge in the ensuing trial heard testimony from experts on the dangers of radiation and nuclear waste and on the history of civil disobedience. Eventually he dismissed the charges on the basis of a technical flaw in the indictment. The case received wide publicity within the antinuclear movement, where it was hailed as a great victory; broader civil disobedience campaigns followed. Perhaps the most visible was in Seabrook, New Hampshire. The first action in August 1976 resulted in 18 arrests and little publicity, but it set a precedent for the movement. By the following May, a similar action at Seabrook resulted in 1,414 arrests and generated a great deal of publicity. The tactic of nonviolent civil disobedience spread throughout the movement.[24]

This choice of tactics encouraged the further decentralization of leadership. In order to support this intense level of personal commitment and risk, affinity groups of 10–40 people became the backbone of the movement. This ensured that all participants would receive some training in nonviolence (often sponsored by older peace groups like WRL, FOR, and AFSC) before participating in actions, as the movement attempted to guard against either zealot or government-inspired violence. Networks of affinity groups grew up around power plants; the largest of these was the Clamshell Alliance formed to oppose Seabrook. This network style of organization was replicated by other alliances, including the Shad and Abalone alliances in New York and California respectively. The alliances themselves were given a national profile and some coordination by environmental organizations like the Friends of the Earth, movement journals such as *Critical Mass,* and a few media-anointed spokespeople, most notably Jane Fonda and Ralph Nader.

The 1979 accident at the Three Mile Island nuclear plant near Harrisburg, Pennsylvania, gave the national antinuclear movement added impetus, media attention, and much greater public support. Shortly following the March 28 accident, a demonstration in Washington, D.C. on May 6, drew between 65,000 and 125,000 people and a great deal of publicity. President Carter, a presidential commission headed by John Kemeny, and the Nuclear Regulatory Commission all endorsed what they termed justified public concern about nuclear safety. Stricter regulations resulted in increased construction costs. This, in conjunction with the then falling cost of oil and greater energy conservation, made nuclear power development an increasingly unattractive prospect for energy companies. The apparently effective end of the line for the next generation of nuclear plants, and the institutionalization of explicit safety concerns, demobilized much of the antinuclear forces, although active campaigns continued at construction sites.[25]

Although the movement against nuclear power had its roots in older nuclear disarmament groups, weapons issues were generally subsumed by a focus on nuclear power. A few campaigns stressed the link between these issues, but as the movement grew they became notable as exceptions.[26] Strategic considerations about goals provided an ongoing debate within the movement, and the spread of opposition to nuclear power led many groups to downplay or ignore nuclear weapons. With the exception of Rocky Flats, which produced weapons-grade plutonium, there appeared to be few easily visible targets, and it was more difficult to mobilize people on national defense issues. Many activists thought the weapons issue would be so divisive it was best left untouched.[27] Mass media aided in separating the issues; although the May 1979 demonstration was directed against both nuclear power and nuclear weapons, for example, both mainstream and left media virtually ignored any demands about nuclear weaponry.[28] As late as 1981, a regular column in WRL's *WIN* magazine, "International Nuke Notes," dealt almost exclusively with protest against nuclear power.

RECREATING A PEACE MOVEMENT

The new nuclear disarmament movement showed its first flashes of life within the coalition against nuclear power. While the public face of the antinuclear power movement grew to overshadow peace activism, during the 1970s activists established organizations and campaigns that would be instrumental to the development of the nuclear freeze campaign. The clearest attempt to link issues of nuclear power and nuclear weapons was the Rocky Flats Action Group, founded in 1974. Coordinated by Mike Jendrzejczyk of FOR and Pam Solo of AFSC, the Rocky Flats group tried to use local activism to address both local and national policy issues. They tried to use public fear about nuclear production nearby to engage in political education about a larger picture. The effort was exemplified by the slogan "Rocky Flats: Local Hazard/Global Threat." The first Rocky Flats protest in 1975 drew only 25 protestors; but subsequent demonstrations and actions were significantly larger as the movement against nuclear power grew, and the Rocky Flats group gained support from other organizations. An April 1979 demonstration drew 15,000 people for a period of five days, including physicist Michio Kaku, who emphasized the scientific and economic connections between nuclear weapons and nuclear power.[29]

Mobilization for Survival (MfS) took much the same approach. Modeled after the Mobilization Committee to End the War in Vietnam, MfS was a coalition of more than 280 affiliated groups, including 40 national organizations, most active in the antiwar movement, in an attempt to "put back on the political agenda what had been lost in the Vietnam years: an awareness of the threat of nuclear holocaust."[30] The Mobilization's political agenda was never limited, however, to the threat of nuclear holocaust. The impetus for organizing a new peace coalition had come from an article by antiwar veteran Sidney Lens in *The Progressive*. In a long piece outlining the history and basic tenets of U.S. nuclear policy, Lens proclaimed, "Americans need defense against their own leadership more than they need defense against a foreign invasion."[31] He called for a national movement with an international orientation and for a demonstration to commemorate the upcoming United Nations Special Session for Disarmament. His call led to a series of meetings among veteran antiwar activists, including representatives from WRL, AFSC, CALC, and WILPF. Representatives from more than 100 local, regional, and national groups attended a larger organizational meeting in the spring of 1977. The formation of MfS was then announced by Lens, David Dellinger, Sid Peck, Dave McReynolds, Peggy Duff, and Daniel Ellsberg, all experienced in leading the antiwar and/or civil rights movements of the 1960s.[32] MfS was eager to emphasize these links and in doing so both established its credibility within the peace movement and limited the scope of its appeal beyond.

In preparation for the UN Special Session, MfS organized interim events to commemorate the anniversary of the Hiroshima and Nagasaki bombings in August of 1977. This was followed by a petition campaign calling for a nuclear moratorium on both weapons and power, a series of 200 teach-ins on nuclear weapons and power issues, and in December MfS's first national conference in Chicago, attended by some 400 activists. MfS established four goals to define its efforts: "zero nuclear weapons, ban nuclear power, reverse the arms race, meet human needs."[33] The four goals were always defined broadly enough to allow and encourage a wide range of political activity linking many issues. MfS became the first national peace organization to emphasize the connection between nuclear weapons and nuclear power.

The UN's first Special Session on Disarmament, pushed onto the General Assembly's agenda by the nonaligned bloc, took place in May 1978. The General Assembly, unsurprisingly and to little effect, agreed that halting the arms race was a necessary and worthwhile goal. Meanwhile, MfS coordinated a range of activities outside the UN, including a demonstration with an estimated 15,000–25,000 participants.[34] Although the number pales in comparison to the 1 million who would march at the Second Special Session just four years later, it marked the beginning of the peace movement's resurrection as a political force.

The demonstration firmly established MfS's presence as an organized force between the center and left of the peace movement. MfS represented the commitment of a peace coalition to push its efforts beyond single-issue, single-producer, or single weapons systems campaigns, like the one that then appeared to have killed the B-1 bomber. It was a concerted attempt to unite the antiwar movement of the 1960s with the peace movement that preceded it. No single goal or campaign appeared on the horizon, however, that could successfully accomplish this. Following the May demonstration MfS's constituent groups, following the pattern of previous movements, directed their efforts primarily to local campaigns coordinated by decentralized leadership. They were generally unable to attract much publicity or incite mainstream mobilization.

The low profile and limited success resulted from several factors, some related to political opportunities, others to strategic decisions. On the larger political landscape, Jimmy Carter simply did not engender the fear and concern about nuclear weaponry that his successor would. MfS's appeal was also confined largely to the left edge of the political spectrum. Indeed, the prominent presence of figures such as Ellsberg and Chicago Eight defendant Dave Dellinger may have preempted a large share of moderate or mainstream support. Political coherence and clarity, however, were more important to MfS than turning out more softer support; its commitment to broaden the peace movement's analysis probably contributed to its failure to broaden the movement's popular appeal. Local organizations especially were willing to link controversial political issues as diverse as housing, social service budgets, and superpower intervention in the Third World with opposition to nuclear weapons. MfS was also willing to work in coalition with unpopular "fringe" groups, again hurting its mainstream appeal. Further, MfS's commitment to being a progressive and provocative force on the edge of an already marginal movement contributed to the development of a noncompromising agenda that appeared to have little appeal beyond the traditional peace movement. As one Congressional aide wrote, the Mobilization's call for no nuclear weapons and no nuclear power was "fine for pacifists, but would never wash with the public."[35] MfS was a precursor, however, to the nuclear freeze movement, breaking ground and laying tracks for a larger campaign.

BUILDING ON FOUNDATIONS

By the end of the 1970s and the Carter presidency, a new social movement was not visible, but the possibility for one was evident. Previous campaigns and established organizations had left a mark on the political landscape as well as an infrastructure and a tradition that could support new and broad mobilization. Previous protest movements left behind a number of political organizations, each maintaining its own constituency, style, resources, and a set of political tactics. Those organizations available to the nuclear freeze movement include several broad groupings. First, and most obvious, there are the organizations that had constituted the Test Ban and anti-ABM movements, including both the arms control wing: FAS, CLW, SANE, and UCS; and the traditional pacifist or peace movement organizations: AFSC, FOR, WILPF, WRL, Women Strike for Peace, and now the MfS coalition. Additionally, although not clearly a member of either camp, PSR remained, albeit in a smaller form. Helen Caldicott had begun to revive the organization in 1979, using it as a platform to oppose nuclear power.[36] These groups offered a wide range of political resources to an incipient movement concerned with nuclear issues, if some sort of unifying idea could mobilize them.

The potential constituency for a disarmament or arms control movement also reached significantly beyond the traditional peace and arms control communities. An antinuclear movement could forge alliances with religious organizations beyond the established peace churches. In this case, the movement would have to present an idea for disarmament apparently simple and fair enough to over-come the natural reluctance of large established religious institu-tions to engage in political activity. The potential to engage the vast social networks and extensive political resources of mainstream churches was strongly suggested before the freeze movement, for example, by Pope John Paul II's statements on the nuclear arms race, the National Council of Churches' decision to engage in nu-clear education projects, and by the Riverside Church's new disarm-ament program, coordinated by the Rev. William Sloane Coffin.[37] Coffin also represented another connection, the antiwar movement. CNFMP and CALC, for example, had developed in opposition to the war but represented a larger set of issues, which could easily include nuclear armaments. Environmental organizations such as the Sierra Club and Friends of the Earth could also be drawn to the issue, as could other groups opposed to nuclear power.

The election of Ronald Reagan and the new president's combination of defense, domestic, and economic policies drew the net of potential allies even wider. Reagan's assault on the rights of women and minorities, for example, dramatically heightened the desire of groups such as the National Organization for Women and the Southern Christian Leadership Conference to find an effective means to mobilize opposition to the president. Cuts in federal spending on education and social welfare gave teachers and social workers, and their organizations, reason to dissent. Reagan administration policies drew the ire of many other constituencies, making those groups more accessible to mobilization, including many trade unions, organizations of the elderly like the Gray Panthers, Nader-style citizen lobbies, and the National Lawyer's Guild. The inability of the Democratic Party to represent a viable opposition to the new president also encouraged traditionally Democratic constituencies to look for more forceful ways to engage in political action. The freeze movement would attempt to tap into all this frustration.

The nuclear disarmament, civil rights, and antiwar movements of the 1960s had established a network of organizations from which the nuclear freeze movement would draw support and also had developed an inventory of tactics. The social movements of the 1970s, including conservative and reactionary movements such as antibusing and antitax campaigns, although more generally scattered, decentralized, and locally based, had also demonstrated a broad range of political tactics and mobilization styles available to a new social movement. Previous arms control and disarmament movements alone had utilized a broad range of activity, including trespass on nuclear test sites, tax resistance, expert scientific testimony before Congress, public education campaigns on the dangers of nuclear radiation and war, site-based campaigns against nuclear weapons deployment, lobbying Congress, political education through drama and fiction, and large demonstrations. Other social movements, while using many similar tactics, augmented this already large tactical arsenal. The civil rights movement, for example, successfully used the church as a political ally, and demonstrated the efficacy of massive civil disobedience in dramatizing issues and attracting media attention. The antiwar movement used large demonstrations dramatically and coordinated teach-ins on college campuses and elsewhere. Both the antiwar and civil rights movements also explored the potential of using litigation to achieve movement goals, both for individual remedy and broad political statements.[38]

The movements of the 1970s, learning from their predecessors, developed new styles of organization, frequently community based with more decentralized decision making and entirely different notions of leadership. The women's movement enlivened all subsequent campaigns, forcing organizations to come to terms not only with so-called feminist issues but also with new ideas about democratic participation. The movement against nuclear power, with its affinity group structure and formally rotating leadership, is perhaps the most dramatic example of a new organizational style.[39] The antitax and consumer movements of the 1970s took advantage of provisions for state referenda, mobilizing public support in opposition to state legislatures and other elected officials. This tactic became a cornerstone of the freeze campaign.[40]

Earlier movements left an impact on history and policy and on those who participated in them. Most of those involved in the freeze leadership were not political neophytes, and their experiences in past movements influenced the decisions they made about the freeze. The founders of MfS, for example, were almost all veterans of the movement against the Vietnam War. Randy Kehler, the first national coordinator of the Nuclear Weapons Freeze Clearinghouse, had spent nearly two years in federal prisons for draft evasion during the 1960s and for most of the 1970s had engaged in community organizing in western Massachusetts, not far from where Sam Lovejoy toppled a weather tower.[41]

The political education of participating in earlier protest movements was not limited to the new antinuclear leadership. Protest movements of previous decades had touched many people directly, people who were ready and eager to engage in activism again. Many were probably searching for a vehicle for action. E. P. Thompson tried to tap into this group, publishing an article in *The Nation* in January 1981, just as Ronald Reagan was inaugurated president. Invoking the movements of the past, Thompson called for Americans to protest the deployment of Pershing II and cruise missiles in Europe. Andrew Stiller, one such activist wrote plaintively in reply, "those of us who marched . . . to end the Vietnam war a decade ago are still here. We still guard at least the embers of the values so painfully acquired in those days." Agreeing with Thompson about the need for protest, Stiller almost desperately called for direction, "FOR THE LOVE OF HUMANITY, TELL US WHAT WE SHOULD DO (emphasis original)."[42]

Finally, each successive movement had established its own communications network, enabling organizations to coordinate activity and disseminate information as well as appeals for action. The dialogue above illustrates that *The Nation* is one part of this network, along with a host of other left/liberal national publications, including *The Progressive, In These Times,* and *Mother Jones.* Even more important for reaching activists, virtually all the older organizations have their own organs for disseminating information. Some, such as the *Bulletin of the Atomic Scientists,* reach considerably beyond their sponsor's membership. Beyond formal publications and local newsletters, many of the political organizations and churches had traditions of cooperation and experience in reaching and mobilizing not only their constituencies but each other as well. The resources for a protest movement in place, the nuclear freeze proposal proved to be the galvanizing force that united and mobilized them.

NOTES

1. On the infrastructure necessary for building a movement, see Jo Freeman, *The Politics of Women's Liberation: An Emerging Social Movement and Its Relation to the Policy Process,* New York: David McKay, 1975, pp. 48–49.

2. Lawrence Wittner, *Rebels against War: The American Peace Movement, 1933–1983,* Philadelphia: Temple University Press, 1984.

3. For overviews of U.S. peace movements, see Charles Chatfield, ed., *Peace Movements in America,* New York: Schocken, 1973; Charles DiBenedetti, *The Peace Reform in American History,* Bloomington: Indiana University Press, 1980; C. Roland Marchand, *The American Peace Movement and Social Reform, 1898–1918,* Princeton, NJ: Princeton University Press, 1972; Wittner, *Rebels against War.*

4. James Clotfelter, "Disarmament Movements in the United States," *Journal of Peace Research,* June 1986, pp. 97–101.

5. Paul Boyer, "From Activism to Apathy: The American People and Nuclear Weapons," *The Journal of American History,* March 1984, p. 823; Seymour Feshbach and Michael J. White, "Individual Differences in Attitudes towards Nuclear Arms Policies: Some Psychological and Social Policy Considerations," *Journal of Peace Research,* June 1986, pp. 129–39; Ute Volmberg, "Folie a Deux: Peace Movement and Deterrence Experts on Their Way to the Abyss?" *Bulletin of Peace Proposals* 15 (1984): 37.

6. Boyer, "From Activism to Apathy," p. 823.

7. Kim Salomon, "The Peace Movement: An Anti-Establishment Movement," *Journal of Peace Research,* June 1986, pp. 115–27; Frank Parkin, *Middle Class*

Radicalism, New York: Praeger, 1968.

8. Russell Johnson, "AFSC Peace Work from the '50s to the '80s," *Peacework*, September 1983; Donna Warnock, "Feminism and Militarism: Can the Peace Movement Reach Out?" *WIN*, April 15, 1982, pp. 7–11.

9. Thomas B. Elliot et al., "What Are the Implications for U.S. Defense Policy of Growing Nuclear Dissent in the United States?" The Naval War College National Defense University Strategic Study, April 1983, p. 3; Wittner, *Rebels against War*, pp. 144–47, 165.

10. Boyer, "From Activism to Apathy," p. 823; Elliot, "Implications," p. 8; H. Jack Geiger, "Learning from the PSR: Successful Methods for Major Impact," in Steven E. Miller, ed., *The Nuclear Weapons Freeze and Arms Control*, Cambridge, MA: Ballinger, 1984, pp. 41–43; Robin Herman, "Protestors Old and New Forge Alliance for Antinuclear Rally," New York *Times*, June 4, 1982, p. B6; Steven Pressman, "Nuclear Freeze Groups Focus on Candidates," *Congressional Quarterly*, May 5, 1984, p. 1023; Warnock, "Feminism and Militarism"; Wittner, *Rebels against War*, pp. 243–45, 276.

11. For a comprehensive history of SANE, see Milton S. Katz, *Ban the Bomb: A History of SANE, 1957–1985*, New York: Praeger, 1986.

12. Ibid., pp. 838–40; Wittner, *Rebels against War*, pp. 257–60. On the purge, see Katz, *SANE*, pp. 46–62 passim; Rael Jean Isaac and Erich Isaac, "The Counterfeit Peacemakers: Atomic Freeze," *The American Spectator*, June 1982, p. 15; Barbara Deming, "The Ordeal of SANE," *The Nation*, March 11, 1961.

13. Boyer, "From Activism to Apathy," p. 821; Harvard Nuclear Weapons Study Group, *Living with Nuclear Weapons*, New York: Bantam Books, 1983, pp. 10, 200–2.

14. Boyer, "From Activism to Apathy," pp. 835–36; Wittner, *Rebels against War*, pp. 272, 278.

15. This same shift in focus occurred after 1963 in European antinuclear movements. Parkin, *Middle-Class Radicalism*; Nigel Young, "The Contemporary European Anti-nuclear Movement Experimentation in the Mobilization of Public Power," *PRIO Papers*, March 1983, p. 3.

16. Robert Leavitt, "Freezing the Arms Race: The Genesis of a Mass Movement," unpublished Kennedy School of Government Case Study, Harvard University, 1983, pp. 5–6.

17. Joel Primack and Frank von Hippel, *Advice and Dissent: Scientists in the Political Arena*, New York: Basic, 1974, pp. 59–73, 178–95, 210.

18. Primack and von Hippel, *Advice and Dissent*, p. 190.

19. Dorothy Nelkin, "Antinuclear Connection: Power and Weapons," *Bulletin of the Atomic Scientists*, April 1981, pp. 37–38; Pam Solo, interview with author, June 31, 1987.

20. Harry C. Boyte, "The Formation of the New Peace Movement: A Communitarian Perspective," *Social Policy*, Summer 1982, p. 5; Paul Wehr, "Nuclear Pacifism as Collective Action," *Journal of Peace Research*, June 1986, p. 104.

21. Nick Kotz, *Wild Blue Yonder: Money, Politics, and the B-1 Bomber*, New York: Pantheon; Pam Solo, *From Protest to Policy: Beyond the Nuclear Freeze to Common Security*, Cambridge, MA: Ballinger, 1988, pp. 29–30; Doug Waller, *Congress and the Nuclear Freeze: An Inside Look at the Politics of a Mass Movement*, Amherst, MA: University of Massachusetts Press, 1987, p. 27.

22. Nelkin, "Antinuclear Connection," p. 36.

23. Lynn E. Dwyer, "Structure and Strategy in the Antinuclear Movement," in Jo Freeman, ed., *Social Movements of the Sixties and Seventies,* New York: Longman, 1983, pp. 148–61.

24. Ann Morrissett Davidson, "The U.S. Antinuclear Movement," *Bulletin of the Atomic Scientists,* December 1979. To prevent an even larger civil disobedience action the following June, Seabrook owners and New Hampshire officials negotiated with the Clamshell Alliance to allow protestors to demonstrate on the construction site under the condition that they would not engage in civil disobedience. Under these terms, more than 20,000 people demonstrated in June 1978.

25. Dwyer, "Structure and Strategy."

26. Pam Solo and Mike Jendrzejczyk, "Nuclear Watergate: Radiation Roulette in Nevada," *The Nation,* June 2, 1979; Ann Morrissett Davidson, "Letter," *Bulletin of the Atomic Scientists,* October 1981, p. 62.

27. Steven E. Barkan, "Strategic, Tactical, and Organizational Dilemmas of the Protest Movement against Nuclear Power," *Social Problems* 27 (October 1979): 25; Nelkin, "Antinuclear Connections," p. 36. Ironically, the debate about linking issues would be repeated and reversed within the nuclear freeze movement.

28. See, for example, "Editorial," *The Nation,* May 19, 1979.

29. Davidson, "U.S. Antinuclear Movement"; Solo and Jendrzejczyk, "Nuclear Watergate"; Nelkin, "Antinuclear Connection"; Solo, *From Protest to Policy,* pp. 30–34.

30. Tom DeLuca, "The Cutting Edge of Survival: Mobe Looks at Mobe," *The Mobilizer,* May 1982.

31. Sid Lens, "Doomsday Strategy," *The Progressive,* February 1976, p. 35.

32. Alexander Cockburn and James Ridgeway, "The Freeze Movement versus Ronald Reagan," *The New Left Review* 137 (January/February 1983): 6; Davidson, "U.S. Antinuclear Movement"; Robert Moore, "Letter," *Bulletin of the Atomic Scientists,* October 1981, p. 61.

33. DeLuca, "Cutting Edge"; Tony Palomba, "Mobilization Nurtures Grassroots Activists," *Peacework,* January 1983; Solo, *From Protest to Policy,* p. 31.

34. Louise Bruyn, "June 12: A Look at How It Was Organized," *Peacework,* July/August 1982; DeLuca, "Cutting Edge"; Patrick Lacyfield, "Thousands Rally at UN on May 27th," *WIN,* June 15, 1978, pp. 4–6; Sid Peck, "The Danger and the Choice: Why Your Presence Is Needed at the United Nations on June 12," *Peacework,* April 1982; Sid Peck and Kathy Matthews, "A Question of Survival," *WIN,* August 28, 1978, pp. 4–8.

35. Waller, *Congress and the Nuclear Freeze,* pp. 29–30.

36. Davidson, "U.S. Antinuclear Movement"; Geiger, "Learning from the PSR"; Peter G. Joseph, "Doctors Speak Up," *Bulletin of the Atomic Scientists,* March 1981, p. 17; Pressman, "Nuclear Freeze Groups," p. 1023; Solo, *From Protest to Policy,* p. 36.

37. Herman, "Protestors Old and New."

38. Joel F. Handler, *Social Movements and the Legal System: A Theory of Law Reform and Social Change,* Orlando, FL: Academic Press, 1978.

39. Jane Dibblin, "The Author and the Activist," *END Bulletin,* February/March 1983, pp. 27–28; Salomon, "The Peace Movement," p. 125; Wehr, "Nuclear Pacifism," pp. 105–8.

40. David D. Schmidt, "Taking the Initiative, 1982," *WIN*, November 1982; Women's Action for Nuclear Disarmament, *Turnabout: Emerging New Realism in the Nuclear Age*, Boston: WAND Education Fund, 1986, p. 22.

41. Cockburn and Ridgeway, "The Freeze Movement," pp. 6–7.

42. Andrew Stiller, "Letter," *The Nation*, February 14, 1981.

9

DEFINING AND UNIFYING THE NUCLEAR FREEZE MOVEMENT

In December 1979 Randall Forsberg addressed 600 activists at Mobilization for Survival's annual convention and asked that all the affiliated groups agree to work on the nuclear freeze proposal. Forsberg realized the potential for a mass movement demanding dramatic changes in U.S. nuclear policy and also recognized that the necessary political resources were already available. What was missing was a vehicle for mobilizing and uniting the existing networks of groups and activists. In preparation for the MfS meeting, Forsberg wrote the *Call to Halt the Arms Race,* in which she proposed a bilateral nuclear freeze on the production, testing, and deployment of nuclear weapons and delivery vehicles. The freeze appealed to a wide range of organizations, to a large degree, because it was easily accessible and salable to the general public. Expressing a first step toward resolving a host of difficult problems in moderate and clear language, the nuclear freeze encouraged grassroots political mobilization, simultaneously tapping into a vein of populist antielitism that runs deep in U.S. political culture.

THE NUCLEAR FREEZE PROPOSAL: RADICAL SENSIBILITY

Forsberg was not alone in urging greater cooperation among peace groups or the development of a set of common goals. Indeed, MfS had originally been conceived as a vehicle for that purpose. When Forsberg proposed the freeze to MfS, the coalition was already working on a nuclear moratorium petition campaign with CALC. MfS was also planning to expand its own efforts during the following year by organizing student participation through a "Survival Summer." Organizers conceded that the moratorium proposal, however, failed to generate either massive support or much attention. There was a widespread desire to rethink strategy.[1]

Mike Jendrzejczyk and Pam Solo, who had achieved some success with the Rocky Flats campaign, were looking to expand their program to other sites and give it a national profile.[2] Steve Ladd, working with the War Resister's League, wrote to Solo and Jendrzejczyk proposing a larger national campaign, perhaps focused on a campaign for a comprehensive test ban, "I think we need to develop a unified national campaign and strategy to stop the new generation of nuclear weapons, a campaign that would possibly involve people working at all levels and in all communities. . . . I had originally hoped that Survival Summer could be the initiator of something like this."[3]

As the presidential campaign began in 1980 many peace groups were distressed by the rightward drift in national politics yet over-whelmed by the sheer number of issues. There were too many potential fronts on which to do battle, none clearly mandating priority. In an internal memo, for example, FOR seemed swamped by political options, including work to improve U.S. relations with the Soviet Union, opposition to Soviet troops in Afghanistan, a campaign to dump Carter's hawkish national security advisor Zbigniew Brzezinski, stopping military aid to Pakistan, improving U.S. energy policy in relation to the Middle East, protesting increased military spending, campaigning against the reinstitution of draft registration, and supporting the freeze proposal.[4] Executive Director Richard Baggett Deats was meanwhile working to get established religious institutions, in particular the National Council of Churches, involved in some organized campaign for nuclear disarmament, possibly a negotiated moratorium on nuclear weapons.[5] AFSC held a special consultation during the winter of 1979–1980 at the Princeton Club to discuss new options for action in light of the failure of SALT II and what was viewed as the worsening political climate.[6]

The nuclear freeze was not the only strategy for action circulating within the peace community, nor was it a strictly original idea.[7] Before Forsberg's *Call to Halt the Arms Race,* a nuclear freeze had most recently been proposed in the spring of 1979 by Senator Mark Hatfield (R-OR) as an amendment to SALT II. During the same year Richard Barnet made a similar proposal in an article published in *Foreign Affairs*. Barnet suggested that previous arms control efforts had failed to gain widespread support because their objectives were not sufficiently comprehensive nor clear, noting that the ultimate goal of "general and complete disarmament" had been abandoned by the United States long ago. He proposed a "three year moratorium on procurement, testing and deployment of all bombers, missiles and warheads," in conjunction with the adoption of a "no first use" nuclear policy by both superpowers.[8]

The roots of the idea of negotiated freezes on weapons systems are much deeper, however, and can be traced at least to 1922, when the United States, Great Britain, and Japan agreed to cut their battleship forces in half and freeze new battleship construction for ten years. President Lyndon Johnson and Defense Secretary McNamara proposed a nuclear freeze to Soviet General Secretary Brezhnev in 1964, when the United States enjoyed a considerable advantage in both strategic weapons and nuclear weapons technology; no one was surprised when Brezhnev refused.[9] On June 17, 1969, Senator Edward Brooke (R-MA), along with 39 cosponsors, introduced a resolution in the Senate calling for a freeze on the flight testing of multiple warhead missiles. At President Nixon's urging, the proposal was modified into a more general strategic freeze that would allow the United States to develop MIRV technology; the resolution passed in the Senate on April 9, 1970, by an overwhelming 73–6 margin. Gerard Smith, then director of ACDA under Nixon, and chief U.S. SALT I negotiator, later revealed that he had privately suggested that President Nixon propose a nuclear freeze to the Soviets in 1969. The "Stop Where We Are" proposal, according to Smith, would work to the advantage of the United States whether or not the Soviets accepted. "It was not at all clear that the USSR would accept such a proposal," Smith later explained, "but by proposing it we could take the 'high ground' psychologically and, if necessary later, move to something more modest if that was the most the Soviets would accept." There is no evidence that President Nixon ever proposed such a freeze.[10]

The Soviet Union proposed a bilateral freeze on new nuclear weapons systems and nuclear testing on September 28, 1976. General Secretary Brezhnev repeated this proposal at the 25th Communist Party Conference on November 2, 1977, then again on May 26, 1978, at the United Nations. Although the United States had no official response at that time, former President Jimmy Carter later revealed that the Soviet Union had actually rejected the comprehensive nuclear freeze on production and deployment he had proposed in June 1979.[11] Apparently, both superpowers had seen advantage to both proposing and rejecting nuclear weapons freezes.

The public appeal of a nuclear freeze, as Smith had suggested, was immediately obvious. Unlike virtually all other arms control proposals, it was strikingly simple, intelligible to the general public as well as to arms control experts. Also unlike other arms control proposals, it promised an end to the arms race, rather than a continued and difficult struggle to manage ongoing international competition. Beyond its public relations appeal, the comprehensive nature of an agreed freeze, given sufficient political will, would be easier to negotiate and verify than more complicated agreements. There was one crucial additional dimension to Forsberg's freeze proposal: it was intended not only as an arms control proposal but also as the centerpiece of a protest movement. This critical double role for the freeze was instrumental in gaining the proposal quick support. The freeze was a simple and salable idea, for one did not have to understand strategic doctrine, become immersed in the minutiae of nuclear weapons hardware, or even assess blame for the arms race to support it. These same characteristics, however, would also prove to be a weakness, making the proposal vulnerable to ostensibly friendly redefinition by both allies and opponents.[12]

The idea of organizing around a freeze proposal began circulating early in 1979 through a series of discussions among long-time peace activists. Seeking a campaign vehicle to stop the development of the next generation of nuclear weaponry, a group asked Forsberg, who along with the Boston Study Group had just completed a book calling for a radical restructuring of U.S. military forces, to draft a proposal.[13] She drafted the *Call,* the heart of which became the nuclear freeze proposal:[14]

> To improve national and international security, the United States and the Soviet Union should stop the nuclear arms race. Specifically, they should adopt a mutual freeze on the testing, production, and deployment of nuclear weapons and of missiles and new aircraft designed primarily to deliver nuclear weapons. This is an essential, verifiable first step toward lessening the risk of nuclear war and reducing the nuclear arsenals.

For Forsberg, the nuclear freeze was always a first step in a sustained effort to bring about a series of bilateral and multilateral agreements making the world safer and more just. Immediately after the implementation of the freeze she envisioned, the same antinuclear movement that had rallied behind the freeze would push the superpowers to agree to end intervention in the Third World and then cut standing nuclear and conventional forces by half. These steps would be followed by strengthened economic development and human rights in the Third World and in Eastern Europe and then by the abolition of military alliances and foreign military bases. Eventually all nuclear weapons and then all national military forces could be abolished.[15]

Even the first step of a nuclear freeze, however, represented a radical departure from the established practice of arms control. While previous arms control agreements had set numerical limits on weaponry and allowed technological modernization, the freeze would end both numerical increases and technological improvements in nuclear forces. It was not an attempt to manage the arms race but to end it.[16] Said Forsberg, "There is a prevailing idea among the experts about arms control in which, in effect, we stand to engage in the arms race indefinitely and that concept is in fundamental disagreement with the goals and purposes of the peace movement."[17] Forsberg's freeze meant an end to the technological arms race, nuclear weapons production altogether, and ultimately extended deterrence and the world political system that extended deterrence supported. It is doubtful that most freeze supporters or opponents gauged the full scope of the proposal. As Michael Kazin would later write of the freeze, "It is a thoroughly rational idea with radical implications."[18]

The nuclear freeze was also a domestic political strategy, and here again, by putting issues normally left to professionals and the military on the democratic agenda, the idea had radical implications not always immediately visible. Forsberg believed that the changes she wanted to see in military policy could be brought about by a majority movement composed primarily of mainstream and moderate people drawn by the strength of the idea, people who were not normally engaged in political activism. This necessitated a clear and incrementally staged approach, based on persuasive common-sense proposals and rational argument that would make nuclear issues accessible to the general public.[19]

Putting nuclear arms issues on the democratic agenda became a key feature of the freeze movement. By pursuing the freeze through traditionally democratic processes and imbuing virtually every activity with populist rhetoric, both the movement and proposal gained legitimacy and tapped into classic U.S. antielitism. For example, Senator Tom Harkin (D-IA), an early Congressional supporter, intoned that U.S. citizens would no longer "allow their lives to be held in constant peril by the decisions of an elite group of generals, politicians, and scientists." Toby Moffett, then a Democratic U.S. representative from Connecticut, used the same sort of rhetoric: "The people are sick and tired of leaving their fate totally in the hands of experts," he said; "the experts have failed." Said Common Cause's Fred Wertheimer: "The issue of nuclear war and nuclear arms control belongs to the people. . . . These experts talk beyond the comprehension of the average citizen of this country, and that's just plain wrong." By claiming the democratic high ground, freeze advocates forced opponents to retreat to condescending and antidemocratic rhetoric that devalued public opinion.[20]

The nuclear freeze proposal was well-crafted for gaining public support, but it was still necessary to mobilize a network to disseminate the idea, organize action, and represent the cause politically. Before it could reach the public, the freeze had to win support from the leadership of established peace groups. There had been no single overriding cause uniting these groups since the end of the Vietnam War, and their efforts before the emergence of the freeze were splintered and often marginalized. Some organizations were involved in long-term programs seeking comprehensive changes in the political and economic system of the United States while others were working within established political institutions for more modest reforms. Convincing groups pursuing a wide variety of goals that the nuclear freeze merited top priority was no easy task. Forsberg's first presentation of the freeze proposal to MfS received mixed responses. MfS was then busy with its own nuclear moratorium proposal and was more inclined to press for unilateral initiatives in any case.[21]

In January 1980 Forsberg founded the Institute for Defense and Disarmament Studies (IDDS), which she intended to develop as a think tank modeled after the Stockholm International Peace Research Institute (SIPRI), where she had previously worked. Forsberg hoped IDDS would serve as an information resource for the peace movement and military analysts and provide a factual groundwork for her disarmament proposals.[22] It would also serve as the first clearinghouse for the nuclear freeze campaign. Forsberg also continued to revise the *Call* and to seek support for the nuclear freeze idea among peace activists. She did not have to persuade these sympathetic groups that there was something wrong with the nuclear arms race but, rather, that the nuclear freeze was a viable means of doing something about it. A speech given at the World Council of Churches' International Public Hearing on Nuclear Weapons and Disarmament in November 1981 gives some idea of Forsberg's argument:

> While the notion of stopping the production of nuclear weapons has been with us since 1945, it has never been the primary focus of disarmament efforts. Instead, past efforts have been splintered around many competing goals. Moreover, these goals have clustered around the extremes, some emphasizing quite limited measures which, even if successful, would not stop the arms race; others requiring the total abolition of nuclear armaments or of warfare and armaments generally. . . . We need a dramatic, simple, moderate, but still effective proposal to mobilize the middle class, to give them hope and to bring them actively into the ranks of those who oppose the arms race. . . . [This] would show that human beings can direct their own destiny; that we can harness the arms race; that, together, we are stronger than the military industrial complex; that human will can prevail over the technological imperative. It would demonstrate that we can "democratize" and therefore eventually abolish the ancient, pernicious, elite institutions of warfare and exploitative foreign policy.[23]

The freeze began to receive support from the older peace and religious activist groups in 1980. Harvey Cox, of Harvard Divinity School, presented the *Call* to the Peace and Social Concerns group of U.S. National Council of Churches (NCC), which endorsed the proposal, as did the NCC at its summer convention. Other religious groups were quick to endorse the freeze. Carol Jensen of CALC was an early supporter, and she worked to push the *Call* to potentially sympathetic groups. Jensen formed an ad hoc freeze task force, which worked to get initial endorsements from prominent individuals and from groups that could help the campaign.[24] By the summer of 1980 the Riverside Church Disarmament Program, Pax Christi, the Coalition for a New Foreign and Military Policy, World Peacemakers, and Sojourners had joined the effort. AFSC published 5,000 copies of the *Call* as a four-page flyer in April 1980 and began distributing it through its own network. CALC and FOR also endorsed the proposal and aided in the production and distribution of another 20,000 copies. That spring, the Council for a Nuclear Weapons Freeze formed to coordinate these efforts.[25]

DEFINING THE NUCLEAR FREEZE

In order to build a coalition that would expand beyond these religious and pacifist groups to reach the political mainstream, discussion and organizing efforts had to remain focused on the nuclear freeze proposal itself, a proposal Forsberg believed represented a moderate and intermediate-range goal. She was particularly concerned that her allies did not have disproportionate influence in defining the scope and rhetoric of the campaign, fearing that the campaign could be coopted by more radical peace groups espousing a "pacifist-vegetarian anti-corporate value system" and emphasizing direct action and civil disobedience. She saw her role as keeping the focus of the campaign in the political center, working within established political institutions, and maintaining the freeze's middle-class middle-American appeal.[26]

The desire to stay in the middle, that is, to keep the early activist groups in a coalition supporting the freeze proposal while still allowing for growth toward the political center, created a tension that dogged the campaign throughout its life. This conflict was manifest in many different ways, most clearly through debates within the coalition about defining the freeze proposal and hammering out a political strategy. These issues were necessarily related because those who saw the freeze as a moderate reform designed to inject some element of appreciation for the arms control process into Reagan administration policy were comfortable with more conventional means of political participation, such as lobbying, electoral campaigns, and holding press conferences. Their goals could conceivably be achieved through organized participation in conventional politics. Others, who saw the freeze as an attempt to remake society by starting with nuclear policy, were understandably less sanguine that their goals could be achieved this way. Conflicts about these larger issues were often played out in smaller battles about the structure and organization of the campaign, particularly about the decision making process .

Early freeze supporters were forced constantly to justify their tactics and their proposals to critics on both sides: those who thought the freeze was too ambitious and others who believed it was so moderate that it really did not merit support, especially as it might preempt support for a more comprehensive agenda. In 1980, when the presidential race was underway, the freeze did not grow beyond the first few endorsements from religious activist groups and a select few politicians already publicly committed to left/liberal positions on military issues, most notably Democratic Congressmen Ronald Dellums of California and Ted Weiss of New York.[27]

Forsberg insisted that endorsement of the freeze proposal be kept separate from the succeeding steps she envisioned so that no additional agenda, including her own, would cloud the freeze and alienate potential supporters.[28] Even so, support from the liberal arms control community, which had seemed the most likely ally, was particularly slow in coming. The Federation of American Scientists (FAS), Center for Defense Information (CDI), Arms Control Association (ACA), Council for a Livable World (CLW), and SANE all refused to endorse the nuclear freeze proposal in 1980, preferring, according to Forsberg, to push for more traditional arms control measures, specifically, negotiated percentage reductions in the number of nuclear warheads. They were all apparently reluctant to sign on to a proposal as comprehensive as the nuclear freeze and to join in coalition with the groups already supporting it. Jerome Grossman of CLW, which later endorsed the freeze, explained this early reticence in terms of the group's desire to maintain its credibility and working relationships with the political establishment, "We had to be dragged kicking and screaming to support the freeze."[29]

Absent the support of established liberal and arms control oriented groups, the freeze coalition was effectively limited to groups that, for the most part, advocated broader and more comprehensive reforms of U.S. policy, including AFSC, CALC, CNFMP, FOR, the Institute for Policy Studies (IPS), MfS, the United States Peace Council (USPC), WILPF, Women Strike for Peace, and WRL.[30] Even within this coalition, however, many of the groups had doubts about the proposal. Freeze founders were faced not only with the reluctance of more moderate groups to accept the idea but also with the hesitation of their affirmed allies to push it aggressively. Within the

AFSC some argued that the emergence of the freeze might eliminate unilateral initiatives from the agenda of peace activists, although AFSC itself had been calling for unilateral disarmament since 1958.[31] WRL struggled even with endorsing the proposal because, as David McReynolds told *Newsweek*, "The problem is that the freeze presents an arms-control position, not a disarmament position."[32] FOR also stayed in the coalition but continued to endorse unilateral initiatives. MfS endorsed the nuclear freeze early but never gave it much support because its leaders were dissatisfied with the proposal's failure explicitly to address economic issues and military intervention in the Third World. Although its leaders supported the freeze, they saw MfS's role as looking beyond it.[33]

Indeed, virtually all the groups endorsing the nuclear freeze proposal were looking beyond it in some way, attempting to link the freeze to other issues, and consequently were often frustrated when coalition partners resisted these linkages. Each additional issue added to the freeze agenda, while possibly strengthening the clarity of the campaign's message or the support of one contingent, also risked alienating supporters and potential supporters. This concern about gaining moderate support and forging a majority movement led freeze leaders to eschew developing the "anti-imperialist, antiracist, antisexist, and anti-interventionist agenda" some critics demanded.[34]

The conflict would remain throughout the life of the freeze coalition, as groups would emphasize different aspects and implications of the nuclear freeze. AFSC, for example, linked the freeze to the economic implications of the arms race, arguing for a redefinition of U.S. budgetary priorities and increased funding for social services. Later in the campaign some freeze supporters would argue that additional funds should be allocated to conventional weaponry. Partisans of both the pro-choice and antiabortion positions argued that the freeze movement had to be linked with their respective causes in order to be consistent and effective.[35] Gay rights also became a potentially divisive issue, as some activists argued that gays were being pressured to keep a low profile within the movement in order to avoid alienating the ever-elusive political mainstream.[36] Many argued that the freeze movement should also oppose nuclear power, although more generally the movement abandoned this issue as divisive and unnecessarily controversial.[37] Forsberg particularly worked to keep the freeze issue separate from other divisive issues and to broaden the scope of the freeze coalition, insisting that a wide range of groups be invited to the first national freeze conference, "All you have to do to come is support the freeze."[38]

It was not always clear, however, what support for the freeze meant. The major political disputes hinged on defining the nuclear freeze and on reaching a working consensus on the political goals of the campaign. Pam Solo explained that she and Jendrzejczyk had not seen the freeze as the vanguard of a progressive political movement, as some activists argued it should be, but as a campaign to change U.S. foreign policy.[39] For Solo, however, that included many issues that others within the campaign were reluctant to address. Without doubt the most virulent debates were over issues most closely related to the activists' various views of foreign policy and public opinion. Within the freeze coalition, forces like MfS consistently pushed the movement to address explicitly the draft, development and procurement of specific weapons systems, and superpower intervention in the Third World, particularly U.S. intervention in Central America and the Middle East.[40]

Quelling the concerns of both the left and the right within the freeze coalition resulted in a politics of expediency. Implicitly acknowledging the criticisms of both groups, the leadership fell back on the position that the nuclear freeze was essentially the most comprehensive proposal they could advance without shattering the coalition. To critics on the left, leaders responded that the freeze was able to achieve a far greater audience than any previous efforts and was particularly effective in enlisting new activists whom other groups could work to educate and radicalize. To critics on the right, freeze leaders responded that the proposal already had broad public support and attention that was unlikely to be matched, support that could be translated into pragmatic arms control measures. Mark Niedergang, who coordinated the freeze campaign in its earliest days, wrote such a defense to the *WIN* audience — comprised mostly of those on the left wing of the freeze movement's core constituency. He writes:

> The bilateral nature of the freeze comes from recognizing the fears, insecurities and belief systems of a majority of the American people. It acknowledges public distrust of a unilateral initiative, and maintains some elements of the status quo, but despite its seemingly conservative platform for communicating a deep political analysis. . . . Calling a halt to the arms race seems a goal small enough to be achievable yet large enough to be significant.[41]

Niedergang acknowledged that the freeze had not advanced a comprehensive analysis of the arms race or U.S. society but countered that groups that do present such analyses are inevitably marginalized. Within the freeze coalition, he argued, groups could raise other issues. Further, the campaign would give those groups and activists with a broader analysis an avenue to the political center that was generally foreclosed to them; he argued, "The freeze provides progressives with an opportunity to criticize political and economic relations from within the mainstream."[42] With the freeze movement, left activists could work effectively in conventional politics and in the electoral system and, as a result, achieve real successes. Not only would the freeze movement benefit those with broader agendas, he argued, but the presence of such groups and individuals would enliven and energize the movement as a whole. Diversity within the coalition would enable the movement to "avoid poles of isolation and cooptation."[43] Essentially, political conflicts had to be managed on pragmatic grounds.

Niedergang's reply did not satisfy activist critics on the left. Ada Sanchez and Normon Solomon, responding to Niedergang, argued that the freeze was not only too weak ideologically but was also politically misinformed. The prevalent definition of the freeze was too narrow for the "magnitude and momentum" of mass concerns and, they claimed, could be easily undercut or coopted by arms control negotiations, allegations of Soviet intransigence, and mainstream politics. "Freeze organizers pride themselves on their astute comprehension of *realpolitik,* but the freeze drive is being thawed by the predictable dynamics of political compromise." Eager to settle for "half a loaf," the authors warned, freeze activists "will get crumbs. . . . They can expect Reagan administration officials to repeat their refrain that 'a freeze isn't good enough — the world needs substantial reductions in nuclear weapons arsenals'."[44] The narrow freeze, they argued, sold the broad and growing movement short, and would ultimately compromise its potential efficacy.

Divisions on political analyses of international relations and the arms race were further exacerbated by vastly different views of U.S. domestic politics and the potential influence of a protest movement. The first freeze strategy, written by Forsberg and George Sommaripa, reflected an ambivalence about activist politics. Forsberg had just left a graduate program in arms control and defense policy and had spent seven years at SIPRI working on extremely technical defense issues. Even though she had substantial differences with the basic tenets of arms control orthodoxy, she respected the complexity of the issues and the expertise and influence of arms control experts. She chose a movement strategy for grounding her ideas with some reluctance and only because she believed that politicians and policy makers would not address broader issues arms control and disarmament issues unless forced to do so by popular pressure. The freeze movement, for her, was the only way to do this. Political necessity, she believed, would create a climate in which experts would be willing to reevaluate established policies and contemplate radical changes. The reason this had not occurred in the past, she argued, was that the expert elite had not yet found an agreeable first step toward disarmament.[45]

Public support could force the experts to consider the freeze proposal; Forsberg was confident that it could withstand their scrutiny and eventually command their support. She believed the inherent sense of the proposal would ultimately win the day. The initial strategy paper reflected these beliefs and called for grassroots support really only as a means for reaching the arms control elite. The paper proposed winning endorsements from large mainstream interest groups, including universities, business, and organized labor, followed by close work with journalists, editors, and television producers to establish the legitimacy of the freeze idea. Key events would include a technical colloquium of established experts who would work out the details of implementing a freeze, a press conference of "prominent Americans" who supported the freeze, and the use of nationally syndicated television programs to disseminate and discuss the ideas.[46] Winning public attention and expert support would translate into significant, although not necessarily majority support in Congress, which could then be brought to bear on whoever was president, forcing him to propose a freeze to the Soviet Union. By continuing to press for what they saw as an intermediate-range goal (a nuclear freeze), movement strategists argued, the movement could hope to win smaller victories along the way, and stop deployment of the MX, Trident II, and Euromissiles.[47]

NOTES

1. Robert Leavitt, "Freezing the Arms Race: The Genesis of a Mass Movement," unpublished Kennedy School of Government Case Study, Harvard University, 1983, p. 11; Pam Solo, *From Protest to Policy: Beyond the Freeze to Common Security*, Cambridge, MA: Ballinger, 1988, pp. 42–45.

2. Pam Solo and Mike Jendrzejczyk, memo, August 1980, IPIS archives.

3. Steve Ladd, letter, August 4, 1980, Institute for Peace and International Security (IPIS) archives.

4. FOR, memo, "Analysis of Current International/Domestic Situation and Discussion of Policy Alternatives," February 20, 1980, IPIS archives.

5. Richard Baggett Deats, memo, June 18, 1980, IPIS archives.

6. Alexander Cockburn and James Ridgeway, "The Freeze Movement vs. Ronald Reagan," *New Left Review* 137 (January/February 1983): 6.

7. *Freeze Focus*, December 1984; Franklin A. Long, "A Rapidly Negotiable First-Stage Nuclear Freeze," in Steven E. Miller, ed., *The Nuclear Weapons Freeze and Arms Control*, Cambridge, MA: Ballinger, 1984, p. 22; Pam Solo, *From Protest to Policy*, p. 44; Jeremy J. Stone, "Legislating Bilateral Freeze Restraints," in Miller, ed., *Nuclear Weapons Freeze*, pp. 186–295.

8. Richard Barnet, "U.S.-Soviet Relations: The Need for a Comprehensive Approach," *Foreign Affairs*, Spring 1979, pp. 788–90.

9. Warner R. Schilling, "U.S. Strategic Nuclear Concepts in the 1970s: The Search for Sufficiently Equivalent Countervailing Parity," *International Security*, Fall 1981, p. 56; Stone, "Legislating Bilateral Freeze Restraints."

10. Stone, "Legislating Bilateral Freeze Restraints," p. 192.

11. Jimmy Carter, *Keeping Faith: Memoirs of a President,* New York: Bantam, 1982, pp. 245–46, 535.

12. Adam M. Garfinkle, *The Politics of the Nuclear Freeze,* Philadelphia: Foreign Policy Research Institute, 1984, p. 77; Morton H. Halperin, "The Freeze as Arms Control," *Bulletin of the Atomic Scientists,* March 1983, p. 2; Solo, *From Protest to Policy,* pp. 24–25.

13. Boston Study Group, *The Price of Defense: A New Strategy for Military Spending,* New York: New York Times Books, 1979. On Forsberg, see Suzanne Gordon, "The Woman Behind the Freeze," *Mother Jones,* September/October 1982, p. 64.

14. *Freeze Focus,* December 1984; Solo, *From Protest to Policy,* pp. 42–45.

15. George Sommaripa and Randall Forsberg, "Strategy for a Concerted National Effort to Halt the Arms Race," August 25, 1980, p. 1, IPIS archives. For Forsberg's analysis see her articles, "A Bilateral Nuclear-Weapons Freeze," *Scientific American,* November 1982, pp. 52–61; "The Freeze and Beyond; Confining the Military to Defense as a Route to Disarmament," *World Policy Journal,* Winter 1984, pp. 285–318.

16. Forsberg, "Bilateral Nuclear Weapons Freeze"; Jan H. Kalicki, "Arms Control and the Nuclear Weapons Freeze," in Miller, ed., *Nuclear Weapons Freeze,* p. 14.

17. Randall Forsberg, interviewed by Pam Solo, 1985.

18. Michael Kazin, "How the Freeze Campaign Was Born," *The Nation,* May 1, 1982, p. 523.

19. Leavitt, "Freezing the Arms Race," p. 2.

20. Garfinkle, *Politics of the Nuclear Freeze,* pp. 25–27.

21. Leavitt, "Freezing the Arms Race," p. 11.

22. Ibid., p. 16.

23. Randall Forsberg, "If We Can Share a Single Goal, We Can Stop the Arms Race!" *Christianity and Crisis,* January 18, 1982.

24. Leavitt, "Freezing the Arms Race," pp. 16–17.

25. *Freeze Focus,* December 1984; Sommaripa and Forsberg, "Strategy for a Concerted National Effort," p. 2.

26. Leavitt, "Freezing the Arms Race," p. 23.

27. Solo, *From Protest to Policy,* pp. 47–49; Sommaripa and Forsberg, "Strategy for a Concerted National Effort," p. 2.

28. Wendy Mogey (AFSC), letter to Solo and Jendrzejczyk, April 15, 1980, IPIS archives.

29. Interview with author, February 9, 1989.

30. Garfinkle, *Politics of the Nuclear Freeze,* p. 1; Nuclear Freeze Steering Committee Meeting Minutes, December 8, 1980, IPIS archives.

31. Russell Johnson, "AFSC Peace Work from the '50s to the '80s," *Peacework,* September 1983.

32. *Newsweek,* "A Matter of Life and Death," April 26, 1982, pp. 20–25.

33. Leavitt, "Freezing the Arms Race," pp. 25–28. Also see Tom DeLuca, "The Cutting Edge of Survival: Mobe Looks at Mobe," *The Mobilizer,* May 1982, who argues that in supporting the nuclear freeze, MfS should focus on "a major reduction in the nuclear arsenal and/or unilateral steps toward disarmament."

34. See, for example, Jon Saxton, "Nuclear Freeze Campaign: Disarmament in a Vacuum," *WIN,* December 1, 1981, pp. 10–16.

35. Patty Edmonds, "Antibomb Equals Antichoice," *Nuclear Times,* February 1984, p. 15. *Peacework,* February 1982, printed notice of group "Pro-lifers for survival," whose membership included notable antinuclear activists Rev. Daniel Berrigan, Robert Aldridge, and James Forest. Also, Donna Warnock, "Feminism and Militarism: Can the Peace Movement Reach Out?" *WIN,* April 15, 1982, p. 7.

36. Eric Kristensen, "Homophobia, Gay Liberation, and the Movement," *Peacework,* July/August 1982.

37. See, for example, Frank Brodhead, "The Peace Movement Today," *The Mobilizer,* May 1982.

38. Leavitt, "Freezing the Arms Race," p. 23.

39. Solo, interview with author, June 30, 1986.

40. Also see Brodhead, "Peace Movement Today"; Cockburn and Ridgeway, "The Freeze Movement," pp. 13–15; *Peacework,* January 1983, special issue on the "deadly connection" between nuclear weapons and superpower intervention in the Third World.

41. Mark Niedergang, "Freeze: Beginning Is Half," *WIN,* November 1982, p. 7.

42. Ibid., p. 8.

43. Ibid., pp. 10–11.

44. Ada Sanchez and Normon Solomon, "Anti-Freeze: The Dangers of Moderation," *WIN,* November 1982, pp. 11–12.

45. Leavitt, "Freezing the Arms Race," p. 13.

46. Sommaripa and Forsberg, "Strategy for a Concerted National Effort," pp. 9–10.

47. Carol Jensen, "Notes on a Strategy to Achieve a Nuclear Weapons Freeze," memo, July 14, 1980, IPIS archives.

10

A STRATEGY TO
REACH THE PUBLIC

Once the freeze proposal established a base of support among peace groups, supporters tried to incorporate it into their ongoing projects, to reach the general public, and to enter the political system. Experimentation with several different strategies led activists to emphasize local organizing. Initial attempts to push the freeze nationally met little success, but the public response in local venues was extremely encouraging. By building a strong grassroots base of support, the freeze movement gradually percolated back up to national politics, where politicians were compelled to respond to it.

FIRST STRIKE: THE DEMOCRATIC
NATIONAL CONVENTION

The first attempt to bring the nuclear freeze to mainstream U.S. politics was at the 1980 Democratic National Convention in New York. Partly this was a result of strategy, but it also reflected a geographic coincidence. AFSC was among the nuclear freeze's strongest supporters early in 1980, and its primary disarmament effort, the "New Manhattan Project," was based in New York. AFSC had made a commitment early in March, a month before printing *Call to Halt the Arms Race,* to propose a nuclear moratorium at both the Democratic and Republican national conventions.[1] By May the "Delegates' Campaign" had been redefined to include the nuclear freeze proposal, which activists hoped to incorporate into the platforms of both parties. The effort to influence the Republican convention dissipated as the Democratic convention became a top priority. In preparation, between April and June of 1980 the AFSC distributed the *Call* in 38 Congressional districts in New York and New Jersey.

The *Call* quickly won some support from people prominent and well respected by the left of the Democratic Party, including Representatives Dellums and Weiss, Shirley Chisholm, Harvey Cox, Bernard Feld, Philip Morrison, John Kenneth Galbraith, Theodore Sorenson, and Gloria Steinem, but the campaigns of both Jimmy Carter and Edward Kennedy worked to keep the issue off the agenda.[2] When the freeze resolution was defeated 78–51 in the platform committee, Frank Askin, a New Jersey delegate, took the resolution to the floor and tried to win support for a minority plank in the platform:

> In order to stop the nuclear arms race while awaiting the completion of negotiations on strategic arms limitation, the Democratic Administration will pursue an immediate freeze, applying to all nuclear weapons states, on all further testing and deployment of nuclear weapons and delivery systems, within the limits of verifiability.

The language, modified slightly from the *Call,* reflected the qualifications of bilateralism and verification that would be present in every successive freeze resolution. Overshadowed by the bitter nomination fight, with organized support from neither camp, the resolution quietly won support from 40 percent of the delegates.[3] Although a substantial achievement, this must have seemed a hollow victory as the campaign got underway and Democratic nominee Jimmy Carter, while attacking candidate Reagan's hawkish proposals, promised that if reelected he, too, would abandon SALT II, budget large increases for the military, modernize the strategic arsenal with counterforce weapons including the MX and Trident II missiles, and place new intermediate-range nuclear missiles in Europe. Arms control, much less disarmament or the nuclear freeze, were completely excluded from the mainstream political debate. The election results, including Reagan's landslide victory and Republican victories in the Senate, also appeared to be further repudiation of antinuclear and peace activist efforts. The election forced a substantive reevaluation of movement strategy.

The election also created the political space, however, necessary for the movement to emerge within the mainstream. President Reagan and his allies dramatically moved U.S. military policy to a far more aggressive and expensive posture, aided by the timidity of Congressional Democrats in opposing the new administration's initiatives. This effectively left proponents of arms control or military reform, including interest groups, activists, scholars, and politicians, without the access or appearance of potential influence they had earlier enjoyed. Excluded from the halls of policy making, they were now accessible to protest mobilization. The nuclear freeze proposal, although perhaps not initially appealing to all as an arms control strategy, could be an effective vehicle for expressing discontent with Reagan's policies.

It seems likely that if the elections had turned out differently, if Reagan's victory margin had been narrower or if the Democrats had retained control of the Senate and some amount of political confidence, the freeze would have found the struggle to reach the mainstream and grow far more difficult. More radical groups would have been even less willing to compromise their aims to achieve a unified and comprehensive movement. Liberal groups would have been warier about entering this kind of coalition altogether. Finally, with a marginally warmer reception from the Democratic Party leadership or Congress, the freeze leadership would probably not have pushed the campaign to the grassroots to the extent that it did.

Activists quickly recognized Reagan as an asset for their efforts. By moving government policy and political rhetoric so far to the right, he created room for the movement to emerge. In the context of Reagan's policies, one freeze strategist argued, the freeze could present itself "as a bilateral plan . . . conservative and modest." Reagan's economic policies would enable the antinuclear activists to use the military budget and the issue of budget transfers to organize and expand their base of support. "And as the economy gets worse (which more military spending will do to the economy)," Dan Ebener wrote in a memo to activists the day after Reagan's election, "new solutions such as ours will be looked at with a new openness, especially by moderate Democrats who will be more willing to criticize the new president."[4]

A GRASSROOTS BASE

The November 1980 election also provided the fledgling freeze campaign with a new approach that would prove to be the cornerstone of its activities during the next two years: local referenda. In three western Massachusetts state senate districts, voters had the opportunity to consider a nonbinding nuclear freeze resolution. Question 7 passed in 59 of 62 towns with a total of 59 percent of the vote, even though Ronald Reagan had carried all three districts and 33 of the towns. Within the scope of the Reagan landslide, this tiny victory provided an element of hope for freeze activists, as well as a model for organizing.[5]

In 1979 Sister Judith Scheckel, representing AFSC, and Randy Kehler, who had founded the Traprock Peace Center earlier that year, began organizing the referendum effort independently of Forsberg and the national freeze committee. Kehler, a long-time activist, was anxious to address the nuclear weapons issue, but was not comfortable with Mobilization for Survival's style of organizing or the nuclear moratorium; he believed that such a broad strategic focus caused people to "burn out."[6] He had learned of Hatfield's proposed freeze amendment to SALT II from Jim Wallis, editor of the pacifist journal, *Sojourners,* who had picked it up from the Institute for Policy Studies.

Traprock and AFSC coordinated the campaign, which easily gained the 1,200 signatures needed in each senate district by setting up tables in front of supermarkets and shopping centers. Activists used the signature gathering to begin building their organization and to engage in a very limited kind of political education. ("We could only begin to explain," Kehler and Scheckel wrote, "that 'those Russians' don't want a nuclear war any more than we do.") Once the petitions were certified, activists organized study groups and house meetings, researching and discussing various aspects of the arms race, particularly its economic implications. According to the organizers, the campaign accelerated during the summer of 1980, even as the Democratic Party rejected it, gaining support from local religious leaders and college students. In the fall freeze supporters showed films and gave presentations to all kinds of local groups, including public school classes.

Sometime in the fall organizers realized that the campaign might benefit from a relationship with the national effort. In a fundraising letter Kehler promised that a referendum victory could spur a larger national campaign. "Clearly," he wrote, "our efforts here in Western Massachusetts are part of something already large and just beginning to grow." The referendum, he continued, will be a "bellwether for public reaction to the idea."[7] National groups and activists took interest in the western Massachusetts campaign and contributed their efforts. Daniel Ellsberg, for example, visited the area and gave several speeches on behalf of the freeze referendum.[8] Kehler's emergency fundraising appeal also drew more than $15,000 from outside the area; virtually all of it went into publicizing the referendum. There were broadcasts on local radio and television, bumper stickers, billboards, and a series of signature ads in local newspapers. One signed by 150 health care professionals addressed the medical consequences of nuclear war; another with signatures from nearly 100 human service workers condemned the economic costs of the arms race.

News of the referendum victory was carried by UPI although only the nearby Boston *Globe* picked it up. Many small left and peace journals, however, jumped on the story. The western Massachusetts referendum victory, the only positive note in an otherwise dismal cacophony of conservative victories, established the nuclear freeze resolution as a viable vehicle for organizing and expressing opposition to the newly ascendent right. Not only was the freeze given legitimacy as a standard for the opposition to the Reagan agenda, but the referendum campaign also demonstrated a set of effective organizing tactics. Perhaps most significantly, the western Massachusetts effort defined the nuclear freeze as the answer to both a widespread fear of nuclear war and the political alienation of the left. Kehler and Scheckel concluded in their report on the referendum:

> With our victory at the polls came victorious expressions of personal growth and self-worth from those who had taken on tasks they had never done before. The referendum campaign gave us a legitimate and tangible reason for us to approach other persons and groups, and as we encountered them we grew in clarity and purpose. We gained a sense of power, of strength and confidence in ourselves and in the peace movement. And we discovered that most people really are against nuclear weapons and nuclear war.[9]

There is an element of willful political naiveté in this. While small victories are necessary to build a core of activists and organizations, it is dangerous to divorce those institutions and confidence-building exercises from a political context. The nuclear freeze had to be about more than establishing a sense of self-worth and personal growth for activists. Further, the referendum campaign was never confronted with any organized opposition. Freeze supporters were able to define their resolution very loosely, often as little more than an expression of fear or distaste for life in a nuclear world. This approach helped gain a great deal of support at the time, but a softness in much of it would eventually contribute to the diffusion of the campaign.

BUILDING ON A VICTORY

Fear of nuclear war became the centerpiece of early freeze organizing. Activists tapped into reasonable concerns about the possibility of accidental nuclear war, for example, as a problem the freeze could solve.[10] Other events nourished this fear, including the well-publicized case of Howard Morland who, after months of litigation and over government opposition, published an article describing the basic plans for building a nuclear device. Involving issues of free speech and prior restraint, daily newspapers gave the case extensive coverage.[11] Aided by Reagan administration rhetoric, antinuclear groups would feed on these fears, often funneling freshly terrified people into local freeze efforts.[12]

PSR is the best example of an antinuclear group that stoked public fears and then utilized them in support of antinuclear efforts. Australian pediatrician Helen Caldicott had revived the group in Boston at the time of the Three Mile Island accident. A powerful speaker, she detailed the effects of nuclear radiation or nuclear explosions on the human body, generally whipping audiences into frenzied anger. The reborn organization was initially cast in her image, expanding dramatically from a few hundred doctors mostly in the Boston area in 1979, to more than 10,000 contributing members in 1981, when PSR endorsed the nuclear freeze. PSR speakers went on "bombing runs," in which they described the effects of one nuclear bomb dropped on the city or town they were addressing. Freeze advocates would follow the speech with strategies for political action.[13]

Following the western Massachusetts victory, the freeze became the most visible expression of antinuclear and anti-Reagan fears. The then-small national nuclear freeze coalition worked to cultivate this identity, to build a national political organization, and to ensure the proposal's political viability. Over Forsberg's initial opposition, CALC's Carol Jensen worked to organize the campaign's first national convention, to be held in March 1981. Political and personal strains in the initial working group began to show as the movement attempted to move from its original supporters on the political margins toward the mainstream.

Forsberg insisted, for example, that the names of many of the groups in the early freeze coalition not appear on invitations to the first national strategy meeting. "We believe that if known, that the current peacenik/radical/religious-pacifist composition of groups in the steering committee might dissuade other middle-of-the-road constituencies from participating," she wrote in a memo to the steering committee. The invitations, dated December 12, 1980, eventually went out over Forsberg's own name and the signatures of Richard Barnet, Elise Boulding, Harvey Cox, Richard Falk, Bernard Feld, and Philip Morrison.[14]

Even at this early stage, however, the patterns of organization established in the campaign's short history would affect the way in which the nuclear freeze was presented to the public. The New Manhattan Project's Delegates' Campaign had already begun organizing freeze supporters according to Congressional districts; the western Massachusetts effort established the value of organizing nuclear freeze activism locally and the use of referenda. Both procedures were established as a framework for organizing the campaign well before the first national strategy meeting.[15]

On March 20–22, 1981, 300 activists attended the strategy conference at Georgetown University's Center for Peace Studies. The conference adopted a national strategy and created the structure that would evolve into the National Nuclear Weapons Freeze Clearing-house (NWFC), initially quartered at Forsberg's IDDS in Brookline, Massachusetts. The strategy called for a four-step campaign that would span a period of 3–5 years. Step one, "demonstrate the potential of the freeze," included documenting the growth of the proposal's appeal, winning endorsements from organizations and prominent individuals, winning electoral support for the proposal in select areas of strength, and gaining media coverage. Step two, "broaden the base of public support," called for expanding all the activities in step one, developing a higher profile in national politics and media, and winning support from the international community, including Europeans and the nonaligned nations, and gaining support in Congress. In stage three, "focus public support of the freeze on policymakers so it becomes a matter of national discussion," the campaign would work with Congressional supporters to pass legislation that would, for example, stop the MX, the Euromissiles, plutonium production, and nuclear testing. Stage four, the product of all the previous work, would be "adoption of the freeze."[16]

The campaign, especially at the outset, was deeply rooted in local organizations and the efforts of grassroots activists, unusual for a social movement explicitly concerned with issues clearly national and international in scope. The strategy made sense, however, given the limited resources available and the strength of the probable opposition at the national level. In a memo on the necessity of extensive local organizing, Gordon Faison and Randy Kehler argued that if the campaign sought national support initially "we will fail to win over [national] policy-makers if they know there's no pressure from large numbers of their constituents." A strategy based on local initiative would maximize political participation, they contended, would train large numbers of activists and offer the intermediate victories needed to sustain participation. It would also allow organizers to choose tactics most likely to be effective in their own areas. Perhaps most important, it would enable the movement to avoid "heavy" opposition.[17] A series of local victories would build organizational support for a larger effort, effectively laying the foundation for winning at the national level.

The decentralized ethos of the freeze campaign, reinforced by necessity, also called for using established organizations and their events to the greatest extent possible rather than for establishing new organizations and independent events. Freeze advocates piggybacked on the efforts of all sorts of local groups, arranging to address organizations at their regular meetings and bringing tables and information to all sorts of events.[18] This strategy had several clear benefits. First, by tapping into the efforts of larger, more established groups, the freeze was able to gain an outreach and a public face far more extensive than its own resources alone could provide. Second, this kind of piggybacking granted the movement legitimacy and an entree to media attention. Third, the focus on cohesive subgroups, such as local churches, clubs, social and service organizations, created a self-sustaining network that, often absent concrete political achievements, provided personal satisfaction to activists and encouraged continued participation. Fourth, use of established organizations with their own varieties of constituencies and purposes allowed the movement to develop a diverse leadership and to gain admission to a variety of social and political niches, effectively expanding the political space available for mobilization. Finally, the movement's approach encouraged a broad spectrum of organizations to undertake an even wider variety of activity in the name of the nuclear freeze, heightening the movement's public profile and multiplying the number of options available to potential activists.

The first stage of the freeze program, demonstrating the idea's potential to attract support, produced remarkable successes, as reflected in *The Freeze Newsletter*. Edited by Mark Niedergang and published by IDDS during 1981, the earliest editions demonstrated both the amateurishness and energy of the movement. The newsletters were photocopied, included typographical mistakes, and were almost all hand-addressed by IDDS's small research staff in flurries of activity. In 1981 the newsletter chronicled an ever-growing list of endorsements from local and national "notables" and the general infusion of the freeze idea into a wide variety of communities and organizations. It reported on freeze resolutions passed by several state legislative bodies, the involvement of local and national churches, several large demonstrations and civil disobedience actions, and nuclear freeze petition campaigns growing in 17 states. The Mother's Day Rallies of the Women's Party for Survival in 15 states earned newsletter coverage, as did Seattle Archbishop Hunthausen's call for tax resistance, prayer vigils at Ellsworth Air Force Base, and the efforts of several local groups in campaigns against the Trident and MX missiles. Randall Forsberg wrote updates of U.S. military plans on counterforce weaponry and the Euromissiles for the newsletter, which also provided coverage of growing antinuclear movements in Western Europe. New organizing ideas also received prominent coverage, such as the Virginia freeze campaign's booth at a state fair (featuring the "knock a nuke" game) and advice from organizers on how to collect signatures on freeze petitions.

The newsletter reported that town meetings in several New England states, a vestige of direct democracy, proved to be an excellent forum for freeze advocates. A relatively small amount of organization and preparation by just a few residents enabled entire towns to place the freeze on the Democratic agenda along with a wide range of local issues. The freeze almost always passed by a wide margin. During the spring of 1981, more than 20 towns in Vermont, New Hampshire, and Massachusetts endorsed freeze resolutions at their annual meetings.[19] Local organizing efforts generated immediate benefits, creating a diversity of activity generally infused with a populist enthusiasm.

The newsletter also reported the responses of elected officials, generally warmest from politicians furthest removed from any responsibility or influence on the process of making military and nuclear policy. In March 1981, for example, the City Council of Cambridge, Massachusetts ordered its civil defense director to stop all participation in federal emergency plans for evacuation in the event of a nuclear war, to cease distribution of such plans, and to prepare a pamphlet describing "why no step short of nuclear disarmament by all nations could protect Cambridge citizens against a nuclear war."[20] The Evanston, Illinois, Board of Aldermen passed a resolution calling for Illinois' U.S. Senators Percy and Dixon to support a nuclear freeze. In June 1981, the State Assembly in New York, the State House of Representatives in Oregon, and both Houses of the Massachusetts Legislature voted overwhelmingly for nuclear freeze resolutions, with proponents arguing that favorable votes demonstrated opposition to high military spending and a commitment to finding federal funds for domestic priorities. Other state legislatures would soon follow suit. Governor Brendan Byrne of New Jersey proclaimed October 24–31, 1981, "Mutual Nuclear Freeze Week."[21]

Politicians in the federal government were generally more wary about embracing the movement, excluding the few early allies in the House of Representatives. The response of Senator Paul Tsongas (D-MA) was more typical. After meeting with representatives from nuclear freeze groups in his state, he refused to take a stand on the proposal, stating that such complicated issues deserve deeper consideration, although he encouraged the activists to continue their work.[22]

In 1981 the Clearinghouse at IDDS could do little more than transmit information on issues and activities, and it was strained even in fulfilling that task. Relevant freeze stories at this point included virtually every bit of opposition to the Reagan administration's nuclear policies and a range of political activity from direct action to letter-writing campaigns, as well as everything in between. The newsletter consistently devoted attention to the most disparate and colorful aspects of the movement, including, in the October 1981 issue alone, nuclear freeze fundraising facts; an open letter from a professor of business at MIT's Sloan School asking colleagues and former classmates to join him in supporting the freeze; a report on a peace march across the United States and somehow across the Atlantic and Europe to Moscow; and a group of 12 Los Angeles rabbis calling on Jews to use Tisha B'Av, a traditional fast day, to commemorate the bombings of Hiroshima and Nagasaki. It was all too much for IDDS's public education division to handle, Niedergang admitted, writing, "So much exciting material has come in that we decided to expand this edition of the Freeze newsletter from 16 to 24 pages — and even then we couldn't fit in all the successful events and creative ideas that are worth sharing. Thanks is due to local organizers — the heart and soul of the Freeze Campaign — for their energy and commitment."[23]

Just as local activist groups and national organizations in coalition animated the nuclear freeze movement, the freeze also helped its constituent groups. PSR grew from several hundred members in 1979 to more than 30,000 in 1984, including a seven-fold growth in membership during the first ten months of 1982. The Council for a Livable World increased its membership list to more than 80,000 in 1984; SANE also reached a level of 80,000 contributors, more than four times its 1980 total. The *Bulletin of the Atomic Scientists* increased its circulation by nearly 50 percent in two years, according to its own records, from less than 22,000 at the end of 1979 to nearly 32,000 in 1983. A new publication, *Nuclear Times*, was founded to satisfy growing demand for information on nuclear issues and the antinuclear movement. In addition to reviving old organizations, the movement created numerous new groups, mushrooming to number more than 1,400 in 1982. In May 1981, after a conference on nuclear issues organized at Harvard, a group of participants formed Business Alert to Nuclear War, shortly followed by the creation of Educators for Social Responsibility, Nurses Alliance for the Prevention of Nuclear War, High Technology Professionals for Peace, Lawyer's Alliance for Nuclear Arms Control, Artists for Survival, Communicators for Nuclear Disarmament, Computer Professionals for Social Responsibility, and literally hundreds of other groups, each carving out its own peace program.[24] All this activity was seen nationally as part of a movement, effectively much greater than the sum of its parts.

EMERGING AS A NATIONAL MOVEMENT

The freeze campaign, while attempting to define itself as the unifying face of the broad movement against nuclear weapons, had yet to emerge as such on the national stage. Its variety of actions, organizations, and leaders made it less attractive or obvious for national media to cover. Not until the fall of 1981, after large antinuclear demonstrations in many Western European capitals, did mass media and political leaders begin to look for the national face of the movement in the United States. By publicizing the European antinuclear movements in their journals, and even arranging solidarity tours of European activists, freeze supporters portrayed their efforts as part of a growing worldwide movement. They had established a groundwork for the campaign that would allow it to emerge as a national movement.

In characteristic fashion, the opportunity for this emergence was provided by an event organized by other groups, many of which had not endorsed the freeze. The Union of Concerned Scientists, in alliance with several other organizations, modeled the Veteran's Day Convocation on November 11, 1981, after the teach-ins on the Vietnam War in 1965. Freeze activists publicized the event, and even though they had not organized it, they used the convocation as their own, turning out freeze supporters and publicizing their proposal. More than 150 campuses held events attended by an estimated 100,000 people. The UCS organizers intended only to inform the public debate and discuss issues of nuclear war and weaponry, but, by virtue of their efforts, freeze advocates turned the event, and to an even larger degree public perception of the event, into a freeze affair.[25]

The freeze organization meanwhile groomed itself to fit the image the national media was presenting — that of a national and moderate movement based in grassroots America. A key step in this process involved moving the NWFC out of IDDS and, indeed, out of New England and the apparent influence of older peace groups. Freeze leaders decided to site campaign headquarters in St. Louis, roughly the symbolic and geographic center of the country, in an attempt to broaden the base of the movement and reinforce its grassroots character. The choice of Middle America rather than Washington, D.C., was meant to distinguish the movement from the numerous Washington-based lobbying groups concerned with arms control. By locating the NWFC in St. Louis, freeze leaders wanted to show that the movement still saw its primary work as building support among the people of the United States rather than simply among politicians and policy makers.[26]

The NWFC also hired a professional staff, headed by Randy Kehler as national coordinator. The job title, as coordinator rather than director or president, reflected the organizers' view that the Clearinghouse would serve as a resource for local groups, providing information and resources rather than strong leadership and direction. Kehler's background as a local organizer and his experience with the first referendum campaign made him a natural choice for the job. Kehler saw his own job as maintaining the fragile freeze coalition, while still allowing it to continue to grow toward the political center. This came to mean defining the movement and its goals in increasingly narrow terms, eschewing issues or analyses that might jeopardize moderate support. Kehler later explained, "My job was to hold the movement together, to resolve tension, to find a middle road that could hold this movement together."

Kehler and Mark Niedergang set up the national clearinghouse's offices in St. Louis during January 1982, attempting to professionalize the political management of the movement, give the campaign a national face, and to expand its base of support.[27] The new freeze newsletter, published in St. Louis, was typeset with professional graphics, logos, and editing. Its content was also far more selective than that of its predecessor; it focused specifically on the efforts to win public acceptance of the freeze proposal through referenda, local government resolutions, petitions, and similar activities. The same upgrade in quality was noticeable in educational materials provided by the national office. They looked more professional but were also more expensive to produce. The NWFC made new demands on grassroots campaigners for direct support beyond activism. Almost apologetically, the newsletter asked for money from the local groups, "We realize that you are devoting much time and energy to peace work. A strong national Freeze Campaign will enhance your own efforts; the money you contribute today may be returned in another form in the future. The energy and hope the Nuclear Weapons Freeze Campaign arouses may also spill over to other, seemingly unrelated, efforts for peace and justice."[28] Interestingly, the newsletters published in St. Louis omitted the "What You Can Do" item that had appeared on the back page of every newsletter published by IDDS. As the campaign professionalized, the support needed from the grassroots was defined far more narrowly.

Both local organizations and national groups in the freeze coalition were, as usual for protest movements, financially pressed to fund their own activities. The national campaign increasingly turned toward traditional sources of funds for liberal causes: generally supportive foundations like the Stern Fund, the Field Foundation, Stewart Mott, the CS fund, and the Rockefeller Family Foundation; wealthy individuals like Alan Kay and Harold Willens; and direct mail fundraising to likely contributors defined as educated and middle to upper-middle class. Between December 1981 and August 1982, fully 86 percent of the NWFC's funds came from large donors and foundations, while individual contributions (up to $1,000) totalled only 6 percent, with the remaining 8 percent made up of direct mail contributions.[29] Funders and financial supporters became yet another crucial constituency to be placated and maintained within the freeze coalition, and this necessitated certain stylistic and political modifications.

Stylistically, presentations, publications, and all sorts of educational materials became increasingly sophisticated and increasingly similar to those of other organizations. "The movement has grown up," said Richard Pollock, of David Fenton Communications, a media consulting firm. "They realize that they're taking on the big boys eye-to-eye, and their presentations must be as professional as possible."[30] This meant increased use of professional consultants like Pollock, direct mail firms, pollsters, and various other professionals who would consume an ever-increasing share of freeze funds.

Politically, the dependence on funders meant defining the movement to attract potential donors. Specifically, connections to controversial political issues were eschewed and the freeze itself became narrower. The campaign even dodged conflicts about the new generation of counterforce weapons in development, the issue that had initially provoked the *Call*. The freeze itself, if implemented bilaterally, would end development of the Trident and MX missiles and stop the deployment of Pershing II and cruise missiles in Europe. National freeze leadership maintained a focus on the freeze, refusing to address specifically the weapons it could affect, often creating political conflicts with apparently natural allies.[31] When asked by Western European antinuclear leaders about the freeze's position on Euromissile deployment, Kehler explained, "At the moment [February 1983] . . . the freeze campaign has no official position about suspending new U.S. weapons. Many of our Congressional supporters view that as unilateralism and they are opposed to it, so it's a very controversial issue."[32]

While the national campaign was busy dodging controversy and negotiating acceptable political and rhetorical compromises, the movement gained wider public attention through the efforts of other groups. During the first week of March 1982, nearly 200 New England town meetings considered the freeze proposal. Coordinated by the AFSC, the town meeting effort was a huge political success, drawing national coverage and broad support, requiring little money or national effort, and setting off scores of copycat efforts. On March 2, the nuclear freeze passed in 155 Vermont towns, was rejected in 22, and tabled without a vote in 8, bringing the total of Vermont town endorsements to 177. By June 1982, the freeze had also been endorsed by 107 Massachusetts town meetings, 54 meetings in New Hampshire, 25 in Connecticut, 62 in Maine and 2 in Delaware. In what one observer called a "resurgence of participatory democracy," the town meeting spirit spread even to New York City, where nearly 3,500 Manhattan residents held neighborhood meetings to endorse the freeze. By this time, the proposal had won the support of 144 city councils, 31 county councils, and 8 full state legislatures.[33]

By tapping into traditional democratic structures and values, the nuclear freeze built not only support but also political legitimacy. Through town meetings, where coordinated opposition on foreign policy issues was unlikely and organized small groups could win, the movement built a record of successes, established and reinforced a network of local organizations, and won national media attention. This tactic reinforced the image of the nuclear freeze as moderate, mainstream, and majority. Politicians followed the groundswell of public support. By December 1981, the nuclear freeze had won the support of 24 U.S. Representatives and one U.S. senator, Claiborne Pell (D-RI). By June 1982, after a round of town meeting victories, the freeze counted the support of 169 U.S. representatives and 25 senators.

The town meetings, state and local referenda, and the introduction of the nuclear freeze proposal in Congress on March 10, 1982, all contributed to give the proposal and the national freeze organization the public face of a much broader antinuclear movement, with substantial wings on both its left and right. Initially this worked to the freeze's benefit. In April 1982, for example, when Roger Molander's Ground Zero coordinated a week of local and national educational events on nuclear weapons issues, it was widely seen as a freeze event. The national freeze organization made a concerted attempt to take advantage of the Ground Zero events, as they had the UCS Convocation, and succeeded in translating the week of events into a successful publicity and legitimacy coup for the freeze. Most media coverage focused on moderates who had come to the movement rather recently, if at all, like Molander, Bishop Thomas Gumbleton, Dean of Harvard Medical School Howard Hiatt, and author Jonathan Schell. Even key figures within the freeze were used to emphasize this theme of moderation. According to *Newsweek*, "Forsberg hopes that the movement will avoid the mistake of going too far." Quoting her, "One of the strengths of this movement is that it does not call for nuclear disarmament right now."[34]

This portrayal would continue to follow the nuclear freeze, as the role of original coalition groups in the movement diminished. Conflicts between these original supporters and more establishment arms control-oriented organizations — including the freeze's own national organization — became more heated and difficult to resolve. Ironically, this is most clearly demonstrated by the movement's high-water mark, the June 12, 1982, demonstration in New York City.

A NATIONAL DEMONSTRATION AND INTERNAL CONFLICT

The June 12 demonstration was planned to commemorate the UN's Second Special Session on Disarmament and featured the broadest antinuclear coalition the movement would assemble, including the MfS coalition that had organized the first SSD demonstration, the left religious organizations who had given the freeze proposal early support, moderate establishment-oriented arms control organizations, environmental and antinuclear power groups, New York-based minority organizations, and marginalized left parties. Among the endorsers were Greenpeace, Harlem Fightback, MfS, the Unitarian Universalist UN office, Ground Zero, the SHAD Alliance, Pax Christi, WIN, WRL, the Riverside Church, the United Church of Christ, the United States Peace Council, the Communist Worker's Party, WILPF, the United Presbyterian Church, the National Conference of Black Mayors, SANE, Maryknoll

Missionaries, PSR, People's Anti-War Mobilization, the Communist Party, Democratic Socialists Organizing Committee, the National Black United Front (BUF), AFSC, and the National Education Association, along with dozens of other groups.[35]

It is not surprising that a coalition this diverse would have difficulties in negotiating a political platform, agreeing on a list of speakers, and even establishing an organizational structure and a decision-making process acceptable to all involved. These difficulties were exacerbated by the legitimacy and widespread media attention the nuclear freeze had only recently won. The demonstration would be large and extensively covered, regardless of many of the decisions organizers made, and therefore it represented an opportunity for all kinds of groups to tap into the political momentum created by the freeze movement and to present their organizations and their views to newly mobilized activists and national media. As such, it was a demonstration that no organization would pass up, regardless of how vitriolic the conflicts in planning. Further, the location of the demonstration in New York, where many groups had local and national headquarters, increased the number of participating organizations located near enough to attend planning meetings. Many organizations had a claim on left politics in New York City, and none were willing to sacrifice their territorial prerogatives.[36] The planning coalition included 80 national groups as well as 150 local organizations.

Conflicts within the June 12 coalition began to surface almost as soon as planning began in the fall of 1981. In the interest of gaining a large turnout, any group interested in endorsing the demonstration was welcome to join the planning. As the freeze movement grew to occupy an increasingly prominent place on the national scene in the early months of 1982, however, and the stakes for the demonstration grew higher, tensions increased and several times threatened to put an end to planning for the demonstration altogether. There were numerous conflicts and a general dissatisfaction with the time-consuming meetings, initially run by consensus, but the major rift was between the more established older peace organizations including SANE, AFSC, FOR, and the NWFC, and a coalition of local left and minority groups.

This latter group, represented by the Third World and Progressive Peoples Coalition (TWPPC), was led by the Reverend Herbert Daughtry and his Brooklyn-based Black United Front (BUF). The BUF wanted a number of issues added to the explicit agenda of the demonstration, including racism and economic injustice in the United States, a call to end U.S. military intervention in the Third World, and a demand for U.S. unilateral nuclear disarmament. The peace groups backed away from much of this and from a broader agenda generally.[37] The TWPPC was incensed by what its leadership saw as the lack of political relevance to the more moderate approach. Joe Morrison of the South African Military Refugee Aid Fund, part of TWPPC, criticized the dominant groups, "If we water down the coalition too much, it can be diluted to the point that we haven't changed anything."[38]

Agreement about how much watering down the coalition could stand was not easy to reach. The older peace organizations had conflicts among themselves about how broadly to frame the demonstration's demands. A difficult and long debate had produced a fragile consensus around two slogans: "Freeze and Reverse the Arms Race" and "Redirect Resources from the Military to Meet Human Needs." Even the latter slogan, however, was problematic for some groups hesitant to risk the political controversy inherent in addressing the budget, even though the freeze campaign had earlier been eager to make this connection. The more moderate groups were primarily interested in having the demonstration reach a wide audience that would build the movement toward the center of the political spectrum. Mark Roberts of Greenpeace explained, "A significant issue was trying to attract middle America . . . this rally can't be too far left. . . . I personally would like to see more right-wing and conservative groups involved."[39]

The original planning committee fell apart after a March 6 meeting, when Greenpeace, SANE, and Riverside decided that they could not work with some of the left groups, including the BUF. Art van Redmundt, of Greenpeace's Washington office, sent a letter to 37 groups proposing a new executive committee and specifically excluding the BUF. The demonstration had to reach a broad cross-section of people, he argued to justify the exclusion, and "to achieve this result the rally must appear favorable to the new mainstream constituencies."[40] Several of the groups were uncomfortable with this approach, particularly MfS, WRL, and those on the left of the coalition that was to remain. These organizations had their own disputes with the BUF, but they were sensitive to the politics of exclusion and to charges of racism against the traditional peace movement.

All of the groups involved were able to paper over their differences long enough to hold the June 12 coalition together for the demonstration, but the conflicts reflected real problems within the emerging peace movement, conflicts that would not be resolved and would continue to divide the movement. John Collins of CALC explained:

> A lot of the difficulties arise out of the fact that the peace and environmentalist movements tend to be white and middle-class and to a certain degree, racist. Not in the sense of the KKK or that kind of thing. It's just that a lot of people in white groups don't know how to relate to and work with third world groups. Also, with the new upsurge in the disarmament movement

coming from the political center, the danger is that the center will turn around and say to the left, "Okay, we don't need you."[41]

The June 12 demonstration was big enough for every group to find some way to demonstrate its own strength. In a sense it was a triumph in diversity, as Central Park and the streets of New York literally overflowed with people. While the 1 million people attending the June 12 demonstration (plus another 50,000 in a sympathy demonstration in San Francisco) reflected a broad diversity of opinion, both the national media's portrayal of the freeze and the freeze movement's self-portrait indicated that Collins's fears were being realized. The organizers did a good job of avoiding being coopted by the left, but they were not nearly as successful with the mainstream and the right. Organizers attempted to prevent political opportunists from taking advantage of their demonstration. Edward Kennedy and Mark Hatfield were not asked to speak from the platform because the June 12 coalition made a blanket decision to exclude potential presidential candidates. During the demonstration Mayor Ed Koch, virtually alone among New York City Democratic politicians in refusing to endorse the freeze, appeared backstage with a personal police escort. Although he was prepared to speak, union-supplied marshals dissuaded him from attempting to reach the podium.[42]

The most prominent speakers included Democratic U.S. Representatives Edward Markey (MA), Tom Downey (NY), Mickey Leland (TX), Ted Weiss (NY), and Toby Moffett (CT), former Representatives Bella Abzug and Father Robert Drinan, New York City Council President Carol Bellamy, Corretta Scott King, and union leader Victor Gotbaum. Although Ted Kennedy was excluded, his niece Kathleen Kennedy Townsend was featured as a representative from Americans for Democratic Action. Celebrities abounded, including Bruce Springsteen, Holly Near, Orson Welles, Pete Seeger, Linda Ronstadt, Rita Marley, and Sara Miles. Although more radical speakers, including Daughtry, David Dellinger, Seymour Melman, Winona La Duke of the American Indian Movement, and Norma Becker of the War Resister's League, were given time at the podium, they faded into a background of unity above all else.[43]

Many speakers emphasized organized freeze participation in the electoral process. Randall Forsberg's speech particularly was notable for its frequently repeated refrain, "We will remember in November." Forsberg clearly linked the freeze to federal budget issues, demanding, "How can we spend $20 billion a year on these stupid weapons when infant nutrition and school lunches are cut back; student loans are cut back; the elderly are forced to go without hearing aids and eat dogfood; and 20 percent of the black population is unemployed?" In retrospect, however, her prescription for action seems timid: voting against freeze opponents.[44] It would become more problematic as increasing numbers of legislators endorsed some version of the freeze. Although it is unfair to read too much into a rally speech, the omission of any recommended action beyond voting is striking and significant.

Another striking omission was mention of the Israeli invasion of Lebanon that had occurred just one week earlier. The freeze coalition had become much too large and unwieldy to respond rapidly to changes in the political scene; activists, with the notable exceptions of freeze outsiders Dellinger and Noam Chomsky, deliberately avoided discussing Lebanon, reluctant to risk confronting the difficult issues it raised — particularly within their own coalition.[45] This omission further alienated supporters on the left of the freeze and demonstrated the movement's dogged determination to avoid controversy. Joe Gerson of AFSC later wrote that he had attended the New York demonstration after returning from a fact-finding tour in Israel and Lebanon and was disappointed by the planners' decision not to mention the Israeli invasion. "If the June 12 march was one of the greatest successes of the American peace movement," he wrote, "it was also one of our notable failures."[46]

The conflict about intervention was not anomalous. Indeed, the June 12 demonstration represented the end of the first freeze coalition. Groups at the left of the coalition, while still nominally supporting the nuclear freeze, broadened the scope of their attention to address other issues, including U.S. military intervention in Central America and a wide variety of budget issues, and continued to use nonconventional means of political participation, such as large demonstrations and civil disobedience. These groups worked to escalate the political analysis and often the tactics, campaigning against development of specific weapons, crisis relocation plans, weapons research, or for the establishment of "nuclear free zones."[47]

The national freeze, at the same time, distanced itself from all of this in a continuing effort to seize the political center. This split is clear even immediately following the June 12 demonstration. In its report on the event, WRL's *WIN* magazine gave extensive coverage to a large civil disobedience action on June 14, in which more than 1,600 protestors were arrested outside the U.S., Soviet, French, British, and Chinese missions to the UN while attempting to "Blockade the Bombmakers."[48] In stark contrast, the national freeze's newsletter did not mention the civil disobedience.

THE BROADEST COALITION POSSIBLE

Like most of the organizations on its left, the NWFC wanted to ensure that the freeze resolution was not appropriated by the

Democratic Party's mainstream; however, it rejected the aggressive approach of other groups. Freeze leaders argued that in order to prevent the Democratic Party from seizing control of the issue, they had to move even further toward the center of the political spectrum. After the demonstration Randy Kehler emphasized his view that the freeze had to remain bipartisan or nonpartisan. "The answer, in my view, is not to try to discourage Democrats from supporting the Freeze," he wrote. "On the contrary, we should very much welcome their support, not as Democrats, but as fellow citizens and as national leaders. At the same time, we must redouble our efforts to increase the support and participation of those of our fellow citizens who happen to be Republicans."[49] In treating party affiliation and politics generally as an insignificant condition, Kehler underscored the dramatic depoliticization the movement was embracing. The new slogan printed on all future editions of the newsletter and the National Clearinghouse's stationery also reflected this approach: "The Nuclear Freeze. . . . Because nobody wants a nuclear war." The original slogan, "The Future is in Our Hands," had a far more populist tone.

Virtually everything in subsequent newsletters dealt exclusively with the effort to win broader public acceptance of the freeze proposal and the resolution's growing support across the United States and in Congress. Reports from Western Europe, on particular weapons systems, on local organizing strategies, and on related issues such as military intervention or budget transfers, all but disappeared from the newsletter and from the national effort. Instead, the newsletter reflected a nonpolitical opposition to nuclear war and weaponry and a confidence in the ability of the people of the United States and their government to end the nuclear threat by adopting the nuclear freeze.

Meanwhile, the strategies of political participation became more conventional and effectively conservative: referenda, lobbying, contributions to sympathetic candidates, candidate forums, petitions, and targeted voting. Increasingly, the NWFC, which had begun as a movement coalition, viewed itself as an established and continuing force in conventional politics. The National Committee's new strategy, adopted at a conference in Atlanta late in June 1982, reflected this, stressing that "The Freeze Campaign should, following the November elections, begin to develop the necessary structures, resources, and strategies to concentrate even greater effort on raising the issue of a comprehensive, bilateral freeze and bilateral reductions during the *1984 election period* (emphasis original)."[50]

Although the freeze campaign won many of the battles it picked in 1982, it had handicapped its ability to mobilize and win in the future, as its emphasis shifted from the grassroots base of local organizers, who still supplied the core of activism, to Congress. The November 1982 elections, claimed as a huge success by many within the

movement, reinforced the movement's commitment to a Congressional focus. In November the Democrats gained 26 seats in the House
of Representatives, effectively ending the working majority of
Republicans and Southern Democrats supporting the Reagan
initiatives. Although the actual impact of the movement on any of
these Congressional races is unclear, the freeze clearly won
dramatically in its referenda campaigns. The freeze won
overwhelming support on the ballot in California, Massachusetts,
Michigan, Minnesota, New Jersey, North Dakota, Rhode Island, and
Washington, D.C., as well as in numerous other cities, towns, and
counties. Its only ballot losses were narrow defeats in two counties in
Arkansas and Colorado and in the state of Arizona, where Senator
Barry Goldwater and the Reagan administration orchestrated a
sophisticated opposition campaign.[51]

The effort not only to win passage of nonbinding referenda but also
to demonstrate overwhelming margins of support for the freeze
encouraged the national movement to adopt a least common
denominator style of politics. This movement was aided by the
political structures of the national freeze movement, emphasizing
strong local participation and the attempt to build consensus and by
the politics and personalities of its leadership. Controversial issues
were eschewed, and, as the coalition grew, the number of issues that
might be considered controversial increased. The effort to win
acceptance from the mainstream meant that the movement's center
of gravity moved steadily rightward. Freeze leaders like Kehler
dodged virtually any issue that might jeopardize the support of the
hypothetical moderate Republican. Attempting to keep everyone on
board, it became virtually impossible to move the campaign forward.
Theo Brown, executive director of Ground Zero defended this
approach.

> We in the antinuclear movement must not be sidetracked from
> proclaiming the urgency and uniqueness of the nuclear
> threat. . . . Linking other issues to our agenda makes it harder
> — not easier — for new people to become involved in the effort
> to prevent nuclear war. . . . The more baggage we add to our
> central concern about nuclear war, the more obstacles we put
> in the way of new people who would come to the issue. . . .
> There are not enough liberals to save this country from
> nuclear war.[52]

In attempting to gain moderate and conservative supporters, the
movement constantly struggled to hold its own natural constituency.
To maintain the support of the left and liberal groups that still
constituted the largest part of the movement, the national freeze
published fact sheets and educational materials addressing the

federal budget, counterforce weaponry, and foreign military intervention. These educational efforts, however, were divorced from the organization's political efforts, and this was problematic for the freeze. "Keeping education separate from strategy," Pam Solo later observed, "was like giving the movement a lobotomy."[53]

The statewide referenda campaigns of 1982 reflected the shift in the movement's center of gravity and the deliberate attempts made by activists to simplify further the politics of Forsberg's original proposal. Of these efforts, the largest and most visible campaign was in California. Buoyed by the support of millionaire Harold Willens and highlighted by the participation of numerous figures from the entertainment industry, the California campaign attracted widespread support and a great deal of media attention. This approach, defining the freeze narrowly and conservatively enough to preempt opposition, generated substantial electoral victories for referenda across the country. It also served to obscure the meaning of those victories. As the freeze resolution steamrolled across the country and through Congress, it won wide support, but what the vast majorities endorsing the freeze thought they were supporting was less and less clear.

NOTES

1. Wendy Mogey, AFSC appeal for action, March 3, 1980; Wendy Mogey and Patsy Leake, memo, May 21, 1980, IPIS archives.

2. Patsy Leake, letter, July 24, 1980; George Sommaripa and Randall Forsberg, "Strategy for a Concerted National Effort to Halt the Arms Race," August 25, 1980, p. 2, IPIS archives.

3. Frank Askin, letter to delegates, July 14, 1980; Mike Jendrzejczyk, memo, July 3, 1980, IPIS archives; Pam Solo, *From Protest to Policy: Beyond the Freeze to Common Security*, Cambridge, MA: Ballinger, 1988, p. 49.

4. Dan Ebener, "Strategy Development Meeting, Nuclear Weapons Freeze Proposal: 'The Day After'," November 5, 1980, IPIS archives.

5. Harry C. Boyte, "The Formation of a New Peace Movement: A Communitarian Perspective," *Social Policy* 13 (Summer 1982): 6; *Freeze Focus*, December 1984; Randall Kehler and Judith Scheckel, "Yes: The People Decided," *Sojourners*, March 1981; Solo, *From Protest to Policy*, pp. 49–50. The freeze resolution passed by a margin of 94,000 to 65,000.

6. Randy Kehler, interview with Pam Solo, 1985, pp. 17, 27.

7. Randall Kehler, letter, October 15, 1980, IPIS archives.

8. Robert Leavitt, "Freezing the Arms Race: The Genesis of a Mass Movement," unpublished Kennedy School of Government Case Study, Harvard University, 1983, p. 21.

9. Kehler and Scheckel, "The People Decided."

10. Also see James E. Muller, "On Accidental War," *Newsweek*, March 1982, p. 9. A report of numerous near misses released by the U.S. Senate supported this effort: Senators Gary Hart and Barry Goldwater, *Recent False Alerts from the*

Nation's Missile Attack Warning System, Washington, D.C.: U.S. Government Printing Office, 1980.

11.   See Howard Morland, "The H-Bomb Secret," *The Progressive*, November 1979, pp. 14–36; and *The Secret That Exploded*, New York: Random House, 1981; Lawrence Tribe and David H. Remer, "Some Reflections on the *Progressive* Case: Publish or Perish," *Bulletin of the Atomic Scientists*, March 1981, p. 20; A. De Volpi et al., *Born Secret: The H-Bomb, the Progressive Case, and National Security*, New York: Pergamon, 1981.

12.   Women's Action for Nuclear Disarmament, *Turnabout: Emerging New Realism in the Nuclear Age*, Boston: WAND Education Fund, 1986, p. 11; Ute Volmberg, "Folie a Deux: Peace Movement and Deterrence Experts on Their Way to the Abyss?" *Bulletin of Peace Proposals*, 15 (1984): 37.

13.   Leavitt, "Freezing the Arms Race," pp. 30–31; Solo, *From Protest to Policy*, p. 67.

14.   Randall Forsberg, memo, December 2, 1980, IPIS archives.

15.   Also see Patsy Leake, memo, December 18, 1980, "Local Organizing around the Freeze," and letter inviting organizers to a conference, December 29, 1980, IPIS archives.

16.   Strategy Drafting Committee, "Strategy for Stopping the Nuclear Arms Race," March 1981, IPIS archives. Also, *The Freeze Newsletter*, July 1981; Solo, *From Protest to Policy*, pp. 57–61.

17.   Gordon Faison and Randy Kehler, memo, July 22, 1981, IPIS archives.

18.   Leavitt, "Freezing the Arms Race," p. 31.

19.   *The Nuclear Freeze Newsletter*, July 1981; Mary Ellen Donovan, "Plainfield, NH, 1981: Against the Arms Race, New York *Times*, March 28, 1981.

20.   *The Freeze Newsletter*, July 1981.

21.   *The Nuclear Freeze Newsletter*, October 1981.

22.   Ibid.

23.   Ibid.

24.   David Corn, "A Directory of Antinuclear Groups," *The Nation*, May 1, 1982; Adam M. Garfinkle, *The Politics of the Nuclear Freeze*, Philadelphia: Foreign Policy Research Institute, 1984, p. 115; Leavitt, "Freezing the Arms Race," p. 31; Steven Pressman, "Nuclear Freeze Groups Focus on Candidates," *Congressional Quarterly*, May 5, 1984, pp. 1022–23; Solo, *From Politics to Policy*, pp. 67–69. See Institute for Defense and Disarmament Studies, *Peace Resource Book 1986*, Cambridge, MA: Ballinger, 1986, for a comprehensive listing of groups.

25.   Billy Kreuter, "Veteran's Day Anti-nuke Teach-Ins," *Peacework*, December 1981; Paul Walker, "Teach-Ins on American Campuses," *Bulletin of the Atomic Scientists*, February 1982, p. 10.

26.   *Freeze Update*, December 1981; Solo, *From Protest to Policy*, pp. 63–64.

27.   Kehler, interview with Solo, p. 34; Leavitt, "Freezing the Arms Race," pp. 33–34.

28.   *Freeze Update*, December 1981.

29.   "Nuclear Weapons Freeze Campaign, Inc., Contribution Analysis," August 31, 1981, IPIS archives. Direct mail generated $26,402.74; individual contributors (excluding donations over $1,000) gave $22, 449.41; and foundations and large donors contributed $301,047.97, totalling $349,900.12.

30. Quoted in Judith Miller, ". . . And Now a Disarmament Industry," New York *Times*, June 25, 1982.

31. *Freeze Update,* June 1982.

32. Mary Kaldor, Randy Kehler, Mient Jan Faber, "Learning from Each Other," *END Bulletin*, February/March 1983, p. 23.

33. Boyte, "Formation of the New Peace Movement," p. 4; *Freeze Update,* June 1982; Leavitt, "Freezing the Arms Race," Section C, p. 3; *Peacework,* April 1982; Solo, *From Protest to Policy,* pp. 83–84, 98.

34. *Newsweek,* "Who's Who in the Movement," April 26, 1982. Also see "Nuclear Weapons Freeze Campaign 1982 National Strategy: Broadening the Base and Creating a New Political Reality," IPIS archives.

35. Jonathan D. Auerbach, "Nuclear Freeze at a Crossroads," Boston *Globe,* June 22, 1986, p. A19; Dave Lindorff, "War in Peace: The Fight for Position in New York's June 12 Disarmament Rally," *The Village Voice,* April 20, 1982, p. 12; *Peacework,* May 1982, "Special Issue on the Upcoming Demonstration."

36. There was already a great deal of antinuclear activity based in New York. During 1982 and 1983, Susan Jaffe published a regular column in *The Village Voice* listing numerous disarmament or "survival" events each week, including lectures, rallies, teach-ins, and workshops.

37. Louise Bruyn, "June 12: A Look at How It Was Organized," *Peacework,* July/August 1982; Robin Herman, "Protestors Old and New Forge Alliance for Antinuclear Rally," New York *Times,* June 4, 1982, p. B6; Lindorff, "War in Peace"; Murray Rosenblith, "June 12 — A Million March for Peace," *WIN,* August 15, 1982, pp. 6–7.

38. Lindorff, "War in Peace."

39. Ibid.

40. Ibid.

41. Ibid.

42. Rosenblith, "June 12." On Koch and the freeze, see Jack Newfield, "Freeze Leaves Koch Cold," *The Village Voice,* April 27, 1982.

43. Alexander Cockburn and James Ridgeway, "Peace in Central Park," *The Village Voice,* June 22, 1982, p. 21; Herman, "Protestors Old and New"; *The Freeze Newsletter,* July 1982; Rosenblith, "June 12."

44. Forsberg's speech is reprinted in *Freeze Newsletter,* July 1982.

45. Alexander Cockburn and James Ridgeway, "The Freeze Movement versus Ronald Reagan," *The New Left Review* 137 (January/February 1983): 13; Solo, *From Protest to Policy,* pp. 87–89.

46. Joe Gerson, "Defuse the Nuclear Triggers," *Nuclear Times,* February 1984, pp. 11–12.

47. Also see Marta Daniels, "Connecticut Residents Visit Vermont 'Hosts'," *Peacework,* November 1982; John Demeter, "NFZ Campaigns: Moving against Nuclear Dollars," *Nuclear Times,* February 1984; Mark Hare, "New York: Home Is Where the Bomb Is," *WIN,* April 1, 1982, pp. 4–9; "Nuclear Free Zones Declared, Civil Defense Challenged," *WIN,* July 1983.

48. Cockburn and Ridgeway, "Peace in Central Park"; John Miller, "Over One Million Protest Nuclear Arms as UN Special Session Opens," August 1, 1982; and "June 14: Disobedience for Disarmament," *WIN,* August 15, 1982.

49. *Freeze Newsletter,* July 1982.

50. Ibid.

51.   Cockburn and Ridgeway, "The Freeze Movement," p. 15; Jamie Kalven, "Bulletins," *Bulletin of the Atomic Scientists,* May 1982, p. 65; Solo, *From Protest to Policy,* p. 98.

52.   Theo Brown, "Don't Confuse the Issue," *Nuclear Times,* February 1984, p. 13.

53.   Solo, interview with author, June 30, 1987.

11

BEFORE, BESIDE, BEYOND THE FREEZE: ERUPTIONS OF ACTIVISM

While the nuclear freeze campaign channeled its efforts increasingly toward institutional politics, other activists expressed opposition to U.S. nuclear policy in different arenas. Skeptical of achieving substantial gains through Congress, the electoral process, or through work with formal interest groups, small groups pursued direct action strategies, civil disobedience, and litigation. Direct action and legal challenges to the nuclear arms race preceded the freeze campaign's emergence and continued throughout the movement's life and beyond. By addressing related issues in more dramatic and colorful ways, these actions drew public attention to antinuclear concerns and animated the more conventional wing of the movement. The institutional and extra-institutional wings of the disarmament movement enhanced each other's appeal and prospects. As the freeze gained mainstream support and legitimacy, it gradually but deliberately distanced itself from the site-based protests and civil disobedience actions that had earlier served as its exclamation points. The growing distance between the two wings of the movement limited the political prospects for both.

Advocates of direct action against weapons producers or military bases accept that the prospects for much media attention or massive public support are generally not good. The likelihood of achieving an immediate or even noticeable impact on U.S. politics or policy is also usually slight. Recognizing the difficulties of affecting U.S. nuclear policy through conventional participation in the political system, however, small groups of people attempt to affect the instruments of that policy through direct and usually dramatic action. Individuals engage in such actions as pouring blood on weapons systems, trespassing on a nuclear test site, or attempting to block entrance to the Pentagon for a variety of reasons. This kind of direct action always carries a large element of personal risk and demands great commitment. People often make these commitments because political efficacy is less important to them than moral witness. While they recognize that smashing a missile nosecone with a hammer is unlikely to dismantle the U.S. nuclear arsenal, it may be the most that an individual can do and as such is, in itself, preferable to silent acquiescence or conventional politics, which advocates often view as much the same anyway.

This does not mean that people engaged in direct action have no concern for political efficacy. Direct action often represents a protest movement's cutting edge, dramatizing issues and galvanizing a network of groups into action.[1] A dramatic action may draw a great deal of attention not only to itself but also to larger political issues. By demonstrating the convictions of the participants, it may inspire others to undertake political action, sometimes in imitation but more frequently in less dramatic ways. Seemingly desperate and marginal acts can often set into motion a series of events leading to a powerful social movement, generally far beyond the activists' wildest expectations. The long-term political impact of the Boston Tea Party or Rosa Parks' refusal to move to the back of a segregated bus or the demonstrations accompanying the 1968 Democratic National Convention, for example, could not have been reasonably anticipated by the activists themselves. It is clear, however, they served as rallying points for emerging social movements that altered the face of U.S. politics.

DIRECT ACTION AGAINST THE ARMS RACE

Establishing such a rallying point is probably what Grace Paley and ten others affiliated with the War Resister's League had in mind on Labor Day, 1978, when they were arrested on the lawn of the White House while unfurling a banner with the message, "No nuclear weapons, no nuclear wars."[2] Resistance actions like this came from the margins of the U.S. political landscape and throughout the 1970s remained there. As the decade drew to a close, however, bursts of similar antinuclear activism erupted, albeit in a limited way, into mainstream political attention, generating sparks of life for the disarmament movement.

The Women's Pentagon Actions (WPA) in 1980 and 1981 were larger attempts to demonstrate concern about Carter's and Reagan's military buildup and to provide an impetus for antinuclear and antiwar mobilization. The first action grew out of a Women and Ecology Conference held at the University of Massachusetts at Amherst in May 1980 and was given organizational assistance by AFSC and MfS. More than 1,300 women, mostly from the Northeast, participated in the first weekend protest from November 14–17, 1980. As in the movement against nuclear power, the women organized in small affinity groups run by consensus. The affinity group structure provided for a diversity of activity including street theater dramatizing and mourning the plight of battered women, educational workshops, and screaming in anger at the Pentagon. Grace Paley read a statement of unity, expressing the protestors' solidarity with a broad spectrum of women and oppressed people. The mostly white, middle-class protestors explicitly stressed their allegiance to women of color and lesbians and affirmed their intention to create a new world. "Life on the planet has become intolerable," the women proclaimed, as they set to "exorcise evil spirits from the Pentagon," but the concerns were not all metaphysical. "Defense spending, racism, sexism, violence against women and the weapons and military policies that could well mean curtains for us all," were the broad targets of the action.[3] Civil disobedience was the final stage of the protest, as the women blocked the steps to three of five Pentagon entrances, resulting in 124 arrests.

The WPA network grew over the next year, and more than 3,000 women participated in the second demonstration in November 1981. The WPA actions, according to one activist, helped to "crystallize a political perspective of feminist anti-militarism."[4] The participants expressed solidarity with the antinuclear movements in Western Europe just beginning to receive coverage in the United States and linked their antinuclear efforts to a wide variety of political issues. One participant reported, "We talked about budget cuts in human services, the ERA [equal rights amendment], racism in society and in ourselves, the draft, the growing social controls which threaten us, Three Mile Island, World War III." Tying yarn and cloth together, the women encircled the building with a symbolic web of life, discouraging people from entering the building, chanting, "Shame, shame," and "Take the toys away from the boys." Although 60 women were arrested and the Pentagon continued its daily business, many of the women left with a vision of action for the future. Kate Cloud summarized the experience, "The personal is political. . . . Again and again we reminded ourselves that our symbolic protest would develop in significance only if we live out our politics in our lives. The WPA expressed a global vision and a determination to end the obscenity of racist, women hating, death wish governments."[5]

The Women's Pentagon Actions are notable for a number of reasons. First, the protestors made no attempt to winnow their slogans or demands to those that would easily gain widespread support. They were explicitly more interested in articulating their analyses of societal evils clearly and comprehensively than in devising a compromise platform suited to mass consumption. Second, the women involved eschewed conventional notions of politics in their attempt to influence government policy. They chose not to pursue the standard paths of access to politicians or government officials, rejecting both the stylistic and political compromises inherent in such an effort. Finally, while their activities were explicitly directed at the Pentagon, it was always clear that their target audience was much larger and that they hoped to reach sympathetic people across the country and inspire other political activity.[6]

The Plowshares Eight also attempted to express their opposition to the nuclear arms race through direct action, with a greater political fallout. On September 9, 1980, they broke into the General Electric facility at King of Prussia, Pennsylvania, used hammers to smash the nosecones of two Minuteman missiles, and spilled their own blood over blueprints and tools.[7] The action gained national attention at least partly because of the participation of both Daniel Berrigan, SJ, and Philip Berrigan, who had been a Josephite priest. The Berrigan brothers had been frequent and visible civil disobedients during the antiwar movement, and each had been tried and convicted of similar actions several times, serving time in federal prisons. The rest of the group included other Catholic clerical and lay activists: Dean Hammer; Father Carl Kamat, OMI; Elmer Maas; Sister Anne Montgomery, RSCJ; Molly Rush; and John Schuchardt.

According to the Plowshares group, General Electric received $3 million a day in military contracts, "a terrible crime against the poor," as the company, in contrast to its slogan, "actually prepares to bring good things to death." The activists attempted to interfere in this endeavor as effectively as they could, inflicting damage GE estimated to be in the range of $10,000–$40,000. Daniel Berrigan was shortly thereafter released on $50,000 bail. He and the other defendants, with trial pending, continued publicizing their case, encouraging others to take similar actions, and engaging in other civil disobedience actions. The celebrity of the defendants, the changing political climate, and the Plowshares group's prolonged legal defense all brought a disproportionate amount of media and activist attention to the case. The magnitude of the nuclear threat and the immediacy of the social and economic damage inflicted by conduct of the arms race, the Plowshares Eight argued, gave both moral and legal justification to their action.[8] Unlike the WPA, the Plowshares' legal defense was at least as important and visible as the action itself. The actual trial and subsequent appeals kept the Plowshares Eight and their concerns in the news over a period of years, providing a rallying point to others in the movement.

DIRECT ACTION IN THE LEGAL SYSTEM

Although others had tried to use the courts as a vehicle for promoting antinuclear concern or policy reform, the legal system has more generally consumed large amounts of scarce movement resources on relatively narrow issues without providing a prominent public profile. Catholic Action of Hawaii's Peace Education Project, for example, had filed a lawsuit calling for the U.S. Navy to prepare an Environmental Impact Statement disclosing the absence or presence of nuclear weapons at its Pearl Harbor facility. (The navy has a long-standing policy of refusing to confirm or deny the presence of nuclear weapons on any of its ships.) Coordinated by the Center for Constitutional Rights, the suit dragged on for three years and through two reversals after its initial filing in March 1978. The decisions increasingly hinged on narrow legal and administrative issues; the final decision to exempt the Department of Defense from such disclosure requirements was an unambiguous defeat for the antinuclear activists. Activists within the movement had previously considered using the case as a model, but the decision gave little encouragement for similar strategies.[9]

In contrast, the Plowshares action was extremely effective in fulfilling a larger political role, partly because of the notoriety of the defendants and their counsel, former Attorney General Ramsey Clark, and partly because of the ineptitude of trial judge Samuel W. Salus, II. Perhaps most important, the Plowshares group refused to reduce their defense to any technical legal issue. Their "competing harms" defense was based on a claim that the threat of nuclear war, a cornerstone of U.S. military and foreign policy, was so great that virtually any good faith attempt to mitigate it was justified. They sought to use this "necessity defense" less to win acquittal than to present public and publicized expert testimony that would outline the dimensions of the nuclear threat. Judge Salus, while acknowledging their choice of defense, refused to allow testimony on nuclear issues from anyone other than the defendants themselves. Reprimanding the Plowshares Eight, he said: "Nuclear war is not on trial here in this courtroom! You are."[10]

The Plowshares Eight were initially convicted in March 1981, receiving harsh 3–10 year prison sentences. They appealed the verdict, citing a series of procedural violations and Salus' bias. Ruling on these issues, the Pennsylvania Superior Court granted a new trial without addressing larger legal and political issues.[11] Salus had taken the unusual step of giving an interview to the New York *Times* while the trial was in progress, commenting on its unusual nature. The appellate court also cited as evidence of bias a letter the judge had written to an independent film maker who wanted to bring cameras into the courtroom. Before the trial, Salus wrote:

I feel that to make a documentary of such an insignificant situation will make heroes of immature and intransigent people, enhancing their status and importance. It gives them the much wanted publicity which motivated them to do the illogical act in the first place.[12]

The appellate court ruled that Salus was to be excused from any future legal action regarding the Plowshares defendants. Nearly three-fourths of the opinion dealt with the competing harms or necessity defense. While ostensibly admitting this defense under Pennsylvania state law, Salus had prohibited the defense from calling its first witness, Robert Aldridge, who was to testify on the threat of first strike weapons. Salus had ruled that the defendants could present all the relevant information in their personal statements and that expert testimony was unwarranted. The Plowshares activists were also prohibited from reading the full list of expert witnesses who were to have testified on their behalf. A majority of the appellate court ruled that defendants using the competing harms defense were entitled to present expert testimony to support their claim.

Justice Brosky, writing for the majority, explained that in order to prove justification for illegal action, the defense must prove that the defendant believed his actions were necessary to avoid a harm or evil greater than the one that he commits. This need be only an honestly held subjective belief, but such a belief must be objectively reasonable. While Brosky makes no claim of sympathy with the Plowshares group, their political views, or their actions, his opinion calls for defendants in such cases to be given ample opportunity to convince judges and juries of their reasonableness. Although U.S. nuclear policy is not on trial, according to Judge Brosky and the majority, defendants must be given the opportunity to subject it to a jury's scrutiny.

More encouraging was a concurrence filed by Justice Spaeth. In a rambling, although often eloquent, opinion, buttressed by references to Freud, Lewis Thomas, the *Bulletin of the Atomic Scientists,* the U.S. Catholic bishops' pastoral on nuclear weapons, and case law, Spaeth argues that literal interpretation of the law in such a case is far less important than compliance with higher moral values. Proving that a reasonable person might believe that nuclear war is imminent, he continues, is also not a relevant point: the threat of nuclear war *is* imminent. U.S. nuclear policy, he argues, is designed to keep the threat of nuclear war credible and should terrify reasonable people. Unfortunately, he continues, we cannot count upon the courts to champion justice or individuals who take strong moral stands. He adds that too often the court serves as a rubber stamp for illegitimate and immoral decisions made by the legislature, citing the interment of Japanese Americans during World War II as an example. The lesson that we should learn from this, he concludes, is "how an uncritical acceptance of the war power can lead us to abandon liberties we hold dear."[13]

The passionate support Justice Spaeth offered the Plowshares Eight probably encouraged some of the few activists who actually read the opinion. More significant, however, was one point on which Spaeth and the remainder of the majority agreed: the successful invocation of the necessity defense was not contingent upon proving that the single action in question would stop whatever greater harm was at issue. Rather, the majority agreed, to justify the defense of necessity, the action taken may simply be reasonably seen as a modest part of a long and varied political process ultimately resulting in a reduction of the nuclear threat. Although the belief that hammering a few missile nosecones will in itself bring about nuclear disarmament is surely naive, the idea that such a dramatic action might contribute to developing a national debate on nuclear issues is not only reasonable but borne out by the role the Plowshares action played in the emergence of the nuclear freeze movement.

The aftershocks of the Plowshares events spanned a longer period of time than the freeze movement; the initial action occurred before anything resembling a mass movement was evident while Jimmy Carter was president; appeals continued throughout Ronald Reagan's first term. The appellate court's order of a new trial came during the primary season of the 1984 election campaign. Throughout this time the Plowshares defendants were free and engaged in various activities to support their case and their cause, often including other similar civil disobedience actions. The case generated a large amount of media attention, including several long articles in the New York *Times* and three stories on CBS news. The Berrigans were quoted extensively, much more, for example, than freeze leaders Randall Forsberg and Randy Kehler.[14] Left and religious media were even more generous in coverage.

Before this first Plowshares action, Richard Baggett Deats, executive secretary of the Fellowship of Reconciliation, had envisioned a series of Plowshares actions, which would spearhead a religious campaign for a nuclear moratorium, nuclear disarmament, and an end to draft registration.[15] This vision was subsequently fulfilled, as the attack at General Electric was replicated by other small similarly motivated groups throughout the country, many calling attention to their connection by taking the appellation "Plowshares."

In New England the Ailanthus religious community, which included King of Prussia veteran John Schuchardt, staged a series of vigils, demonstrations, and civil disobedience actions at area military contractors, including Draper Laboratories in Cambridge and AVCO industries in Wilmington, Massachusetts.[16] In September 1981, 51 people from religious communities were arrested in front of the Sheraton Hotel in Washington, D.C., where they protested the Air

Force's annual arms display for foreign buyers.[17] In the sixth Plowshares action, seven people were arrested at Griffiss Air Force Base in Rome, New York, where they hammered and poured their own blood on B-52 strategic bombers.[18] Subsequently, Griffiss was the proximate target of the much larger Women's Peace Encampment at Seneca Falls.

General Dynamics' Electric Boat Division in Groton, Connecticut, and the Trident ballistic missile submarine produced there proved to be a veritable magnet for Plowshares-type actions. Protestors regularly attempted to invade the site by land and sea in order to damage new Trident submarines with hammers and their own blood; they were often surprisingly successful with guerrilla-style attacks. While Feminists Against Trident spraypainted "Trident — Omnicide" on Electric Boat's engineering building, four members of the Trident Nein group were able to reach the *USS Florida* by canoe and paint *USS Auschwitz* on the submarine in ten places. In the 45 minutes on the vessel before they were apprehended, they also poured their own blood down the missile hatches. Another group of five simultaneously invaded by land, banging on two sonar bubbles and hanging a banner, *"USS Auschwitz*: An Oven without Walls," over the damaged bubbles. The last group spent some three hours on the site before being arrested by the Groton police. The *USS Ohio,* the first submarine designed specifically to carry Trident missiles, received a similar reception in Bangor, Washington, where 30 boats, ranging in size from 12–54 feet, attempted to blockade its entry to the harbor. This "peace fleet" was dispersed by 53 Coast Guard and Navy ships. All these protests were in the context of a coordinated series of larger, legal demonstrations with the same targets.[19]

Those actions are only a small sampling of the wide variety of direct actions that spread in response to a growing public concern with U.S. nuclear policies. Site-based actions created political targets that served as focal points for an incipient movement. One of the most interesting targets was a moving one, a train that carried nuclear warheads from the Pantex plant in Amarillo, Texas, where they are manufactured, to various deployment sites around the country. The train is painted entirely white. In 1977 activists Jim and Shelley Douglass found a house overlooking the tracks the White Train traveled to enter a Trident submarine base near Bangor, Washington. At the time the Douglasses were looking for a site at which to establish the Ground Zero Center for Nonviolent Action. They rejected the house for Ground Zero, but in 1981 they decided to move their family in and to begin a campaign to stop the train.[20]

For Jim Douglass the White Train was like the boxcars that carried Jews to concentration camps during World War II. He saw it as part of the machinery of the nuclear weapons state and believed that it was a good target for the antinuclear movement. The

Douglasses established the Agape community to coordinate a campaign against the train. From that time Agape tried to track the route of the White Train through its circuitous path across 23 states. Each time it came through Bangor it was met by groups of up to several hundred activists holding candlelight vigils, demonstrating, and frequently attempting to block the tracks. Agape coordinated a network of sympathetic activists across the country to ensure the White Train would receive similar greetings at several sites along its route. In the following years, activists staged vigils across the White Train route, often including civil disobedience. The activists had effectively found a symbol that made the threat of nuclear war visible and addressable.[21]

Other activists argued that the tracks of the nuclear arms race were even more extensive than those of the White Train and that there were ample opportunities to interfere in the operation of the nuclear war system. Seattle Archbishop Raymond Hunthausen, a vigorous supporter of the White Train actions, publicly announced that he would withhold one-half of his federal income tax to protest U.S. nuclear policy. He explained, "Form 1040 is the place where the Pentagon enters all of our lives and asks our unthinking cooperation with the idol of nuclear destruction. I think the teaching of Jesus tells us to render to a nuclear armed Caesar what the Caesar deserves: tax resistance."[22] Although it is difficult to obtain reliable figures on tax resistance to nuclear policy, discussion of the practice and a variety of strategies for pursuing it, increased during the early 1980s.

The results of these actions in the courtroom were mixed. The few limited attempts to have federal judges rule against the Department of Defense or the president on matters of policy (as in the Catholic Action suit), or on the constitutionality of particular nuclear weapons systems, were clearly unsuccessful — at least in the courtroom. In *Greenham Women against Cruise Missiles v. Reagan et al.,*[23] for example, seven British citizens, one American woman living in England, and Congressmen Ronald Dellums and Ted Weiss asked a federal court to declare deployment of cruise missiles in Western Europe unconstitutional. Among other points, the plaintiffs argued that deployment of these weapons would rob Congress of its Constitutional responsibility to decide whether to declare war. The case was dismissed shortly after ground-launched cruise missiles were deployed in Britain, the judge ruling that such issues were essentially beyond the purview and the capabilities of the judiciary. Judges generally avoid controversial political issues like these, preferring, instead, to abdicate authority and responsibility to elected officials.

On occasion the antinuclear movement fared somewhat better in criminal cases, although most judges, through rulings on evidence and instructions to juries, tried to limit the cases to narrow issues, for example, did trespass take place? was property destroyed? Sentences, as in the first Plowshares case, were often harsh. Perhaps equally often, however, in the interest of saving time and money, and of minimizing publicity, charges were summarily dismissed.[24] In a few cases, however, expert witnesses, including Richard Falk, Daniel Ellsberg, Admiral Gene LaRoque (Ret.), Paul Walker, and Howard Zinn were permitted to testify on broader issues, often garnering a great deal of attention for both the defendants and their concerns.[25] Juries sometimes responded to the necessity justification, even against the instructions of the judge, although often timidly. In the Ailanthus Four case, for example, the jury found the defendants guilty of trespass but demanded to make an additional statement, "We found the defendants guilty on narrow legal grounds, but we believe that the case raises important moral and philosophical issues which should be discussed in the widest possible forum."[26]

On at least one occasion, a federal judge responded even more strongly. On October 11, 1984, John LaForge and Barbara Katt were convicted of breaking into the Sperry Corporation's offices in Minnesota, pouring their own blood on two prototype computers for the Trident submarine guidance system and then smashing them with hammers. U.S. District Judge Miles Lord suspended the pair's six-month sentence, contrasting it with a recent case he had presided over involving Sperry.[27] Sperry had arranged to plead guilty to overcharging the Department of Defense $325,000 on a variety of projects although the actual overcharge totaled $3.6 million. No criminal charges were filed. Lord then praised the activists, saying his decision was an attempt

> to force the government to remove the halo with which it seems to embrace any device which can kill and to place, instead, thereon a shroud — a shroud of death, destruction, mutilation, disease and debilitation. . . . [I anxiously await] the protestation of those who complain of my attempts to correct the imbalance that now exists in a system that operates in such a manner as to provide one type of justice for the rich and a lesser type for the poor, one standard for the mighty and another for the meek [a system whose] objectivity is sublimated to military madness and the bomb. . . . Can it be that those of us who build weapons to kill are engaged in a more sanctified endeavor than those who would by their acts attempt to counsel moderation and mediation as an alternative method of settling international disputes. What is so sacred about a bomb, so romantic about a missile? Why do we condemn and hang individual killers while extolling the virtues of the warmongers.[28]

As sympathetic and supportive as he was, Lord could do little more than let the protestors go free. His denunciation of nuclear weapons and weapons producers, however powerful coming from the bench, had no effect on policy.[29] Lord's endorsement, although encouraging, at best allowed the antinuclear activists to continue their work, at least temporarily free. It certainly did not improve their political position. The damage to computer keyboards that the activists had effected and that Lord had allowed to go unpunished was surely minute in the context of the U.S. nuclear arsenal. The suspended prison sentence did not promise other activists that subsequent cases would be handled similarly by other judges, or even by Lord.

The problem is in the nature of the criminal system. Ted Dzielak, who worked with many of the White Train defendants through the National Lawyer's Guild, argues that antinuclear activists need to develop legal strategies that allow them to take the offensive. The best the defendant in criminal court can hope for is acquittal or a light sentence. Even a victory in this context leaves the nuclear arsenal untouched. For example, in one case White Train protestors, charged with blocking the train tracks, argued that the train was operating illegally. The court ruled in their favor; however, the decision hinged not on Nuremberg precedents but on the vehicle's last brake inspection. Again and again, even in victory, the larger issues of concern to antinuclear activists escaped judicial scrutiny. Even sympathetic judges were generally unwilling or unable to rule on the objects of antinuclear protest.[30]

DIRECT ACTION AND THE NUCLEAR FREEZE MOVEMENT

Antinuclear civil disobedience and direct action were important to the movement because activists were able to use dramatic action, inside and outside court, to publicize U.S. nuclear policy and the depth and intensity of antinuclear concern. Mitch Snyder, a well-known activist on behalf of the homeless, accomplished much the same thing without going near a courtroom. Snyder fasted for 62 days to protest the Navy's launching of a new attack submarine and its name, *Corpus Christi*. (The National Conference of Catholic Bishops unanimously voted to request a name change and was joined in its call by 24 Episcopal bishops and 250 other religious orders.) In modest response, the Navy renamed the submarine *City of Corpus Christi*.[31] Many dramatic actions, however, generally involved confrontation with weapons producers and/or some representative of the state. Such affairs often wind up in court, where the legal system may provide ample drama and publicity.

Civil disobedience, direct action, and bold demonstrations were the opening salvos in the antinuclear campaign. As the freeze movement grew, such actions, generally with far more comprehensive demands, were the exclamation points within the movement, highlights that drew attention to everything else. The freeze campaign, in the same way, gave a legitimate face to direct action and offered a political program that required less commitment and intensity for potential participants. The approaches were mutually complementary. The first freeze newsletter showed a cognizance of this and covered such dramatic actions.

As the campaign grew, however, these same civil disobedients and activists were more often ignored. As the *Freeze Newsletter* grew into *Freeze Focus,* its content reflected the changing emphasis of the campaign. Civil disobedience actions, although more frequent, received less and less attention, until virtually everything in the organ dealt directly with the process of winning Congressional support for a freeze resolution. In the interest of winning a majority coalition and moderate support, freeze leaders sometimes even repudiated civil disobedients and unilateralists. Harold Nash, co-chair of the Southeastern Connecticut freeze committee, denounced the Trident Nein activists as vandals. Nash, who had previously designed sonar equipment and torpedoes for the navy, explained that the nuclear freeze movement was mainstream and moderate. As far as civil disobedience, he added, "We want to dissociate ourselves from that as much as possible."[32]

Most freeze leaders were reluctant to be as explicit about dissociation as Nash, but he was certainly not alone in his wishes. While dramatic actions and civil disobedience continued throughout and beyond the life of the nuclear freeze, the campaign itself was increasingly reluctant to give them credence or publicity. Partisans of direct action, in the same way, grew distrustful of the freeze, which appeared increasingly moderate and mainstream. The mutual wariness allowed the movement to be fragmented and ultimately contributed to its demise. Dramatic actions not embraced by the more mainstream wing of the movement were effectively allowed to drop off the margins of political legitimacy, and such actions no longer pointed to a legitimate proposal for mainstream action.

NOTES

1. Jo Freeman, *The Politics of Women's Liberation: A Case Study of an Emerging Social Movement and Its Relation to the Policy Process,* New York: David McKay, 1975, pp. 48–49.

2. *The Nation,* "Editorial," February 10, 1979.

3. Mary Ellen Donovan, "Pentagon Power," *The Nation,* December 6, 1980, p. 597. Ellen Sturgis, interview with author, June 28, 1985.

4. Kate Cloud, "Report on the Women's Pentagon Action," *Peacework*, December 1981.

5. Ibid.

6. The women involved with WPA were generally proud of their activities and relatively optimistic about their potential impact. For a contrasting evaluation, see James Fallows, *National Defense*, New York: Random House, 1981, p. 177.

7. New York *Times*, September 10, 1980, p. 16; December 13, 1980, p. 8.

8. *IFOR Report*, December 1980, p. 20.

9. Center for Constitutional Rights, press release, July 22, 1980; Steve Ladd, letter, August 4, 1980, IPIS archives; *Weinberger v. Catholic Action of Hawaii*, 454 *U.S.* 1981; Melody Wilder, "Weinberger v. Catholic Action of Hawaii/Peace Education Project: Assessing the Environmental Impact of Nuclear Weapons Storage," *Virginia Journal of Natural Resource Laws* 3 (Winter 1984): 335.

10. Robert J. Lifton, "Norristown, PA, 1981: The Plowshares 8," New York *Times*, March 28, 1981.

11. *Atlantic Reporter 2nd* 472 (1984): 1099.

12. Ibid.

13. Ibid.

14. Francis C. Brown III, "Media Coverage of the American Nuclear Freeze and Antinuclear Movement," unpublished thesis, Woodrow Wilson School of Public and International Affairs, Princeton University, 1985, pp. 89–90.

15. FOR Funding Proposal, "Project Plowshares," April 28, 1980, IPIS archives.

16. Suzanne Belote, "Ailanthus Witness at Draper Laboratory," *Peacework*, February 1982; Susan Furry, "Ailanthus Defendants: Guilty on Narrow Legal Grounds," *Peacework*, March 1982; Martin Holladay, "Avco Plowshares Defendants Convicted," *Peacework*, January 1983; Renata Rizzo, "Taking Weapons to Court," *Nuclear Times*, February 1984, pp. 16–26.

17. *Freeze Newsletter*, October 1981.

18. Martin Holladay, "Avco Plowshares."

19. David Burroughs, "Peace Fleet Greets the Trident," *WIN*, October 15, 1982, pp. 4–7; Vincent Kay, "The Trident Nein Disarmament Action: A Nonviolent, Orderly, Even Polite Action," *Peacework*, October 1982; "The Trident Nein Action," *Peacework*, July/August 1982; *Peacework*, December 1982.

20. Jim Douglass, "Tracking the White Train," *Sojourners*, February 1984.

21. Douglass, "Tracing the White Train"; Don Mosley, "This Train Is Bound for . . . ?" *Sojourners*, February 1984.

22. Hunthausen's comments on June 12, 1981, are quoted in Bob Thiefels, "War Tax Resistance," *Peacework*, March 1982. (This column became a monthly feature). Also see Hunthausen and Bishop Leroy Matthiesen, "Bishops at the End of the Line," *Sojourners*, February 1984.

23. 591 *Federal Supplement* (S.D.N.Y. 1984): 1332.

24. Burroughs, "Peace Fleet."

25. Holladay, "Avco Plowshares"; Rizzo, "Taking Weapons to Court," p. 25.

26. Furry, "Ailanthus Defendants."

27. Miles Lord had earned the reputation of an activist and a maverick on the bench for his aggressive conduct in environmental cases dealing with toxic waste and in a liability case involving the Dalcon shield birth control device. See Miles W. Lord, "A Plea for Corporate Conscience," *Harpers*, June 1984, pp. 13–14; "A. H.

Robins Hauls a Judge into Court," *Business Week,* July 16, 1984, pp. 27–28; M. S. Serrill, "A Panel Tries to Judge a Judge," *Time,* July 23, 1984, p. 88.

28. "An Outspoken Judge," *Christian Century,* December 5, 1984, p. 11; Patricia Schraber Lefevre, "District Judge Gives Sperry Software Pair Suspended Sentence," *National Catholic Reporter,* November 16, 1984.

29. It did, however, create a stir in the press. See B. D. Berkowitz, "Justice with a Spin on It," *National Review,* August 9, 1985; Colman McCarthy, "War, Property, and Peace," Washington *Post,* November 11, 1984.

30. National Lawyer's Guild, *Peace and Disarmament Newsletter,* August 1984; Dzielak, interview with author, February 1985.

31. Alexander Cockburn and James Ridgeway, "Kennedy, Hatfield Political Goldrush," *The Village Voice,* May 4, 1982, p. 18; *The Freeze Newsletter,* July 1981; "Corpus Christi: Not in His Name and Not in Ours," *Peacework,* February 1982.

32. Alexander Cockburn and James Ridgeway, "The Freeze Movement versus Ronald Reagan," *The New Left Review* 137 (January/February 1983): 20.

12

THE FREEZE UNDER FIRE: ATTACKS FROM THE LEFT AND RIGHT

Conflicts within the nuclear freeze movement were not all generated internally, for the freeze did not define itself in a vacuum. From the time Forsberg first presented the *Call*, the freeze proposal and the movement faced attacks from both the right and the left. As the movement grew larger, critics of all persuasions beset the freeze. Allies on the left contended that the freeze did not go far enough and pressed for an escalation in tactics and analysis. At the same time, conservative critics within and around the Reagan administration sought to discredit the movement and negate its impact. Although the movement was perhaps too successful at rejecting the pressure from its left, the right was more problematic. The freeze positioned itself to respond to and preempt these criticisms, ultimately diluting its potential growth and influence.

A FREEZE IS NOT ENOUGH

Left critics had both tactical and political differences with the freeze movement as it emerged. Most generally, they argued that by failing to define itself with sufficient clarity and to make certain political connections explicit, the freeze would dilute its message and restrict its potential influence. Among the connections critics considered essential were budget issues, racism, abortion, and most powerfully, military intervention in the Middle East and Central America.[1] There were numerous rationales for moving the rhetoric and politics of the movement further to the left and expanding its explicit concerns. Critics argued that greater definition would yield moral clarity and consistency, would aid in reaching new constituencies, was needed to respond to urgency of a particular pressing issue, would give the movement greater coherence, and would enhance its political efficacy.

The War Resister's League had doubts about the freeze's consistent emphasis on bilateralism, arguing that this emphasis made the movement too soft and cooptable. "The same people who support a freeze did in fact vote for Reagan," WRL director David McReynolds wrote. The danger of the freeze's bilateral approach, he contended, was that it would "lock the movement into the theory that we do not need to move toward disarmament until the Soviets agree to move with us at exactly the same 'frozen pace' — thus giving the hard-liners on both sides the monkey wrench they know so well how to use."[2] Even after endorsing the nuclear freeze WRL continued to emphasize unilateral initiatives to distinguish itself from the larger movement. A fundraising letter, dated June 1981, urged people to contribute to WRL, "If you think freezing the arms race is not enough . . . [contribute] to the only organization calling for unilateral disarmament."[3]

As the movement grew, critics within grew more skeptical of the national campaign's concerted strategy to simplify the issues enough to build a grand coalition. Carl Conetta, for example, wrote that the freeze's "lowest common denominator strategy" risked allowing "nuclear madness," to substitute for the political analysis necessary to plot an effective campaign.[4] David Cortright of SANE argued that the movement had to utilize its strength and opportunity to work to cancel specific weapons systems. Movement leaders had to realize that the movement's strength, Cortwright wrote in October 1982, had only been demonstrated with symbolic victories. Even with the movement's growth and referenda successes, in 1982 Congress approved the largest peacetime military budget in U.S. history, including funding for numerous new nuclear weapons systems. Unless it addressed the budget and relevant weapons, he argued, the freeze would be coopted by its Congressional supporters.[5]

Even at the movement's apparent zenith, on June 12, 1982, many activists were dubious about the freeze's future prospects. Shortly after the demonstration, *The Village Voice* published a critical discussion between antiwar veterans and MfS founders David Dellinger and Sidney Lens. Lens called for the development of a nuclear abolitionist movement to supersede the freeze.

> I think the freeze movement is going to run out of juice fairly soon. We've not yet generated the same kind of idealism of the 60s and 70s on the campuses and among working class youth. They will not really be stimulated in the same way until we start talking about Ban the Bomb. . . . This movement for a freeze is a request to the government. . . . What happens when the government says, Go to Hell. . . . In the Vietnam war, we

didn't make progress until we took an absolutist position on withdrawal.

Agreeing with Lens, Dellinger also argued that the movement had to present a broader analysis.

> You can't avoid the difficult subjects on the theory that you are going to build a stronger movement that way. You might, given the short run, get more people out. . . . We faced that in the Vietnam war . . . there was a time when our [the Mobilization Committee to End the War's] treasurer resigned because he said we were confusing things by bringing in the race issue [specifically, Martin Luther King]. But you simply could not build a sound movement by keeping these things separate.[6]

Freeze leaders were candid among themselves about the problems of a "freeze as floor" approach and recognized the potential liabilities. In a closed retreat they reminded each other about both the difficulty and the necessity of developing an awareness of the extent of grassroots support they would have on other political issues, including military intervention in Central America, nuclear power, conventional armaments, and imperialism in general. Many within the leadership saw the ambiguity of the freeze as a good thing, but there was a general realization that in order for the movement to be successful, according to Mike Casper, "others in the movement have to push more extreme goals, more forcefully." Randy Kehler observed that the freeze was sucking up other things in its wake, "with some sacrifice of diversity." Recognizing that the loss of diversity might ultimately hurt the movement, he advised that "the freeze must know how to use its left, to ensure that pressure is maintained."[7]

For the campaign as a whole, however, the size of the coalition had grown so large and the perception that a victory was possible so widespread, that organizers worked hard to keep divisive issues from surfacing. When activists proposed resolutions that would push the freeze movement forward tactically or to the left politically, the leadership found ways to stifle them. At the freeze's National Conference in Denver during February 1983, for example, resolutions endorsing both radical and moderate (1–3 day delays in filing returns) tax resistance[8] and for promoting a Congressional funding delay on new weapons were tabled and, to the dismay of their sponsors, never reached the general conference. "The momentum of the Campaign is likely to be lost if we confine our efforts to calling for a Senate freeze vote while passively watching both houses approve funding for the new weapons," wrote one disgruntled activist.[9]

Potentially divisive questions dealt not only with tactical escalation but also with goals. *Sojourner's* editor Jim Wallis proposed an "abolitionist resolution," at the Denver conference, asking the campaign to declare that its ultimate goal was the elimination of all nuclear weapons. No level of nuclear weapons was acceptable, Wallis argued, likening the disarmament movement to opposition to slavery more than 100 years earlier. The freeze campaign's strategy task force urged the conference not to vote on the resolution because discussion of long-term goals was not necessary and potentially divisive. "Abolition is only one of a variety of 'ultimate goals' that freeze supporters may share," wrote Jann Orr-Harter in the task force report. The resolution was allocated four minutes for floor debate before it was recommitted to committee.[10]

CONSERVATIVE ATTACKS ON THE FREEZE

The freeze leadership was determined to maintain a moderate profile and a broad constituency at all costs. Although they were wary of attacks from within and from the left, they generally agreed that the more serious and dangerous threat was from the more hostile proliferation of attacks from the right. Allegations of communism or naiveté from the Reagan administration and its conservative surrogates received far more attention from the press and from the movement itself. The freeze had generally been neglected by mainstream politicians in its early phases, but as its size and potential strength increased, the amount and intensity of criticism from the right also increased.

Attacks on the Western European peace movements commenced in the fall of 1981 when the movements showed their strength in large demonstrations and received media coverage in the United States for the first time. The European movements, charged the State Department, were being manipulated by the Soviet Union. Opposition to the neutron bomb, and to deployment of Pershing II and cruise missiles in Western Europe, were signs of a malignant "neutralism" sweeping throughout the youth of NATO allies. The peace movements represented forces that threatened to tear the alliance apart, leaving NATO nations vulnerable to Soviet attack. The culprit behind all of this, the State Department claimed, was the World Peace Council, which funneled money and marching orders from Moscow to the European movements.[11]

Administration attention turned to the freeze only when the movement began to demonstrate its own strength. Immediately following the Kennedy-Bingham press conference announcing the introduction of the freeze resolution into Congress on March 10, 1982, Secretary of State Alexander Haig called a news conference to denounce the resolution. The freeze is "not only bad defense and

security policy," he said, "but bad arms control policy as well."
Congressional freeze proponents were initially delighted by this
attack, and by consistent criticisms from Reagan administration
officials, because they kept the national spotlight on the freeze and
the movement and its Congressional supporters in the public eye.[12] It
was, however, only the opening salvo in a multifaceted and
coordinated offensive.

Shortly following, in April 1982 the State Department buttressed
Haig's allegations by publishing two reports augmenting and
amplifying them. One reviewed the charges against the Soviet Union,
the KGB, and the World Peace Council (WPC), emphasizing
particularly the WPC's interest in instigating and supporting
oppositional movements in the West.[13] The second report was a
direct, although somewhat softer, attack on the nuclear freeze
proposal, stating,

> [T]he U.S. Government recognizes that the proposal represents
> the best of intentions: to reduce the likelihood of nuclear war
> and encourage more rapid progress in a critical and
> exceptionally complex area of arms control. . . . We all share
> those objectives. But . . . we have concluded that a freeze . . .
> would have adverse implications for international security and
> . . . would frustrate attempts to achieve the goals on which we
> all agree: the negotiation of substantial reductions in the
> nuclear arsenals of both sides.[14]

Conservative groups took their cue from the government,
although their assaults on the freeze movement would not be bound
by even the modest conventions of evidence or civility of the State
Department. The first wave of criticism came in the spring of 1982, as
established conservative journals published highly critical articles
about the growing movement. The basic grounds for the attack were
allegations that the Soviet Union was "pulling the strings" of the
disarmament movements in Western Europe and the United States.
Vladimir Bukovsky wrote in *Commentary* that he was not surprised
the Soviet Union would try something like this, but "what was much
more amusing to observe was the ease with which presumably
mature and intelligent people had by the thousands fallen into the
Soviet booby-trap."[15] Bukovsky condemned the movement's lack of
analysis, its sources of information (SIPRI, for example), and
particularly its failure to condemn the Soviet invasion of Afghanistan
in sufficiently strong terms. The reasons for these deficiencies, he
argued, were clear:

> Just as it did in the 1950s, the movement today probably con-
> sists of the same odd mixture of Communists, fellow-travelers,

muddleheaded intellectuals, hypocrites seeking popularity, professional political speculators, frightened bourgeois, and youths eager to rebel just for the sake of rebelling. . . . There is also not the slightest doubt that this motley crowd is manipulated by a handful of scoundrels instructed directly from Moscow.[16]

Bukovsky's boilerplate diatribe included no specific discussion of the proposals, politics, or even the proponents of the nuclear freeze, but other critics would be more specific. Rael Jean Isaac and Erich Isaac published a piece in *The American Spectator* castigating many organizations and individuals involved in the freeze movement. According to the Isaacs the freeze originated with pacifist organizations, which "are centers of radicalism whose relation to nonviolence is highly problematical, since in practice they condone violence to achieve the goals of what the Left defines as the 'liberation movement'."[17] Specifically, they charged, FOR had met with supporters of the Palestinian Liberation Organization (PLO) and had also criticized Henry Kissinger; many of the organizations supporting the freeze are also concerned with economic issues; and the movement as a whole had not repudiated the participation of the small United States Peace Council. Further, AFSC's Terry Provance, they charged, was a member of the World Peace Council. (The WPC actually had used Provance's name years earlier without his permission and against his wishes. Despite his explanation, this allegation dogged him and the movement for more than a year.)[18] The authors called upon the peace movement to purge communists from their midst, as SANE had in 1960.

The American Security Council charged that the freeze was "clearly an integral part of the massive campaign to disarm the West which the Soviets have conducted over the past five years" and that its implementation would cause irreparable harm to democracy and freedom. Citing hawkish nuclear scientist Edward Teller as authority, the report declared that "if the nuclear freeze goes through, this country won't exist in 1990." Clearly the Soviet Union had to be behind all of this, although author Thomas Smith acknowledged "there is no overt data, as such, on the sums being spent by the Soviets to promote the U.S. freeze campaigns."[19]

By the summer of 1982 many new right organizations were taking an active interest in attacking the nuclear freeze, using it as a target for focusing and building their own forces. Jerry Falwell and Phyllis Schlafly added the nuclear freeze to their lists of dangerous and immoral liberal ideas and bought full page ads in major newspapers to proclaim their views.[20] The Moral Majority started what its leaders hoped would become a massive petition campaign against the freeze, explaining the danger the movement posed to the country in a fundraising letter, "Here in America the 'freeze-niks' are hysterically singing Russia's favorite song: *a unilateral nuclear freeze* (emphasis original) — and the Russians are loving it."[21]

As the fall campaign season for both Congress and the freeze referendum efforts intensified, the pace of the anti-freeze attacks accelerated. Ultraconservatives attacked the movement from the floors of both the House and the Senate. Representative Larry McDonald (R-GA) proclaimed that the people who supported the nuclear freeze also supported Vietnamese Communists, the PLO, and terrorists in El Salvador and South Africa. Senator Jeremiah Denton (R-AL) entered into the *Congressional Record* some 45 pages of documents purportedly detailing Soviet influence on the freeze movement. According to Denton, the nuclear freeze "received minimal support from the major disarmament groups until March 1981, following the Brezhnev speech to the CPSU [Soviet Communist Party] 26th Congress." The material was full of overstatement and outright inaccuracies on both large and small matters. What gained the most attention, however, was Denton's assertion that a small group, Peace Links, was a Soviet front. Betty Bumpers and Tipper Gore, both married to Democratic senators, had founded the group, whose membership included the wives of several other Congressmen. Members of both parties took to the floor to defend the women and the integrity of the movement in general.[22]

Reader's Digest published an article charging Soviet manipulation of Western peace movements, excerpted from a book on the KGB by one of its editors.[23] The piece was even less sophisticated and substantiated than most others, but it reached a far larger audience, including the president. Reagan himself got involved in the anti-freeze effort in October. During Ground Zero week in April he had expressed a general sympathy for people opposed to nuclear war, on the recommendation of many of his advisors, who suggested he might coopt the movement in that way. In a radio speech he declared, "To those who protest against nuclear war, I can only say I'm with you . . . heart and soul in sympathy" with the goal of preventing nuclear war.[24] Clearly, however, he had different ideas about how to accomplish this. He had avoided direct criticism of the movement, concerned that it might actually encourage the growth of the freeze campaign. On October 4, 1982, he broke this silence, no doubt concerned about the strong support the freeze had received. Supporters of the nuclear freeze, he said, were being manipulated by "some who want the weakening of America." Subsequently, he softened this line only slightly, allowing that most freeze proponents were sincere but misguided and had unwittingly been tricked by foreign agents into "carrying water" for the Soviets.[25]

The president also employed the Departments of State and Defense in public relations attempts to counter the freeze. State Department officials actively solicited invitations to speak against the freeze in states considering freeze referenda. Between April 1 and September 30, 1982, officials from the State Department participated in 77 speaking tours, which included 220 events dealing with nuclear issues. The pace accelerated in October, and 75 percent of the speeches were in states where the freeze was on the ballot. Retired Admiral Eugene Carroll, who toured Arizona on behalf of the nuclear freeze, said that at every stop he was followed by a National Security Council official who argued against the freeze.[26]

An anti-freeze group, the Coalition of Peace Through Strength, organized events and demonstrations against the movement. Including members of the Veterans of Foreign Wars and the Naval Reserve Association, this group claimed that the public was being misled by the nuclear freeze movement. In fact, spokesmen argued, there was no rough parity between the superpowers; rather, the Soviet Union enjoyed a substantial margin of nuclear superiority. Unable to find evidence to support this analysis, they urged the president to release classified documents that would. Although substantially smaller than the freeze coalition, the anti-freeze coalition gained media attention and legitimation when President Reagan received its representatives at the White House. They reportedly urged Reagan to support General Daniel Graham's "High Frontier" project, a plan for space-based antiballistic missile defenses, as an "alternative to negotiating with the Soviets under . . . unfavorable conditions."[27]

THE INFLUENCE OF ATTACKS

The referenda results, aside from Arizona, seemed to indicate the failure of anti-freeze efforts, but critics had succeeded in putting the movement on the defensive. Activists felt compelled to justify continually the movement's authenticity, sincerity, and sense and to cloak it all with a growing moderation and emphasis on bilateralism. Further, the rabid right wing opened the way for more moderate nuclear freeze critics. *Time* and *Newsweek* both ran editorial pieces praising the independence and sincerity of freeze activists but arguing that the nuclear world was more complicated than the activists realized. "The freeze movement reflects a populist impatience both with the arms race and with the traditional arms control that has failed to stop 'the madness'," *Time* wrote. "The sentiment is understandable, but in the view of many nuclear experts, the proposed solution is impractical and unwise."[28] McGeorge Bundy, a critic of the Reagan administration's military posture, was one of many nuclear experts who noted that the issues were far too complicated to be resolved by a bilateral nuclear freeze, which was a dubious notion in any case.[29]

Ronald Radosh, claiming sympathy with the movement and liberal causes generally, wrote a more insidious version of the Isaacs' article for *The New Republic.* It is impossible for progressives to work with Communists, Radosh contended. The presence of Communists within the freeze coalition, represented most blatantly by the U.S. Peace Council, has given critics an easy avenue for attacking the movement, even though the USPC had no real power within the movement. Radosh repeated Jeremiah Denton's accusations that groups supporting the freeze, the Women's Strike for Peace and WILPF, were Communist fronts. Acknowledging that Denton was wrong, Radosh added, "but it would be correct to describe their leaders as unfailing fellow travelers." Their presence within the movement, and that of Communist Party members, Radosh argued, naming USPC's Michael Myerson as an example, weakens the movement. It prevents the freeze, for example, from directing sufficient criticism at the Soviet Union and its invasion of Afghanistan. The movement must purge the Communists, Radosh argued, and take a stricter anti-Communist line in advocating the freeze. If the freeze does not, he writes, "it will sink into oblivion."[30]

These attacks, regardless of motivation, sophistication, or substance, all left their marks on the movement. Refuting the specific allegations of Soviet funding or influence on the movement was not difficult, but it was time consuming. Although the movement avoided purging troublesome participants in response to red-baiting, there was a more subtle drift away from strategies or analyses that might be considered too radical. The freeze sought to emphasize its moderate nature and patriotism in a way that limited its scope, analysis, and capacity to mobilize. Freeze proponents emphasized the support of establishment arms control experts with strong anti-Soviet credentials, regardless of any other policies these authorities advocated. Former CIA Director William Colby, for example, a founding member of the Committee on the Present Danger, became a frequently quoted authority on the desirability and verifiability of the freeze, even though he contended that implementation must be contingent upon securing substantial funding increases for conventional weaponry.[31]

Advocates often began their presentations by criticizing the Soviet Union, noting the need to stop its strategic nuclear modernization and emphasizing that the freeze was in no way unilateral. Tactically, they emphasized conventional means of political participation.[32] Attacks from the right, and fear of such attacks, effectively kept the movement from escalating tactics or moving to the left. "The pressure of red-baiting," Cockburn and Ridgeway wrote, "had led many of the immensely respectable citizens leading, or more importantly funding, the freeze movement to accept the witch-hunter's premises even while rejecting their specific charges. By indignantly producing proof that they are not agents of the Soviet Union they have conceded the propriety of the interrogation."[33] In attempting to maintain a mainstream and moderate public profile, the movement endorsed a tactical and political timidity, ultimately separating the freeze from the forces that gave it life. In an effort to keep ill-defined "moderate Republican" support, the freeze movement virtually abandoned long-range goals in favor of short-term support. But, as Pam Solo put it, "the short run kept getting shorter and shorter."[34]

When the Soviet Union shot down a commercial Korean flight (KAL 007), incidentally killing freeze critic Representative Larry McDonald, the perceived threat of conservative criticism was heightened. The incident ostensibly demonstrated the malevolent nature of the Soviet Union, the critical factor critics charged freeze advocates did not recognize. Kehler admitted the KAL 007 incident was a "disaster" for the movement.[35] By the end of 1983, the national organization had retreated to a freeze fundamentalism, offering only weak opposition to MX and Trident missile development and to Pershing II and cruise missile deployment in Europe. Instead, it shifted legislative focus to an even simpler "quick freeze," which did not deal with production of nuclear weapons. The new proposal failed to gain widespread support in Congress or from the general public.[36] In a 1984 national freeze executive committee meeting, the Direct Action task force, which had grown out of the earlier Nuclear Weapons Facilities campaign, asked to change its name to the apparently less radical appellation of Citizen Pressure task force. Weary from the red-baiting and political attacks, the executive committee officially considered avoiding future use of the word "nonviolent," because of its possible "negative connotations."[37]

NOTES

1. For a sampling of these criticisms, see Michael Albert and David Dellinger, eds., *Beyond Survival: New Directions for the Disarmament Movement,* Boston: South End Press, 1983; Frank Brodhead, "Sittin' In," *WIN,* November 1982, pp. 20–21; Patty Edmonds, "Antibomb Equals Antichoice," *Nuclear Times,* February 1984; Jeanne Gallo, "The Disarmament and Solidarity Movements and the Central American Connection," *Peacework,* June 1982; Joe Gerson, "Defuse the Nuclear Triggers," *Nuclear Times,* February 1984; Michael T. Klare, "An Open Letter to the Peace Movement," *WIN,* November 1982, pp. 13–14; Jack O'Dell, "Disarmament and Intervention: What Is to Be Done?" *Peacework,* April 1983; Lianne G. Rozzell, "The Arms Race and the Threat to Black Survival," *Peacework,* September 1982.

2. David McReynolds, "Letter," *WIN,* March 15, 1982.

3. War Resister's League fundraising letter, June 1981, IPIS archives.

4. Carl Conetta, "Common Sense for a Mass Movement," *WIN,* November 1982, pp. 15–18.

5. David Cortright, "After November," strategy paper draft, October 1982, IPIS archives. See also Alexander Cockburn and James Ridgeway, "The Freeze: The Trap of an MX Battle," *The Village Voice,* November 16, 1982.

6. Alexander Cockburn and James Ridgeway, "Peace in Central Park," *The Village Voice,* June 22, 1982, p. 21. Lens had opposed inserting a "verification" qualifier in the freeze proposal at the first national conference. See Pam Solo, *From Protest to Policy: Beyond the Freeze to Common Security,* Cambridge, MA: Ballinger, 1988, p. 59.

7. Notes from "Meeting at Blue Ridge Mountain Center," May 13–16, 1982, IPIS archives.

8. At this time Randy Kehler and his wife Betsy Corner had not paid federal taxes in six years. Protesting against war and the military generally, they had filed accurate tax returns but had sent the amount due in federal taxes to local peace and social service organizations. Interestingly, NWFC Coordinator Kehler's personal choice did not emerge as part of the public debate within the freeze campaign. B. J. Roche, "Couple Faces Loss of Home for Refusal to Pay Federal Taxes," Boston *Globe,* March 5, 1989, p. 45.

9. Council for a Nuclear Weapons Freeze, memo, May 13, 1983, IPIS archives.

10. "Report on Proposed Resolutions for Denver Conference," IPIS archives; Jim Wallis, "The Abolitionist Resolution," *The Nuclear Freeze Newsletter,* June 1983. Also see Jim Wallis, ed., *Waging Peace: A Handbook for the Struggle to Abolish Nuclear Weapons,* San Francisco: Harper & Row, 1982.

11. Department of State, "Forgery, Disinformation, Political Operations," Special Report No. 88, October 1981. See also W. Joshua, "Soviet Manipulation of the European Peace Movement," *Strategic Review,* Winter 1983.

12. Doug Waller, *Congress and the Nuclear Freeze: An Inside Look at the Politics of a Mass Movement,* Amherst, MA: University of Massachusetts Press, 1987, pp. 76–77.

13. United States Department of State, "World Peace Council: Instrument of Soviet Foreign Policy," Foreign Affairs Note, April 1982.

14. United States Department of State, "Arms Control and the Nuclear Freeze Proposal," April 1982.

15. Vladimir Bukovsky, "The Peace Movement and the Soviet Union," *Commentary,* May 1982, p. 19.

16. Ibid., p. 32.

17. Rael Jean Isaac and Erich Isaac, "The Counterfeit Peacemakers: Atomic Freeze," *The American Spectator,* June 1982, p. 9.

18. For further reports of red-baiting, see Frank Donner's articles in *The Nation,* "Rounding Up the Usual Suspects," August 7–14, p. 97; "But Will They Come: The Campaign to Smear the Nuclear Freeze," November 6, 1982, p. 456.

19. Thomas Smith, "The Nuclear Freeze Movement," American Security Council Washington Report, June 1982.

20. Waller, *Congress and the Nuclear Freeze,* pp. 187–88.

21. Moral Majority, fundraising letter, June 17, 1982.

22. *The Congressional Record,* September 29, 1982, S12509–12554; Waller, *Congress and the Nuclear Freeze,* p. 145.

23. John Barron, "The KGB's Magical War for Peace," *Reader's Digest,* October 1982, pp. 206–59.

24. Elizabeth Drew, "A Reporter in Washington, D.C.: Sketchbook," *The New Yorker,* May 3, 1982, p. 141.

25. Quoted in Women's Action for Nuclear Disarmament, *Turnabout: Emerging New Realism in the Nuclear Age*, Boston: WAND Education Fund, 1986, p. 27.

26. Jon Sawyer, "Reagan Moves to Blunt Nuclear Freeze Drive," St. Louis *Post-Dispatch*, October 17, 1982; Waller, *Congress and the Nuclear Freeze*, p. 164.

27. Gregory M. Lamb, "Other Side of Freeze Debate: 'Peace Through Strength'," *Christian Science Monitor*, March 9, 1983. On High Frontier, see Daniel O. Graham, *High Frontier: A New National Strategy*, Washington, D.C.: Heritage Foundation, 1982.

28. "Freeze No, Deployment Yes," *Time*, April 18, 1983. See also Samuel Cohen, "A Plea for Nuclear Isolation," *Newsweek*, April 26, 1982.

29. Robert Leavitt, "Freezing the Arms Race: The Genesis of a Mass Movement," unpublished Kennedy School of Government Case Study, Harvard University, 1983, Section B, p. 8.

30. Ronald Radosh, "The 'Peace Council and Peace," *The New Republic*, January 31, 1983.

31. Morton H. Halperin, "The Freeze as Arms Control," *Bulletin of the Atomic Scientists* March 1983, p. 2.

32. See, for example, Christopher Paine, "The Freeze and Its Critics," *Bulletin of the Atomic Scientists* April 1982, p. 8.

33. Cockburn and Ridgeway, "The Freeze Movement vs. Ronald Reagan," *The New Left Review* 137 (January/February 1983): 17.

34. Solo, interview with author, June 30, 1987.

35. *The Freeze Newsletter*, December 1983. For other reactions within the movement, see Marta Daniels and Maggie Bierwith, "KAL 007: Repercussions for the Peace Movement," *Peacework*, October 1983; *The Nuclear Freeze Newsletter*, November 1983.

36. *Freeze Focus*, December 1984; Solo, *From Protest to Policy*, pp. 157–60; Waller, *Congress and the Nuclear Freeze*, p. 292.

37. "Executive Committee Meeting Minutes," June 19, 1984, IPIS archives.

13

POLITICAL SUPPORT: THE SMOTHERING EMBRACE

Opponents played a critical role in defining the nuclear freeze, but allies were even more significant in shaping the scope of the movement's demands. As the freeze demonstrated popular appeal and the ability to mobilize support, organizations and individuals with a wide variety of purposes seized upon it, attempting to make some use of the support that had grown up around the freeze. Congressional supporters appropriated the movement's language and symbolism, turning the freeze proposal into something much more moderate and less threatening to the bipartisan tradition of arms control. By convincing freeze supporters that these modifications were in their best interest, purported allies convinced the movement to cooperate in its own demobilization. Apparent access to conventional channels of political participation cut into the legitimacy and intensity of extra-institutional protest.[1] The redefined freeze was further diluted, as critics and supporters alike found ways to express both their shared concern and their unequivocal opposition to nuclear war.

ANTINUCLEAR CONCERNS

Perhaps the most striking example of this was President Reagan's decision to adopt General Daniel Graham's High Frontier project as his own. On March 23, 1983, Reagan gave a nationally televised address proposing a Strategic Defense Initiative (SDI), soon popularly known as Star Wars. In it, after criticizing the freeze as a reward to the Soviet Union, he questioned the morality of nuclear deterrence, arguing that defense would be better. Said Reagan, "Wouldn't it be better to save lives that to avenge them?" SDI "could pave the way for arms control measures to eliminate the weapons themselves. . . . Our only purpose — one which all people share — is to search for ways to reduce the dangers of nuclear war."[2] The televised address came just before the nuclear freeze resolution was scheduled for floor debate in the House of Representatives for the second time. At first Congressional freeze advocates viewed the Reagan initiative as an opportunity, for it enabled them to stop defending their hazy version of the freeze against its critics and take the offensive in a counterattack against the president and his military policies. Representatives Tom Downey and Ed Markey took to the House floor and railed against Reagan's attempt to find a deus ex machina ending not for the arms race but for the nuclear freeze.[3]

Although the House later passed a nuclear freeze resolution, the Reagan speech demonstrated the movement's weaknesses in defining its own terms and goals. Star Wars enabled the president and all sorts of freeze opponents to sound like antinuclear activists, and this marked the beginning of the end for the movement. Star Wars became a cornerstone of the Republican campaign during the 1984 election, effectively preventing Democrats from claiming the peace issue. Randy Kehler remarked on this after watching a videotape about SDI shown at the Republican National Convention in 1984. "It was just like ours," he said. "It said how deterrence is folly and immoral, and economically the arms race is killing us, and there's no defense against nuclear weapons anyway."[4] Certainly most freeze advocates were not convinced by the Reagan approach, and indeed opposition to Star Wars became a new and significant element in the disarmament movement.[5] But by changing his rhetoric and looking toward the end of the nuclear arms race, the president was able to put his critics on the defensive and regain command of the language of debate and, in the process, dilute the perceived urgency of the antinuclear movement.

SDI was hardly the most subtle or even the most effective way in which politicians and arms controllers tried to coopt the freeze movement, putting to their own uses its high public profile and vast grassroots support. Indeed, opponents of the movement were far less effective and dangerous in this regard than apparent allies, who redefined the freeze to allow strategic nuclear modernization, for example, or to be nothing more than a plea for traditional arms control. The movement must bear some of the responsibility for failing to maintain control of its identity and goals, but this failure must be understood in the context of the assault it endured from friends and foes alike.

Given the context of Reagan's military and arms control policies, many arms control professionals initially welcomed the movement, the pressure it put on the administration, and the attention it brought to arms control. The movement and the resolution were seen as a way to force the Reagan administration to maintain an arms control regime. Representative Les Aspin (D-WI), who eventually and reluctantly came to support the freeze, frequently commented, "If we had a President who was genuinely interested in arms control . . . we would need no [freeze] resolution at all." He hoped that the resolution would keep the prospects for arms control alive during Reagan's term.[6]

Similarly, Albert Carnesale, a SALT I negotiator and Harvard University dean, reported that arms control advocates initially viewed the freeze movement as a "godsend," believing it would bring attention to arms control and build support for subsequent agreements. At the same time, he cautioned, there was a concern that the movement, by seeking unrealistic goals and overselling the potential of a freeze, might pass without influence.[7] Freeze activists were not always responsive to the attempts by arms control experts to remake the freeze into something experts thought would be more useful and achievable.

In addition to those who hoped to use the freeze to make political points for their causes, there was a larger number apparently interested in using the movement to make personal political gains. In his history of the freeze, Representative Markey's former legislative aide Doug Waller is candid about this:

> Peter Franchot, Markey's administrative assistant, was the first in the office to run across a copy of Randall Forsberg's *Call to Halt the Nuclear Arms Race*. . . . Franchot immediately took to the freeze. He had done enough public interest work to become a fair judge of grass-roots campaigns and how they could catch fire — and of how a politician could ride the crest of a movement's wave, if he or she were willing to take a few chances. "The freeze is going to sweep this country," he told us time and again. . . . "And there's no reason why we shouldn't be in the middle of it."[8]

According to Waller, the freeze was exactly the vehicle Markey needed to broaden his base of support and increase his visibility.[9] Waller supported Markey's interest in the proposal but insisted that the Congressman present the freeze as a nonbinding resolution expressing the sense of Congress, not as a bill with potential policy impact. "We should make it clear," he said, "that we are introducing a symbolic measure." This first of many qualifications incorporated, Markey sent a "Dear Colleague" letter around Congress on February 5, 1982, asking for support; within five days 28 Democrats responded with offers to cosponsor a nuclear freeze resolution.[10]

The movement's leadership, however, was wary about jumping into the Congressional fray, and Markey was not its only alternative. By the end of 1981 a number of more prominent legislators, including

Senators Claiborne Pell (D-RI), Mark Hatfield (R-OR), and Patrick Leahy (D-VT), and Markey's Massachusetts colleagues in the House, Representatives Silvio Conte (R), Nicholas Mavroules (D), and Gerry Studds (D), had signed on to the freeze. Several had already offered to introduce the resolution, but the campaign wanted to make sure that it had first built sufficient public support, referring to the original strategy paper that called for a wait of 2–5 years. A strategy paper written in February of 1982, just days after Markey's "Dear Colleague" letter, expressed this reluctance clearly: "Let us be careful about moving too rapidly into these other phases before we have a sufficiently large and broad base of support. While the issue is filled with urgency, we can do more harm than good by a premature attempt to win at the national level."[11]

While movement leaders attempted to negotiate with Congressional supporters to develop a legislative strategy, Senator Edward Kennedy, whose unannounced (and ultimately unrealized) 1984 presidential campaign had been building for more than a year, seized upon the freeze. Kennedy's staff saw the freeze as an opportunity for the senator. Said one aide, "We could all see that the movement was on the verge of a breakthrough. . . . The Senator just wanted to get on top of it, harness all that energy, and bring it to Washington instead of just letting it go on."[12] Although freeze leaders wanted to wait, Kennedy did not. He promised to introduce a freeze with or without the movement's support. The campaign worked with him because it did not really seem to have a choice. The freeze decided to work with Kennedy and other Congressional supporters rather than choosing the impossible task of trying to restrain them.[13]

THE FREEZE IN CONGRESS

On March 10, 1982, with the support of the national freeze leadership, Kennedy and Representative Jonathan Bingham (D-NY) held a press conference at American University to announce their introduction of the nuclear freeze resolution into Congress. Kennedy introduced the freeze in the Senate with Mark Hatfield and 18 cosponsors; Bingham, Markey, and Conte presented the resolution in the House, with 115 cosponsors, including Speaker Tip O'Neill. Suddenly the movement was given massive national attention and a dramatic infusion of professional political support, much of it generated by Kennedy's office, including endorsements from well-respected establishment figures Frank Church, William Colby, Averell Harriman, Henry Cabot Lodge, Gerard Smith, and Paul Warnke.[14]

The profile of the movement and the content of the resolution had changed. Kennedy deliberately wrote his freeze proposal in vague language to attract moderate support, perhaps considering the right wing of the Democratic Party. The nonbinding resolution called upon the president to "decide when and how to achieve a mutual verifiable freeze on the testing, production, and further deployment of nuclear warheads, missiles, and other delivery systems."[15] Freeze leaders and early supporters were dubious about the new language. Said Randall Forsberg, "The resolution was watered down, it has so many minutes of caveats . . . it represented virtually nothing."[16] George Rathjens, Forsberg's thesis adviser at MIT and an early freeze supporter, reported that after reading the Kennedy-Hatfield resolution he almost "fell off the wagon." The number of qualifiers, including the "when and how" clause, made the resolution "a prescription for going nowhere," he said. The Reagan administration could have easily coopted the movement at that point by endorsing the freeze and beginning negotiations, simultaneously rejustifying its nuclear modernization programs as necessary "bargaining chips," Rathjens observed, "but they weren't smart enough to do that."[17]

Kehler agreed but was characteristically more optimistic. Commenting on the wording of the Congressional freeze, he said,

Here I think we have a problem and I hope it's not a problem that we can't correct soon. In fact, the original wording of the freeze proposal said "immediate freeze." For some reason that I don't understand myself, the word immediate was taken out at our founding convention. Then, to make matters worse . . . [Congressional sponsors] deliberately made it vague in order to win additional support.[18]

Not only the vision of realpolitik, but also the goals of Congressional leaders, differed dramatically from those of the freeze initiators.

While Forsberg and the early freeze supporters saw the freeze as a first step toward ending the nuclear arms race, and as a radical departure from previous arms control efforts, Congressional activists viewed it as a vehicle to pressure the Reagan administration to return to the established arms control processes it had eschewed and to improve their own electoral prospects.[19] Democratic presidential aspirant Walter Mondale endorsed this view on the eve of the resolution's introduction in Congress. Responding to a question about the freeze, he explained, "I think it is a very useful initiative as an expression of concern. This administration has broken with the bipartisan tradition that's existed since the bomb first went off by which our leaders have solemnly sought to restrain nuclear arms buildups."[20]

While pushing the Reagan administration back to an arms control posture compatible with previous U.S. policy, Congressional supporters also reaped less policy-oriented benefits from their embrace of the freeze. Kennedy particularly was seen by many as a leader of the freeze movement, and he worked to encourage this perception. During 1982 he sponsored his own nuclear freeze rallies, at which he was the featured speaker. He also coauthored a book with Hatfield about the freeze. (It was actually drafted by aides Robert Shrum and Corey Parker.) Drafted in about a week, the book was initially published in a paperback run of 200,000 copies. Proceeds were to go to the Freeze Foundation, a conduit the senators had established ostensibly to gain Congressional backing for the freeze resolution. Markey also established his own antinuclear PAC, the U.S. Committee Against Nuclear War, which raised more than $1 million between 1982 and 1984. Other political action committees raised substantial sums of money by putting the freeze resolution on their agendas and in their appeals. Support for the freeze made good financial sense, and Democratic politicians were eager to politicize the freeze in a way that was profitable for them.[21]

For Congressional advocates, however, endorsing the freeze entailed redefining the movement and the resolution into something they found easier to support; specifically, the freeze was an expression of discontent with the Reagan program, not an alternative. Unsurprisingly, movement leaders were not enthusiastic about this definition. Wanting to press their views more forcefully, freeze leaders proposed a coordinated campaign against appropriations bills for new nuclear weapons systems at their June 1982 national convention in Atlanta. Congressional allies, represented by aides from Markey's and Kennedy's offices, were able to dissuade the national campaign from adopting this strategy, arguing that it would harm chances for passing their freeze resolution. In a memo to Waller, Markey's aide Howard Homoroff acknowledged that "it seemed strange for our office to be a moderating influence on anything" and expressed concern about problems in the future should the campaign not be willing to adapt to Capitol Hill realities.[22]

Congressional freeze supporters were themselves confronted by opponents who attempted to coopt their language to weaken the resolution and the movement. Within three weeks of the Kennedy-Hatfield freeze resolution's introduction, conservatives proposed a freeze of their own — to be negotiated *after* both sides had engaged in very substantial reductions like those President Reagan had proposed in his attempts to avoid arms control. The president strongly supported this version, introduced into the Senate by a bipartisan slate of conservatives, including Democrats Henry Jackson (WA), Robert Byrd (WV), Sam Nunn (GA), and Lloyd Bentsen (TX), and Republicans John Warner (VA), Howard Baker (TN), Richard Lugar (IN), and William Cohen (ME). The so-called Jackson-Warner freeze, or "phony freeze" to critics, was antithetical to the goals of the movement and even to the Kennedy-Hatfield version. By appropriating the language of the freeze and putting it in the service of the administration's plans, freeze opponents tried to confuse and diffuse the movement. In Washington it was widely assumed that the proposal had been written by top Reagan adviser Richard Perle, who had previously worked for Jackson. At least in the Senate, the strategy worked, winning 61 cosponsors, some supporting the proposal because, according to Elizabeth Drew, "they wanted to sign everything in sight that had the word 'freeze' in it and because they wanted, as they say in Washington, to 'buy political protection'."[23]

This strategy, introducing substitutes for movement-backed legislation with freeze-style language, would be repeated throughout the nuclear freeze resolution's legislative life. Congressional politicians who opposed the freeze wanted alternatives to support instead. Gary Hart's STOP, William Cohen's build-down, "no first use" proposals, percentage reductions, test bans, and numerous other proposals appeared in Congress whenever the freeze was discussed, effectively muddying the issues; many legislators supported mutually contradictory pieces of legislation. In June of 1982 there were 32 pieces of legislation on arms control before Congress.[24]

In 1982 at least, the basic debate in Congress was between the Kennedy-Hatfield and Jackson-Warner freezes. *Congressional Digest* described the nuclear freeze as the "current vehicle for debate over nuclear weapons policy," explaining the conflict as being between war avoidance and deterrence. "The controversy over the nuclear freeze proposal centers on whether to halt arms programs first and then reduce quantity, or reduce to an equitable level and then halt production." While both resolutions were filled with loopholes and loose language, in testimony before Congress Forsberg and Kehler argued that the Kennedy-Hatfield version was far preferable because, if implemented, it would end the modernization of nuclear forces; whereas it was unclear that Jackson-Warner would do anything.[25] The Senate Foreign Relations Committee rejected the Kennedy-Hatfield freeze on July 12, 1982, by a vote of 12–5, supporting the Jackson-Warner resolution and Reagan's START proposals instead.[26]

The real legislative fight was in the House. Jonathan Bingham effectively shepherded the resolution through the House Foreign Affairs Committee, which reported the resolution favorably on June 23, 1982, by a vote of 28–8. The freeze resolution reached the floor of the House on August 5, 1982, where Republican critics attacked the vague wording and ambiguity that supporters had deliberately built into it. Ultraconservative Henry Hyde (R-IL) asked movement supporters, for example, how they could call for a freeze first and concurrent negotiations to achieve that freeze. Representative William S. Broomfield (R-MI) offered an amendment based on the Jackson-Warner bill. The amendment was adopted by a vote of 204–202, before the resolution passed overwhelmingly. While the Broomfield amendment effectively killed the freeze in 1982, the extremely close vote made many freeze advocates optimistic and reinforced their faith in a Congressional strategy.[27]

The entire legislative record on nuclear weapons and foreign policy issues provided much less evidence for optimism. The Coalition for a New Foreign and Military Policy tracked 11 key votes, noting defeats on nine. The vote on the nuclear freeze resolution was close, but attempts to reduce the military budget and to delete funds for the B-1 bomber, Trident missiles, Pershing II missiles, civil defense planning for nuclear war, and airfield construction in Honduras all lost by large margins. For the most part, these bills were introduced by strong freeze supporters, including Markey, Tom Downey, Tom Harkin (D-IA), Nicholas Mavroules, and Ronald Dellums. Dellums also offered an amendment to the military budget to delete some $50 billion allocated for "first strike weapons," including many of the weapons listed above, as well as cruise missiles and nuclear-powered aircraft carriers. It was defeated 55–348, although certainly it more clearly expressed what Forsberg had in mind when she drafted the freeze.[28] Ironically both victories, deleting funding for MX procurement and banning the production of binary nerve gas, were overturned by Congress the following year.

For activists, however, the year ended with several hopeful notes. Freeze referenda passed with large margins of support virtually everywhere they appeared on the ballot. The close vote on the Broomfield amendment led many activists and organizations to focus their efforts on the 1982 elections. Although the movement's direct impact on the elections is unclear, Democrats and freeze supporters gained 26 seats in the House of Representatives, virtually ensuring, or so it seemed, passage of the resolution in the House in 1983. As a result, many within the freeze coalition argued that the movement should look beyond passing the resolution to other objectives, particularly stopping the development and deployment of counterforce weapons and the Euromissiles. Pam Solo and Mike Jendrzejczyk wanted the movement to focus on the appropriations process, using its apparent strength, support in the House of Representatives, to prevent funding for particularly provocative programs. They argued that this could be done within the bilateral approach, making funding suspensions contingent upon reciprocal restraint by the Soviet Union. Funding for Pershing II and cruise missile deployment, for example, would be deleted as long as the Soviet Union suspended its own deployment of SS-20s. They also wanted to tighten the language in the freeze proposal, particularly to eliminate the "when and how" clause.[29]

Doug Waller reports that he and Jan Kalicki, Kennedy's legislative aide, were shocked when activists discussed this more aggressive approach at their February 1983 national conference in San Francisco. They worked to convince freeze leaders that it would be hard enough to get the freeze adopted without the burden of new language. Jonathan Bingham's retirement had cost the movement a strong and respected legislative supporter, they contended, and House Foreign Affairs Committee Chairman Clement Zablocki (D-WI) had agreed to manage the resolution in committee only on the condition that the language be identical to the previous year's resolution. The Congressional aides were even more adamant that the freeze not be too closely connected with efforts to stop Euromissile deployment. There was no support in Congress for addressing this issue, Waller argued, "The missiles were a European problem to be settled by European governments, not the U.S. Congress." The national freeze agreed to support the older and more vaguely written resolution and endorsed compromise wording on the Pershing II and cruise missiles, criticizing both U.S. and Soviet intermediate-range missiles.[30]

These compromises, although acceptable to Congressional freeze advocates, exacerbated already growing rifts within the national leadership of the movement. In a memo to Forsberg and Kehler, Jendrzejczyk and Solo discussed the importance of connecting the freeze movement to concrete achievements, raised questions about the willingness of staff members, particularly lobbyists, to adhere to the national committee's strategy, and questioned whether the freeze organization was becoming beholden to Kennedy and Markey. "Do we cater too much to what Jan Kalicki and Doug Waller think our priorities should be?" they asked.[31] "Kalicki was a tough bargainer," Kehler later conceded, "and we didn't always realize when he said we can't budge, that it was a bargaining stance."[32]

Along with Forsberg and Melinda Fine (NWFC's liaison with Western European disarmament groups), Solo and Jendrzejczyk pushed the freeze to take an unequivocal stand against Euromissile deployment. While the national committee adopted their proposal to endorse a one-year deployment delay, contingent upon Soviet cooperation, freeze lobbyists never emphasized the issue. The national freeze organization eventually endorsed antideployment demonstrations organized by AFSC, MfS, and other groups, but its influence was belated and barely visible.[33]

Meanwhile, the freeze resolution's movement through the House in 1983 seemed to demonstrate activists' worst fears about the movement being coopted and trivialized. When passage of the resolution became the national freeze organization's primary objective for 1983, the movement pulled out all stops to achieve that goal, coordinating a large lobbying effort on March 7 and 8. The "Citizens' Lobby" drew 5,000 activists to meet with legislators and to demonstrate both the movement's moderation and its strength. It was an impressive effort, as the movement was able to claim the support of the United Farm Workers, the National Education

Association, and the YWCA, as well as numerous unions and organizations that are key elements in the Democratic Party coalition. Speakers at a small rally included Markey, Kennedy, Forsberg, Caldicott, Dellums, Kehler, Senator Alan Cranston (D-CA), Washington Mayor Marion Berry, and actress Colleen Dewhurst.[34] Unsurprisingly, the rally drew extensive and generally sympathetic coverage, emphasizing the movement's strength and its moderation. Mary McGrory wrote, "It was just like the old days. What was missing from all the milling and rhetoric and fervor was anger. The new peaceniks are older, more settled. They are not mad, just determined. They don't want to trash the system or yell at anybody. They merely want to say they will not go away."[35]

They did go away, however, before the freeze resolution was even considered in the House Foreign Affairs Committee. At President Reagan's urging, Chairman Zablocki agreed to postpone mark-up of the resolution until after the West German elections, in which deployment of the Euromissiles figured to be a major issue. Zablocki and Reagan agreed that they did not want to send a message to the West German electorate that might help the antinuclear Greens at the polls.[36] This was the first of many delays. House freeze supporters chose to debate the resolution under an open rule that did not strictly limit debate and that would allow amendments from the House floor. Opponents organized effectively and drafted scores of amendments, all intended to weaken the resolution, extend the debate, and effectively stall the rest of the Democratic leadership's legislative agenda. The freeze became a vehicle for a sort of Republican filibuster in the House. After more than 30 hours of debate and four postponements, the resolution was sent back to the House Rules Committee, which gave it a new rule limiting debate to 14 additional hours. Debate eventually stretched to more than 50 hours.[37]

Freeze proponents defended the resolution by using their majority to amend the proposed amendments, further clouding the issues. Eventually 24 amendments were adopted, including support for maintenance of parity "at present and in the future"; a call for the START talks to seek a nuclear freeze; the exemption of submarines from consideration as delivery vehicles; a call for on-site inspection as means of verification; a clause assuring "nothing in this resolution shall be construed by United States negotiators to mandate any agreement that would jeopardize our ability to preserve freedom"; a commitment that in absence of a freeze, Pershing II and cruise would be deployed; a disclaimer that "nothing in this resolution shall be construed to supersede the treaty-making powers of the President of the United States"; nor would it "prevent measures necessary for the maintenance and credibility of the United States nuclear deterrent"; nor even "prevent whatever modernization and deployment of United States weapons . . . required to maintain the credibility of the

United States nuclear deterrent"; and the further qualification that "any item both sides do not agree to freeze would not be frozen."[38]

For some reason, none of these restrictions bothered Congressional freeze supporters, although another amendment did. Offered by freeze opponents Elliot Levitas (D-GA) and Henry Hyde, it provided that the freeze would be revocable if not followed by negotiated reductions "within a specified reasonable period of time." The Levitas amendment was passed before the Democratic leadership could decide what position to take on it; claiming victory, many freeze opponents now supported the amended freeze resolution. The wide margin of victory, 278–149, reflected less the strength of support for a freeze than the ambiguity of the resolution.[39]

In this regard, statements of Congressional freeze supporters were far more damning than the allegations of critics. Anxious to win passage of the freeze, they consistently degraded its political significance. The long hours of debate over seven weeks gave ample opportunity for advocates in the House to demonstrate their ambivalence and often their ignorance about the resolution as some became uncomfortable with the notion that a freeze might conflict with support for the B-1 bomber, for example. One reporter recalled that Zablocki saw the freeze as a purely symbolic expression of discontent with Reagan's lack of attention to arms control: "His people told me their main message was not to freeze the testing, production, and deployment of nuclear weapons. Their message was to tell the President they wanted something done on arms control. Representative Les Aspin told us the same thing. He said he wanted the headlines to read 'House Passes Nuclear Freeze.' And he didn't care what was said under that."[40]

Proponents were equally candid on the floor. As interpreted by supporters, the freeze would apply only to weapons for which both superpowers could agree on verification terms. Zablocki emphasized that like START, the resolution required nothing to be frozen until a negotiated treaty was ratified by the Senate. Parren Mitchell (D-MD), a liberal freeze supporter who grew frustrated with the debate, sought support by emphasizing the innocuous nature of the resolution, which "did not mandate anyone to do anything . . . a powerless piece of legislation."[41] Indeed, the freeze language was so diluted that it could easily be compatible with Reagan's START, strategic nuclear modernization, Euromissile deployment, or any number of programs and weapons. Amazed that anyone would oppose it, Leon Panetta (D-CA) emphasized the political benefits of its vague wording: "Whether you are a hawk or a dove or something in between. . . . When you go back home . . . you can say anything you want about this resolution."[42]

Nonetheless, Congressional advocates proclaimed the final vote a great triumph for the movement. According to Waller, activists were also elated. The debate had so successfully muddied the issue, however, that activists were much less clear about the victory and certainly far from elated. As both opponents and supporters of the freeze claimed victory, freeze leaders had little opportunity to celebrate; rather they had to explain to activists that they had actually won something.[43]

Everything surrounding the House resolution, however, belied claims about a significant movement victory; its hollowness was underscored by the resolution's dismal prospects for passing in the Republican controlled Senate. Discussion in the Senate was dominated by Senator William Cohen's (R-ME) new entry in arms control obfuscation, the nuclear "build-down." Supported by both the Reagan administration and many freeze supporters, including Senator Gary Hart, Frank Church, William Fulbright, George Ball, and Father Theodore Hesburgh, the build-down allowed strategic modernization as long as each side dismantled two nuclear warheads for each new one deployed. Senator Kennedy eventually introduced his version of the freeze in the Senate on October 31, 1983, as a rider on a bill to increase the debt ceiling. The amendment was quickly and easily defeated 40–58.[44] Freeze leaders suspected that the Reagan administration gave tacit approval to the House freeze resolution in exchange for support on other programs. Said Kehler, "[Richard] Perle in effect gave his stamp of approval to a positive vote on the nonbinding Freeze with the understanding that the next vote would be MX and they would turn that one back."[45]

COUNTERBALANCING THE FREEZE: THE REVIVAL OF MX

Less than three weeks after passing the nuclear freeze resolution, the House approved funding for MX missile procurement, 239–186; the Senate followed suit shortly afterward, 59–39. These votes were particularly harsh blows to the freeze movement, as the MX was among the most politically vulnerable of the Reagan administration's strategic programs. Originally conceived as a mobile complement to U.S. ICBMs, the MX would theoretically enhance deterrence by making a disarming Soviet first strike impossible. Military planners had made the MX so big (10–14 warheads), however, that a mobile basing plan became impractical for numerous financial and political reasons. Less than six months earlier, the House had taken the highly unusual step of rejecting funding for MX procurement, even after the president had pressed for it. Reagan had proposed closely based stationary deployment in missile fields. This so-called Dense Pack plan, openly criticized by three of the five Joint Chiefs of Staff, belied the original rationale for the weapon. After the 1982 election, the House rejected funding for Dense Pack basing, 245–176.[46]

Kehler tried to rationalize this defeat to freeze supporters by pointing out that the national organization had not specifically lobbied against the MX and, after all, 186 representatives had voted against the system.[47] Clearly, however, this was a difficult situation to present optimistically. It showed that national political figures, including self-proclaimed freeze allies, took neither the movement nor the proposal seriously. The resurrection of the MX missile system in the wake of the nuclear freeze demonstrates the magnitude of the obstacles to political change on military issues.

Although Speaker Tip O'Neill opposed the MX, there was an element of ambivalence in his stance: antinuclear forces were particularly strong in Massachusetts and his district, but the project would bring money and jobs into the state. The rest of the Democratic leadership was split, so the party made no concerted effort either to endorse or defeat the system. In the absence of party leadership, the key figure in the MX battle was Representative Les Aspin, who had fashioned a reputation as a pragmatic military reformer. Aspin was a late and reluctant supporter of the nuclear freeze; at a Democratic Party conference in Philadelphia in June 1982, he had unsuccessfully tried to get the party to endorse SALT II ratification instead of the freeze. He was also among the majority that voted against Dense Pack basing for the MX the previous December.

Following the MX defeat, President Reagan worked to revive the weapons system by establishing a special bipartisan commission to justify the MX. Chaired by General Brent Scowcroft, who had served in the three previous administrations, the commission included Carter's Defense Secretary Harold Brown and James Woolsey, who had also served under Nixon and Carter.[48] Perhaps most significantly, Woolsey was a good friend of Aspin, and the two met regularly to discuss the commission's business and the future of U.S. strategic modernization.[49]

During the early months of 1983 Aspin and Woolsey arranged a series of meetings between members of the Scowcroft Commission and Congressional Democratic leaders with an interest in arms control issues, including Thomas Foley (WA), Norman Dicks (WA), Vic Fazio (CA), Dan Glickman (KS), Richard Gephardt (MO), and Albert Gore (TN) — who was then pushing for the development of a smaller, single warhead mobile missile, the Midgetman. Aspin assured his Congressional colleagues that the eventual report would consider their positions on arms control and strategic modernization and that the MX would only reemerge in a bipartisan context. He then helped orchestrate the presentation of the Scowcroft Report, suggesting, for example, that Defense Secretary Caspar Weinberger appear dissatisfied with the commission's recommendations. The report called for the eventual development of a Midgetman-type missile and further arms control negotiations; in the interim, however, the report concluded, the MX would be an adequate, if imperfect, solution to the problem of strategic vulnerability.[50]

Aspin also convened the same group (plus Defense Undersecretary Richard Perle) for a series of meetings to plan a strategy to bring the MX to the House floor. The group worked behind the scenes to improve the Reagan administration's approach to Congress on this issue. Gore and some of the others, for example, helped Reagan write a letter to Congress promising that the Scowcroft findings would be incorporated into the START negotiations and affirming a commitment to the arms control process. They then arranged to ensure a favorable climate for the MX vote in the House by delaying its presentation. The vote would follow a vote on the budget resolution (most Democrats would vote to cut military budget authority), Senate confirmation on Reagan's appointment of Kenneth Adelman to head ACDA (which Democrats would oppose), and the nuclear freeze. Explained Aspin, "People will then have voted three dove votes. The usual pattern of this place is that people begin to get a little uncomfortable if they've gone too far one way and start looking for a way to pop back the other way. . . . We wanted it [MX] to come up a little bit after the freeze."[51]

By supporting the MX, Aspin argued, the Democrats would inject themselves into the administration's policy-making process and influence Reagan's conduct of arms control. Aspin also contended that it was not in the party's long-term interests to kill the weapons system because it would make the Democrats appear anti-defense, clearly an electoral liability. Aspin's strategy and arguments worked with enough Congressional Democrats to save the MX. Les AuCoin (D-OR), an MX opponent, explained, "There is a tendency in this place to try to have it both ways. When you have a Ronald Reagan in league with a Les Aspin, then you find cover."[52] In the Senate, Sam Nunn and William Cohen, who had previously opposed the missile, supported the MX, along with arms control negotiations and the nuclear build-down.[53]

In the House, the Aspin group claimed that influence on arms control would be worth the trade of MX support.[54] Critics were outraged. During the debate, AuCoin castigated his former allies, "I am amazed at those Democrats who entered into this bargain with the Administration. . . . The President gets an MX missile and the country gets a statement of sincerity about arms control. . . . If that is a bargain, all I can say is . . . I am just pleased they are not negotiating with the Soviet Union."[55]

THE FREEZE CAMPAIGN AFTER THE MX

For the freeze movement the MX vote was a sobering and divisive experience. "You think you have expert support," Randy Kehler reflected, referring to Aspin and his group, "but the experts are just using you as a wedge to hit Reagan, but they don't really support your position. . . . And to the extent that we told people that two-thirds of the House of Representatives was with us on the freeze, we misled them and we misled ourselves."[56] Within the national organization, freeze leaders used the experience to justify their positions on future action. Forsberg blamed the national lobbyists for not pushing Congressional allies on the MX, arguing that the movement should lobby forcefully against specific weapons systems, particularly the Euromissiles.[57] Others argued that even raising such issues as the MX threatened to cost the movement its legitimacy and Congressional support.[58] Kehler, trying to hold the movement together by finding a middle ground, argued for lobbying against the MX and making new decisions about addressing specific weapons systems in the future. He stressed, however, that the movement's top priority should be ensuring a strong vote for the freeze resolution in the Senate.[59]

The freeze coalition was coming apart, and despite Kehler's best efforts, it became increasingly difficult to find a middle ground within the movement. Congressional lobbying consumed a progressively larger share of the NWFC's resources, with less visible results. Winning additional Congressional support for the resolution meant expanding the movement's base of support to areas in the West and the South where it was weak. This called for tactical moderation. At the same time, in the Northeast and other areas of strength, activists were eager to escalate their tactics and demands; they had already passed local referenda and convinced their representatives to support the freeze; they felt the campaign was stagnating. The national campaign, however, was reluctant to encourage these groups to push nuclear issues in ways that would jeopardize subsequent growth. It seemed an irresolvable dilemma.

Many of those who had served in the freeze campaign from the beginning were frustrated, tired, and generally burned out. Kehler, for example, was physically exhausted from trying to hold the coalition together and from living between St. Louis and Washington. Privately and without success, he tried to resign and then to redefine the national staff to reduce his responsibility, proposing on one occasion the creation of four national co-coordinators.[60] Forsberg was frustrated with both the slow decision-making process and the least common denominator politics that afflicted the campaign. She concluded that in seeking support the movement had strayed too far from her original vision of a nuclear freeze. "People in the Washington office were not clear about what they were for and against," she later reflected. "There's no doubt in my mind that I would never do it that way again personally. I will never get involved in a movement where I give away my ability to be right in the center of arguing and making decisions and to influence things."[61] By the end of 1983 she began to limit her participation. In a memo explaining, she emphasized that she needed to devote most of her time to establishing IDDS. The Institute supported the freeze, she wrote, but it also "has its own longer-term goals." Establishing IDDS's reputation as an "objective source of information and analysis" was in conflict with Forsberg's continued active promotion of the freeze. She explained that she would continue to support the freeze, but her efforts would be more circumscribed.[62]

In the wake of the legislative record of 1983, disappointing even with House passage of the freeze resolution, the freeze coalition frayed as participating organizations redefined their own strategies and goals. The national committee cast about for a new way of galvanizing and mobilizing its unraveling support. Proposals for activity circulating before the national conference at the end of 1983 included the direct action and tax resistance campaigns proposed earlier and such diverse approaches as continuing to push the freeze; shifting focus to U.S. adoption of a no first use strategy; addressing specific weapons systems in a more cogent way, including the MX, Trident II, Pershing II, ABM, and antisatellite weapons; calling for a test ban; and addressing military intervention in the Third World.[63]

While many grassroots groups pushed to escalate tactics and include more direct action and large demonstrations, key figures within the national leadership were apprehensive. Barbara Roche, coordinator of the national strategy committee, explained this reticence in a 1984 memo opposing a direct action and civil disobedience strategy similar to the civil rights movement:

> I generally do not respond positively to direct action tactics. . . .
> I think the Freeze movement is a *majority* movement among people who already have *access to* and in many cases, are part of — *the decision-making structures*. I think that makes us different from most of the historical precedents you cite, which were minority movements and/or the focus of which was to secure a voice within the decision-making process . . . our task is to motivate or provide ways for as many of those people [among the majority who already support the freeze] as possible to take some action. And I think that more 'flamboyant' actions . . . will scare those folks away. (emphasis original)[64]

Underscoring the NWFC's move toward more conventional politics, Kehler wrote a memo to some of the organizations working with the national freeze, calling for closer cooperation and less "institutocentricity." The organizations receiving the memo were, for the most part, those with a strong Congressional orientation, including SANE, Common Cause, Freeze Voter, CLW, UCS, and

FAS. Excluded were many of the organizations with a stronger emphasis on extra-institutional activity or more radical analyses, including Jobs with Peace, AFSC, WILPF, FOR, and MfS.[65] This only heightened the sense of disaffection with the nuclear freeze among organizations in the excluded group, even though they had been among the freeze proposal's earliest supporters. Kehler tried to make amends with the coalition by recirculating the memo (with an apology) to all the endorsing groups, but the initial mistake reflected the changing reality: the campaign was moving from protest mobilization toward more conventional political participation.

The legislative strategy in 1984 reflected the coalition's disarray. Although the national leadership endorsed the goal of passing a less comprehensive but more forceful quick freeze, the campaign was never able to build any kind of momentum on Capitol Hill. According to Chap Morrison, this reflected the movement's increasing and unhealthy reliance on Senator Kennedy's office. Kennedy dissuaded Senator Alan Cranston (D-CA) from writing his own quick freeze bill and never really pushed the weaker version he eventually proposed. In drafting the bill, Kennedy compromised much of the substance of the quick freeze in any case. Mark Hatfield refused to support the bill unless it did not include the word "freeze." Representative Jim Leach (R-IA) promised to withhold his support from any legislation dealing with the Pershing II missile. Kennedy eliminated both from the bill. When Randy Kehler indicated his disapproval and indicated that the campaign might not support this stripped-down version, Kennedy's office replied that the senator would introduce the bill anyway. Evaluating the year's disappointments, Morrison philosophically and reluctantly urged the campaign to support Kennedy's bill and "lay the groundwork for our effort next year when we will hopefully have something closer to a freeze Congress."[66]

NOTES

1. Jo Freeman, "A Model for Analyzing the Strategic Options," in Freeman, ed., *Social Movements of the Sixties and Seventies*, New York: Longman, 1983, p. 198.

2. Televised address, March 23, 1983, *Public Papers of the President: Ronald Reagan, 1983*, Washington, D.C.: U.S. Government Printing Office, 1983, pp. 439–43.

3. Doug Waller, *Congress and the Nuclear Freeze: An Inside Look at the Politics of a Mass Movement*, Amherst: University of Massachusetts Press, 1987, pp. 189–91.

4. Randy Kehler, interviewed by Pam Solo, 1985, p. 49.

5. See, for example, Marta Daniels, "Stopping Star Wars: The Sky's Not the Limit," *Peacework*, June 1984.

6. Adam M. Garfinkle, *The Politics of the Nuclear Freeze*, Philadelphia: Foreign Policy Research Institute, 1984, pp. 103–5, 147; Waller, *Congress and the*

Nuclear Freeze, p. 153.

7. Robert Leavitt, "Freezing the Arms Race: The Genesis of a Mass Movement," unpublished Kennedy School of Government Case Study, Harvard University, 1983, Section B, p. 7.

8. Waller, *Congress and the Nuclear Freeze*, pp. 46–47.

9. Markey had already established something of a national reputation in dealing with issues of nuclear power and nuclear proliferation. He was also candid about his own political ambitions. Edward J. Markey and Douglas C. Waller, *Nuclear Peril: The Politics of Proliferation*, Cambridge, MA: Ballinger, 1982.

10. Waller, *Congress and the Nuclear Freeze*, pp. 52–54.

11. "Nuclear Weapons Freeze Campaign, 1982 National Strategy: Broadening the Base and Creating a New Political Reality," February 8, 1982, IPIS archives. Also see *Freeze Update*, December 1981.

12. Leavitt, "Freezing the Arms Race," Section B, p. 1.

13. See Christopher Paine quotation, ibid. Also see Waller, *Congress and the Nuclear Freeze*, p. 60.

14. "The Nuclear Freeze Proposal: Pro and Con," *Congressional Digest*, 8–9 (1982): 197; Leavitt, "Freezing the Arms Race," Section B, p. 2; Nuclear Weapons Freeze Clearinghouse, "Press Release," March 10, 1982; Waller, *Congress and the Nuclear Freeze*, pp. 65–67.

15. NWFC, "Press Release," March 10, 1982.

16. Randall Forsberg, interview with Pam Solo, 1985, p. 4.

17. Leavitt, "Freezing the Arms Race," Section B, pp. 7–8.

18. Mary Kaldor, Randy Kehler, and Mient Jan Faber, "Learning from Each Other," *END Bulletin*, February/March 1983, p. 22.

19. Elizabeth Drew, "A Reporter in Washington, D.C.: Sketchbook," *The New Yorker*, May 3, 1982, p. 137.

20. Walter Mondale, "Letter," *The Village Voice*, May 11, 1982.

21. Alexander Cockburn and James Ridgeway, "Kennedy, Hatfield Political Gold Rush," *The Village Voice*, May 4, 1982, p. 18; Edward M. Kennedy and Mark O. Hatfield, "Freeze! How You Can Prevent Nuclear War," New York, 1982; Leavitt, "Freezing the Arms Race," Section B, p. 3; Steven Waldman, "The Hiroshima Hustle," *Washington Monthly*, October 1986, pp. 35–40; Waller, *Congress and the Nuclear Freeze*, pp. 108–9.

22. Waller, *Congress and the Nuclear Freeze*, pp. 106–7.

23. Drew, "Sketchbook," pp. 137–38; Garfinkle, *Politics of the Nuclear Freeze*, p. 183; Christopher E. Paine, "The Freeze and the United Nations," *Bulletin of the Atomic Scientists*, June/July 1982, p. 10.

24. *Freeze Update*, June 1982; Leavitt, "Freezing the Arms Race," Section B, p. 4; Waller, *Congress and the Nuclear Freeze*, pp. 86–90.

25. Forsberg's testimony is reprinted in *Freeze Update*, June 1982.

26. "Pro and Con," *Congressional Digest*, pp. 193–224; Garfinkle, *Politics of the Nuclear Freeze*, p. 183.

27. "Pro and Con," *Congressional Digest*; John David Isaacs, "The Freeze: Election, 1982," *Bulletin of the Atomic Scientists*, October 1982, p. 9; Garfinkle, *Politics of the Nuclear Freeze*, pp. 184, 232–34; Waller, *Congress and the Nuclear Freeze*, pp. 147, 170.

28. Coalition for a New Foreign and Military Policy, "Legislative Scorecard, 1982," IPIS archives.

29. Pam Solo and Mike Jendrzejczyk, "1983 Strategy Proposal," presented February 4–6, 1983, IPIS archives; Waller, *Congress and the Nuclear Freeze,* pp. 147,166.

30. Waller, *Congress and the Nuclear Freeze,* pp. 167–77; Solo, *From Protest to Policy,* pp. 114–22.

31. Pam Solo and Mike Jendrzejczyk, memo, July 5, 1983, IPIS archives.

32. Kehler, interview with Solo, 1985, pp. 7–10.

33. Barbara Roche, "Memo to National Committee Members on Euromissile Strategy," June 3, 1983, IPIS archives; Solo, *From Protest to Policy,* pp. 111–14. On the Euromissile demonstrations, see, for example, Steven Moss, "Thousands Take Stand against Euromissiles," *Peacework,* November 1983.

34. *Freeze Update,* April/May 1983; Solo, *From Protest to Policy,* p. 127; Waller, *Congress and the Nuclear Freeze,* pp. 185–87.

35. Mary McGrory, "GOP Senators Burned Trying to Freeze the Freeze Movement," Washington *Post,* March 10, 1983.

36. Waller, *Congress and the Nuclear Freeze,* p. 191.

37. Ibid., pp. 253–57, 283–85.

38. Garfinkle, *Politics of the Nuclear Freeze,* pp. 234–38.

39. Karin Fierke, "Overwhelming Victory for the Freeze in the House," *Freeze Newsletter,* June 1983; *Freeze Update,* May 1983; Garfinkle, *Politics of the Nuclear Freeze,* p. 283; Leavitt, "Freezing the Arms Race," Section C, pp. 5–6.

40. Women's Action for Nuclear Disarmament, *Turnabout: Emerging New Realism in the Nuclear Age,* Boston: WAND Education Fund, 1986, p. 24.

41. Waller, *Congress and the Nuclear Freeze,* pp. 237, 261.

42. Garfinkle, *Politics of the Nuclear Freeze,* pp. 198–99.

43. Leavitt, "Freezing the Arms Race," Section C, pp. 5–6; Waller, *Congress and the Nuclear Freeze,* p. 287.

44. Christopher E. Paine, "Breakdown on the Build-Down," *Bulletin of the Atomic Scientists,* December 1983, p. 4; Waller, *Congress and the Nuclear Freeze,* pp. 241–42, 290.

45. Kehler, interview with Solo, p. 7.

46. Elizabeth Drew, "A Political Journal," *The New Yorker,* June 20, 1983, pp. 45, 68.

47. *Freeze Newsletter,* August 1983.

48. General Scowcroft had been Henry Kissinger's deputy on the National Security Council during the Nixon administration and had succeeded Kissinger as National Security Advisor to President Ford. He had also served on a general arms control advisory committee to President Carter. Shortly after winning the presidency in 1988, George Bush named Scowcroft as his National Security Advisor.

49. Drew, "Political Journal," p. 46.

50. Ibid., pp. 50, 55–56; "Report of the President's Commission on Strategic Forces," Washington, D.C.: Office of the Secretary of Defense, 1983.

51. Drew, "Political Journal," p. 55.

52. Ibid., p. 74.

53. Ibid., pp. 63, 68.

54. See Aspin's argument in "The MX Bargain," *Bulletin of the Atomic Scientists,* November 1982, p. 52.

55. Ibid., p. 74.

56. Kehler, interview with Solo, 1985, pp. 45, 69.

57. Randy Forsberg, memo, June 22, 1983, IPIS archives.

58. For an example of the difficulties of getting the freeze to address the Euromissiles, see Barbara Roche, memo to national committee members, June 3, 1983, IPIS archives. Debate on this effort bogged down in disputes on a variety of issues, including numbers of Soviet missiles.

59. *Freeze Newsletter,* August 1983.

60. Randy Kehler, confidential memo, September 29, 1983, IPIS archives.

61. Forsberg, interview with Solo, 1985, p. 8.

62. Randy Forsberg, memo to Marguerite Beck-Rex, October 4, 1983, IPIS archives.

63. Randy Kehler and Chap Morrison, memo on national policy alternatives, November 29, 1983, IPIS archives.

64. Barbara Roche, memo on direct action and the freeze, July 2, 1984, IPIS archives.

65. Randy Kehler, memo, February 22, 1984. Compare Pam Solo and Mike Jendrzejczyk, memo criticizing Kehler's memo, March 22, 1984, IPIS archives.

66. Chap Morrison, "Re-Evaluation of the 1984 Legislative Strategy," IPIS archives.

14

CHANGING THE POLITICIANS

Absent consensus within the nuclear freeze coalition on strategies or tactics, the 1984 elections loomed largest on the horizon. Even many activists skeptical about the movement's capacity to make gains with an electoral strategy endorsed the approach as a means of unifying the freeze coalition. Albany activist James Driscoll, for example, proposed electoral participation as an interim compromise for the movement. In a memo to Barbara Roche, Driscoll argued that the movement was "talking too much to the converted . . . we have a majority of the people on our side already. Our task is to mobilize the converted, not to win new allies." An all-out electoral effort in 1984, he contended, would present the easiest strategy around which to build consensus. Driscoll believed it would also demonstrate the futility of such an approach and build support for a civil disobedience campaign in 1985. Regardless of the strategy chosen, however, he stressed, "Just please let's have a simple, clear task for all of us to work on. . . . A two-hour consensual discussion about priorities does not meet that criterion and yet that is what most groups are stuck with every month as a result of these fragmented and shifting messages coming from St. Louis."[1]

At its national conference in December 1983, the national freeze did redefine its objectives, albeit not with the clarity that Driscoll and others demanded. Concluding that the freeze proposal was too vague and gave the president too much latitude to engage in prolonged and nonproductive negotiations, the national organization shifted its focus to the budget and to Congress, where it had demonstrated some support. The leadership also called for a concentrated effort to elect a pro-freeze Congress in 1984 and to work to elect a president who would support the freeze. Recognizing that defeating Reagan would be difficult, the national committee also resolved to engage in a better coordinated and more effective lobbying effort, which could offer campaign support to legislative allies. This, they argued, would hold representatives accountable to the freeze, preventing a reprisal of the MX debacle. The national committee also decided to form an independent Political Action Committee, Freeze Voter '84, to manage campaign contributions and the electoral effort generally.[2]

THE PEACE MOVEMENT IN ELECTORAL POLITICS — 1982

Although the disarmament movement had played a role in influencing the debate and rhetoric in many races during the 1982 election, very little of this was through organized participation in campaigns. The existence of a movement forced Congressional candidates to be more aware of nuclear issues and caused many to reconsider their positions on key votes. This was, however, more clearly the result of popular mobilization and media attention than of a targeted electoral effort.[3] SANE made endorsements in selected races in 1982, and Representative Markey's U.S. Committee Against Nuclear War (USCANW) made a few very small contributions to candidates, but most influence on Congressional campaigns was indirect.[4]

One exception, the Council for a Livable World, had long made electoral participation its primary focus. By making campaign contributions to freeze supporters, it intended to change the composition of the Republican controlled anti-freeze Senate. In 1978 CLW had contributed $187,453 to Senate candidates; in 1980 it increased its contributions to $256,663. Benefiting from the freeze movement, in the 1982 election cycle, CLW contributed $460,606 to Senate candidates, plus another $73, 293 through its new PeacePAC to House candidates. This total, surpassing half a million dollars, more than doubled the Council's previous efforts. The increase in campaign contributions reflected, more than anything else, how spreading public concern had made it easier for arms control and peace groups to raise money. CLW claimed a huge success in 1982, pointing out that its candidates won in 11 of 19 Senate races, and in 37 of the House contests.[5]

The election results were, however, much less clear. Many of the House victories reflected Democrats reclaiming traditionally Democratic seats that had fallen to Republicans, aided by Ronald Reagan's long coattails, in 1980. It is, of course, difficult to isolate single or clear causes in any race, as elections generally hinge on numerous factors including media coverage, candidate image and personality, campaign strategies, funding, endorsements, and local issues. Nonetheless, it is disingenuous for CLW to claim a major role in the overwhelming victories of freeze supporters George Mitchell

(D-ME) and Paul Sarbanes (D-MD); each won more than 60 percent of the vote in his contest. It is doubtful that CLW contributions, totaling less than $50,000 in each race, proved the deciding factor in either case. Among campaigns in which the Council committed "major support," only two were close — decided by less than 2 percentage points. In both cases CLW-endorsed candidates, Democrat Harriet Woods in Missouri and Republican Millicent Fenwick in New Jersey, lost. In campaigns in which CLW gave "moderate" or "modest" support, there were two close races in which CLW supported the winners, incumbent Republicans John Chaffee (RI) and Robert Stafford (VT). Again, it is not clear that freeze support was the key factor in either campaign. Nor is it clear that, in an attempt to remain bipartisan, the interests of the movement were best served by aiding Republican incumbents who faced strong Democratic (and more liberal) challengers, thereby helping the Republican Party maintain control of the Senate.

CLW and PeacePAC also learned how to exploit the Federal Election Commission rules to maximum effect. They had, for example, discovered how to circumvent FEC contribution limits of $5,000 for each campaign by asking their contributors to write checks directly to endorsed candidates. The PACs then delivered the bundled contributions to the candidates, with only direct mail expenses charged against the $5,000 limit. Such signs of political expertise were heralded as harbingers of new-found sophistication and influence.[6]

At the national freeze's December 1983 conference in St. Louis, Randy Kehler announced the establishment of Freeze Voter, which was intended to build on this increasing sophistication and influence. Said Kehler, "Freeze voters around the country are really feeling an appetite for getting involved in the political process." Freeze Voter director Bill Curry proclaimed the slogan of the new group, "We're Not Just Going to Change the Politicians' Minds, We're going to Change the Politicians."[7]

THE FREEZE AND THE 1984
CONGRESSIONAL ELECTIONS

Freeze Voter was not alone in making electoral participation a top priority. Other peace groups adopted the same approach, forming PACs and making campaign contributions. In addition to CLW, PeacePAC, and Freeze Voter '84, Women's Action for Nuclear Disarmament (WAND), SANE, and Friends of the Earth (FOE) formed PACs to support the freeze with campaign contributions in 1984. Together the antinuclear PACs raised more than $6 million from both individual donors and direct mail.[8] The money and the national effort were intended to replace freeze foes in Congress with supporters, to build stronger ties with sympathetic legislators, and to defeat Ronald Reagan's bid for reelection.

The Congressional efforts consumed most of the Peace Pacs' resources and efforts in 1984, but as in 1982, results were hard to evaluate. It is clear that the PACs raised and spent a great deal of money. The Council for a Livable World raised and distributed more than $1.8 million, including approximately $745,000 in bundled contributions. PeacePAC raised and donated more than $200,000, about three-fourths of it in bundled contributions. SANE PAC raised $251,452 and donated $148,898 spread among 73 candidates. WAND PAC raised $34,926, donating $32,919 to candidates. FOE PAC raised $168,722 and spread $56,051 across 75 Congressional campaigns. Most surprising was the national Freeze Voter '84, which raised $1,490,549 but distributed only $17,147 to candidates.[9]

Freeze Voter was not the only PAC to consume most of its funds in raising more funds. Markey's USCANW raised $1.3 million between 1982 and 1984, distributing only $40,000 to candidates in that time. The motivations behind these few contributions themselves were also dubious. Nearly half of the 34 candidates winning USCANW's support received less than $250. Powerful chair of the Appropriations Committee Jamie Whitten (D-MI), however, who supported both the MX missile program and a number of amendments to weaken the freeze, received nearly $1,000. Markey clearly had ulterior motives for his PAC, primarily funding an eventual Senate campaign. Raising money ostensibly for the freeze was an effective way for him to develop his own mailing lists of donors. Virtually everything he raised was plowed back into the fundraising process, paying consultants, direct mail firms, and copywriters. The approach was effective for Markey; in the early months of 1984 as a Senate candidate he outstripped his opponents in fundraising, drawing $270,299 in the first three months of his campaign, more than one-fourth of it from outside Massachusetts.[10] Since Freeze Voter was not contemplating a Senate run, however, its record is somewhat more problematic.

Freeze Voter's distribution of only slightly more than 1 percent of its funds to candidates raises the issue of campaign overhead. CLW, PeacePAC and WAND were able to channel almost all their funds directly into campaigns through bundled and in-kind contributions. They limited fundraising expenses by piggybacking on their affiliated organizations, making use of offices and mailing lists, for example. FOE and SANE were somewhat less successful in this regard. They also risked diluting their efficacy by spreading their campaign contributions so thinly. Freeze Voter claimed to be different from these more conventional PACs, promising to contribute volunteers instead of funds to Congressional campaigns. It spent fully 97 percent of its budget for overhead, additional fundraising, and public education. This was intended to keep the identity of the freeze movement separate from that of either party or any candidate and to make use of the movement's greatest resource, public support. From the outside, however, these efforts appeared to be absorbed by the individual campaigns and thus contributed to the impression that the freeze had lost its capacity to mobilize. Canvassing for a candidate, for example, was certainly less visible than demonstrating. Freeze Voter helped the movement fade from the national media, obscured by the electoral campaigns of 1984. *Time* magazine reporter Joelle Attinger observed, "Reporting on social movements is faddish. The nuclear freeze was the story in 1982. Editors decided that Jesse Jackson was the liberal story last year (1984)."[11]

Even while the movement sacrificed its national visibility, endorsed candidates were not satisfied that the freeze organization helped their campaigns very much. There was general acknowledgment that the nuclear freeze issue motivated many volunteers, but it was much less clear that Freeze Voter had much to do with this. To demonstrate its own organizational efficacy, Freeze Voter worked semi-independently of many campaigns, sending busloads of volunteers into Congressional districts for weekends of voter education and registration. Candidates argued that much of this work was not well planned, however, often conflicting with their own campaign priorities. They generally preferred to have campaign staff and volunteers working directly under their supervision, implementing their campaign strategies.[12]

The political efficacy of Freeze Voter's approach was debatable. While Freeze Voter claimed to have won in 25 of 37 House races, 20 of those winners were incumbents, and more than 96 percent of all House incumbents were reelected anyway. Only two of six candidates endorsed by Freeze Voter in races for open House seats won. In close elections, in which the margin of victory was less than 4 percent and the support of Freeze Voter is most likely to have played a role, Freeze Voter won 9 of 15 races, but 7 of those victors were incumbents. In the 1984 Senate elections, Freeze Voter claimed to have won with 4 of its 8 endorsed candidates; however, only one race was close. In Illinois Democratic challenger Paul Simon, endorsed by Freeze Voter, defeated incumbent Charles Percy with slightly more than 50 percent of the vote.[13]

As in all campaigns, however, many other factors influenced the outcome. Percy faced a strong primary challenge from the right wing of the Republican Party. Although he won renomination, the effort took a great deal of time and money and forced him to portray himself somewhat more conservatively than he otherwise might have. In response, Simon tried to move closer to the political center that Percy had vacated and to devote little attention to nuclear issues. Simon's campaign manager David Axelrod recalled that this created conflicts with Freeze Voter, "We decided not to emphasize the freeze issue because Percy was trying to attack Simon as a weak liberal. When we decided to downplay the freeze, the peace activists were furious. Some called to say they hated us. Others quit volunteering."[14]

While some candidates supporting the nuclear freeze were less than enthusiastic about the kind of help Freeze Voter offered, others, particularly Republicans, felt that the freeze had forgotten them. The electoral approach challenged the freeze campaign's expressed commitment to bipartisanship. Freeze Voter endorsed Democratic challenger Mary Wentworth over incumbent Sylvio Conte in western Massachusetts, even though Conte had introduced the original nuclear freeze resolution in the House. In Iowa, Freeze Voter endorsed incumbent Republican Jim Leach and challenger Kevin Ready, alienating both camps in the process. In Oregon local activists split over whether to endorse incumbent Senator Mark Hatfield or Democratic challenger Marge Hendriksen. WAND endorsed no one, but the national Freeze Voter endorsed Hatfield, irritating Oregon Democrats upon whom the campaign depended for support.[15]

Conte, Hatfield, and Leach all won handily anyway and unsurprisingly were subsequently cold toward the freeze and its legislative agenda. This underscored the dilemma of bipartisanship. While some activists argued that the freeze should align itself with the Democratic Party, others contended that the commitment to bipartisanship simply demanded more careful attention and tolerance for Republican allies. Endorsing this view, CLW president Jerome Grossman said, "Never trade in an old friend for a new one who makes promises. Stick with the incumbent if he or she had done a good job, especially if it's a Republican who has taken political risks for you."[16]

Participation in electoral politics presented divisive dilemmas to the freeze movement. Becoming an ancillary to the Democratic Party, or more accurately, to one wing within the party, meant institutionalizing least common denominator politics and political compromise to the extent that the freeze itself would disappear, as the movement's experience with Kennedy and Markey clearly indicated. Approaching the electoral process as a traditional PAC, rewarding friends and trying to punish opponents, as Grossman suggested, meant effectively isolating the nuclear freeze from a broader agenda, demobilizing the freeze constituency, and committing movement organizations to the continued courting of monied supporters who would fund their efforts. Many activists were ambivalent about electoral politics to begin with, and the purist versus pragmatist debates, whether to endorse mediocre candidates who might win over more attractive ones who would not, hardly encouraged wider participation in the movement. Grossman's approach was clearly a long-term strategy that would, at best, yield only incremental reforms in military policy.

THE 1984 PRESIDENTIAL CAMPAIGN

The Congressional elections presented difficult and divisive problems for the nuclear freeze movement, but the presidential election was an even tougher hurdle. The first step in the process for the movement entailed working in the Democratic primaries to ensure that the party and the eventual nominee supported the freeze. This proved to be problematic; although seven of eight Democratic hopefuls ostensibly supported the nuclear freeze, the freeze they endorsed was defined extremely loosely. All were interested in wooing freeze activists without committing themselves to positions they believed would be politically untenable in the final election. Former Senator George McGovern, without much money or prospects of winning, felt free to endorse a strongly worded freeze platform, including cutting military spending by 25 percent, canceling the deployment of new nuclear missiles in Europe, and implementing a one-year U.S. unilateral nuclear freeze, pending negotiations with the Soviet Union. The Reverend Jesse Jackson similarly was able to support the freeze in conjunction with real cuts in military spending, a one-year delay in deploying the Euromissiles, and a reduction in U.S. conventional forces and troops stationed in Western Europe. In an attempt to broaden his rainbow coalition and forge an alliance with the freeze movement, Jackson asked Forsberg to serve as his advisor on military issues; she declined.[17]

Presidential hopefuls in office tempered their peace platforms to a greater extent. The most assiduous in courting freeze support was California Senator Alan Cranston. Cranston proclaimed his support for the resolution early, often, and forcefully, and his voting record on military issues was stronger on the freeze platform than that of almost any of his colleagues. Most notably, he called for a unilateral test ban, pending Soviet compliance, a delay on Euromissile deployment, and limiting military spending to the inflated Reagan-era levels. There were also blemishes on the Cranston record; he had consistently supported funding for the California-made B-1 bomber, perhaps the least popular weapon in the Reagan buildup. He had also supported the Jackson-Warner version of the freeze, as had Ernest Hollings and John Glenn. He endorsed adoption of a no first use posture only after a buildup in conventional forces — as did Hollings and Gary Hart. Nonetheless, late in 1983, Jerome Wiesener and Harris Wofford, also early freeze supporters, formed a Peace Committee for Alan Cranston.

Among the other candidates, the peace platforms were weaker. Ruben Askew was alone among Democratic hopefuls in opposing the nuclear freeze; he also supported a real increase in military spending of 5 percent annually. Ernest Hollings supported the freeze, but only in conjunction with strategic nuclear modernization, a contradictory position shared by John Glenn, Walter Mondale, and Gary Hart.[18] Hollings advocated real increases in the military budget of 3 percent annually and had only recently withdrawn his support for the B-1 bomber and MX missile. John Glenn had also abandoned his support for MX only recently and still supported the B-1 bomber, Euromissile deployment, and annual spending increases in the military budget of 5–7 percent. He had opposed ratification of SALT II and adoption of a nuclear no first use posture.

Professional politicians and mass media dismissed the chances of all these candidates after the New Hampshire primary, leaving only Gary Hart and Walter Mondale for consideration by pragmatic freeze advocates. The choice here was unpleasant and far from clear. Within Congress Hart had been strong in his opposition to the MX and B-1 bomber. He had also established himself as a member of a military reform coalition that called for a redefinition of military priorities and an increase in spending on conventional forces. Overall, he favored real military spending increases of 4.5–5 percent annually. He came to support the freeze reluctantly, at a relatively late date, and endorsed strategic modernization along with it. He also supported a series of contradictory arms control resolutions, including his own STOP and the nuclear build-down.[19] Mondale had supported the MX as vice-president and now supported deployment of a mix of Euromissiles and development of the Midgetman and Trident II missiles, as well as a 4.3 percent increase in military spending.[20]

While the freeze movement successfully elicited detailed positions on a wide variety of military issues, the coalition was split about what to do next. All the Democrats promised at least a marginal improvement over Ronald Reagan, who was candid in his opposition to the nuclear freeze and no first use, and who also supported the B-1, Trident II, MX, and the Euromissiles, along with a 17 percent real increase in military spending. Indeed the prospect of a second Reagan term was a major motivation for many activists to engage in campaign politics.[21] Beyond the general agreement that another Reagan term would be the worst alternative, there was no consensus within the freeze, nor in Freeze Voter. Activists were divided between those who advocated a programmatic approach that called for endorsing and aiding the strongest advocate of freeze concerns and those who endorsed a pragmatic approach of endorsing the candidate most likely to beat Reagan. A poll of activists in February 1984 showed that while most considered George McGovern an ideal candidate, few thought he could win the Democratic nomination, much less the November election. In contrast, only 9 percent thought Walter Mondale was an ideal candidate, and most said they did not trust him. Still, 41 percent said they would recommend the former vice-president as the Democratic nominee — a much greater margin of support than any other candidate enjoyed.[22]

Freeze Voter's director Bill Curry, a Democratic Party activist and Mondale supporter, favored the latter approach and in doing so alienated himself from much of the freeze leadership. Forsberg, who was president of Freeze Voter, was determined that the freeze not be bought off by hollow rhetoric and taken for granted by the Democratic nominee. She argued that her approach was really the pragmatic one. In a letter sent to all the Democratic hopefuls, she wrote, "To tip the balance against Reagan in November, it will not be sufficient for the Democratic candidate to give lip service to the freeze while supporting traditional arms control. This is what Jimmy Carter did in 1980. Merely 'supporting arms control' does not inspire enthusiasm among the public."[23]

Subsequent events proved Forsberg right. Although Ronald Reagan may have brought many activists into the electoral process to work against him, apparently few signed on to elect Mondale because of a confidence in the challenger. Karen Mulhauser was one who did; she left Citizens Against Nuclear War to work full-time in the Mondale campaign. Said Mulhauser, "When I tried to get local activists to attend Mondale rallies with freeze signs, I inevitably had to spend several hours trying to convince them that there was a real difference between Mondale and Reagan. They often said they'd vote for Mondale but they couldn't 'stomach' working for him."[24]

On military and nuclear issues, Mondale's success would depend upon his ability to portray his opponent as being so dangerous that voters would overlook their misgivings about Mondale to vote against Reagan. Jimmy Carter had tried the same approach four years earlier. Reagan simply did not look that dastardly, and the policy differences were not large enough and sufficiently clear to provide a clear choice to most voters. The Reagan campaign worked to ensure that this was so, for Republican polling in 1983 had shown the president vulnerable on nuclear issues. In response, Reagan launched the Star Wars program, met with Soviet foreign minister Gromyko, and campaigned against the Soviet Union, trying to reduce public fear of nuclear war and increase distrust of the Russians.

The president solved most of his rhetorical problems, and Walter Mondale proved to be the solution to the policy problems. In the 1984 presidential debates Reagan and Mondale displayed relatively marginal differences on policy. The president supported his own strategic program, although his language was somewhat more temperate than it had been before the freeze movement's emergence. He expressed his hope for world peace and condemned the notion that a nuclear war could be fought, claiming that Star Wars, which Mondale opposed, would eventually end the threat of nuclear war. He scaled his proposed military budget down to annual increases of 8 percent above the rate of inflation.

In Walter Mondale, there was little contrast. Mondale supported the freeze and advocated building the Trident II and Midgetman missiles, deploying the Euromissiles, and possibly imposing a "quarantine" on Nicaragua. Unlike the president, he favored "reasonable" annual increases in military spending of 5 percent above inflation. He argued that he was far more responsible in dealing with the Soviet Union, that he would never trust the other superpower, and that he would always stand firm against communism in protecting the global interests of the United States. Essentially he embraced every foreign policy goal expressed by Ronald Reagan, offering marginally softer means of pursuing them. Voters who supported the Reagan agenda would be understandably reluctant to vote for a pale copy of the original. Voters who doubted the Reagan foreign policy agenda were given little choice and perhaps turned their attention to other issues on which the differences between the candidates were clearer.

Ronald Reagan won reelection by nearly 7 million votes, with 59 percent of the vote. Mondale carried only his home state of Minnesota and the District of Columbia. The freeze movement had tried to make Mondale its standard-bearer, but he continually dropped the flag. Trying to choose between strong candidates and strong advocates, the movement and the Democratic Party got neither. By investing heavily and publicly in the electoral effort, however, the freeze had precipitated its own demise.

Randy Kehler saw hopeful signs. Trying to put the best light on Reagan's overwhelming victory, he wrote that the movement could find solace in its successes. The freeze had been a major issue in the 1984 campaign. The Ronald Reagan who won reelection in 1984 was considerably more moderate than the one who assumed office in 1981. The president now talked about arms control and not limited nuclear wars. The Democrats had "adopted a pro-freeze platform and nominated a pro-freeze candidate." Kehler, as always, claimed to be optimistic.[25]

NOTES

1. James Driscoll, letter to Barbara Roche/Strategy Committee, October 1, 1983, IPIS archives.

2. *The Freeze Newsletter,* December 1983.

3. Douglas C. Waller, "The Impact of the Nuclear Freeze Movement on Congress," in Steven E. Miller, ed., *The Nuclear Weapons Freeze and Arms Control,* Cambridge, MA: Ballinger, 1984.

4. James David Isaacs, "The Freeze: Election, 1982," *Bulletin of the Atomic Scientists,* October 1982, p. 9.

5. Council for a Livable World, *1982 Election Report.*

6. Betsy Taylor, "If We Can't Change the Politicians' Minds . . . Let's Change the Politicians," unpublished study, August 1985, pp. 1–4.

7. Steven Pressman, "Nuclear Freeze Groups Focus on Candidates," *Congressional Quarterly,* May 5, 1984, p. 1021. The freeze had been discussing this strategy for some time before establishing Freeze Voter; see David J. Newburger, memo to Ben Senturia, June 6, 1983; Freeze Executive Committee Minutes, May 18, 1983, IPIS archives.

8. Taylor, "If We Can't Change"; Doug Waller, *Congress and the Nuclear Freeze: An Inside Look at the Politics of a Mass Movement,* Amherst: University of Massachusetts Press, 1987, p. 294.

9. Taylor, "If We Can't Change," p. 9.

10. Steven Waldman, "The Hiroshima Hustle," *The Washington Monthly,* October 1986, pp. 35–40.

11. Taylor, "If We Can't Change," p. 9.

12. Ibid., p. 5.

13. Freeze Voter '84, "Marginal Races and Outcomes," IPIS archives.

14. Taylor, "If We Can't Change," p. 13.

15. Ibid., p. 12.

16. Ibid.

17. David Corn, "Candidates Vie for Peace Votes," *Nuclear Times,* February 1984.

18. Richard Falk, "The Missing Security Debate: What the Democrats Aren't Saying," *The Nation,* May 5, 1984, p. 529; Adam M. Garfinkle, *The Politics of the Nuclear Freeze,* Philadelphia: Institute for Foreign Policy Analysis, 1984, p. 202; Michael Klare, "The Democrats on National Security," *The Nation,* April 14, 1984, p. 441.

19. Both the build-down and Hart's STOP provided for ongoing strategic nuclear modernization; the freeze was intended to stop technological modernization.

20. Corn, "Candidates Vie"; Falk, "Missing Security Debate."

21. See, for example, Arnie Alpert, "Reagan Driving Activists to Electoral Politics," *Peacework,* February 1984.

22. David M. Rubin, "Can the Peace Groups Make a President?" *Harpers,* February 1984, pp. 16–20.

23. Randall Forsberg, letter to Mondale (and other candidates), March 2, 1984, IPIS archives.

24. Taylor, "If We Can't Change."

25. *Freeze Focus,* December 1984.

15

THE FREEZE
AFTER THE FALL

Ronald Reagan's landslide reelection in 1984 dealt the nuclear freeze movement a crippling blow. Despite massive support in public opinion polls and consistently increasing organizational strength, the movement was unable to mobilize its apparent majority against its prime target. It is not that the movement did not try. Indeed, the electoral effort seemed to overshadow virtually all else once the campaign began. Freeze groups were fully engaged in the presidential race, contributing both money and volunteers to sympathetic candidates. They also raised the rhetorical stakes for the election. Helen Caldicott was particularly visible, urging her audiences to vote as if their lives depended upon the next election. "If Ronald Reagan is reelected," she announced, "accidental nuclear war becomes a mathematical certainty."[1] Women's Action for Nuclear Disarmament (WAND) produced a series of radio advertisements that termed the 1984 presidential election, "the most important vote of the nuclear age."[2]

The freeze invested a great deal of energy and political capital in the campaign, and this investment proved costly. Randall Forsberg reflected, "The grassroots people who poured in thousands of hours over the last four years through their work on the freeze are tremendously disappointed and frustrated. We felt that the degree of commitment and devotion had to make a difference, and the shock of what happened in the 1984 elections left us reeling."[3] Attempts to recapture political momentum proved to be very difficult. Immediately following the election, Caldicott softened her stance somewhat, allowing that accidental nuclear war could be averted during a second Reagan term but only if the peace movement worked hard to ensure the election of a better Congress in 1986. This appeal now lacked credence, however, especially as Reagan proclaimed his victory a mandate for arms control.[4]

Voting against Ronald Reagan seems a timid prescription for action when one's life, and indeed the fate of the earth, is said to be in jeopardy. The emergence of Walter Mondale's presidential campaign as a focal point for much of the freeze movement's activity in 1984 reflects a great deal about the nuclear freeze movement and also about the obstacle course confronting virtually all protest movements in the United States. The sheer number of potential routes of access to government, and apparent influence on policy making, works to fragment and dissipate oppositional movements.

For numerous reasons the freeze was unable to translate its strength as shown in public opinion polls into Mondale votes. Among the obstacles the movement faced were the preponderance of other issues, particularly taxation; the nature of presidential campaigns in the United States, which emphasize a candidate's personal and media appeal rather than political issues; the disproportionate national funding of the two parties; and the extremely weak and damaged candidacy of the Democratic challenger. Perhaps most significant, the Ronald Reagan who ran for reelection was quite different from the one elected in 1980, and surely this was at least partly the result of the nuclear freeze. The president refused to allow the movement to define his positions on military and nuclear security issues. Midway through his first term he and his advisors abandoned much of the troublesome rhetoric about limited nuclear wars and the Soviet Union that had fed the freeze campaign's early growth.

Although Reagan's reelection marked the end of the nuclear freeze in political discourse, activists and political organizations continued their work, including virtually all the types of political action that characterized the movement in earlier years: civil disobedience and direct action, symbolic demonstrations and educational events, and legislative lobbying and electoral campaigns. This variety of activity, however, was no longer united by a common face. Each action was widely perceived as discrete, divorced from other activities and from a larger social and political movement. Mainstream politics fragmented the movement, defusing its potential impact. Essentially, this happened in three ways: marginalization, depoliticization, and cooptation.

FORCED TO THE MARGINS

Partisans of direct action continued their efforts, engaging in dramatic attacks on weapons manufacturers and military installations while calling for the abolition of nuclear weapons. Rarely, however, were these calls connected to any conventional political activity or systematic program. The costs of participation were generally very high; activists often received harsh jail sentences or heavy fines. These high costs, the intensity of commitment required for participation, and the lack of any apparent potential for political efficacy severely limited the number who would participate. Those who did were politically marginalized.

As an example, in November 1984, just after the election, four activists attacked a Minuteman missile silo not far from Kansas City, Missouri. They cut through the fence surrounding the silo, damaged the concrete platform with a jackhammer, and then poured their own blood down the silo hatch. They were sentenced to 18-year prison terms. This was the first of at least a dozen "Silo Pruning Hooks" Plowshares actions, none of which received much attention from either movement organs or mainstream media. Said Helen Woodson, a veteran of the first silo protest, "For the most part, the American media is not interested in the only true disarmament taking place — acts of faith and conscience by nonviolent civil disobedience."[5] By implying that the only way to contribute to world peace entailed this kind of risk, the Silo Plowshares groups did nothing to broaden the base of the movement.

There was probably more such antinuclear civil disobedience after Reagan's reelection than in the years immediately preceding. The White Train protests, directed against the transport of nuclear warheads, continued and grew along the train's route between Bangor, Washington, and Amarillo, Texas,[6] as did site protests directed against weapons producers.[7] Several groups attempted to disrupt nuclear testing by invading the U.S. test site in Nevada, hoping that their presence near ground zero would delay testing and gain publicity for a proposed test ban. Attempts to broaden this campaign by the American Peace Test, however, were largely unsuccessful.[8]

PROTEST WITHOUT POLITICS

Far more visible were activities designed for extensive participation and media coverage. These activities were intended to give people a sense of expression for their concerns without tying their actions to politics in any way. Political analysis and specific demands were sacrificed with the intent of winning a broad spectrum of support. Although such activities often drew large numbers of participants, their political meaning was unclear because they were divorced not only from any arms control or military reform proposal — such as the freeze — but also from either party, any candidate, or any political program. This depoliticization doomed several colorful events to political insignificance.

There was a large national campaign, for example, to create a peace ribbon to commemorate the anniversary of the bombing of Hiroshima in August 1985. Local antinuclear groups and concerned individuals provided 18" x 36" fabric segments for the ribbon, each depicting things they did not want to lose in a nuclear war. These segments were sewn together, and the colorful ribbon stretched more than ten miles; activists wrapped it around the Pentagon and extended it to the Washington Monument. The planning and conduct of the ribbon demonstration drew considerable press coverage, but the only political message that clearly emerged was that many people did not want a nuclear war.[9]

Even worse for the antinuclear groups were similar events that failed to gain support or publicity. The clearest example was the Great Peace March, sponsored by a California-based group, PRO-Peace. The event was intended to span nine months in 1986, as more than 5,000 people would march across the country from Los Angeles to Washington, D.C., under the slogan, "Take 'em Down."[10] PRO-Peace failed to gain significant support from other disarmament groups, who were reluctant to endorse its simplistic politics and slogan and who were concerned that it would siphon money and political resources from their own activities. PRO-Peace proceeded anyway, setting a fundraising goal of $15 million and developing an organization that would consume that ambitious budget, including offices in 12 cities and more than 150 fulltime employees. Two weeks after the march left Los Angeles in March 1986, PRO-Peace's executive director David Mixner acknowledged that the campaign had run out of money, dissolved PRO-Peace, and declared the event over. A number of the marchers continued anyway, reaching Washington in November by raising subsistence support along the way. By failing to live up to its own grand designs, however, the Great Peace March seemed a hollow achievement, with unclear political intentions and minimal impact.

The trend toward apolitical or antipolitical expression of concern about nuclear issues was carried to an extreme by Beyond War, another California group that asked its members to "take responsibility for ending war and nuclear weaponry." Appealing primarily to middle-class and wealthy Californians, Beyond War bore closer resemblance to self-help human development programs such as test than to any of the groups supporting the nuclear freeze. The Beyond War program was based upon three basic concepts: "1. War is obsolete; 2. We are one; 3. One person can make a difference. The way the Beyond War revolution is supposed to unfold is this: once members integrate these three concepts into their thought processes, then they will automatically shift from the 'old mode' to the 'new mode of thinking'."[11] This new mode would then spread until people and nations stop fighting. The approach represented less a rejection of conventional politics than a repudiation of politics altogether. "The whole point of the Beyond War movement," said one participant, "is not to be anti-Reagan or antimilitary or antianything. I mean, who has the right to say whether what our president says is bad or good." "It's not what you do," said another. "It's your attitude."[12] Beyond War is not what peace movement groups became, but an attempt, albeit less politically challenging, to capture the political space the antinuclear movement had occupied, competing with more political groups for participants and support.

ENTERING THE POLITICAL MAINSTREAM

Activities like these had been components of the freeze movement at its height, but divorced from conventional political activity and politics in general, they were robbed of their impact and of any significance. In contrast, Washington-based lobbying groups and political action committees also continued their activity, most significantly stronger, larger, and better-funded than they had been before the emergence of the freeze.[13] To support themselves and their activity, they became increasingly dependent upon their relationships with financial supporters and legislators. This necessarily entailed a moderation in goals and approaches to improve prospects for financial support and legislative success. There is no doubt that this approach, conventional political action in pursuit of moderate goals, could generate some victories in Congress, such as aiding in the election of legislators who support arms control, working to achieve moderate reductions in funding for particular weapons systems, and lobbying for the ratification of future arms control treaties. Such achievements, however, are substantially more modest than the comprehensive approach to nuclear weapons and foreign policy suggested by the nuclear freeze. Abandoning the broader analysis and concerns that had animated the freeze movement, these groups were coopted.

Developing a legislative agenda modest enough to be achievable yet ambitious enough to be significant was a difficult problem for most of the freeze coalition; indeed, the nuclear freeze proposal had initially been intended as a solution. Lobbying and electoral groups needed to demonstrate both their political importance and their efficacy in order to continue to draw support. The NWFC redirected its own efforts to this Congressionally oriented approach, shutting down its St. Louis office, relocating to Washington, D.C., and changing its central demand to the negotiation of a bilateral ban on nuclear testing.[14] Symbolically and actually, this reflected a deemphasis on the grassroots activity and local organizations that had characterized the freeze movement's early growth. The test ban campaign was a deliberate attempt to replicate the successes of the freeze with a more limited, and thus achievable, platform. Organizers made a concerted, and fairly successful, attempt to gain the endorsements of prominent religious leaders. There was also the requisite number of op-ed pieces by notables endorsing the test ban.[15] Just as moving the national office to Washington reflected a greater emphasis on conventional politics, replacing the freeze proposal with a test ban proposal demonstrated a reduction of goals.

This campaign, calling for the smallest part of the original freeze proposal that could be divorced from the whole, gained relatively little support, either in Congress or among the general public. Difficulties with the public stemmed partly from a perception that the movement was retreating. There was also no consensus on goals within the freeze coalition, and several different proposals competed for support on Capitol Hill. Here diversity proved to be a tremendous weakness, as the initial clarity of the freeze agenda was gradually obscured.[16] The failure to gain broad public support and sustain strong grassroots activism hurt the test ban's chances in Congress.

Clearly there were also other factors involved in the failure of the test ban campaign. Political opponents argued that testing was needed to ensure effective deterrence as long as deterrence remained necessary. The Soviet Union had already undertaken a unilateral test moratorium, and critics argued that it would not have done so unless a test ban was clearly in the Soviet interest and not that of the United States. At the same time, the president now consistently expressed an interest in arms control, frequently deplored the nuclear arms race, and repeatedly expressed his apparently new conviction that "a nuclear war cannot be won and must never be fought."[17] As the movement's message fragmented, it was harder to draw sharp distinctions between the government's policies and the opposition's alternatives.

The shift to an emphasis on conventional political participation entailed a corresponding shift in mobilization strategies. Mass public support was less important than Congressional endorsement; public demonstrations and media attention became less significant than financial support. Comprehensive analysis was secondary to legislative salability; political democracy took a backseat to political efficacy.[18] In short, a large segment of the antinuclear movement eschewed extrainstitutional social mobilization in favor of competing within established political institutions. Arms control and disarmament organizations taking this approach needed to cultivate new resources, particularly funding, and correspondingly abandon the tactics that initially had brought them attention and legitimacy and that had enlivened the nuclear debate.

It also entailed competition with more established and better funded lobbying groups and PACs. In her analysis of the antinuclear movement's electoral efforts in 1984, Betsy Taylor notes that corporate PACs were able to outspend the peace PACs by a significant margin. Lockheed contributed $420,000 to Congressional candidates in 1984, topping the list of corporate PAC contributions. The top 12 corporate PACs included three other military contractors: Rockwell, Northrop, and General Dynamics.[19] This funding imbalance is not limited to military contractors and disarmament activists. In 1984, the Republican National Committee, Congressional Committee, and Senatorial Committees outspent their Democratic counterparts by a ratio of nearly 4:1, $246 million to $66 million. The spending advantage of conservative PACs over liberal PACs was even greater. Conservative PACs, led by the National Conservative Political Action Committee (which spent nearly $20 million), spent $55,186,802, compared to $13,069,085 spent by liberal PACs.[20]

As lopsided as they are, these figures exaggerate both the relative strength of liberal PACs and the potential for disarmament activists to achieve broad results through campaign contributions and lobbying. Conservative and Republican Congressmen receive a much clearer message from their funders than do Democrats and liberals. More than 95 percent of Republican contributions come from business, trade associations, and conservative PACs. In contrast, these same conservative interests provide about half the campaign funds for Democratic candidates, the other half coming from organized labor and liberal PACs. As a result, a Democratic representative concerned about funding his or her reelection campaign receives an ambiguous message about political issues and is faced with the need to please a far more diverse constituency than a Republican counterpart.[21] This leads to precisely the tendency to seek a middle-ground, which Les Aspin and his allies played upon in negotiating funding for the MX missile.

Second, the lobbying efforts of military contractors are far more narrowly targeted than those of arms control and disarmament groups. Military contractors may lobby for funding a particular weapons system, or the award of a specific contract, but arms control groups, by the nature of their concerns, have a much broader agenda. General Dynamics and Northrup may compete for the contract to build a particular weapon, for example, while the arms control advocate may seek to cancel the system altogether. Peace PACs, then, have a far larger number of Congressional votes to monitor and attempt to influence. Further, a representative's decision to choose one contractor over another may generate not only a future campaign contribution but also construction and employment in his or her district. The peace PACs' agenda offers no comparable pork barrel potential.

By focusing their efforts on Congressional politics, arms control and disarmament groups chose to enter a political arena and engage in a style of competition in which they were at a tremendous disadvantage. In order to complete successfully with more established and better funded lobbying groups and PACs, according to advocates of this strategy, arms control and disarmament forces needed to develop a new sophistication. This meant moderating political goals, rhetoric, and organizing strategies.

THE ORGANIZATIONAL IMPERATIVE

The freeze's supporting organizations changed their style and goals, fighting for organizational survival as the movement faded. WAND, for example, in a slick report prepared for wide distribution, proclaimed that subsequent membership drives and volunteer efforts should focus primarily on fundraising. Grassroots activism and decentralized democracy, the publication argues, represented old and archaic notions of political action. The disarmament movement should learn from the successes of conservative groups and emphasize professionalism and organizing through fundraising.[22] "Too many progressive organizations are wedded to old-fashioned notions about citizen participation," WAND writes; "they continue to believe hundreds and thousands of volunteers can be persuaded to assume a broad range of organizing tasks." Voluntarism is less important than fundraising, WAND continues, noting that professional organizations with a strong donor base are "far more powerful, enduring, and effective" than more amateurish protest movement groups.[23]

Vastly increased funding is needed not only for political contributions to candidates but also for a generally more professional approach to politics, including expert survey research, marketing, and advertising. The antinuclear movement, WAND argues, must compete with its opponents using the most sophisticated and professional approaches available or resign itself to defeat. This means emulating the tactics of "its rival communicators — television networks, commercial advertisers, [and] political campaigns." If it does not, "the movement will fall behind these other voices, and will find it increasingly difficult to focus Americans' attention on the important issues of its agenda."[24]

WAND's analysis of the movement's prospects for survival was essentially correct. In times of growth for any movement, there is a concomitant proliferation of organizations, which come to compete for the resources available to the movement as a whole.[25] Although the growth of new organizations and the endorsements of established groups enlivened the nuclear freeze movement and produced substantial growth quickly, it came at a price. The freeze came to be equated with the larger peace movement, getting credit for everything done by any group or individual in the cause of arms control or disarmament. Pam Solo writes:

> As a result, established organizations suffered. Those who had submerged their organization's identity to support the coalition lost funding. . . . Those who chose to step away from the pack and distinguish their organization by developing other strategies and a separate identity in the media gained visibility as a result of their organizational individualism. But the potential impact of a coordinated movement was eventually eroded as the media, politicians, and the public were bombarded with mailings and competing messages.[26]

The imperative of organizational survival, however, virtually forces social movement organizations to distinguish themselves from each other and from the movement as a whole. Consequently, as a movement grows and draws more organizations into its wake, each organization is subjected to increasingly powerful pressures to specialize.[27] There is also the additional pressure to institutionalize and to formalize decision making. The nuclear freeze had initially been created as a coalition effort that emphasized decentralized governance, a campaign with "local self-determination and national coordination," but the exigencies of participating in national politics virtually demanded a coherence and unity this broad coalition could not provide. The NWFC quickly evolved into yet another distinct organizational entity, with its own staff, direction, funding needs, and struggle to survive by outlasting the movement. This meant that power and responsibility gradually shifted from the grassroots base to the staffs of the organizations of the freeze coalition. By June of 1983 the primary decision-making responsibility for the campaign had been formally shifted from committees of volunteers and members of other organizations to NWFC staff. This move supported the coalition effort's transformation into a distinct organization, emphasizing the prerogatives of its professional staff rather than the coordination of a political effort among many groups.[28]

This course of professionalization and bureaucratization of movement organizations is endemic to social movements in the United States, and it is problematic. For the trend toward more secure institutionalization entails a redirection of goals toward more modest, and inherently more conservative, objectives.[29] The leading edge of social mobilization almost invariably comes from outside the established organizations. The nuclear freeze idea, as a case in point, was developed largely independently of the numerous established arms control and disarmament organizations, many of which were slow in endorsing or working for the nuclear freeze. The coalition that grew out of their effort, the NWFC, became a distinct entity with its own organizational imperatives. In 1985, desperately seeking survival, the NWFC began negotiations for a merger with SANE, an older Congressionally oriented arms control group. The new organization, SANE/Freeze, has been far less visible than the freeze at its height and has endured a consistent financial crisis.[30]

THE PRICE OF ORGANIZATIONAL SURVIVAL

As the freeze faded, many organizations adapted to the new political environment by redefining their goals in more accessible and limited ways. According to WAND, the movement needed to prioritize "politically relevant and potentially winnable items among those available on the progressive arms control agenda."[31] Effective action would then be contingent upon increased political sophistication, meaning a sort of legislative triage: abandoning the issues unlikely to win Congressional support in favor of increased efforts for those with better chances. Naturally, Congressional allies would play a key role in aiding arms control advocates make these discriminations. These allies, WAND reports, advise deemphasizing emotional appeals based on fears of nuclear destruction and concentrating instead on the Congressional budget process.

There are several problems with this approach for a movement seeking comprehensive political change. First, a focus on incremental modifications in the budget, although responsive to Congressional interests, is unlikely to inspire broad public support, or even interest. In embracing this strategy, arms control and disarmament groups effectively abandon their greatest resource — broad, although perhaps shallow, public support. Popular support and grassroots activism are not only a potential route to influence on Capitol Hill; they also help maintain a powerful and well-financed organization. External support, funding, and resource mobilization generally follow grassroots activism.[32] The Council for a Livable World's fundraising, for example, increased dramatically as the freeze expanded, growing from $187,453 in 1978 to more than $1 million in 1984. Initially funding increased even as the movement faded; CLW raised nearly $1.5 million for the 1986 election cycle. Without grassroots mobilization, however, this rate of growth, and even the level of funding, would prove difficult to sustain. For the 1988 election cycle CLW raised $1,440,447, some $30,000 less than in 1986. The other peace PACs were far less successful, combining to raise less than the CLW total. Including CLW, their combined fundraising totaled about one-half of the 1984 level.[33]

Second, the intricacies of the long budget process require an ongoing lobbying presence, as the numerous committee and floor votes and compromises offer ample opportunity to undo any accomplishment. Developing such a permanent presence and stability is also more responsive to organizational needs than to larger political concerns. Although antinuclear forces could win occasional legislative battles against stronger opponents, the multiplication of significant votes diminishes the chances of making substantial changes in policy.

Third, by virtually granting control of the arms control and disarmament agenda to Congressional leaders, disarmament advocates give up the ability to define themselves and their goals. Rather than injecting new issues and concerns into the political debate, as social movements can, they limit themselves to a competition in which they are weaker than their opponents and over terms beyond their ability to define. "Movements are supposed to do what politicians can't do," said Pam Solo, reflecting on the demise of the nuclear freeze campaign, "which is to imagine a different future."[34] By adopting an institutional focus, the antinuclear movement abdicated this special role in favor of playing a role in which established politicians and interest groups are more comfortable and far more powerful, effectively ceding its sole political advantage.

Fourth, the institutional approach necessitates an even greater dependence upon elite support, redefining not only tactics but also political goals. For the most part, the differences elite arms control supporters and legislators had with the Reagan administration's nuclear and military policies were far more modest than those of the original freeze advocates. Significantly, these differences did not include the process by which defense policy was made. Intending to maintain good relationships with legislators and moderate and mainstream elite supporters, arms control and disarmament groups readily narrowed their agendas, winnowing out potentially controversial aspects from their programs. The notion of putting nuclear security issues on the Democratic agenda — a powerful mobilizing idea — was downplayed. Further, the institutionalized movement was unable to respond effectively to new political issues; it could not, for example, incorporate growing public concern with escalating conflict in Central America or the Middle East or increased public awareness of apartheid in South Africa. Citizens concerned with these issues, including many of those constituencies active in the freeze movement, had to look beyond their old alliances to express their concerns. The freeze coalition forfeited the political space for protest movements to other issues and groups.

Finally, adopting a strategy based in institutional activity means a much lower public profile, again ceding an advantage the movement had previously enjoyed. Even though most media coverage at the height of the freeze had emphasized the movement's activities rather than its ideas, publicity had been a substantial asset. WAND attributed the poor coverage of freeze ideas to a "failed sales job," advocating a more concerted effort to shape media coverage by convincing reporters and arms control experts that the proposals were good.[35] While there is doubtless some truth in this, it is also true that mass media in the United States are more disposed and better equipped to cover events than ideas in any case. The freeze proposal had never actually won much support or credence from arms control experts but had commanded attention only because of its large-scale mobilization.[36] Giving this up meant sacrificing the only leverage the movement had in influencing expert debate on nuclear issues or in the much more ambitious goal of creating a public debate. Emphasizing conventional means of political participation also meant that the movement was ceding not only its self-definition but also the front pages. Less visible and colorful activity meant less media coverage, aiding in the movement's demise.[37]

While the more institutionally oriented wing of the movement chose activities that were essentially less visible, the mass media simply became less interested in the direct action of groups working on the margins. The first Plowshares action (featuring the Berrigan brothers) had received extensive coverage throughout its long history in the courts, but subsequent Plowshares actions were generally ignored. In the few instances they received coverage, the stories usually reflected a human interest perspective rather than any sort of political angle.[38] The fragmentation of movement action facilitated the separation of civil disobedience and direct action from politics.

The movement's overall growth led virtually all the factions within it to emphasize their own activities at the expense of any kind of common agenda. Ultimately the flow of resources to each was compromised by the absence of a viable national identity. As competition for resources within the movement increased, organizations were quicker to distance themselves politically from potential allies. The component parts of the fragmented movement coalition were each more easily institutionalized or demobilized than the movement as a whole.

NOTES

1. Robert Coles, "The Freeze: Crusade of the Leisure Class," *Harper's*, March 1985.

2. Doug Waller, *Congress and the Nuclear Freeze: An Inside Look at the Politics of a Mass Movement*, Amherst: University of Massachusetts Press, 1987, p. 266.

3. New York *Times*, August 19, 1985, p. 22.

4. New York *Times*, November 8, 1984, p. 1.

5. Mary McGrory, "An Unrepentant Mother Imprisoned for Attacking a Missile Site," Boston *Globe*, April 16, 1986.

6. Washington *Post*, February 23, 1985, p. A2.

7. See, for example, Jim Schwartz, "A Conspiracy of Conscience: Michigan Peace Protests against Williams International," *The Nation,* December 8, 1984.

8. Frank Clancy, "Showdown at Ground Zero," *Mother Jones,* November 1986; Pam Solo, *From Protest to Policy: Beyond the Freeze to Common Security,* Cambridge, MA: Ballinger, 1988, pp. 174–76.

9. New York *Times,* March 3, 1985, Section 21, p. 3; August 5, 1985, Section 1, p. 8; Washington *Post,* July 16, 1985, p C7.

10. Howard Cushnir, "The Great Peace March That Couldn't," *Mother Jones,* June 1986.

11. Susan Faludi, "Inner Peaceniks," *Mother Jones,* April 1987, p. 23.

12. Ibid., pp. 21–22.

13. James Clotfelter, "Disarmament Movements in the United States," *Journal of Peace Research,* June 1986, p. 99.

14. Washington *Post,* April 7, 1986, p. C4.

15. See, for example, Eugene Carroll, "Move toward Test Ban," New York *Times,* January 8, 1985.

16. Solo, *From Protest to Policy,* pp. 174–75.

17. McGeorge Bundy, "The Emperor's Clothes," *The New York Review of Books,* July 20, 1989, p. 6.

18. On the conditions for success as an interest group or PAC, see Jeffrey Berry, *The Interest Group Society,* Boston: Little, Brown, 1984, p. 119; Larry J. Sabato, *Pac Power,* New York: Norton, 1984; Kay Lehman Schlozman and John T. Tierney, *Organized Interests and American Democracy,* New York: Harper & Row, 1986, pp. 290–317.

19. Betsy Taylor, "If We Can't Change the Politicians' Minds . . . Let's Change the Politicians," unpublished paper, August 1985, p. 5.

20. Women's Action for Nuclear Disarmament, *Turnabout: Emerging New Realism in the Nuclear Age,* Boston: WAND Education Fund, 1896, pp. 41–44.

21. Thomas Byrne Edsall, *The New Politics of Inequality,* New York: Norton, 1984, pp. 86–90, 235.

22. This route to institutionalization is common among social movements in the United States. For a comprehensive statement, see John D. McCarthy and Mayer N. Zald, *The Trend of Social Movements in America: Professionalization and Resource Mobilization,* Morristown, NJ: General Learning Press, 1973.

23. WAND, *Turnabout,* pp. 38–44.

24. Ibid., p. 24.

25. John D. McCarthy and Mayer Zald, "Resource Mobilization and Social Movements: A Partial Theory," *American Journal of Sociology* 82 (1977): 1224–25.

26. Solo, *From Protest to Policy,* p. 88.

27. McCarthy and Zald, "Resource Mobilization," p. 1234.

28. Solo, *From Protest to Policy,* p. 142.

29. Theodore J. Lowi, *The Politics of Disorder,* New York: Basic, 1971, pp. 51–54; Frances Fox Piven and Richard A. Cloward, *Poor People's Movements: Why They Succeed, How They Fail,* New York: Vintage, 1979, p. xxi; James Q. Wilson, *Political Organizations,* New York: Basic, 1973, p. 31.

30. Renatta Rizzo and R. Harris, "Grass Roots Opt for Unity: Freeze/SANE Merger," *Nuclear Times,* January 1987; Solo, *From Protest to Policy,* p. 176.

31. WAND, *Turnabout,* p. 36.

32. Doug McAdam, *Political Process and the Development of Black Insurgency,* Chicago: University of Chicago Press, 1982, p. 124.

33. Council for a Livable World, election reports, December 1986, 1988.

34. Randy Kehler, interview with Solo, 1985, p. 38.

35. WAND, *Turnabout,* p. 25.

36. Movement leadership was conscious of the lack of support from arms control experts. Strategists argued it was a major weakness for the freeze as a whole. See "Final Draft of Strategy Paper for 1985," December 7–9, 1984, IPIS archives.

37. Todd Gitlin, *The Whole World Is Watching: Mass Media in the Making and Unmaking of the New Left,* Berkeley; University of California Press, 1980, p. 182; Mark Hertsgaard, "What Became of the Freeze?" *Mother Jones,* June 1985, pp. 44–47.

38. Also see Lloyd Grove, "Martin Holladay: In Prison. Paying for His Civil Disobedience," Washington *Post,* August 5, 1986; W. Plummer, "Separated from Her Children, Jailed Nuke Protestor Liz McAllister Says She's Serving Prime Time for Peace," *People,* August 27, 1984.

16

THE CHANGING POLITICAL LANDSCAPE: THE NUCLEAR FREEZE AND PROTEST MOVEMENTS IN THE UNITED STATES

Although the nuclear freeze movement ceased to occupy a prominent place on the U.S. political landscape, that landscape had changed dramatically. This reality makes a facile evaluation of the success or failure of the nuclear freeze movement impossible. The movement did not succeed in translating its explicit demands into policy, but mainstream politics responded to the freeze and its concerns. Movement organizations also changed, modifying their own goals and reaching an accommodation with the government. This dynamic interaction between government, policy, and social movement organizations is the reason neither the breakdown nor the solidarity perspectives are alone sufficient to explain dissident mobilization. We need to look at the interaction between government and the dissidents is needed to explain and analyze any movement effectively.

The nuclear freeze movement grew beyond the efforts of a few relatively small antinuclear and pacifist groups because the Reagan administration gave it the opportunity and the space to do so. President Reagan's policy reforms, making the U.S. military posture marginally more bellicose and substantially more expensive, was only part of the opportunity. Perhaps even more significant was the Reagan administration's exclusion of moderate and liberal forces from the policy-making process. The amount of influence advocates of minimum deterrence, for example, had enjoyed in previous administrations is debatable; their presence, however, was consistent and usually visible. The potential for antinuclear social mobilization was enhanced because other strategies for access were foreclosed.

The effective purging of previously mainstream figures from the circles of policymaking expanded the potential coalition of opposition to Reagan's nuclear policies. The freeze proposal, by avoiding language tied too closely to any other organization or political position, proved to be a good vehicle for uniting this broad coalition. Conceived as both an arms control strategy and as the standard of a social movement, it was both easily intelligible to most people and, at the same time, comprehensive in its implications. It also was well suited to a mobilization strategy that emphasized local control and populist community participation. This decentralized approach allowed the movement to encompass a broad variety of political activities, to expand rapidly, and to avoid confrontation with strong and committed opposition.

By the middle of 1982, the nuclear freeze movement had emerged in national politics. The cumulative impact of many local actions and a few national and regional events, aided by well-publicized support from numerous elite figures, brought the movement to the attention of national media and politicians. This gave the movement both an element of legitimacy and an infusion of political resources, allowing it to continue its rapid expansion. The proposal ostensibly uniting this movement was defined in increasingly vague terms, however, to avoid straining the growing coalition. Many activists embraced a least common denominator strategy regarding the freeze, intending to build the largest and broadest coalition possible. There was no place within this coalition for ideological debate; even the simplest policy positions, such as stands on particular weapons systems, were essentially dodged by the campaign as a whole. The freeze, initially conceived as a first step toward ending the arms race and remaking world politics, came to be seen as a vehicle for expressing opposition to nuclear war and support for the arms control process. Politicians used the freeze to mobilize support, raise funds, and oppose Ronald Reagan, effectively coopting the movement.

Movement leaders participated in this process because they appeared to be making political gains. Moderation in analysis and tactics generated concrete benefits, most significantly access to mainstream political institutions. The nuclear freeze proposal was endorsed by numerous politicians, debated in Congress, and eventually passed by the House of Representatives. Freeze activists were given currency by national media, met with politicians, and attempted to establish themselves as a permanent force in national politics. These gains seemed to justify the political compromises the movement made, and many freeze advocates were unwilling to do anything that might jeopardize their newly achieved access.

The rapid movement of the nuclear freeze, from the margins of political legitimacy to the halls of Congress in less than two years, also created certain problems for the movement. The freeze was subjected to the rigors of legislative compromise very early in its life; policy makers genuinely seemed to be responsive. As a result,

movement leaders were not as wary as they might have been if they
had been forced to spend a longer period of time in the political
netherworld. The open door to political institutions effectively
preempts the development of more powerful dissident movements.

Access, however, does not equal influence. Although political
institutions proved to be permeable for the freeze movement, they
continued to represent an impenetrable barrier between citizen
pressure and public policy — exactly as Madison and the framers of
the Constitution intended. Although both opponents and self-
described freeze supporters in positions of influence were quick to
adopt freeze movement rhetoric, very few were willing to incorporate
or even acknowledge any of the political analysis that had initially
spawned the proposal and the movement. Thus, almost all
politicians eagerly expressed their opposition to nuclear war, but
virtually none were willing to take positions leading to the end of the
arms race.

The political system offered seemingly innumerable opportunities
for antinuclear activists to express their opinions, demonstrate their
support, and target their efforts. Local referenda were followed by
Congressional resolutions, then by electoral campaigns. The many
opportunities for conventional political participation served to
preclude much extra-institutional activity. There was always
another bill or amendment demanding attention or another election
to contest. The closer to policy-making influence each political battle
was, the narrower the scope of conflict, the more difficult the fight,
the stronger the opposition, and the greater the influence of elite
figures and political opponents. Freeze activism moderated as
activists hoped to win in the highest circles of policymaking.

Even as the freeze faded from discourse, movement organizations
grew and were institutionalized, leaving a far more extensive
network of potentially accessible resources than before the
movement's emergence. Nuclear and military issues received
greater attention from politicians and the mass media. Nuclear
education or peace studies programs were established in many
colleges and high schools.[1] All of this meant that expression of
nuclear concern no longer required extra-institutional social
mobilization. No longer were such concerns politically abnormal or
threatening. Antinuclear forces waged a battle of position within
conventional politics.

At the same time antinuclear movements in Western Europe
ostensibly receded, partly as a result of elections and partly as a
result of the deployment of Pershing II and cruise missiles — both
representing failures for the peace movements. Heightened conflict
in Central America, the Middle East, and South Africa also came to
occupy activist concern, drawing movement resources and supporters to other causes. The economic recession lessened in the United

States; significantly, the rebound came as freeze organizations increasingly tied their own fates to business elites and upper-middle-class patrons, those drawing the most benefit from the Reagan-era recovery.[2] The movement had already effectively distanced itself from those constituencies still adversely affected by the new economy, for example, blacks, poor people, and students. Essentially, the strongest patrons of arms control and disarmament groups had somewhat less volatile quarrels with the Reagan administration and its policies. All of these things came to change the shape of the political space the nuclear freeze had occupied.

Perhaps most significant, the ostensibly neglected concerns that provoked the freeze movement were no longer so blatantly neglected. National politicians at both ends of the political spectrum repeatedly voiced their opposition to nuclear war and reaffirmed their firm commitment to ensure that it did not take place. Reagan administration officials tempered their political rhetoric, abandoning talk of "limited nuclear wars" and nuclear "warning shots." Military spending leveled off in fiscal 1985, albeit at the inflated Reagan-era levels. In January 1984 Ronald Reagan announced his intention to resume arms control negotiations with the Soviet Union, explicitly addressing the fear of nuclear holocaust that had fed the freeze movement, and noting that nuclear war cannot be won and must never be fought.

The constellation of political realities that had made the nuclear freeze movement possible had shifted, as had the structure of political opportunity. The military and strategic nuclear policies directly addressed by the nuclear freeze proposal were essentially unchanged, but almost everything else had changed, particularly the image projected by President Reagan. The willingness he expressed to negotiate arms control agreements was matched and exceeded by Soviet General Secretary Mikhail Gorbachev, who came to power several months after Reagan's reelection. Gorbachev challenged Reagan to make good on his own pronouncements about nuclear weaponry and arms control, accepting for example, Reagan's "zero option" proposal for intermediate-range weapons in Europe.[3] By pursuing internal political and economic reforms Gorbachev also robbed Reagan of many excuses for reticence about arms control. Waller, claiming a victory for the movement, contends that the freeze "tempered Mr. Reagan's distaste for arms control . . . it forced his administration if not to achieve concrete results, at last to continue the quest for arms control."[4] The somewhat more conciliatory Reagan stance made the president a more elusive target for arms control and disarmament advocates. It also made negotiations and some modest arms control agreements possible. Domestic political concerns created a willingness to soften foreign policy rhetoric and posture.

Paradoxically, Reagan also used his Strategic Defense Initiative to assuage the nuclear fears that animated the freeze movement.[5] Star Wars allowed the president to alter the terms of the nuclear debate. Calling nuclear deterrence immoral, Reagan urged the development of a system that he claimed would make these instruments of destruction obsolete and allow large reductions in offensive nuclear weapons. It is unlikely that many strong freeze advocates were convinced by these arguments, but in refuting them they were often forced to alter their own, criticizing Star Wars because it would threaten the system of mutual deterrence.[6] Effectively, SDI put the movement in the position of defending the status quo it had decried as terrifying and immoral. In contrast, the president promised to move beyond this nuclear terror to a safer and more peaceful future.

The Strategic Defense Initiative was a controversial program from the moment the president proposed it in March 1983, but it quickly became a firmly established element in the U.S. defense budget. Skillful political management of the initial research awards created an institutionalized bureaucratic and corporate constituency for the programs.[7] Subsequent debates on Star Wars are likely to turn on incremental levels of funding, rather than the desirability of space-based missile defenses. The secure institutionalization of Star Wars programs within the Pentagon and the defense industry is likely one of the legacies of both the Reagan presidency and, in a circuitous way, the nuclear freeze movement. The other apparent victory for the movement is the resurrection of an arms control regime.

Ronald Reagan refused to credit the nuclear freeze movement with influencing his approach to arms control or military policy, repeatedly claiming that reopened arms control negotiations with the Soviet Union resulted from his administration's military buildup and that he had never taken the threat of nuclear war lightly. These arguments are not surprising; politicians are generally and understandably loathe to credit protest movements with influencing their decisions on important policy matters.[8] Given the historical record, however, of a president who vocally opposed every previous arms control agreement, it is reasonable to consider the new Reagan rhetoric and approach to arms control at least partly the result of a strong and visible opposition movement.

The Reagan-Gorbachev detente provided the Soviet leader with the opportunity he needed to allow, and even to encourage, comprehensive political reforms in the Soviet Union and through the East bloc. The scope and pace of these revolutionary political developments have undermined the dominance of the Cold War consensus in the United States. They have also challenged Reagan's successor, George Bush, in his efforts to resist substantive reevaluation of U.S. foreign policy goals and strategies. Absent from national politics, however, are the broad citizen participation and fundamental political debate the nuclear freeze demanded.

The nuclear freeze movement demonstrates both the extent and the limits of popular influence on U.S. military and strategic policy. In one view, the movement is notable for its failures. The freeze proposal demanded a change not only in Reagan's policies but also in those of the United States since the dawn of the nuclear age. It won an apparent return to pre-Reagan policies, with the notable additions of the Strategic Defense Initiative and a substantially inflated base line for military budgets. The freeze was fragmented, institutionalized, and coopted by modest restraints in the Reagan program and the administration's increasingly sophisticated political management of dissent. The arms control process, historically a legitimator of buildups and arms races, has been rescued, and extra-institutional dissent is once again marginalized.

The movement can also be seen as a political triumph. The freeze effectively forced an extremely popular president to return to long-established bipartisan policies he had consistently eschewed and had vigorously criticized. The movement vanished then, when it was no longer necessary. From this perspective, the nuclear freeze movement was a demonstration of a responsive democratic polity and of the limits on executive power. The Ronald Reagan who talked of limited nuclear war and joked of beginning to bomb the Soviet Union in five minutes was replaced by a president committed to world peace, a Ronald Reagan who saw his landslide victory as a mandate for arms control, one who looked forward to the day when "all nations can begin to reduce nuclear weapons and ultimately banish them from the face of the earth."[9] Freeze organizations were institutionalized, providing a more extensive network of support for arms control and disarmament advocates. This may not be enough, but it sets the terms of political conflict for subsequent challenges.

NOTES

1. Also see Dick Ringler, ed., "Nuclear War: A Teaching Guide," *Bulletin of the Atomic Scientists*, December 1984, pp. 1s–32s; Daniel C. Thomas, *Guide to Careers and Graduate Education in Peace Studies*, Amherst, MA: Five College Program in Peace and World Security Studies, 1987; Daniel C. Thomas and Michael T. Klare, *Peace and World Order Studies: A Curriculum Guide*, Boulder, CO: Westview Press, 1989.

2. Thomas Ferguson and Joel Rogers, "Big Business Backs the Freeze," *The Nation*, July 19/26, 1986.

3. The zero option initially won support among Reagan advisors because it promised the appearance of negotiations without the prospect of agreement. By proposing a clear and unacceptable arms control proposal, advocates within the administration hoped to quell opposition to the deployment of new missiles in Western Europe and defuse what they saw as the Soviet Union's propaganda gains.

See Strobe Talbott, *Deadly Gambits: The Reagan Administration and the Stalemate in Arms Control,* New York: Alfred A. Knopf, 1984, pp. 57–63.

4. Doug Waller, *Congress and the Nuclear Freeze: An Inside Look at the Politics of a Mass Movement,* Amherst: University of Massachusetts, 1987, pp. 300–1.

5. Also see Charles Krauthammer, "Who Killed the Freeze?" Washington *Post,* July 26, 1985; Mary McGrory, "Arms Control Gathers Moss," Washington *Post,* May 16, 1985; R. Emmett Tyrell, Jr., "As Star Wars Grows, Interest in Freeze Declines," Washington *Post,* March 4, 1985.

6. Also see George Ball, "The War for Star Wars," *The New York Review of Books,* April 11, 1985; Nancy L. Kassebaum, "Arms Control after the Summit," *Arms Control Today,* November/December 1985.

7. Fred Kaplan, "'Star Wars': The Ultimate Military-Industrial Compact," Boston *Globe,* September 14, 1987.

8. Perhaps the most dramatic example can be found in Richard Nixon's memoirs. As president, Nixon was insistent that antiwar protests would have no impact on U.S. policy in Vietnam. He later revealed, however, that the disruption produced by the movement made escalation in Vietnam politically impossible, forcing him to back down from a threat he made to employ "measures of the greatest consequence" against North Vietnam. *RN: The Memoirs of a President,* New York: Grosset and Dunlap, 1978, pp. 396–404.

9. *Public Papers of the President: Ronald Reagan, 1984, Volume 2,* Washington, D.C.: U.S. Government Printing Office, 1985, p. 1796.

SELECTED
BIBLIOGRAPHY

Blechmann, Barry M., and Stephen S. Kaplan. *Force without War: U.S. Armed Forces as a Political Instrument.* Washington, D.C.: The Brookings Institution, 1978.

Boyer, Paul. "From Activism to Apathy: The American People and Nuclear Weapons, 1963–1980," *The Journal of American History,* Vol. 70, No. 4, March 1984.

Cockburn, Alexander, and James Ridgeway. "The Freeze Movement versus Ronald Reagan," *The New Left Review,* No. 137, January/February 1983.

Dellums, Ronald V., ed., with R. H. Miller and H. Lee Halterman. *Defense Sense: The Search for a Rational Military Policy.* Cambridge, MA: Ballinger, 1983.

DiBenedetti, Charles. *The Peace Reform in American History.* Bloomington, IN: Indiana University Press, 1980.

Drew, Elizabeth. "A Political Journal," *The New Yorker,* June 20, 1983.

Edelman, Murray. *Politics as Symbolic Action.* Chicago: Markham, 1971.

Falk, Richard. "Lifting the Curse of Bipartisanship," *World Policy Journal,* Fall 1983.

Fallows, James. *National Defense.* New York: Random House, 1981.

Forsberg, Randall. "A Bilateral Nuclear Weapons Freeze," *Scientific American,* November 1982.

___. "The Freeze and Beyond: Confining the Military to Defense as a Route to Disarmament," *World Policy Journal,* Vol. 1, Winter 1984.

Freedman, Lawrence. *The Evolution of Nuclear Strategy.* New York: St. Martin's Press, 1983.

Freeman, Jo. *The Politics of Women's Liberation: A Case Study of an Emerging Social Movement and Its Relation to the Policy Process.* New York: David McKay, 1975.

Gaddis, John Lewis. *Strategies of Containment: A Critical Appraisal of Postwar American National Security Policy.* New York: Oxford University Press, 1982.

Gamson, William A. *The Strategy of Social Protest.* Homewood, IL: The Dorsey Press, 1975.

Gitlin, Todd. *The Whole World Is Watching: Mass Media in the Making and Unmaking of the New Left.* Berkeley: University of California Press, 1980.

Institute for Defense and Disarmament Studies. *Peace Resource Book.* Cambridge, MA: Ballinger, 1986.

Kaufmann, William W. *The 1986 Defense Budget.* Washington, D.C.: The Brookings Institution, 1985.

Ladd, Everett Carll. "The Freeze Framework," *Public Opinion,* August/September 1982.

Leavitt, Robert. "Freezing the Arms Race: The Genesis of a Mass Movement." Unpublished Kennedy School of Government Case Study, Harvard University, 1983.

Lipsky, Michael. *Protest in City Politics: Rent Strikes, Housing, and the Power of the Poor.* Chicago: Rand-McNally, 1970.

Lowi, Theodore, J. *The Politics of Disorder.* New York: Basic, 1971.

McAdam, Doug. *Political Process and the Development of Black Insurgency.* Chicago: University of Chicago Press, 1982.

McCarthy, John D., and Mayer N. Zald. "Resource Mobilization and Social Movements: A Partial Theory," *American Journal of Sociology,* Vol. 82, No. 6, 1977.

Michels, Robert. *Political Parties.* New York: Collier, 1962.

Miller, Steven E., ed. *The Nuclear Weapons Freeze and Arms Control.* Cambridge, MA: Ballinger, 1984.

Miller, Steven E. "The Viability of Nuclear Arms Control: U.S. Domestic and Bilateral Factors," *Bulletin of Peace Proposals,* Vol. 16, No. 3, 1985.

Myrdal, Alva. *The Game of Disarmament: How the United States and Russia Run the Arms Race.* New York: Pantheon, 1982.

National Conference of Roman Catholic Bishops. *The Challenge of Peace: God's Promise and Our Response.* Washington, D.C.: U.S. Catholic Conference, 1983.

Parkin, Frank. *Middle-Class Radicalism: The Social Bases of the British Campaign for Nuclear Disarmament.* New York: Praeger, 1968.

Piven, Frances Fox, and Richard A. Cloward. *Poor People's Movements: Why They Succeed, How They Fail.* New York: Vintage, 1979.

Public Agenda Foundation. *Voter Options on Nuclear Arms Policy.* In collaboration with the Center for Foreign Policy Development, Brown University, May 1984.

Scheer, Robert. *With Enough Shovels: Reagan, Bush and Nuclear War.* New York: Random House, 1982.

Schelling, Thomas C., and Morton H. Halperin. *Strategy and Arms Control.* New York: Twentieth Century Fund, 1961.

Solo, Pam. *From Protest to Policy: Beyond the Freeze to Common Security.* Cambridge, MA: Ballinger, 1988.

Talbott, Strobe. *Deadly Gambits: The Reagan Administration and the Stalemate in Arms Control.* New York: Alfred A. Knopf, 1984.

Tilly, Charles. *From Mobilization to Revolution.* Reading, MA: Addison-Wesley, 1978.

Waller, Doug. *Congress and the Nuclear Freeze: An Inside Look at the Politics of a Mass Movement.* Amherst: University of Massachusetts Press, 1987.

Wittner, Lawrence S. *Rebels against War: The American Peace Movement, 1933–1983.* Philadelphia: Temple University Press, 1983.

INDEX

ABOUT THE AUTHOR

DAVID S. MEYER is currently visiting Assistant Professor of Political Science at Tufts University. He was active as a local organizer in the nuclear freeze movement and has worked as a researcher at the Institute for Defense and Disarmament Studies.